National Parks *of the United Kingdom*

This book has been created with the generous support of

Mark Aldridge and Mark Hooper
Harry and Rachel Hampson
Julian and Susie Oakley
Iain and Martha Parham
Håkan and Carina Winberg

This book has been produced in collaboration with National Parks UK.

www.nationalparks.uk

First published in the UK by Max Ström
An imprint of Bonnier Books UK

5th Floor, HYLO,
103–105 Bunhill Row,
London, EC1Y 8LZ

Owned by Bonnier Books
Sveavägen 56, Stockholm, Sweden

ISBN – 978-1-80418-602-2

All rights reserved. No part of the publication may be reproduced, stored in a retrieval system, transmitted or circulated in any form or by any means, electronic, mechanical, photocopying, recording or otherwise, without prior permission in writing of the publisher.

A CIP catalogue of this book is available from the British Library.

3 5 7 9 10 8 6 4 2

Copyright © by Bonnier Books UK
Text: Carey Davies
Main photo library: Nature Picture Library
Photographs: please see picture credits on page 266
Design: Osborne Ross
Repro: Italgraf, Stockholm
Printed and bound in China 2025

Carey Davies has asserted their moral right to be identified as the author of this Work in accordance with the Copyright, Designs and Patents Act 1988.

MIX
Paper | Supporting responsible forestry
FSC® C104723

Every reasonable effort has been made to trace copyright holders of material reproduced in this book, but if any have been inadvertently overlooked the publishers would be glad to hear from them.

www.bonnierbooks.co.uk

National Parks *of the United Kingdom*

Carey Davies

MAX STRÖM ◀ National Parks

National Parks
Locations

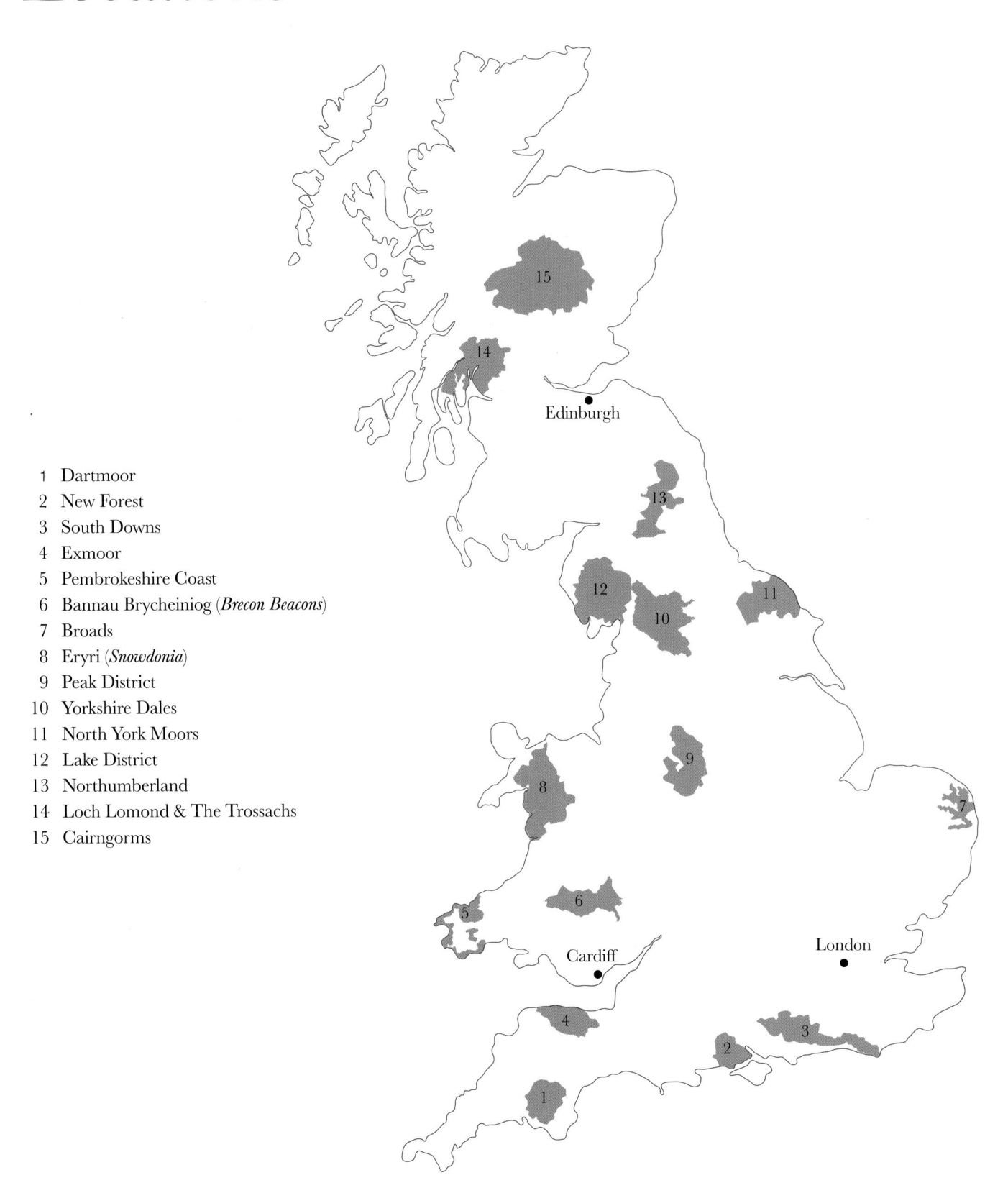

1. Dartmoor
2. New Forest
3. South Downs
4. Exmoor
5. Pembrokeshire Coast
6. Bannau Brycheiniog (*Brecon Beacons*)
7. Broads
8. Eryri (*Snowdonia*)
9. Peak District
10. Yorkshire Dales
11. North York Moors
12. Lake District
13. Northumberland
14. Loch Lomond & The Trossachs
15. Cairngorms

Contents

Introduction	*18*
Dartmoor	*24*
New Forest	*38*
South Downs	*52*
Exmoor	*66*
Pembrokeshire Coast	*80*
Bannau Brycheiniog	*98*
Broads	*114*
Eryri	*128*
Peak District	*150*
Yorkshire Dales	*166*
North York Moors	*180*
Lake District	*192*
Northumberland	*214*
Loch Lomond & The Trossachs	*226*
Cairngorms	*240*
National Parks in brief	*260*

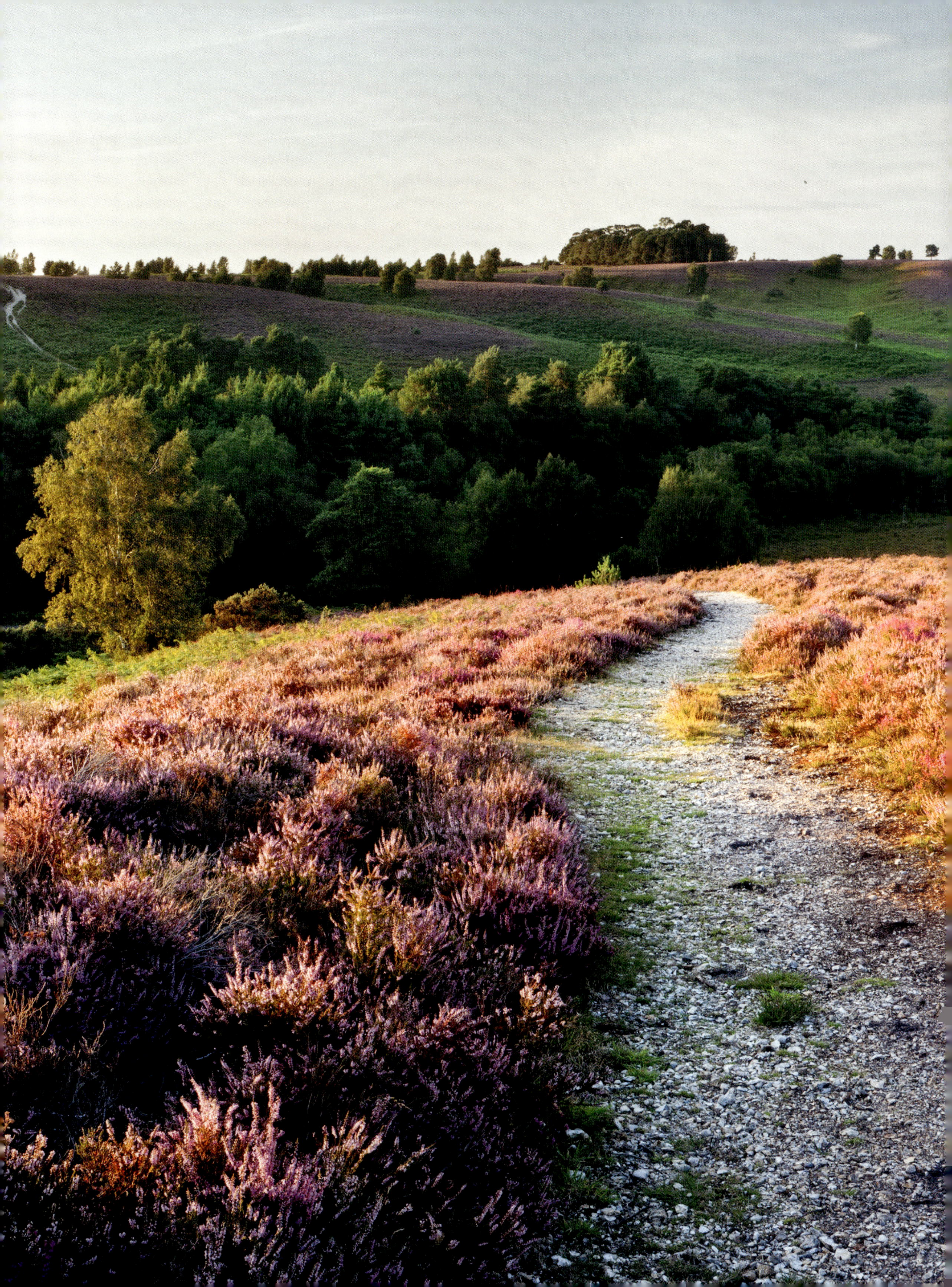

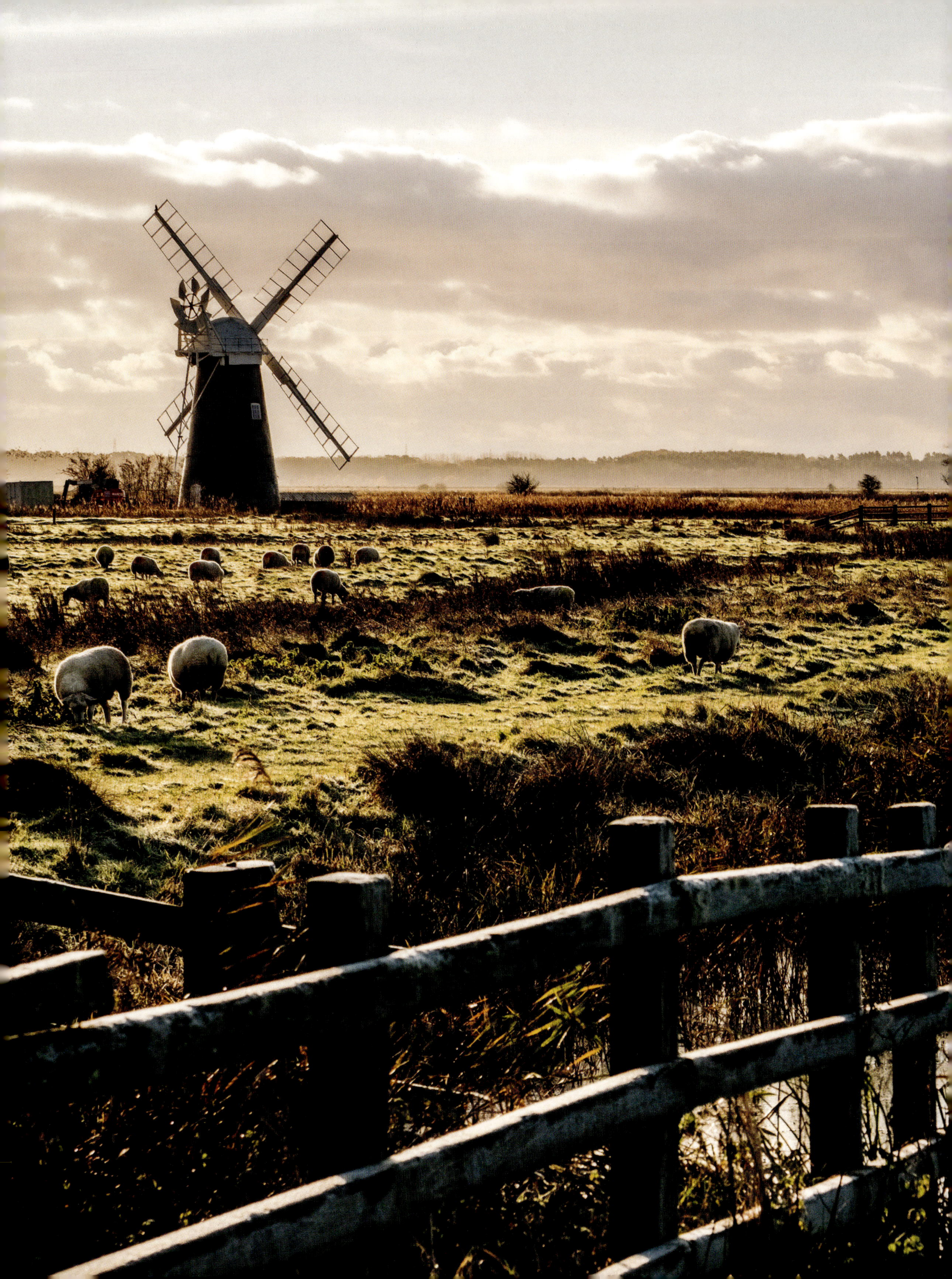

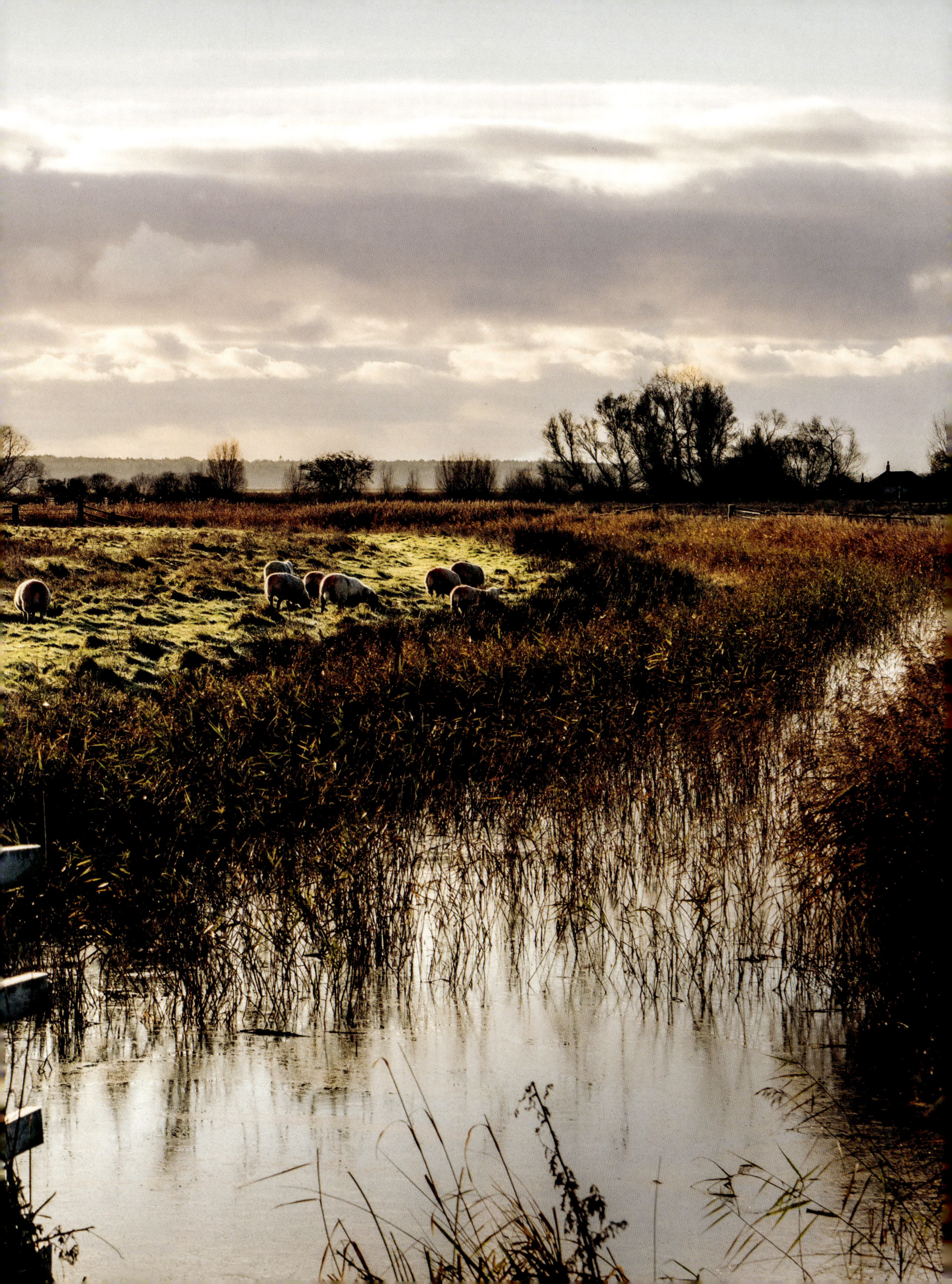

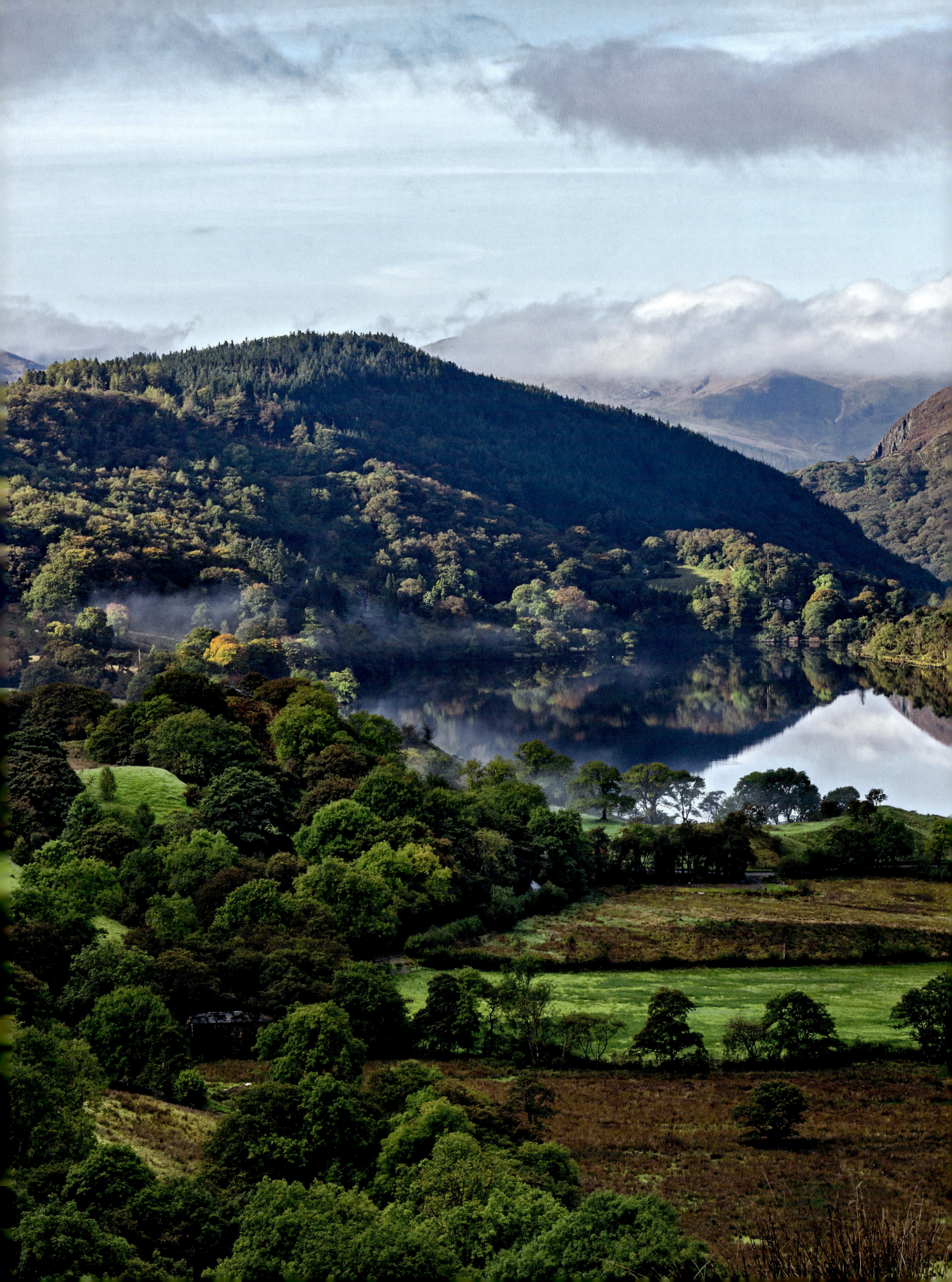

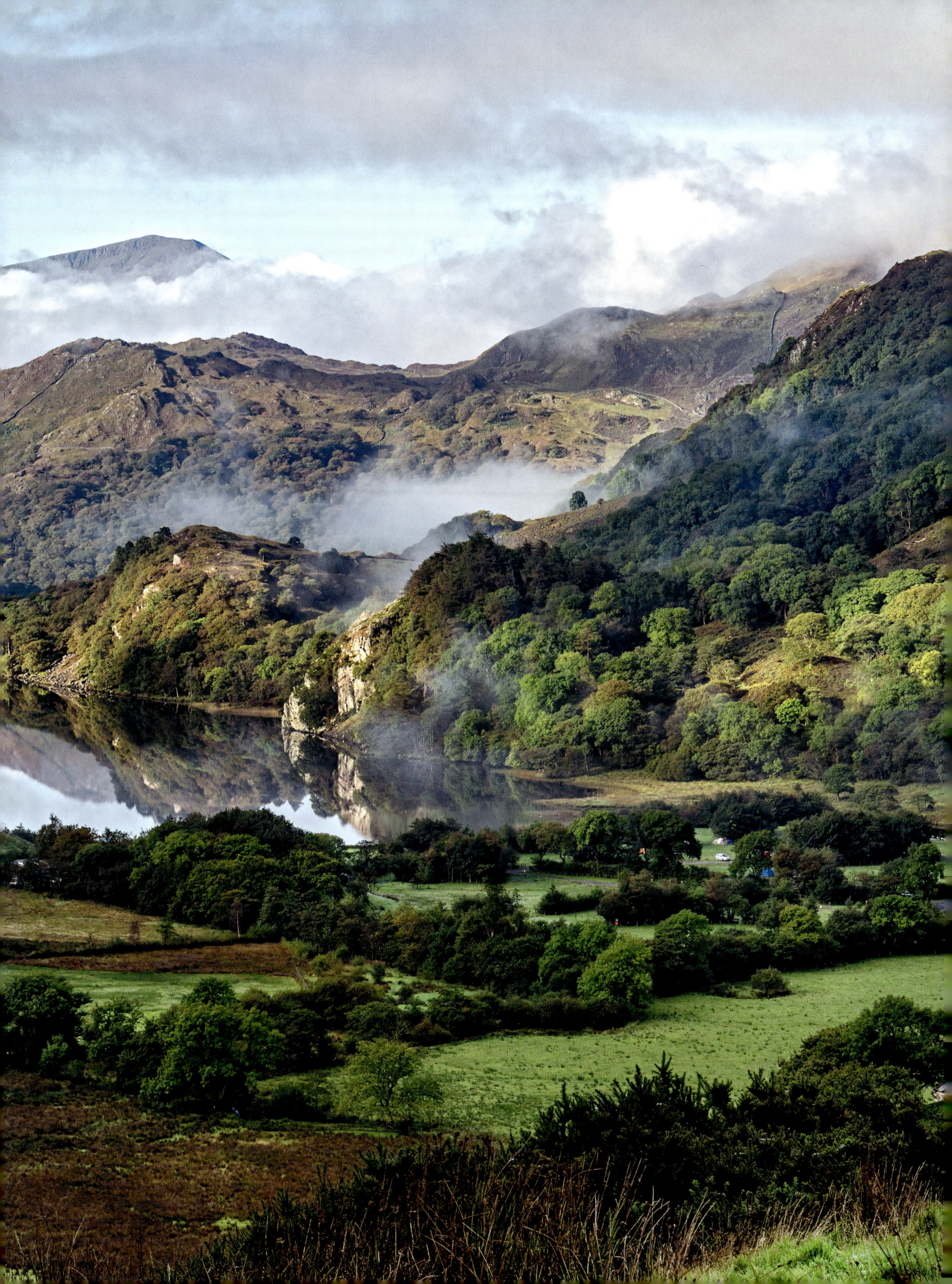

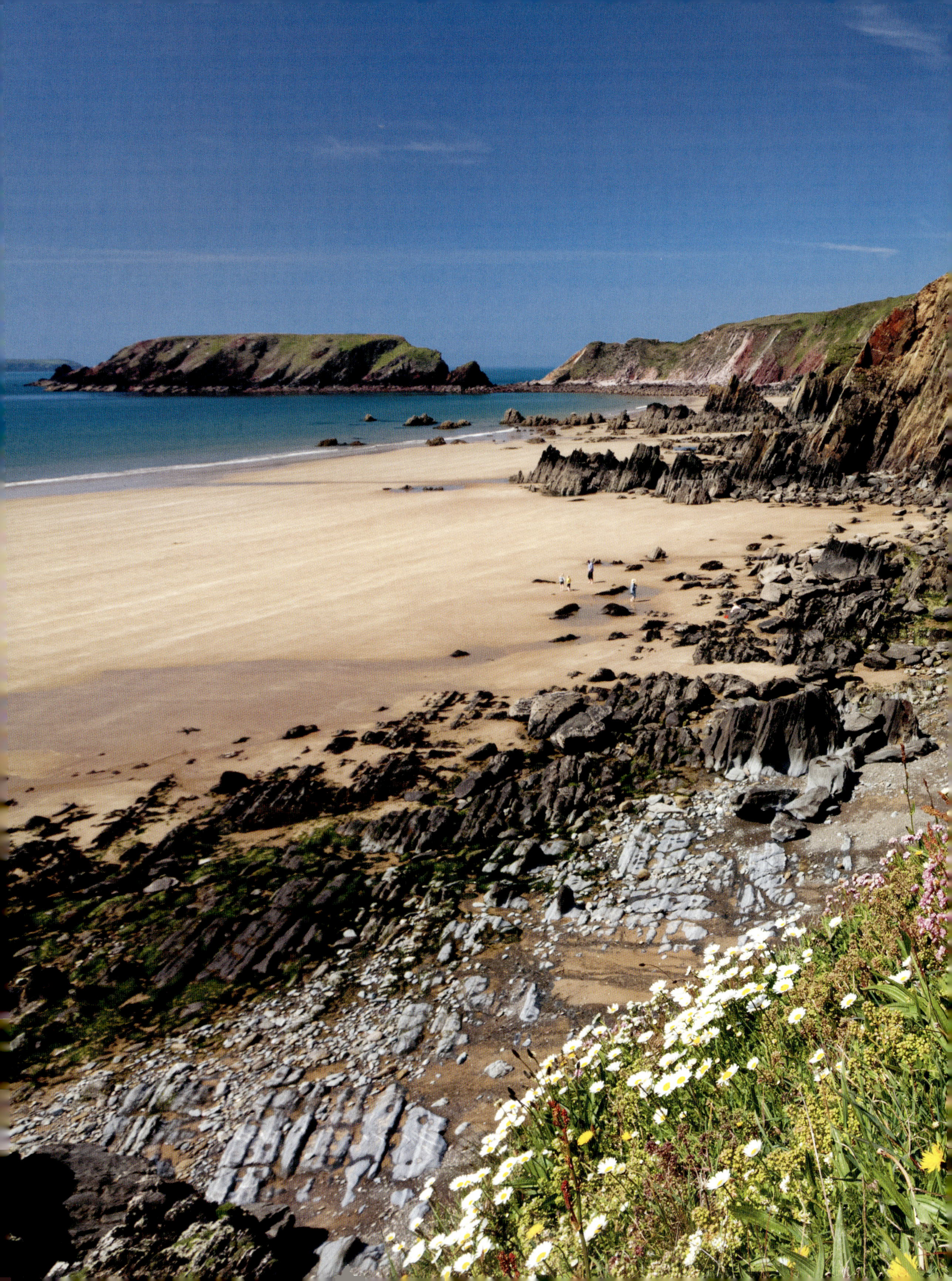

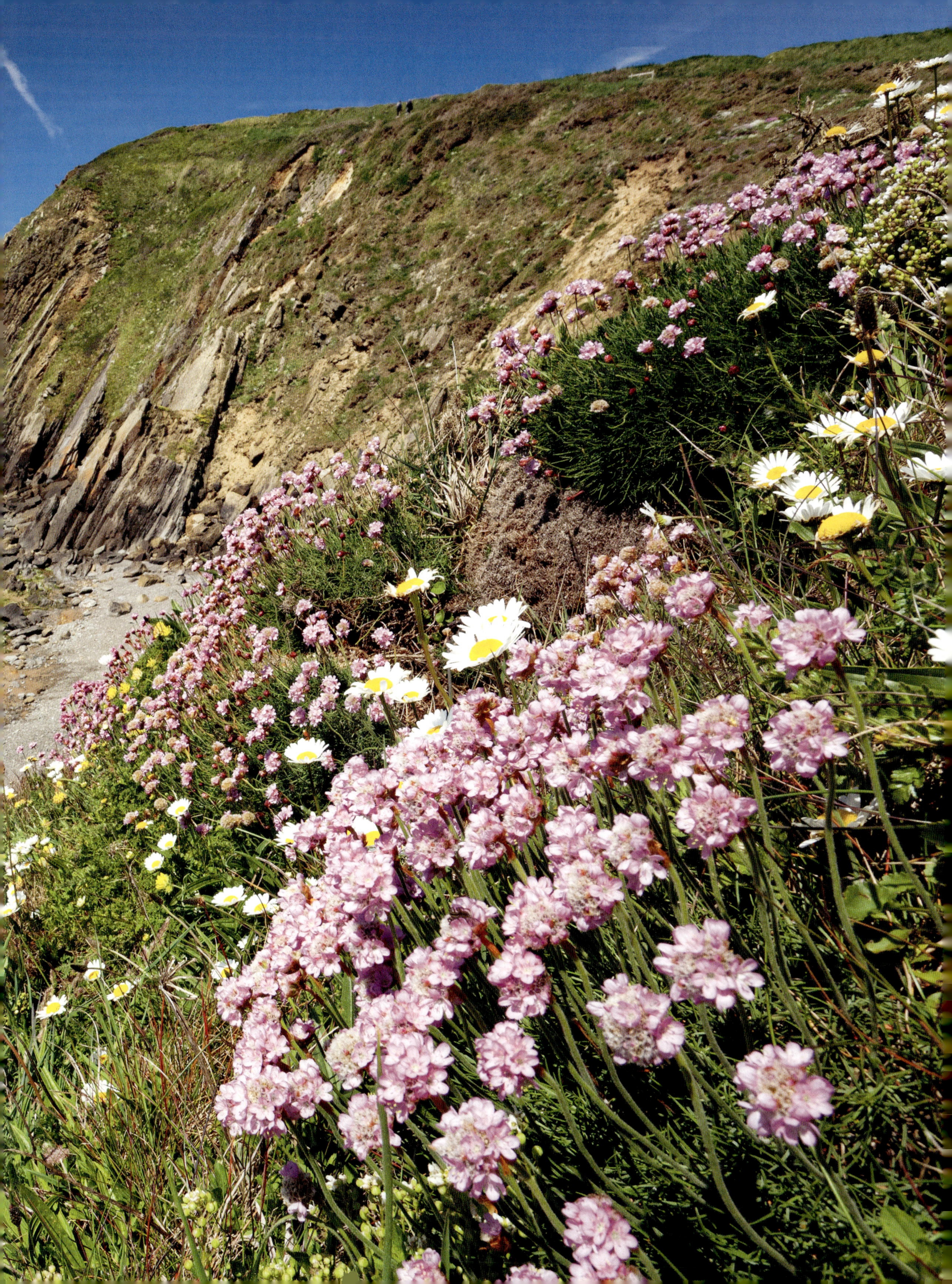

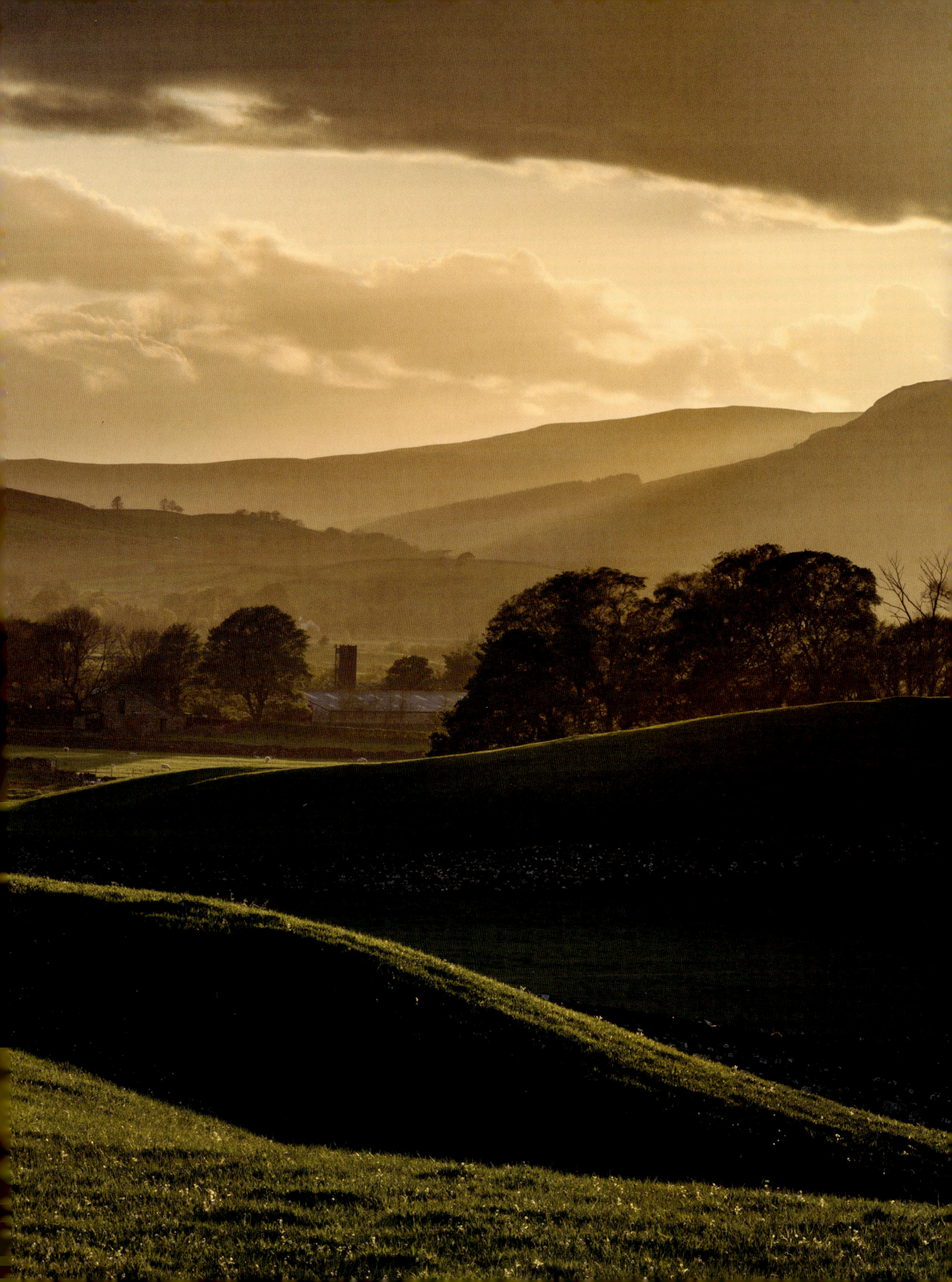

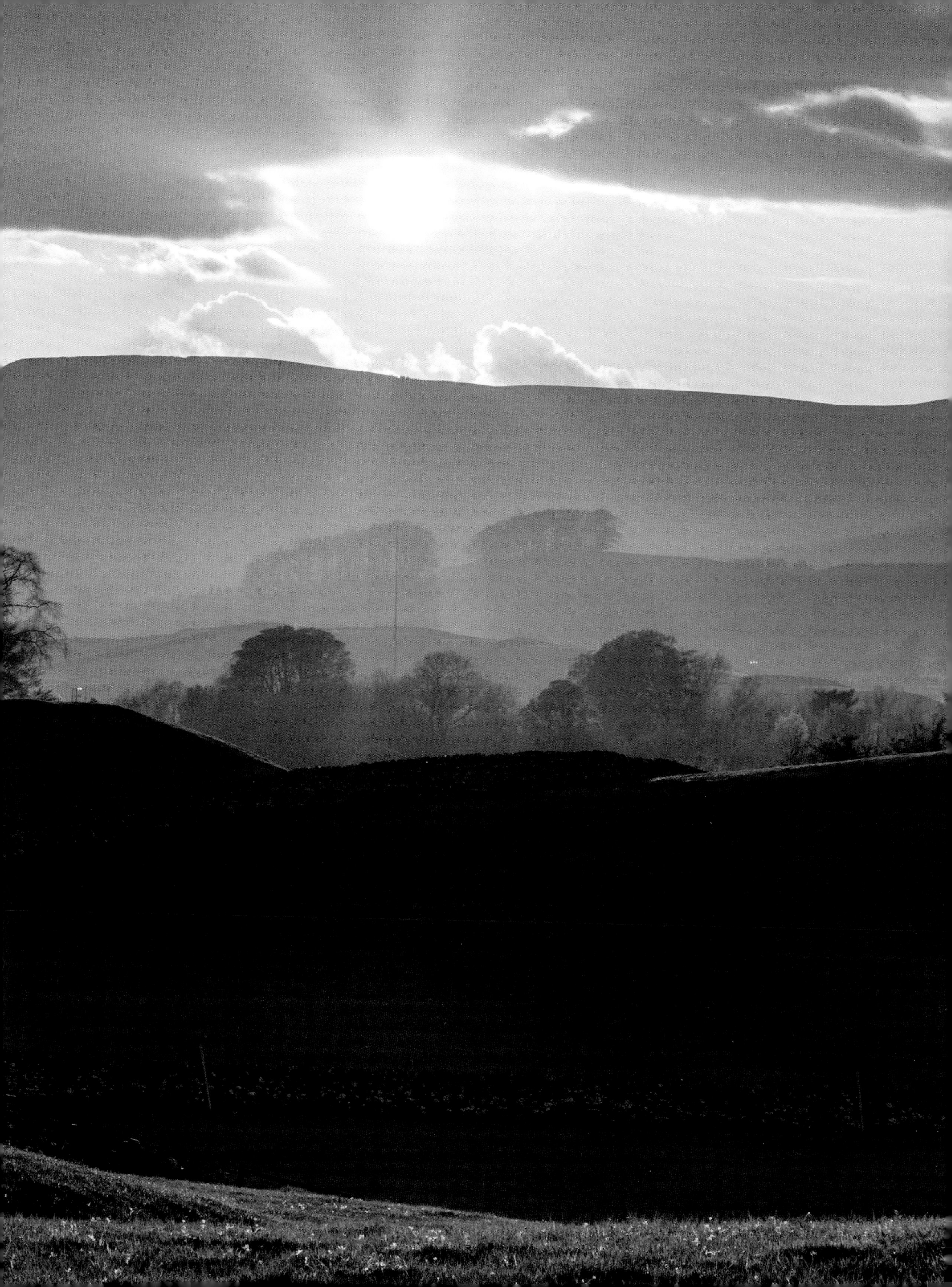

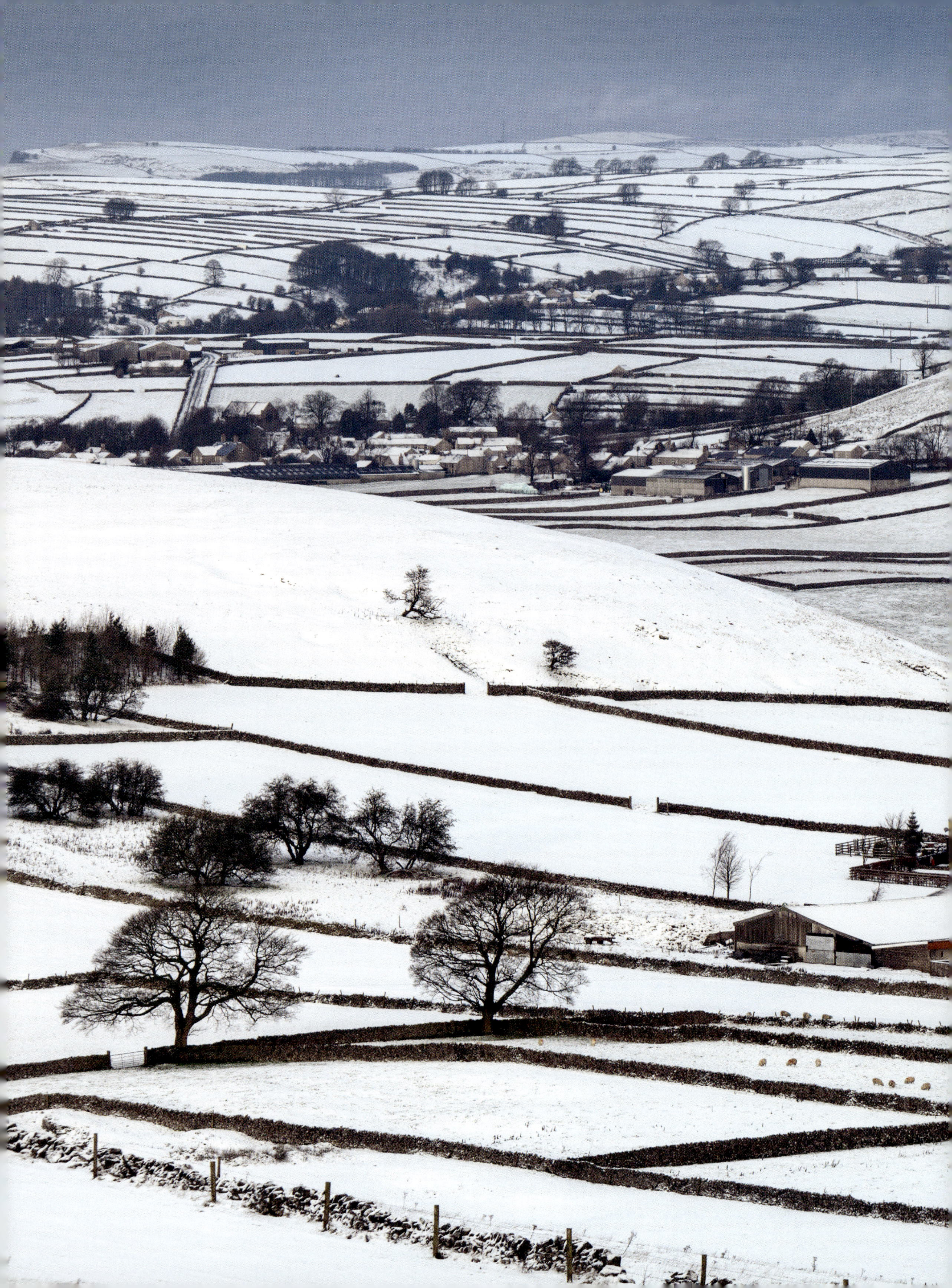

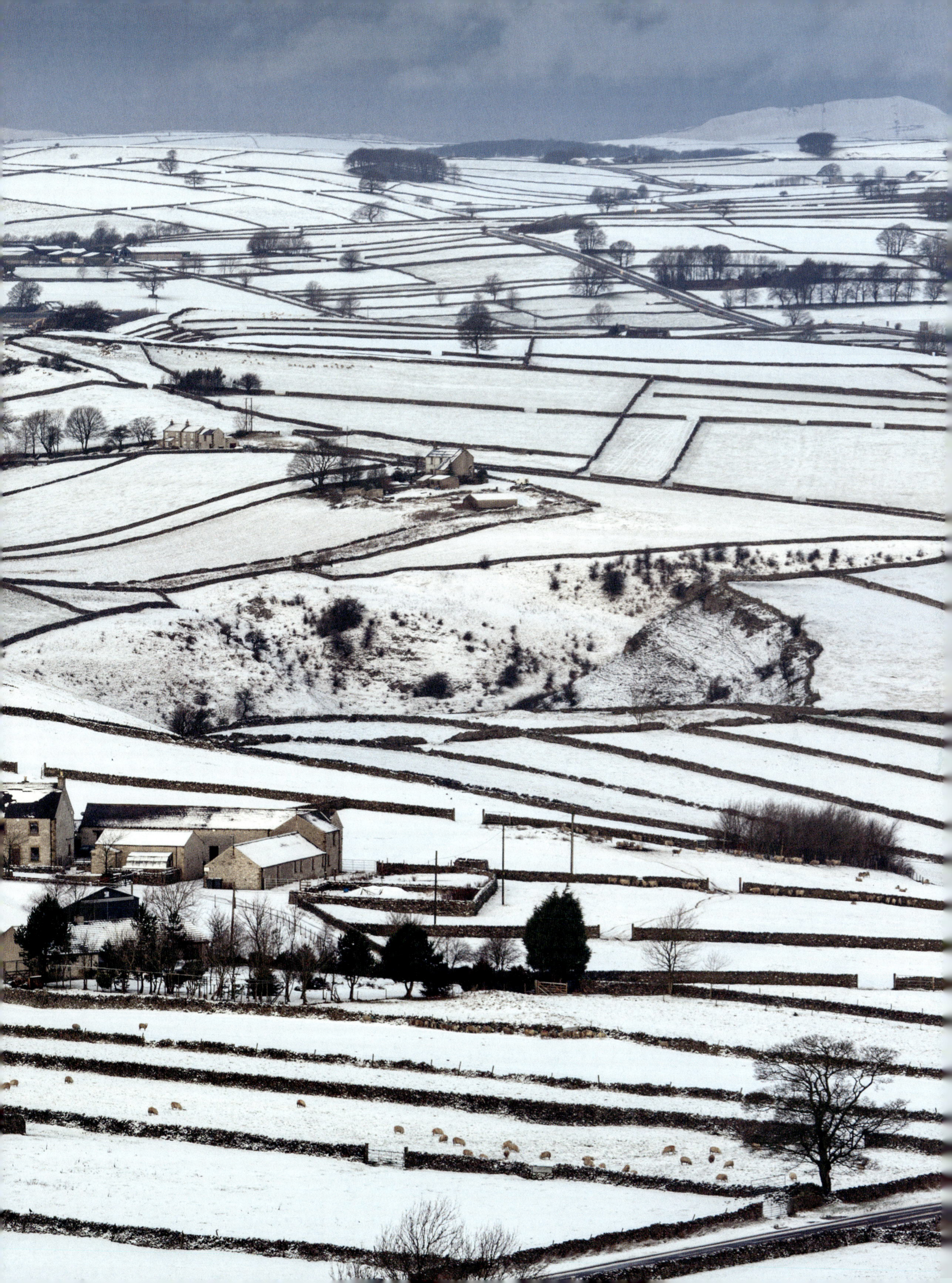

Introduction

Snow-gripped mountain plateaus strafed by 170mph winds. Confetti-coloured wildflower meadows fizzing with bees and butterflies. Cacophonous seabird cities of shearwaters and puffins. Gigantic flocks of starlings strobing above sprawling wetlands. Migrating salmon leaping from foaming river torrents. Golden eagles gliding above ancient pine forests. Leatherback turtles and humpback whales coming so close to shore they can spotted from the coastline.

You may be surprised to learn that not only are all these things found within the borders of the United Kingdom, they can all be seen within our 15 national parks. It is common to think of the extensively farmed and urbanised landscape of the UK as a 'tamed' place, entirely shorn of its natural glories. This books aims to show that this is far from the case.

This Atlantic archipelago has certainly been heavily shaped by human hands for a long time. Around 12,000 years ago, as the climate warmed and the glaciers and tundra of the last Ice Age gave way to forests and grasslands, people also returned to these islands. Thousands of years of agriculture followed, then the Industrial Revolution caused cities to boom, turning a previously rural people into a predominantly urban one for the first time in history.

In the process, there have been significant losses. In the not-too-distant past, wolves and wild cattle roamed across land now hidden under concrete. Brown bears once hunted in our now often-polluted rivers, and lynx prowled in dense forests that have long since been turned into farmland.

Yet the landscapes of these islands, and the countless creatures we share them with, are still capable of inspiring primal feelings of awe and wonder. Much of this wonder is found within the UK's national parks. This family of protected landscapes encompasses a tremendous diversity of environments: from the sub-arctic heights of the Cairngorms to the vineyards of the South Downs; from the jagged mountainous drama of Eryri to the sleepy lowland waterways of the Broads; from the austere moorland of Dartmoor to the lush temperate rainforests of Loch Lomond and The Trossachs; from the wildlife-rich coastline of Pembrokeshire to the UNESCO world heritage site of the Lake District.

Arguably our most accessible and iconic protected landscapes, the national parks are vital breathing spaces sometimes found on the very edge of great cities like Sheffield, Southampton and Glasgow. Celebrated in art and literature for centuries, they inspire our collective imagination.

Unlike in some other countries, our national parks are not designed to preserve tracts of 'wilderness'. After all, with its long history of human settlement, there is no truly untouched ecosystem in Britain; almost every square mile has been worked, planted, grazed, quarried, harvested, or in some other way altered. Rather, these national parks are both cultural preserves and natural refuges. They protect farming methods, traditional forms of architecture, and older rhythms of life which may otherwise have been lost.

Flocks of sheep on the open hills of the Lake District are taught to graze a certain area of land, then pass this knowledge down through generations from ewe to lamb. Free-roaming ponies wander through the New Forest under laws dating back 1,000 years. Thousands of miles of painstakingly built drystone walls striate the glacier-carved valleys of the Yorkshire Dales. Residents of rural villages in limestone regions of the Peak District garland local springs with intricate flower displays every summer. Castles and ancient monuments punctuate the mythology-rich mountains of Bannau Brycheiniog. Each national park is full of character; each has its own distinct atmosphere produced by a unique intertwining of natural and human history.

Today, there is something in the UK's national parks for everyone. Wild mountain landscapes offer worlds of beauty and exploration for hikers. Crags and fast-flowing rivers provide climbers and kayakers with adrenaline-pumping challenges. Wetlands and coasts host internationally important wildlife populations, which delight nature enthusiasts. And for anyone simply seeking to unwind, cosy villages, quiet country and ancient woods provide pockets of calm and a chance to experience the benefits nature can bring to personal wellbeing. Above all, the parks are free to enter and open for everyone to enjoy.

The first national park was created in Britain in 1951. In the years following World War Two the ravages of war were still evident, and a huge effort was underway to rebuild the country. An exhausted population was badly in need of the restorative effects of nature.

The National Parks and Access to the Countryside Act of 1949 was described as 'a people's charter for the open air'. It gave the go-ahead for areas of beautiful, wild and scenic countryside across England and Wales to be designated as national parks. These parks were intended to preserve the unique natural beauty of the designated areas, but above all, they were spaces where anyone could experience freedom, adventure and immersion within nature.

Today we take it for granted that we can freely enjoy these landscapes, but this wasn't always the case. In the 19th century, opposition from landowners meant that the ability of ordinary people to access the countryside could be limited, giving rise to the 'right to roam' movement. The 1949 act was one of the landmark achievements of this long-running campaign for free and open enjoyment of nature.

The Peak District was designated the first national park in April 1951. It was followed by the creation of nine further national parks by the end of the decade across England and Wales. The Broads Authority, with similar powers to a national park, was created in 1988. Scotland's two national parks were designated by the devolved government following the passing of relevant legislation in 2000. The current family was completed with the designation of the New Forest in 2005 and the South Downs in 2010. There are currently no national parks in Northern Ireland, though the idea of designating the Mourne Mountains as one has been mooted for more than 20 years. The total area covered by national parks is almost 10 per cent of the British landmass, and plans are afoot to create more.

All of Britain's national parks share two aims: to 'conserve and enhance the natural beauty, wildlife and cultural heritage of the national park', and 'to promote opportunities for the understanding and enjoyment of the special qualities of the national parks by the public'.

Balancing the two main purposes of the national parks – preservation and public enjoyment – and ensuring they do not conflict with one another can be a constant tightrope act. National parks see over 100 million visits a year, providing a constant inflow of visitors, which support shops, accommodation providers and attractions. In the Lake District alone in 2022, more than 18 million tourists brought £2.1 billion to the region. But balancing the needs of local communities, visitors and the environment requires constant negotiation. Government funding for national parks has fallen by more than 40 per cent in the last decade, making their effective operation increasingly difficult.

There are also lively debates around the preservation and protection of historic human activity and farming practices. Some argue that these practices should be reduced or adapted to allow a more extensive regrowth of nature, which can bring ecologists and conservationists into conflict with farmers and land managers. While there have been some significant reintroduction and nature restoration programmes in national parks in recent decades, some go further, arguing for the reintroduction of lost apex predators like lynx and wolves and a more radical embrace of 'rewilding'.

And despite the fact that national parks are open to everyone, evidence suggests there is still some way to go before everyone feels truly connected with them. Awareness of national parks, what they offer and how to access them is far from universal. Lack of car ownership can present transport difficulties. People on lower incomes or from minority ethnic groups have historically been under-represented among the parks' users. Making everyone feel welcome, and ensuring that there are no barriers to entry, is important for the future.

These important debates are touched on throughout the 15 chapters of this book – one for each national park – but they are not the main focus. The intention here is a simple one: to show the immense breadth of beauty and depth of fascination found in these landscapes. The aim is to inspire more people to visit national parks, in the hope that they will develop a deeper affinity and connection with them. Working from south to north, we start in the high granite world of Dartmoor, a moorland plateau which lost its covering of forest in prehistoric times. We end in another lofty granite landscape, the Cairngorms, where remnants of an ancient forest have survived – and are gradually recovering.

All our national parks, in their different ways, tell important parts of the story of how we came to be on these islands, along with the many other forms of life that we still share them with. They remind us of our closeness to that older, wilder kingdom, of the billions of years of natural history which brought us here. This wild world is interwoven with our lived-in landscape in sometimes startling ways. At their very best, our national parks can be microcosms of how we can live alongside nature without destroying it. In an era dominated by the crises of climate change and collapsing biodiversity, these examples can be inspiring.

Carey Davies

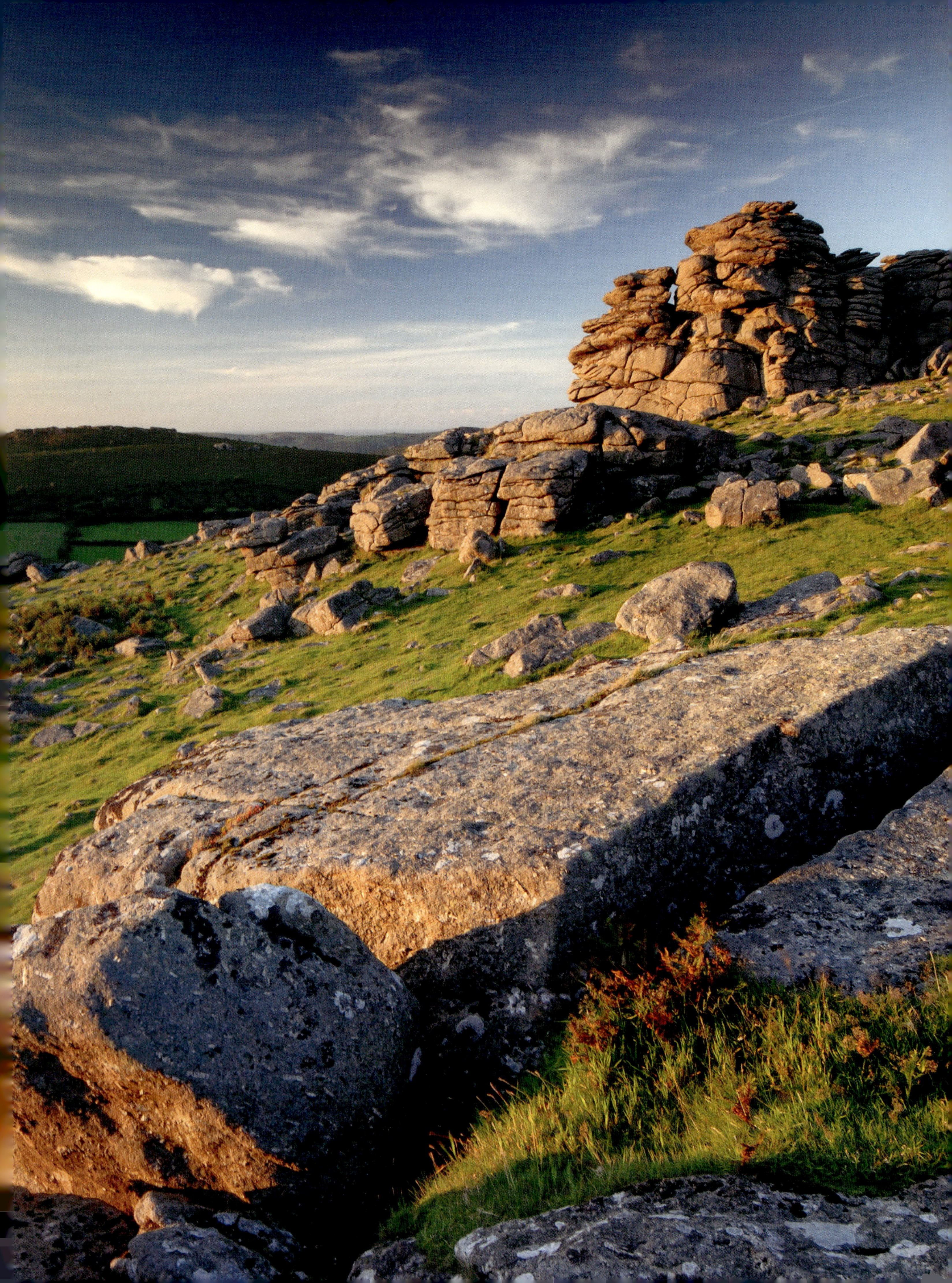

Dartmoor

A wild country ruled by the gods of open space, water, weather and rock. A place of industry and agriculture. A haunted land of ghost hands, hell hounds, big cats and black riders. A holy landscape filled with ancient monuments, sacred circles and stone crosses. A military training ground. A high sanctuary of tranquillity and peace. The site of a prison. An open expanse representing the freedom of the outdoors. A palimpsest of human history which has been worked and reworked for millennia. A place which often gives the impression of enormous emptiness.

Many of these descriptions would seem to contradict each other, but on Dartmoor, they are all true at the same time.

The highest land in southern England, Dartmoor was born underground. It is made from granite, a tough rock formed when molten magma is trapped below the surface of the earth, then slowly cools and crystallises. The 'pluton' (a body of intrusive igneous rock) that Dartmoor is part of was created 300 million years ago, and was slowly exposed to the earth's surface as the softer rocks above it eroded away over millennia. The result is the landform we see today: a broad moorland plateau that rears up conspicuously from the gently pastoral Devon countryside. Its granite bedrock is covered in a layer of blanket peat, which reaches depths of up to 3 metres (10 feet) in places, and the proximity of Dartmoor to the Atlantic, coupled with its altitude, means it gets regular top-ups of rain.

This upland otherworld is one of England's most distinctive, strange and beautiful landscapes. It is moorland: hilly, often boggy terrain with acidic soil, dominated by grasses, mosses and low shrubs. It is not the biggest moor to be found in Britain – a very fit walker could walk across it in one long day – but there are few places in England where the moorland terrain stretches out so far without touching a road, building or other mark of civilisation. The broad granite plateau of Dartmoor is also relatively level and unrelieved by valleys for large distances. At times the sense of space and sky can be almost dizzying, like a reverse vertigo.

Often simply shorthanded to 'the moor', Dartmoor is one of the defining moorland landscapes, its reputation strongly shaped by legend and literature. The most famous literary work set on Dartmoor is *The Hound of the Baskervilles*, a Sherlock Holmes story by Arthur Conan Doyle, where the famous detective investigates reports of a demonic hound said to be responsible for a series of

The granite bones of Dartmoor protrude spectacularly from the land in the form of 'tors', a word thought to derive from the Old Welsh twrr *or* twr, *meaning a cluster or heap. Defining features of Dartmoor, there are 160 of these rocky outcrops dotted across the landscape, often crowning the tops of hills like natural fortresses. This is a world of moors and tors. The wonderfully weathered Hound Tor, shown here, gave its name to the medieval village of Hundetorra, the abandoned ruins of which lie nearby.*

The high plateau of Dartmoor was not always an uninhabited 'wet desert'. These remains at Grimspound are those of a late Bronze Age settlement containing 24 stone roundhouses, encompassed within a boundary wall about 150 metres (500 feet) in diameter. An agricultural society extensively farmed the high reaches of Dartmoor in these prehistoric times, leaving a legacy of stone circles and settlements. But as the forests that once covered the landscape were destroyed to make more room for farming, soil and nutrients washed away, and life on the plateau became unsustainable. The result is the largely treeless and unpopulated landscape we still see today, with monuments like this preserved by the lack of intensive farming since they were built.

grisly deaths. Conan Doyle's novel was inspired by a visit to Dartmoor, where he hiked across the landscape and heard folk tales of phantom canines. Holmes' accomplice, Dr Watson, finds a certain austere beauty in the bleakness: 'The house is banked in with rolling clouds, which rise now and then to show the dreary curves of the moor, with thin, silver veins upon the sides of the hills, and the distant boulders gleaming where the light strikes upon their wet faces.'

The Hound of the Baskervilles has since become a descriptive shorthand for a particular type of Gothic scene: mist-shrouded moorland, lone stunted trees, unseen horrors lurking in the shadows. In fact, Conan Doyle's novel is part of a long tradition in English literature of projecting fears of the mysterious and malevolent on to the moorland landscape, from Emily's Brontë's *Wuthering Heights* to the Old English poem *Beowulf*, where the monstrous antagonist Grendel is described as dwelling on a moor.

But few moors typify this sense of the eerie and uncanny better than Dartmoor. Dartmoor just seems fundamentally *different*, and its sense of apartness even extends into the realm of physics: the structural composition of the underlying granite makes gravity itself weaker on Dartmoor than anywhere else in the UK. Yet walking across Dartmoor can feel anything but effortless: the word 'moor' stems from the same root that also gives us the words 'mire', 'morass' and 'marsh', and there are plenty of all three to be found on Dartmoor.

The Hound of the Baskervilles features the man-eating 'Grimpen Mire', a bog that fatally swallows all who enter, thought to be inspired by the real-life mire of Fox Tor. Local legends tell of unwary folk being sucked to their doom in Dartmoor's bogs, but while these stories may be apocryphal, the most heavily waterlogged expanses are best avoided by walkers. The misleadingly named 'feather beds' are quaking bogs where a wobbling layer of moss and vegetation conceals watery depths beneath; traversing them is like trying to walk across a particularly treacherous bouncy castle.

Yet the image of Dartmoor as an eternally inhospitable and treeless expanse is not quite what it seems. Conan Doyle himself, in a letter to his mother, wrote, 'It is a great place … dotted with the dwellings of prehistoric man, strange monoliths and huts and graves. In those old days, there was evidently a population of very many thousands here and now you may walk all day and never see one human being.'

During the Neolithic and Bronze Age eras, Dartmoor was a centre of human activity – so much so that it is difficult to go any distance on the moor today without encountering remnants of these ancient cultures, preserved over millennia by the relative lack of agriculture and development since.

The story of Dartmoor serves as a microcosm of larger trends in British history. After the glaciers had retreated from Britain following Europe's emergence from the last Ice Age, the arctic-style tundra, which covered Dartmoor during those frigid millennia, gave way to resurgent forests as the temperature warmed. Humans who encountered Dartmoor as they recolonised Britain during that time would have seen a very different landscape to the one we know today: a lush plateau covered in a broadleaved forest of oak, elm and hazel. Then, about 6,000 years ago, a revolution happened. Humans turned from hunter-gathering to farming, swapping an egalitarian, nomadic lifestyle for fixed and hierarchical agricultural societies. On Dartmoor, this meant the beginning of the end for the forest. Early Neolithic farmers are thought to have begun clearing woodland in the lower parts of landscape, probably through burning, to make room for pasture. These people were also builders, rearranging the native granite of Dartmoor into stone circles and stone rows; long-lasting monuments that served as ritual sites and reinforced the new, settled order.

Humans continued living and thriving on Dartmoor into the Bronze Age, the era that defines the Dartmoor landscape to this day. Bronze Age people built stone circles, of which 14 survive, including grand sites like Scorhill and

Dartmoor is strewn with megalithic monuments, including 15 Bronze Age stone circles, like this one known as Down Tor, at Hingston Hill. A ring cairn of 24 stones linked to a stone row that is 350 metres (1,145 feet) long, it is one of the most well-preserved and striking relics on Dartmoor.

Opposite:
Perching impressively on Brent Tor, a conspicuous mound of basaltic rock formed by underwater lava flows about 400 million years ago, St Michael de Rupe is thought to be the highest working church in southern England. Dating back to the 12th century, a legend holds that it was built by the eponymous saint after he was caught at sea in a storm caused by the devil. He promised the Almighty he would construct a church on the highest ground he saw if he survived to reach the shore. The historical record is more prosaic: it was founded by Robert Giffard, a local landowner.

Brisworthy. They constructed fortified settlements, like those at Grimspound and Merrivale, and worked the land through extensive field systems, the boundaries of which are still evident. But as people flourished on Dartmoor, the clearance of the woods gathered pace, resulting in almost total deforestation. Lack of tree cover caused nutrients to leach out of the soils, accelerating the growth of peat bogs and undermining the viability of agriculture. This human-made ecological crisis was compounded by the climate turning colder and wetter. Eventually, life on Dartmoor became unsustainable. People largely retreated from the plateau, leaving a world of bogs and rock behind them.

With the exception of a 300-year period in the Middle Ages, when the climate warmed up enough to allow year-round settlement to return to Dartmoor, this is largely how it has remained since. The deserted village of Hound Tor is a poignant remnant of this relatively brief medieval flourishing, which was cut short by falling temperatures and plague. The history of Dartmoor's deforestation and depopulation is a reminder of the lost worlds that often lie beneath Britain's hills.

Even so, Dartmoor's bog and moorland habitats are not all doom and gloom. Healthy blanket peat bogs have become integral to the ecological make-up of its uplands, supporting distinctive communities of plants, invertebrates and moorland birds like curlew, golden plover and snipe. On a summer day, with dragonflies darting across the peaty pools, yellow asphodel flowering brightly and emerald-coloured sphagnum mosses gleaming in the sun, these boggy places can feel anything but bleak. And as with all such places, Dartmoor's peat bogs play important roles in storing carbon, improving water quality and reducing flood risk.

The expanses of the moors are punctuated by 'tors'; outcrops of granite, that often crown the tops of hills like natural fortresses. They range in size and shape and have sometimes been weathered into fantastic forms over the many epochs

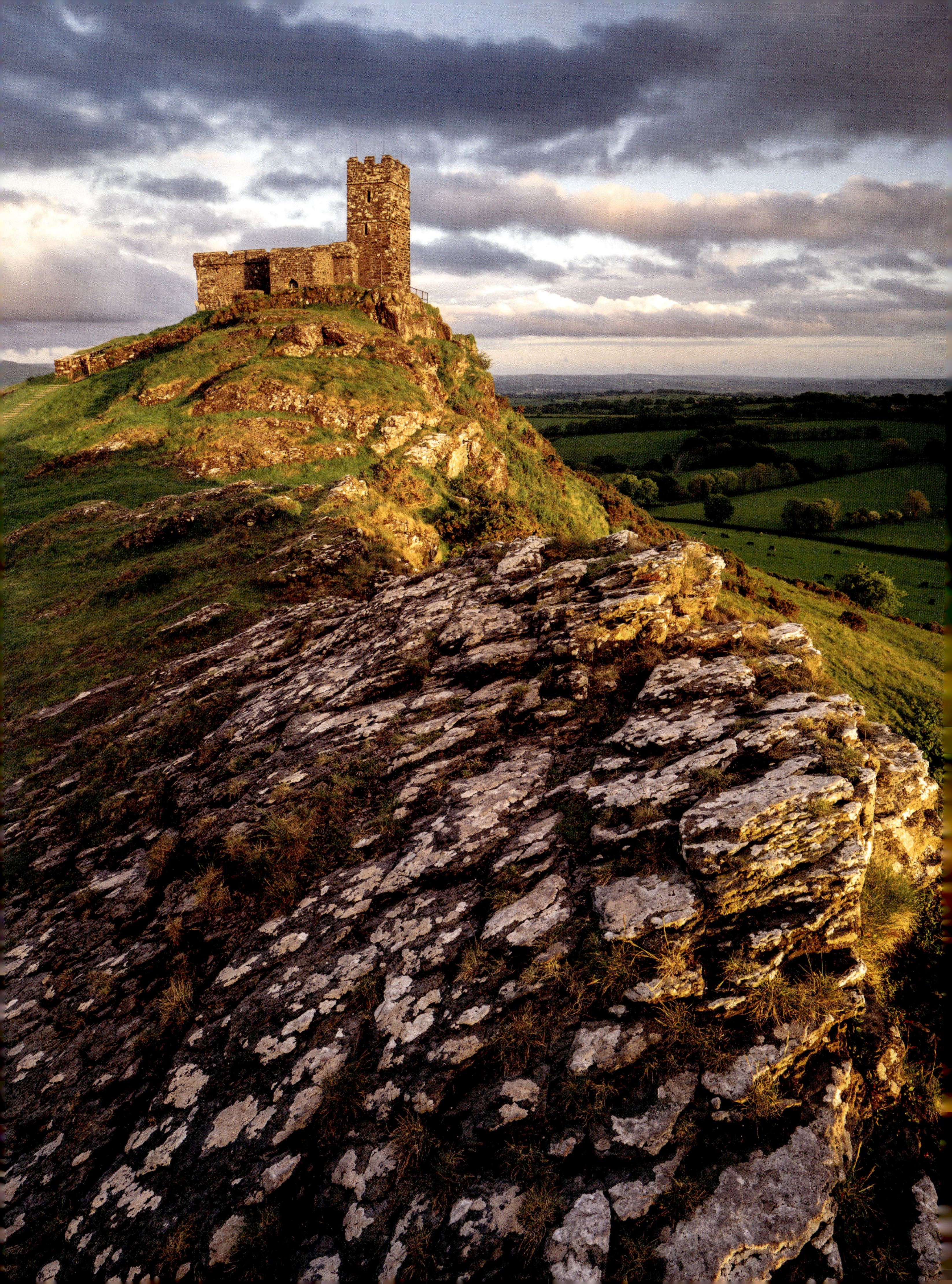

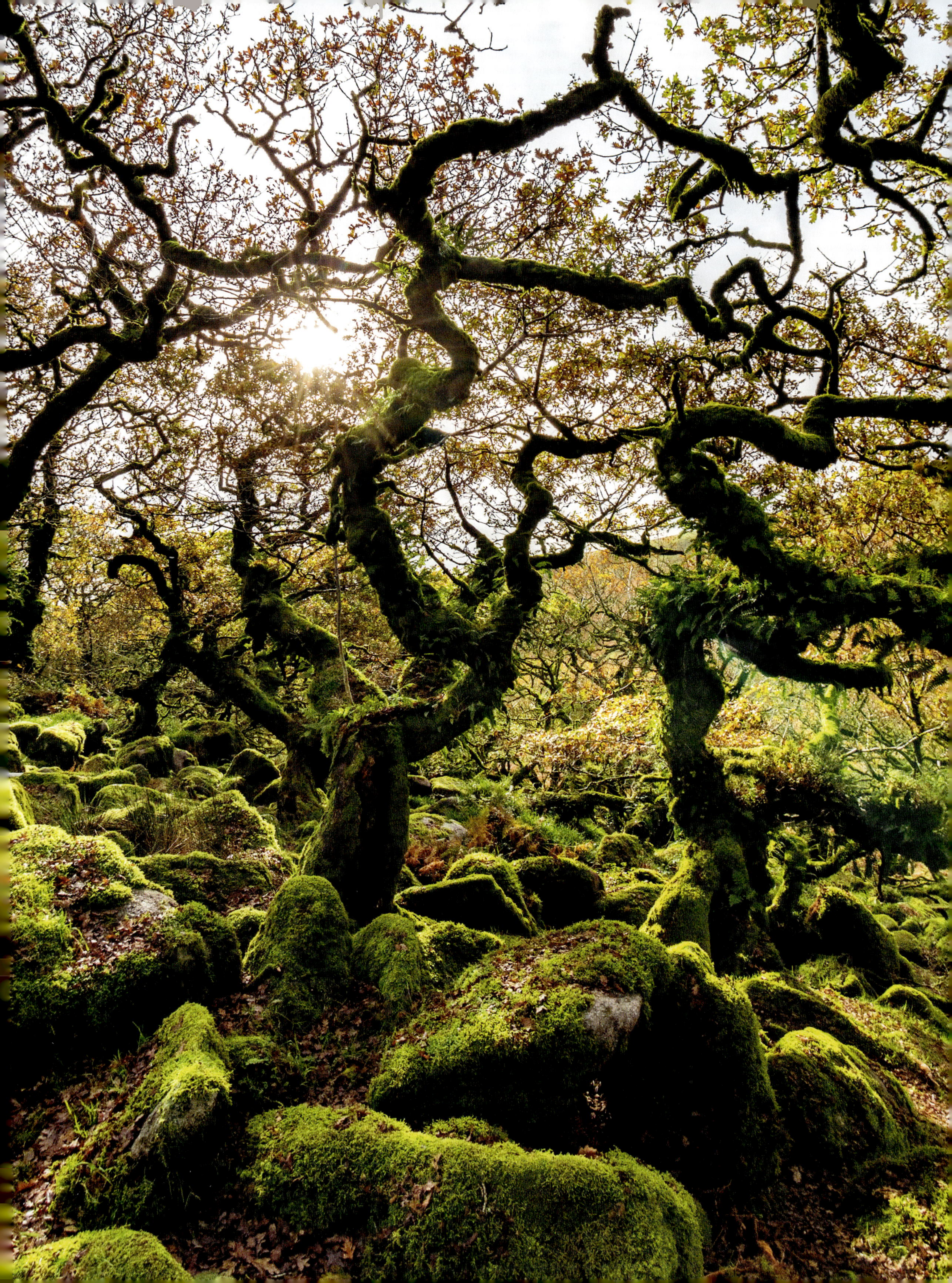

they have been exposed to the atmosphere. These tors have a monumental presence, hinting at a possible source of inspiration for the stone circles and dolmens of Dartmoor.

The original wildwood that covered Dartmoor has also not been completely lost. Fragments of it are believed to have survived in pockets of high-altitude temperate rainforest such as Wistman's Wood and Black-a-Tor Copse. Carefully entering these small, ecologically sensitive and enchanting wonder-woods can feel like stepping back into the Jurassic. Epiphytic plants – plants that grow on other plants – thrive here, producing a glorious intermingled chaos where it can be impossible to distinguish one species from another. Lichens droop like tangled spaghetti from the fantastically contorted arms of weather-beaten pedunculate oaks; tree roots upholstered with mosses sprawl like snakes through fields of lichen-encrusted boulders; fungi and ferns sprout abundantly everywhere. In the height of spring or summer, the vegetation can be so dense that light barely seems to reach the forest floor, instead diffusing into a witchlike green glow.

Dartmoor is a place of two halves: the North Moor and the South Moor, roughly delineated by the B3212 and B3357 roads, which cut across Dartmoor in an X shape. This central corridor is where the handful of farms and settlements dotting the high moor are clustered, the biggest of which is Princetown. At around 430 metres (1,410 feet) above sea level, this is one of the highest villages in Britain.

A significant chunk of Dartmoor's North Moor is used for live firing practice by the military, typically on a few days a month during which it is closed to the public. Dartmoor also holds the slightly dubious distinction of being the only UK national park to contain a prison, HMP Dartmoor, which is close to Princetown. Even so, to many hikers and outdoor enthusiasts, this landscape is a symbol not of restriction or confinement, but of freedom. A local by-law permits wild camping on the 'common land' of Dartmoor, a designation that applies to most of its open moorland. This makes Dartmoor the only place in England where wild camping – practised responsibly, of course, with due respect for the principles of 'leave no trace' – is officially legal. In 2022, after the High Court ruled in favour of a local landowner and effectively banned wild camping on the moor, a public outcry erupted, which included a 3,000-strong protest on the landowner's estate, one of the largest pro-access gatherings in modern times. The High Court's decision was overturned later in the year following an appeal, and at the time of writing, the right to wild camp freely on Dartmoor remains.

On this long lived-upon island, moorland landscapes often occupy several roles. They serve as places of protest; symbols of freedom and escape; sinister, haunted badlands; repositories of the past; unique habitats that play an important role in our ecological fabric. Dartmoor, perhaps England's archetypal moor, is all of these things – and more.

Opposite:
The otherworldly Wistman's Wood is one of only three remaining fragments of high-altitude oakwood on Dartmoor, a glimpse of what much of the wider landscape would once have looked like. At just nine acres in size, it is a small but celebrated example of Britain's 'temperate rainforest'. The contorted branches of dwarf oak trees are wildly festooned with ferns, lichens and mosses, some of which – like the horsehair lichen, found in just two places in Britain – are exceedingly rare.

The gates of Dartmoor prison. The facility was built in 1809 to contain French prisoners from the Napoleonic wars. Its location was originally ten miles from any civilisation, in the remote heart of the moor, but the village of Princetown has since grown up near it. It is still a working prison, used to incarcerate non-violent offenders.

Overleaf:
The high Dartmoor landscape is characterised by the vast open spaces of the granite plateau, seen here from near Belstone, dominated by rough expanses of grass and heather, heathlands and peat bogs. Much of Dartmoor's moorland is 'commons' – areas of unenclosed land that are privately owned, but which other locals have rights to graze livestock like sheep, cattle and ponies, even if it is owned by someone else.

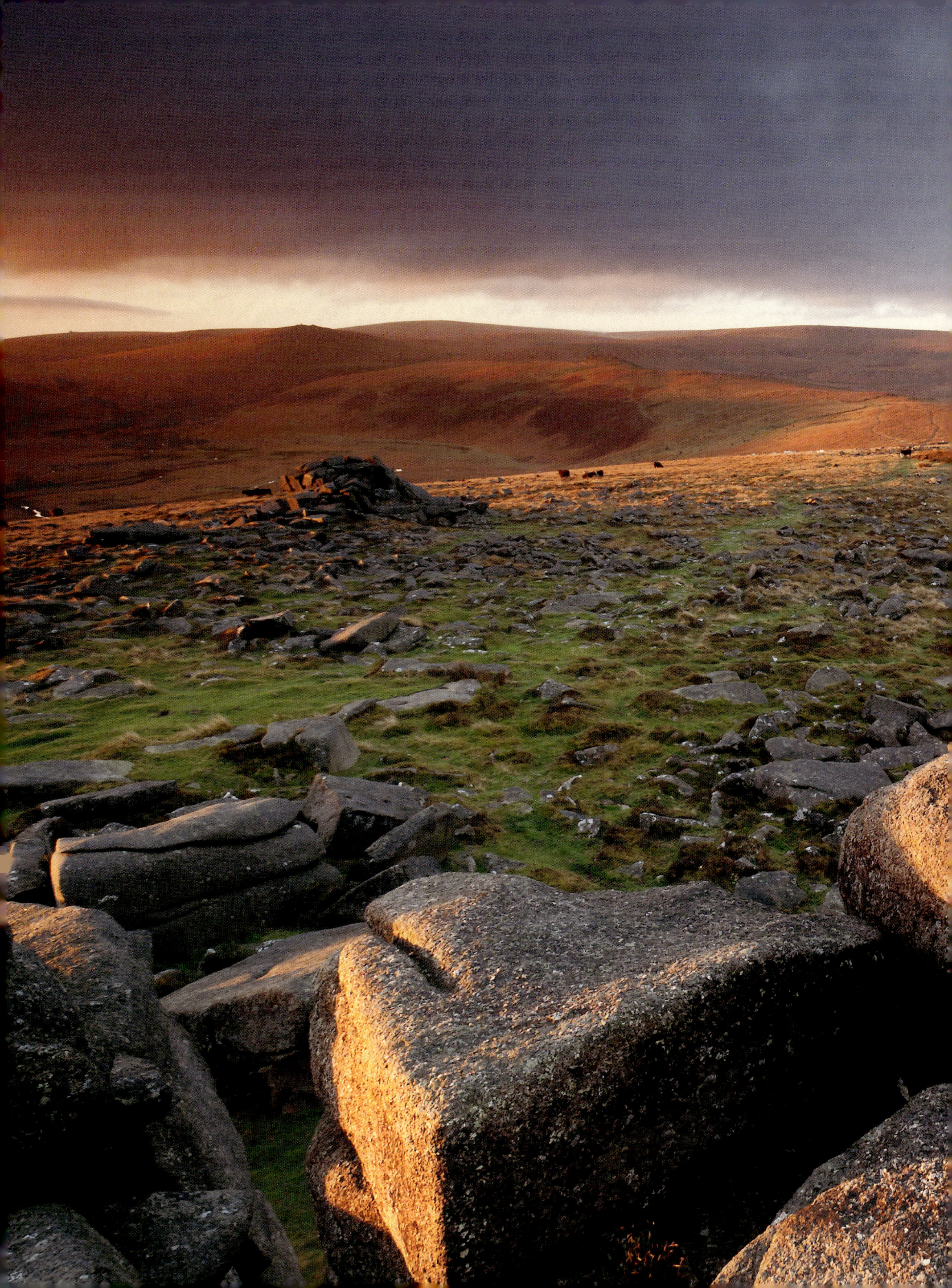

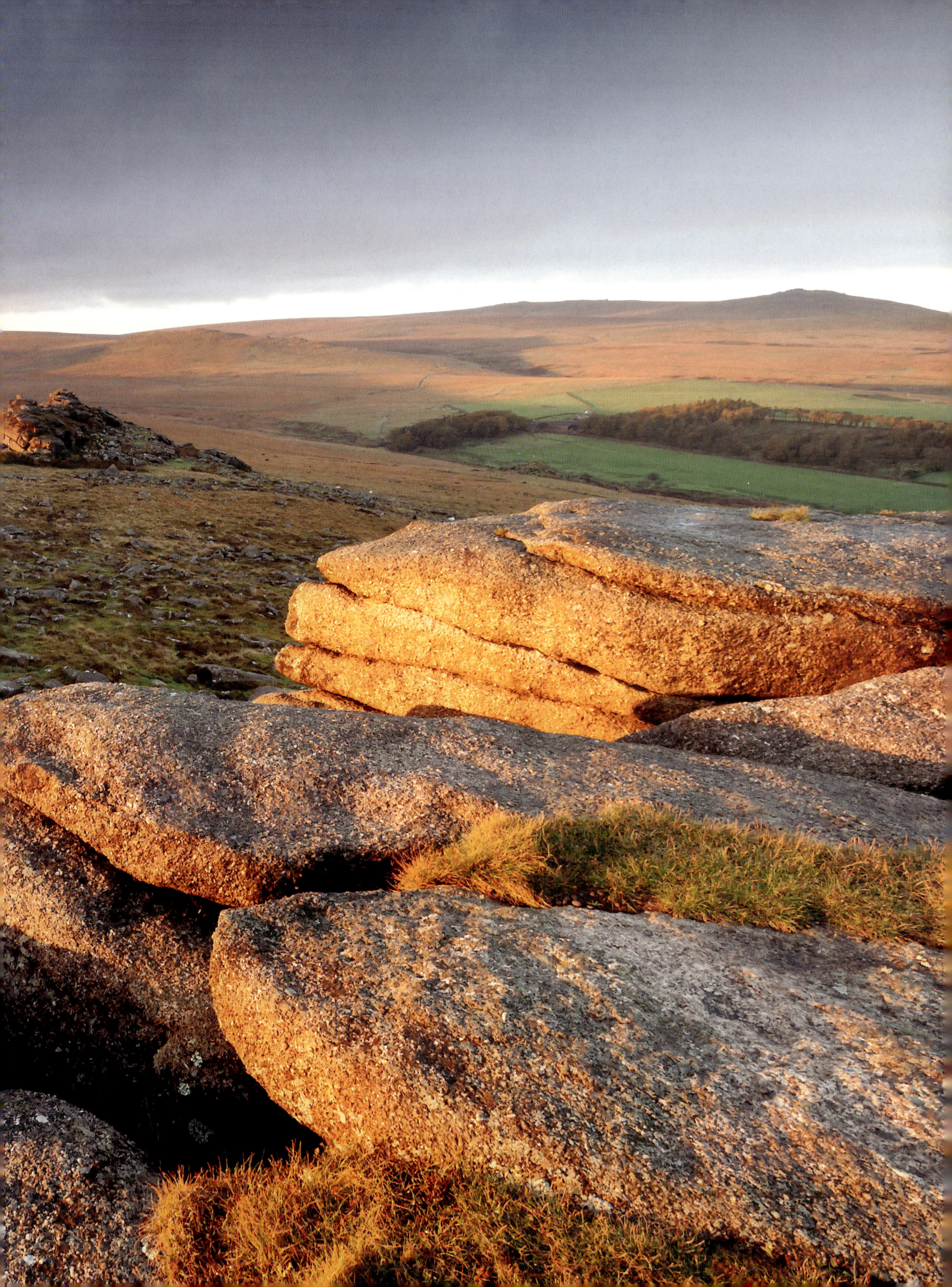

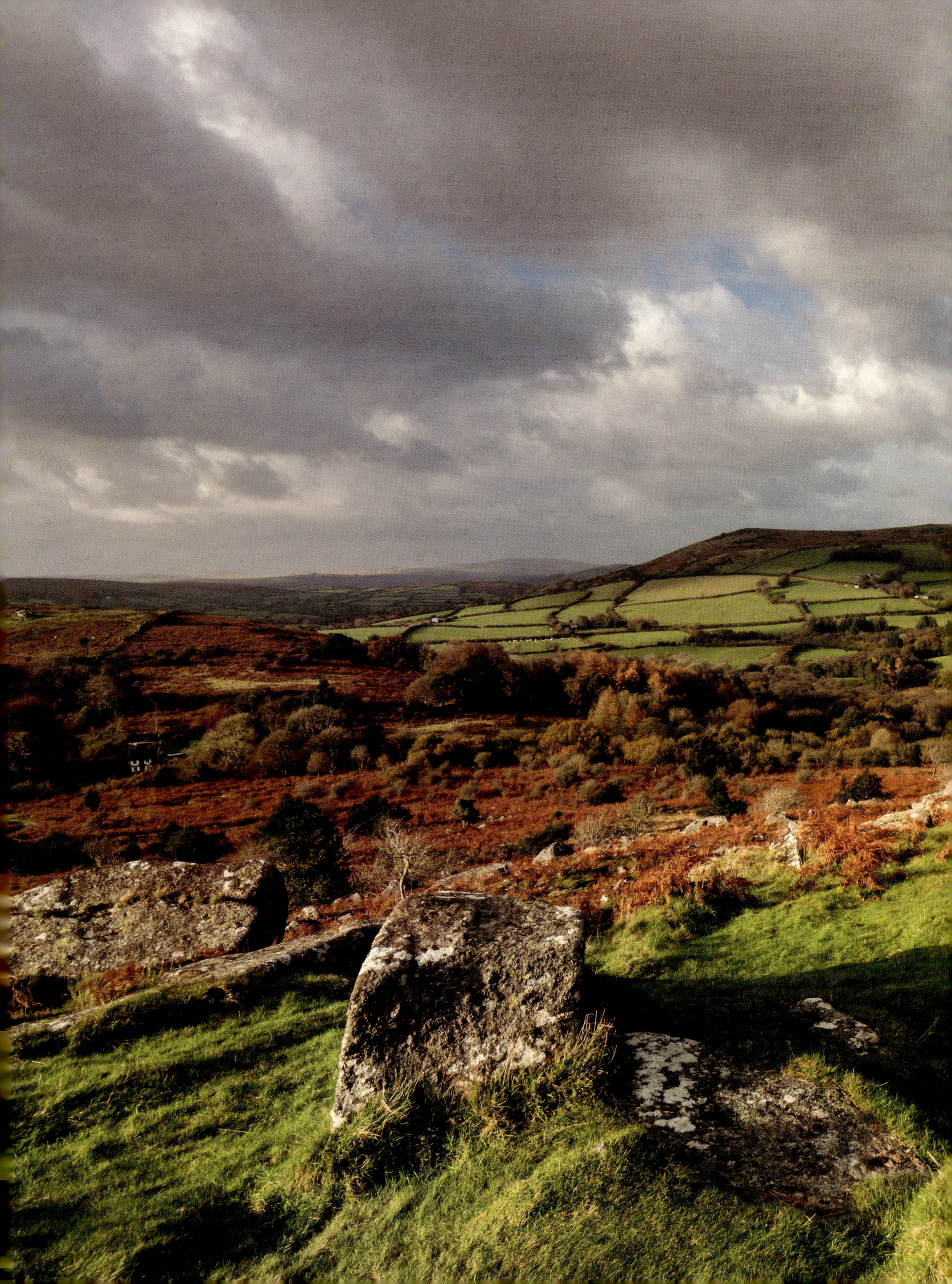

The statuesque Bowerman's Nose near Manaton is a natural granite formation, the hard core of a heavily eroded tor, but its totemic appearance – with its crowning boulder's faint resemblance to a human head – has invited more fantastic accounts of its creation. The eponymous Bowerman was said to be a medieval hunter who was turned to stone by a coven of witches after he overturned their cauldron. His unfortunate dogs are said to have also been petrified, creating the nearby Hound Tor. Myths and folklore often cling to Dartmoor's rocky outcrops; Crockern Tor, in the west of Dartmoor, is said to be the home of Old Crockern, a 'spirit guardian' of the moor who, according to legend, chased away an industrialist-turned-landowner from Manchester who attempted to enclose part of the landscape. Old Crockern has been invoked in recent protests over another wealthy landowner's legal battle to overturn a historic right to wild camping on the commons. The significance of the tors to Neolithic and Bronze Age peoples is debated, but some scholars have suggested the monuments and dolmens they built could have been intended to imitate or echo the tors. Today, these outcrops are natural gathering places and orientating landmarks, often serving as the focus for events and challenges.

Overleaf:
As well as prehistoric monuments, Dartmoor is rich with relics that reflect more recent traditions of worship. This one is known as Nun's Cross, or Siward's Cross, and is one of a host of medieval stone crosses marking a 37-kilometre (23-mile) route across the moor between the monastic centres of Buckfastleigh and Tavistock.

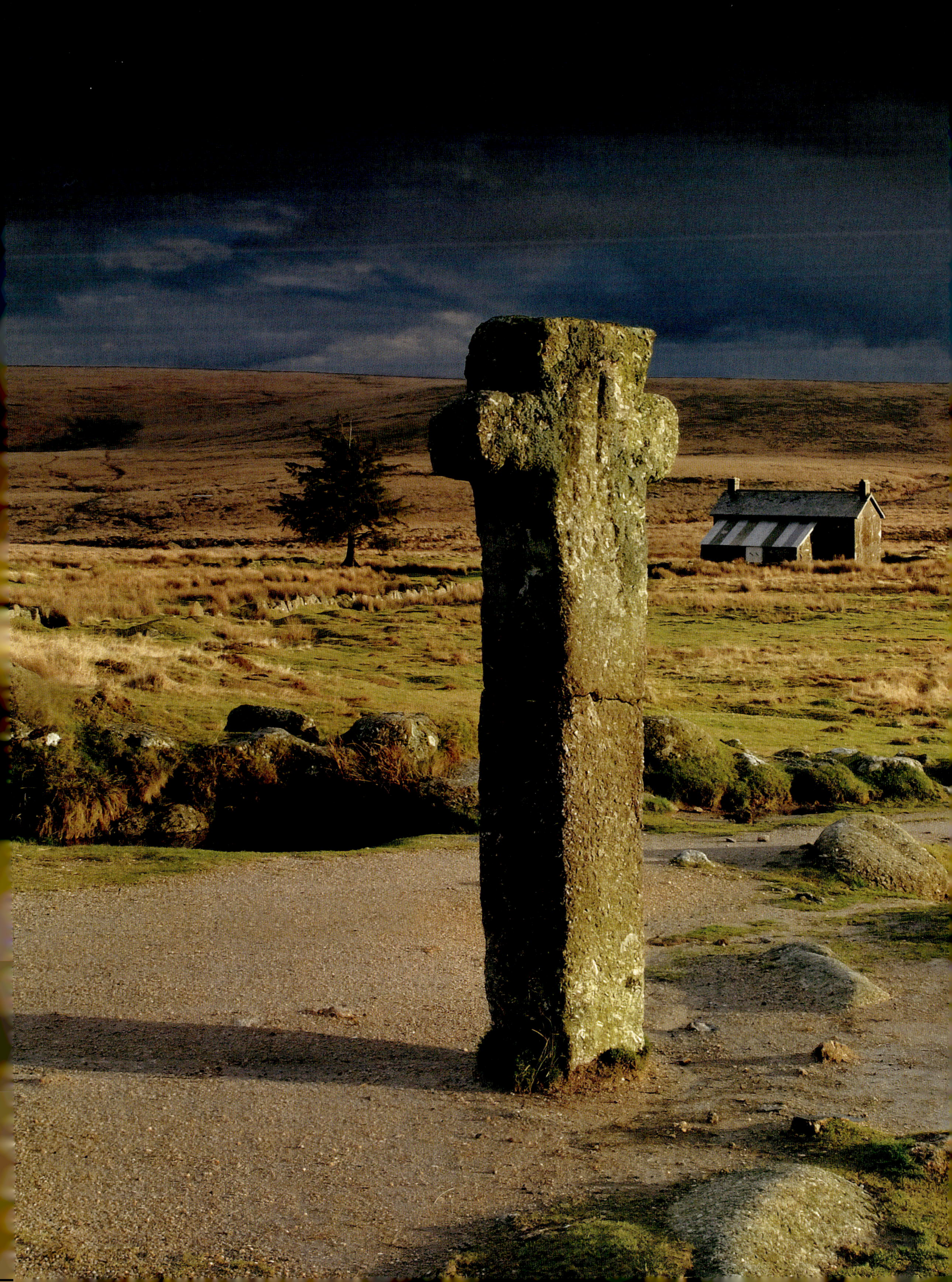

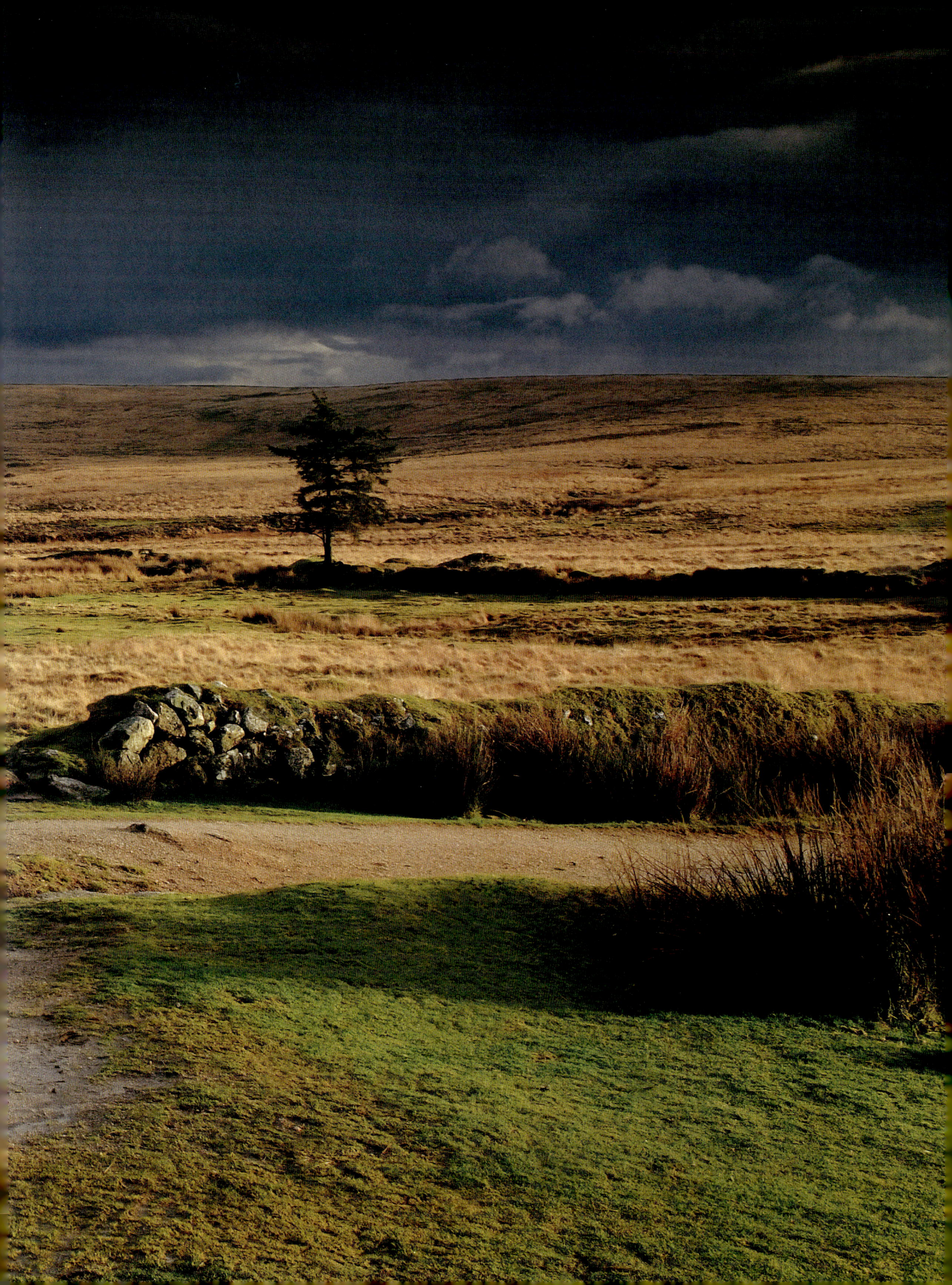

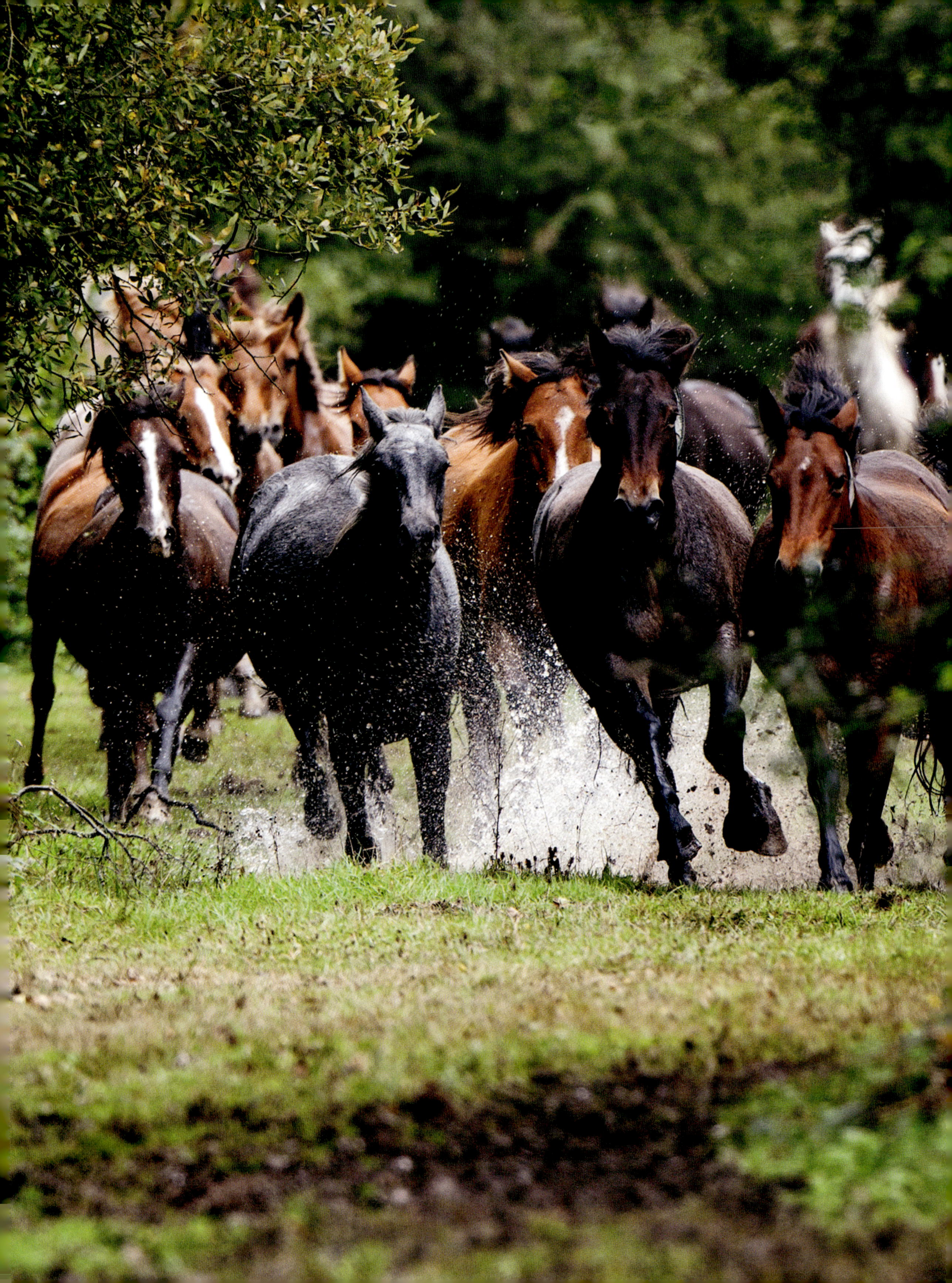

New Forest

On arriving in the New Forest for the first time, you might feel like you have wandered into a realm where people are merely guests. The ruling inhabitants here, you quickly realise, are the ponies. These gentle-tempered animals roam through the winding roads of villages, munching at grass verges, while queues of drivers wait for them to move on. They ramble freely through the sprawling woods, sometimes obliging you to step aside as they pass. Although they have become mixed with breeds from elsewhere, the New Forest ponies have a lineage dating back thousands of years, to before the last Ice Age. They are not strictly 'wild', but owned by locals who have historical grazing rights, a tradition stretching back to William the Conqueror. The ponies are an important component of this unique national park, a last bastion of open farming traditions which are thousands of years old. In a sense, the New Forest is also a relic of something much older: it retains an echo of the largely vanished 'wildwood', the original forest that would once have covered these islands before Neolithic peoples began clearing the landscape for agriculture. It is a refuge of relative wildness on the populous south coast of England.

The name 'New Forest' is something of a double misnomer. It is not only a forest, nor is it new. The moniker derives from William the Conqueror, who made this 'Nova Foresta' a royal hunting ground after the Norman conquest of England in the 11th century. The meaning of the word 'forest' in this medieval context did not simply suggest trees – although there would have been plenty there at the time – but rather connoted a game preserve for hunting. In that respect, this is England's oldest 'protected' landscape, though originally for very different reasons to today.

The New Forest National Park, by some estimates, contains the highest concentration of ancient trees in western Europe. Some of these trees were probably alive and even mature at the time William made his designation: the yew tree in St Nicholas's churchyard near Brockenhurst, for example, is thought to be more than 1,000 years old. Other venerable individuals include the Knightwood Oak, a 500-year-old veteran that has been a tourist attraction since at least Victorian times. In spring the floors of broadleaved woodlands are awash with the colours of bluebells, wild garlic, wood anemones and celandines, while the oldest forest fragments support rare or unusual – and evocatively named – woodland plants like bastard balm and butcher's broom. In autumn the canopy of the woods turns a million opulent shades of gold, copper and bronze, while the fruiting bodies of fungi emerge in the forests and heaths in countless numbers; the New Forest is home to around 2,700 species of fungi.

New Forest ponies are often described as the 'architects' of this unique landscape. Largely free to roam, their itinerant grazing is intrinsic to the character of the New Forest, helping to maintain its distinctive open patchwork of woodland and heath. In an arrangement dating back to the Norman conquest, the animals are owned by 'commoners' who have grazing rights, supervised by ten 'verderers' who oversee the system.

Oak woodland with a bracken understorey in Broomy Inclosure. Walking through the same inclosure in 1934, author Joan Begbie wrote in her nature memoir Walking in the New Forest: *'It is a bewitching wood and was in the pleasantest mood that day. Brightly painted, tiny flowers were generously sprinkled about the short grass of the ride; the oaks, tall and freely spaced, made the sun a welcome guest.'*

Opposite:
A large hen-of-the-woods fungus growing at the base of a veteran pedunculate oak tree. This large fungus is a weak parasite which targets old-growth trees of the sort that are found throughout the New Forest.

Even though this national park contains some of the most extensive continuous tracts of forest in England, around half the landscape is made up of open 'heathland'. As the name suggests, most heathland is dominated by heather, a dense, low-growing woody shrub, which carpets huge tracts of ground, creating spectacular reefs of purple when it blossoms in late summer. Scattered across the heather are trees like pine, birch and holly, as well as clumps of gorse, whose blazing yellow blooms smell of coconut biscuits in the spring sun. In places it resembles a kind of English savannah. While upland heath, or moorland, is relatively common across the UK, lowland heath of the sort found across the New Forest is much rarer – in the last 150 years, around 85 per cent of it has disappeared, lost to agriculture, development, or commercial forestry. But the New Forest remains a sanctuary for lowland heath and the life it supports. It is a habitat perfectly suited to reptile species: the open areas allow the cold-blooded animals to bask in sunshine to replenish their body heat, the underlying sandy soils heat up quickly, and the mix of vegetation provides plenty of cover to retreat into when danger threatens. As a result, the national park is one of the few places that is home to all six of the UK's reptile species: common lizard, sand lizard, slow worm, smooth snake, grass snake and adder.

Folds and depressions in the heathland landscape also contain waterlogged morasses full of mosses, cotton grass, alders and willows. These permanently wet and acidic valley mires may not be the most famous feature of the national park, but in terms of sheer rarity they are its most important habitat: 90 of the 120 remaining such mires in North-West Europe are sited here. The national or regional rarity of the plants found in these places matches the scarcity of the habitat: bogbean, bog pimpernel, or the beautiful coral necklace, found only in a few other locations in the UK.

This mix of heathland habitats, combined with the similarly diverse woodland, form a complex mosaic of environments. Although some boundaries can be found in the park, the relative absence of fences, fields, intensive agriculture or

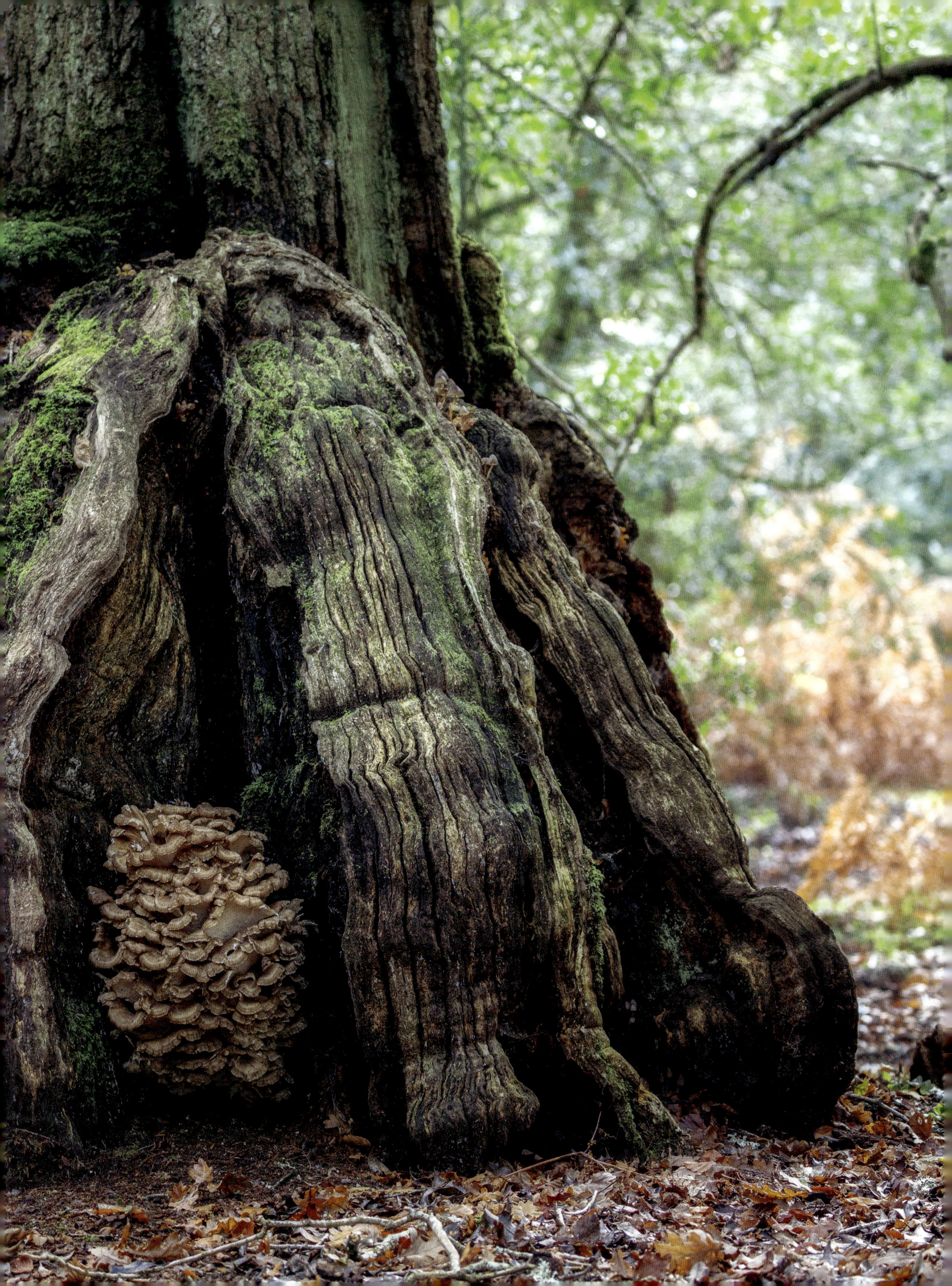

A golden-ringed dragonfly resting on bog myrtle in the New Forest. Found near acidic heathland and moorland streams, this voracious insect is the UK's longest dragonfly, and targets large insects like, bees, beetles, and even other dragonflies. Dragonflies are the world's must successful hunters, with more than 95 per cent of their chases resulting in a kill.

walls means you can weave through the patchwork landscape on foot or bike with a sense of freedom that is rare in these islands. You pass through arcades of ancient trees, emerge into open heaths, then disappear back into the woods again; trace the lines of meandering paths through the furze and heather; follow the routes of winding clay rivers for miles, with huge dragonflies flitting through the trees; and happen upon secretive glades with white horses grazing in them like a scene from Arthurian legend.

Scattered throughout this patchwork are historic villages like Brockenhurst, Beaulieu and Lyndhurst, places full of fine houses, antique shops, good cafés and intriguing museums. The underlying structure of the landscape, with its geology of sand, gravel and clay, is rarely anything more than gently rolling; although the northern parts of the park contain the tallest topography, the highest point of the New Forest is the modest hill of Pipers Wait at only 140 metres (460 feet). Combined with an extensive network of paths and tracks – including a host of accessible and stile-free trails – this is one of the most obliging parks for people with mobility limitations and those just getting started exploring the outdoors. It is also one of the most family friendly.

A family who did have a hard time of it in the New Forest – albeit a fictional one – were the Beverleys, the main protagonists in Frederick Marryat's 1847 children's novel *The Children of the New Forest*. Orphaned by the civil war, with their house burned by Parliamentarian soldiers, the four siblings are taken in by a local verderer and learn to survive on their own in the forest.

The New Forest ponies are sometimes dubbed 'architects' of the landscape. Traditionally, their itinerant grazing has been intrinsic to the character of the landscape, suppressing the regrowth of forest in the open areas and creating the habitat mix that is characteristic of the region. Under the same arrangement as the ponies, you may also see cattle and donkeys grazing on the heaths and pigs snuffling through the oak woods during the 'pannage' season in the autumn, hoovering up the mast of fallen acorns, beechnuts and chestnuts covering the ground.

Outside of the New Forest's ancient woodlands, many woodland areas here are more recent, and owe their existence to human needs. Around 84 square kilometres (32 square miles) of the park are covered by 'inclosures' – forest plantations, fenced off from grazing animals, which were created at different times over the last 300 years to provide sources of timber. The establishment of the earliest inclosures was driven by the voracious demand for sturdy hardwoods like oak to meet the shipbuilding needs of the British navy. In the Napoleonic era it took 4,000 oak trees to build a single ship of the line. As the demand for oak subsided with the rise of metal ships in the 19th century, the inclosures began to be populated with non-native conifers, particularly when there was a need for rapid timber replenishment after the two world wars. Into the mix have also gone around 3,000 ornamental or 'exotic' trees planted by the Victorians, which often form part of 'ornamental drives' like Bolderwood and Rhinefield. These specimens include the likes of Californian redwoods, giant sequoias and Douglas firs, some of which have grown to towering proportions. These non-native introductions, as well as looking spectacular, can provide valuable wildlife habitat in some situations, but much of the lower-value conifer planting has been removed in recent decades in favour of open habitat or native woodland.

On the southern edge of the national park, the land gives way to a 42-kilometre (26-mile) stretch of coastline overlooking the waters of the Solent strait. This relatively unheralded dimension of the New Forest contains some of the park's most significant wildlife habitats. The internationally important Lymington and Keyhaven Marshes Nature Reserve is a mix of marshes, mudflats, lagoons, wetlands and shingle banks where hundreds of species breed, feed or roost across the course of a year. Gulls and terns dominate in summer, amply

Pre-dawn mists drift through the rolling heathland of Ibsley Common. Although a tranquil place today, the now-vanished RAF Ibsley was an important airfield in World War Two, and the crumbing remnants of buildings associated with it can be found on Ibsley Common. Relics from the extensive use of the New Forest in World War Two can still be found across the landscape.

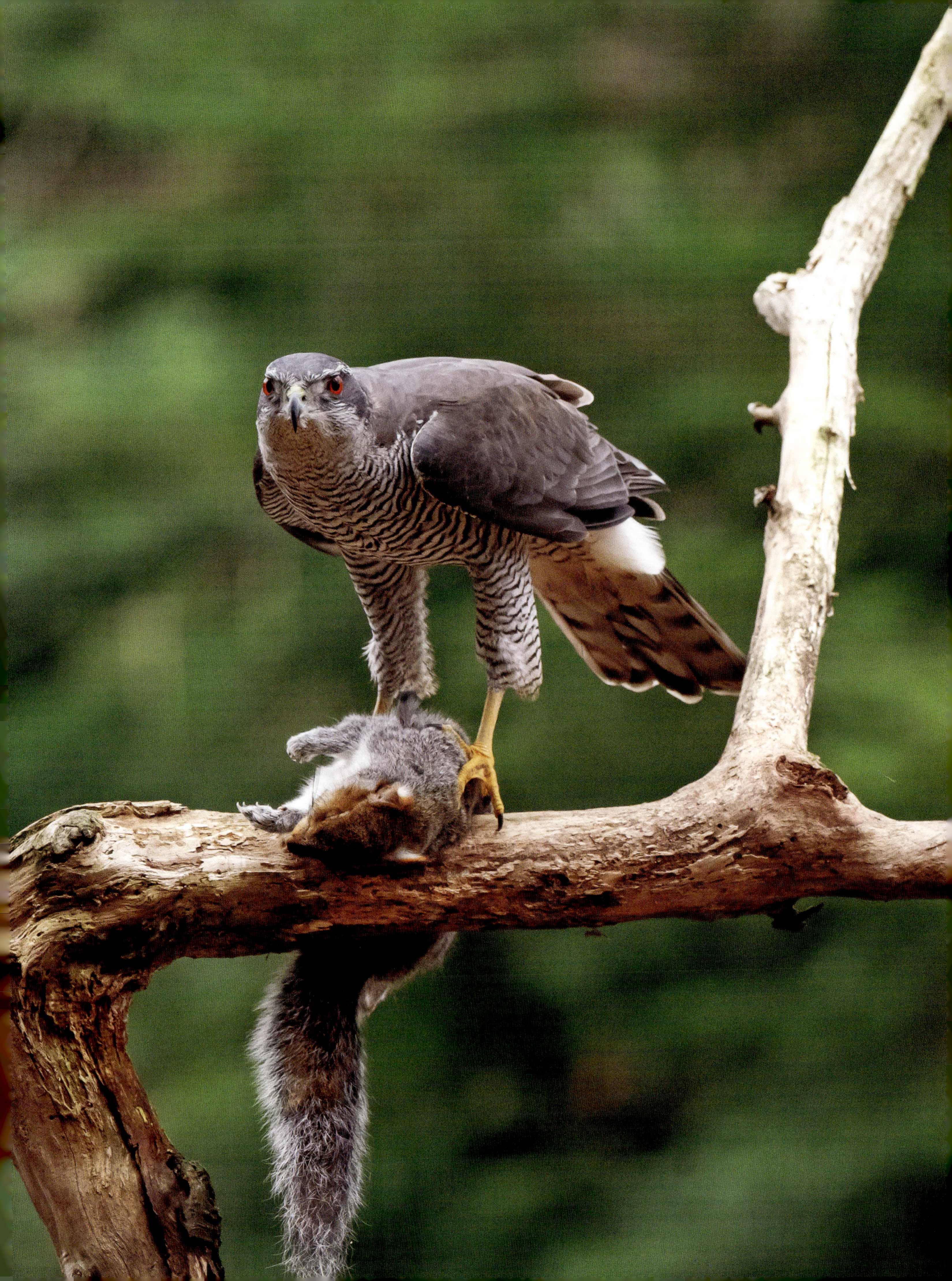

nourished by fish and shellfish in the coastal waters, while overwintering wading birds like redshank, egrets, plovers and curlew are most noticeable in the colder months. Birds of prey like marsh harriers stalk the skies, while the rare Dartford warbler can often be seen and heard in the shrubs and gorse. Although it may be hard to imagine on a bright autumn day, with the mudflats gleaming in the sun and the calls of thousands of birds mingling through the air, all this teeming abundance belies a very different past: in the 18th century, Keyhaven was a booming centre of salt production, and these now-tranquil marshes would have been a gritty industrial scene of salt pans and boiling houses.

The New Forest coastline has also played a significant role in world history. On 6 June 1944, thousands of troops disembarked here as part of the largest seaborne invasion ever seen, tasked with storming the heavily defended Normandy beaches. With its extensive tree cover and access to the coast, the New Forest served as a crucial venue for massing troops, vehicles and materiel in the run up to D-Day, and vestigial remains of the structures and engineering can still be found across the region, particularly on Lepe beach.

It is a poignant reminder that human history has always played a defining role in the New Forest – a place which was, after all, heavily shaped by the aftermath of another invasion 1,000 years ago, one that came in the opposite direction across the English Channel. As is often the case on this island, the tapestry of the landscape interweaves nature's peace with the not-always-peaceful history of how we came to be who we are.

New Forest ponies graze on a partially flooded Hatchet Moor, near Beaulieu.

Opposite:
Sometimes called 'the phantom of the forest', the elusive northern goshawk – seen here with a non-native grey squirrel kill – is a deft high-speed hunter of the woods, skilled at weaving between trees and shrubs in pursuit of prey. The species disappeared from the New Forest for more than a century but returned in 2002, with the population since growing to almost 50 breeding pairs.

Overleaf:
Beech trees blazing with autumn colour in the popular area of Bolderwood. Forming high, cathedral-like canopies, beeches are common across the New Forest. Their autumn foliage provides some of the richest, fieriest hues of any tree, particularly spectacular when paired with an understorey of copper-coloured bracken.

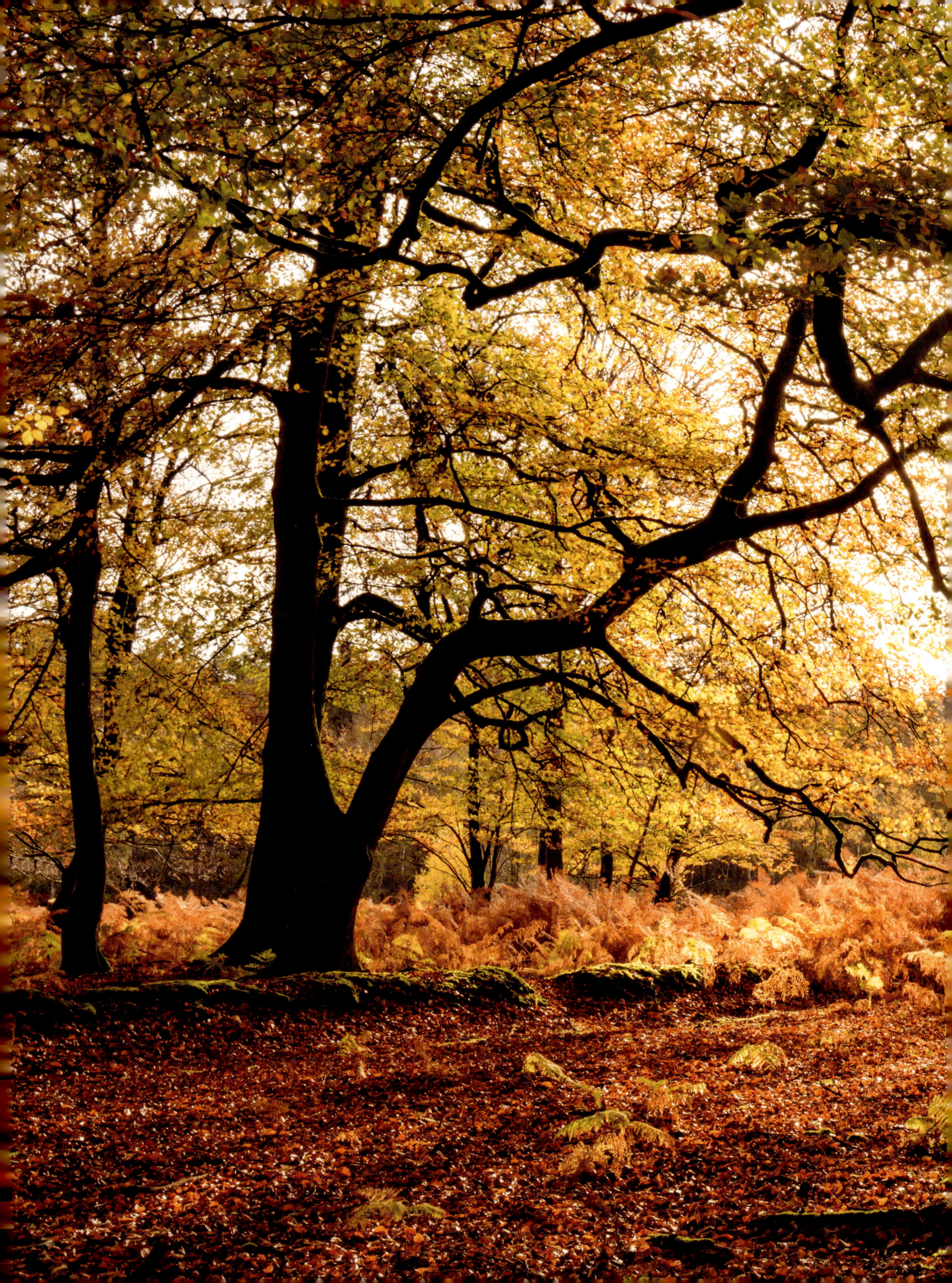

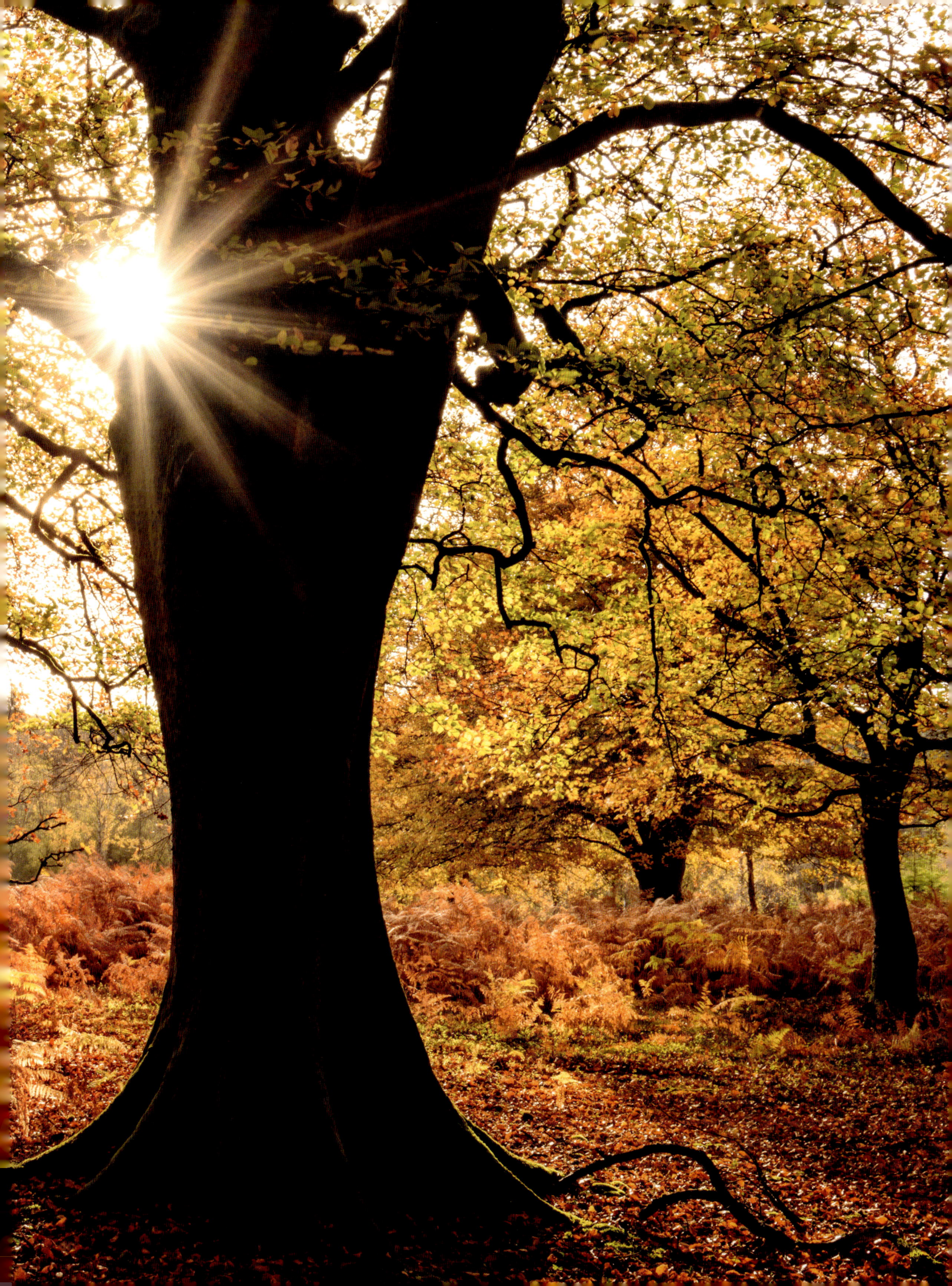

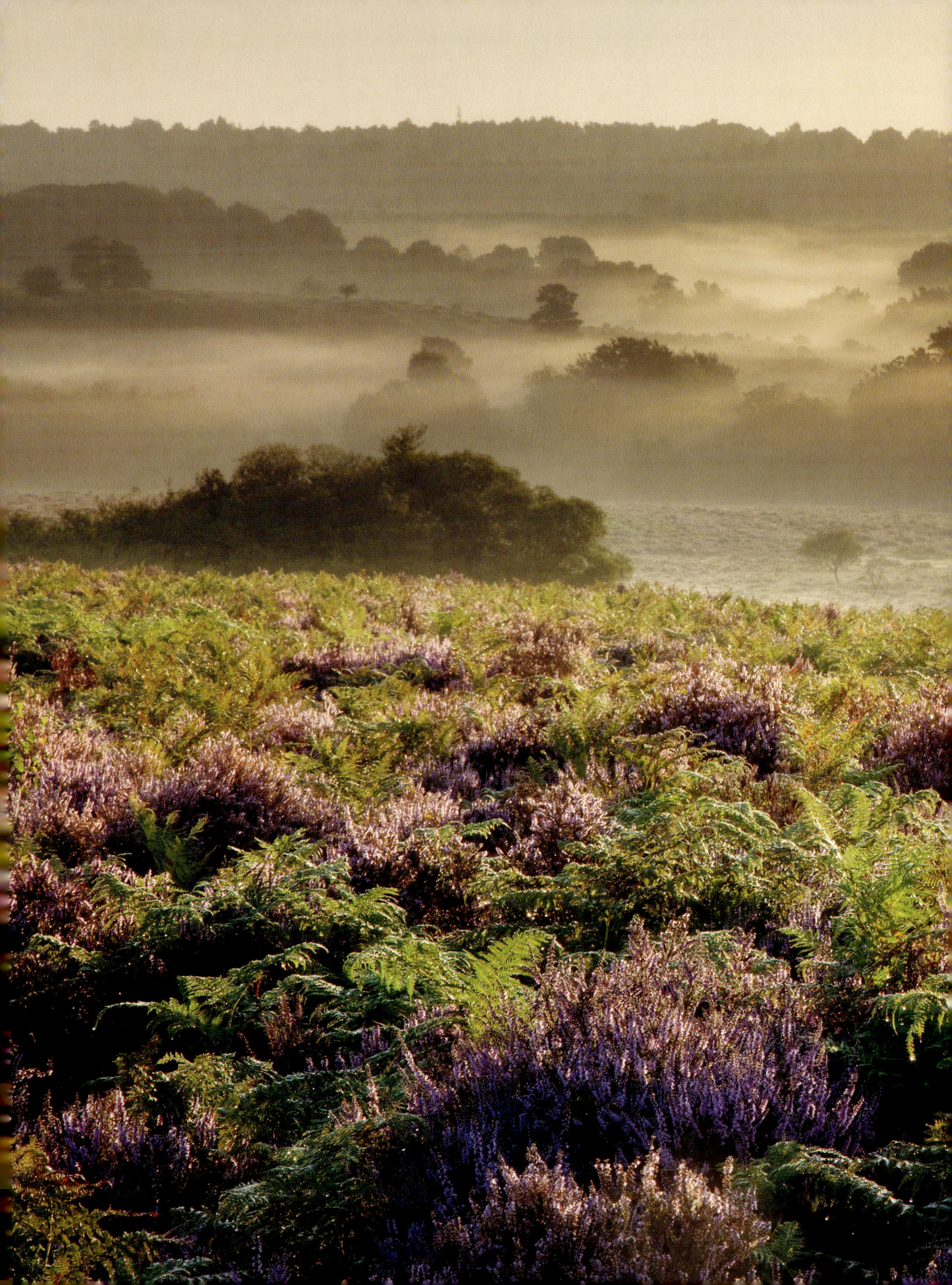

A summer dawn over the tree-scattered heathland of Fritham, with ling and bell heathers at their spectacular blooming best. In August, the heaths of the New Forest light up with purple colour.

Overleaf:
The unsung coastline of the New Forest contains some beautiful places. Shingle spits, salt marshes and wetlands provide prime habitat for wildfowl, wading birds and curlew. There are also slivers of beach, like the one at the end of Tanners Lane, shown here. Further east along the coast, Lepe beach was one of the places used to launch the Allied invasion of Normandy in World War Two.

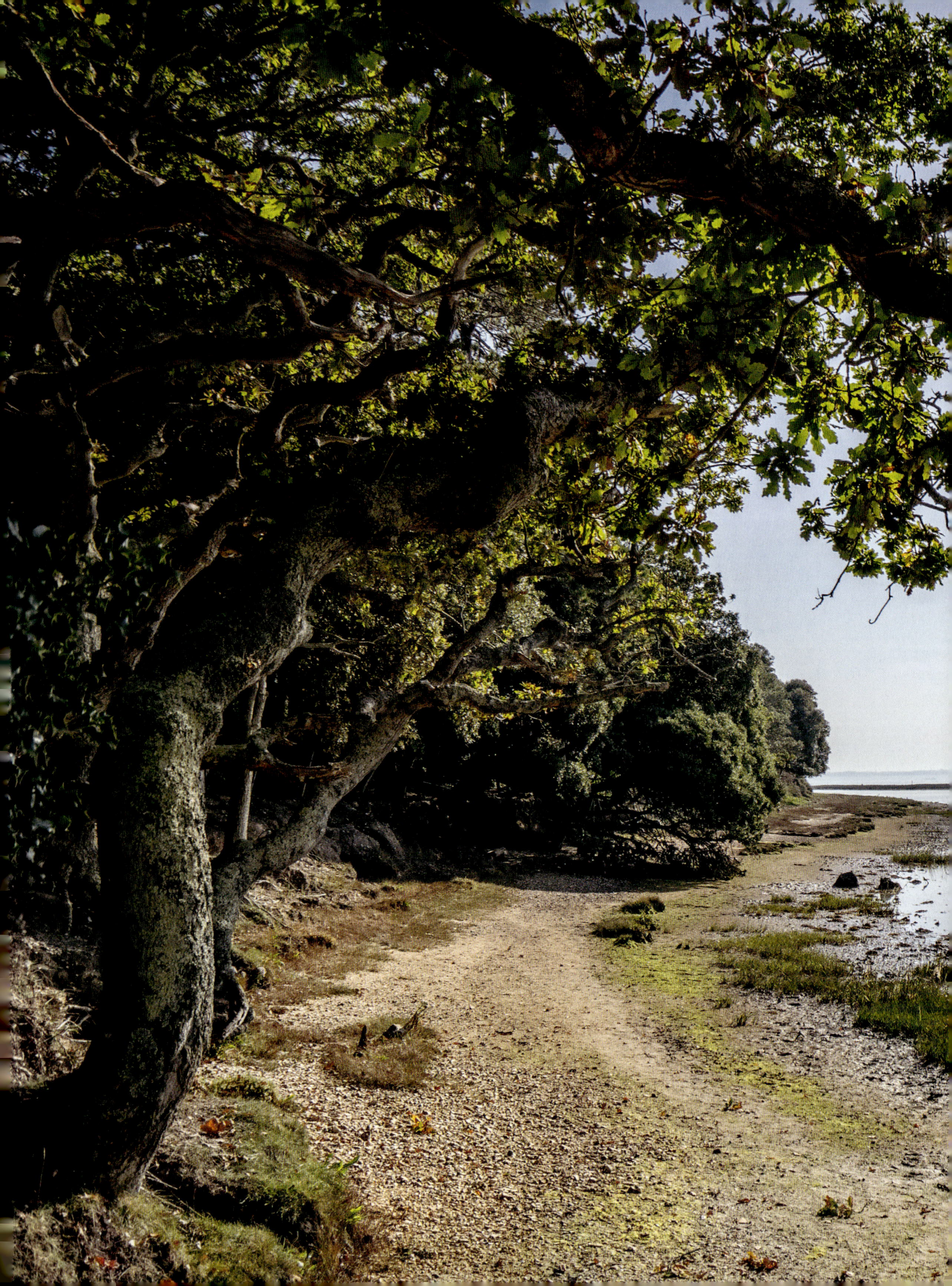

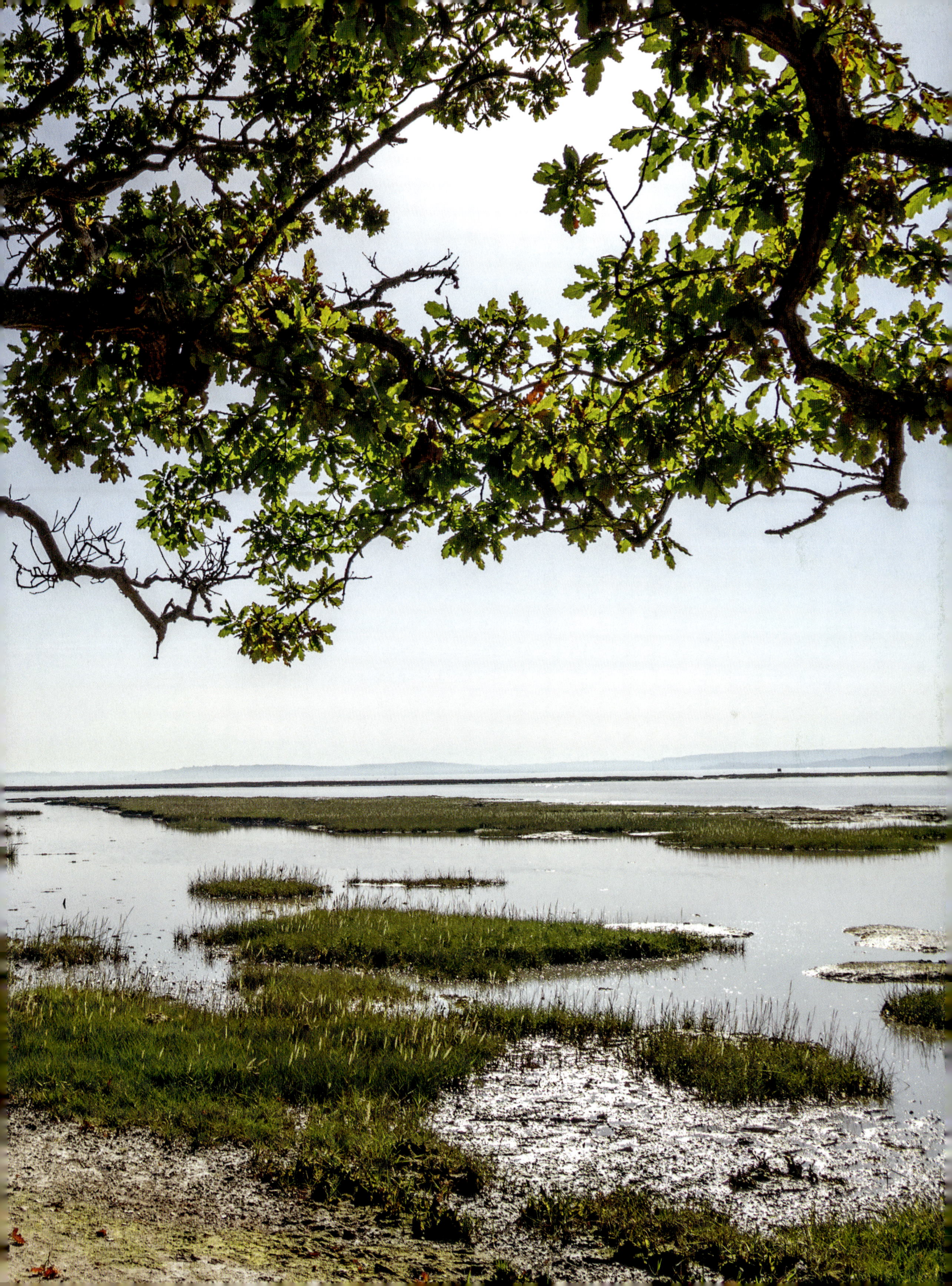

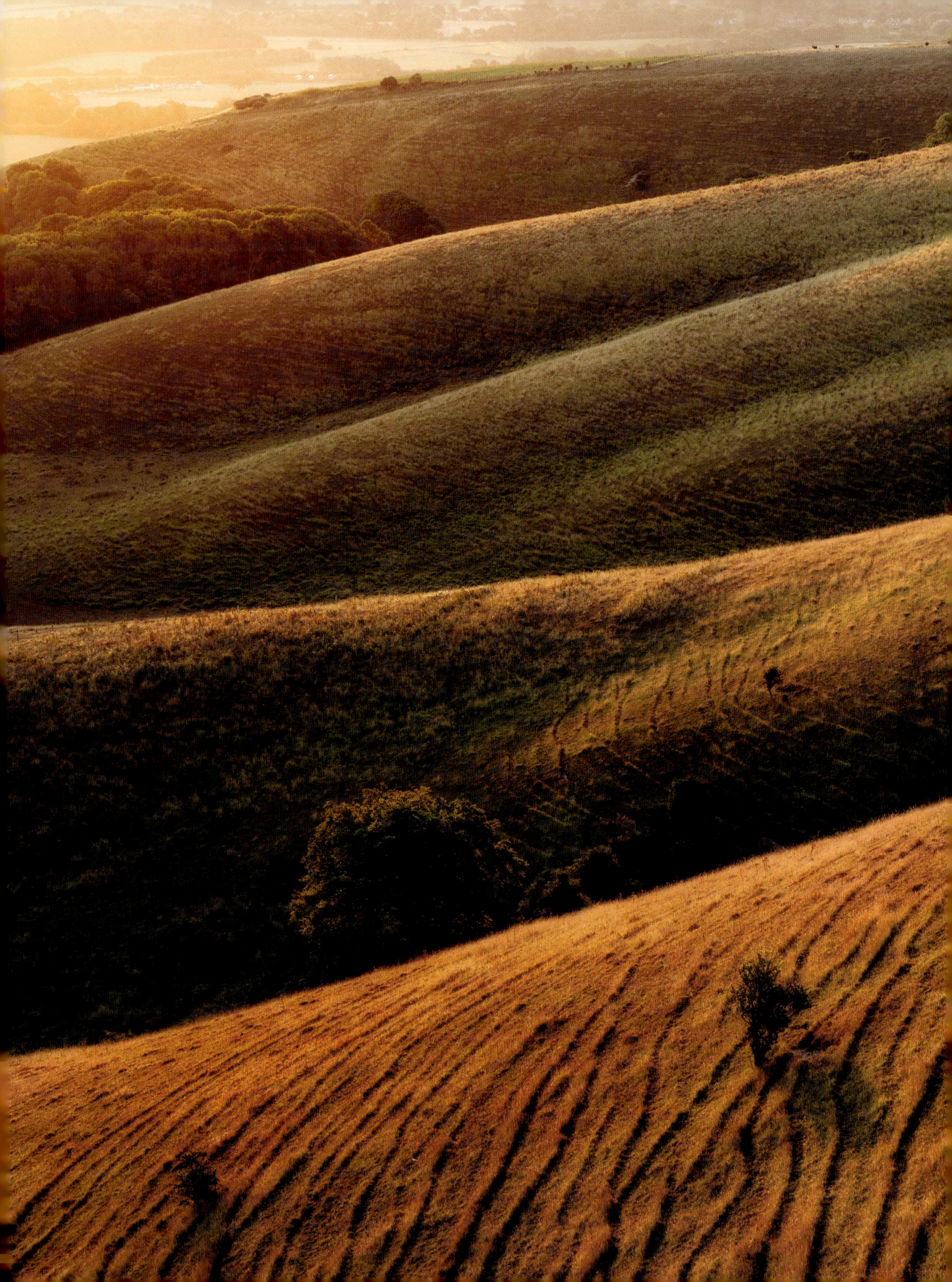

South Downs

Imagine walking through the chalk hills of South East England in the warm embrace of a sunny June day in 1935. Thick, confetti-coloured meadows full of wildflowers carpet the hillsides, with dozens of species per square metre. Field verges foam with daisies and yellow clouds of lady's bedstraw. Adonis blue butterflies flit across the ground, feeding on horseshoe vetches and wild marjoram; wild bees drone between the blooms of clovers and mignonettes. Orchids push up from the earth in clusters of hundreds. Hazes of fragrance drift through the early summer air, carrying the intermingled scents of vanilla, marzipan and thyme. Clicking grasshoppers and crickets form a gentle background din. The world feels light, floating, brimming with possibility.

Much of England would once have been like this. Similar scenes can be found today on the South Downs in places such as Lewes Downs, Malling Down or Old Winchester Hill, but they are much rarer than they used to be. Wildflower-rich chalk grassland once covered large swathes of the South Downs – up to 50 per cent in its eastern section – but now covers just 4 per cent. This shrinkage is part of a wider decline, which has seen England lose around 98 per cent of its species-rich meadows and grasslands since World War Two, including 80 per cent of its chalk grasslands, largely as a result of new farming practices aimed at increasing food production. Fortunately, the protection and restoration of grassland within the South Downs and its neighbouring areas was part of the reason for this landscape's designation as a national park in 2010, pointing to a more hopeful future for its multicoloured meadows.

The South Downs are a range of rolling chalk hills that run in a wide belt across the southern edge of the country. 'Down' in this context comes from 'dun', an Anglo-Saxon word for hill related to the word 'dune'. This feels fitting: the forms of these hills can be as rounded and flowing as wind-sculpted sand. At their western extent, they begin on the outskirts of Winchester and undulate east for around 140 kilometres (87 miles), roughly parallel with the English Channel coastline, before finally terminating at the Seven Sisters cliffs near Eastbourne, where the underlying soft white rock has been exposed in spectacular fashion by the erosive power of the sea. Although this national park is named after the South Downs, it also encloses parts of the Western Weald, a geologically distinct landscape whose patchwork of small-scale farming and ancient woodland has changed little since early medieval times.

With the towns and cities fringing the southern coast of England and the edges of London just under 65 kilometres (40 miles) to the north, this is the most

The gently flowing topography of the South Downs is underlain by soft chalk, giving rise to smoothly contoured hills. Lauded by some as one of the most quintessentially English landscapes, these 'mountains green' may have inspired William Blake's visions of a 'green and pleasant land'.

Common spotted orchids in a thriving meadow near Washington.

Opposite:
One of the mind-bogglingly ancient yew trees of Kingley Vale. With some individuals believed to be as much as 2,000 years old, these are some of the oldest living things in Britain.

The Duke of Burgundy butterfly is one of the UK's fastest-declining species as a whole, but careful restoration of its habitat on the South Downs over the last 20 years has fuelled a local resurgence.

populous of all the UK's national parks. Around 117,000 people live within its boundaries, and the region is webbed with roads and railways. This has been an extensively lived-in landscape since at least Roman times, when imperial invaders laid down roads and left significant remains, like the villa at Bignor. Yet the old woods, lofty ridges and lazy chalk streams still preserve their essential tranquillity, forming an oasis of calm within easy reach of millions of people.

Despite only gaining national park status in recent years, the South Downs are often seen as one of the most quintessentially English landscapes. The Romantic-era poet and painter William Blake's description of a 'green and pleasant land' is thought to have been inspired by the Downs, and has since entered the lexicon as a byword for England – even if its original context was at least partly ironic. Later Victorian and early 20th century writers eulogised the Sussex landscape as an idealised English heartland: Rudyard Kipling wrote of 'our blunt, bow-headed, whale-backed Downs' and supported campaigns to save parts of the landscape from development. Modernist writer Virginia Woolf found great joy in walking on the Downs, describing them as 'too much for one pair of eyes, enough to float a whole population in happiness'.

While the South Downs are known for the open expanses of sheep-grazed, grassy downland often found on top of the hills, the wider landscape is a rural patchwork influenced by millennia of settlement and agriculture. A typical walk in this national park might take you across flower-topped hills; into beautiful little villages with Tudor buildings and old coaching inns; across the sites of Iron Age settlements or Bronze Age barrows or through fertile fields of swaying wheat or rows of grapevines. Meadows, heathlands and woods are interwoven throughout, along with remarkable ancient survivors: some of the gnarled and knotted yew trees in the grove at the heart of the beautiful Kingley Vale forest are thought to be up to 2,000 years old.

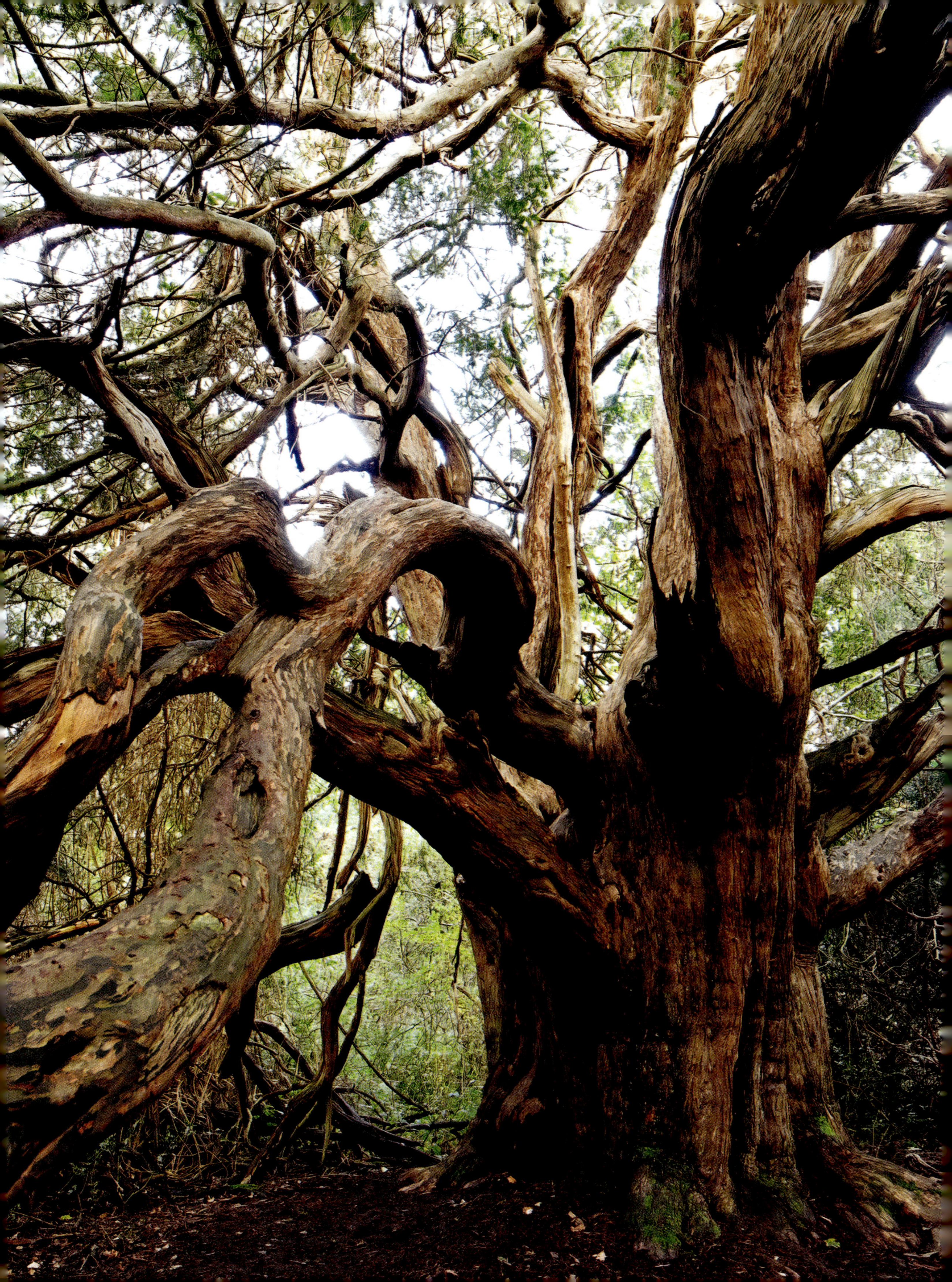

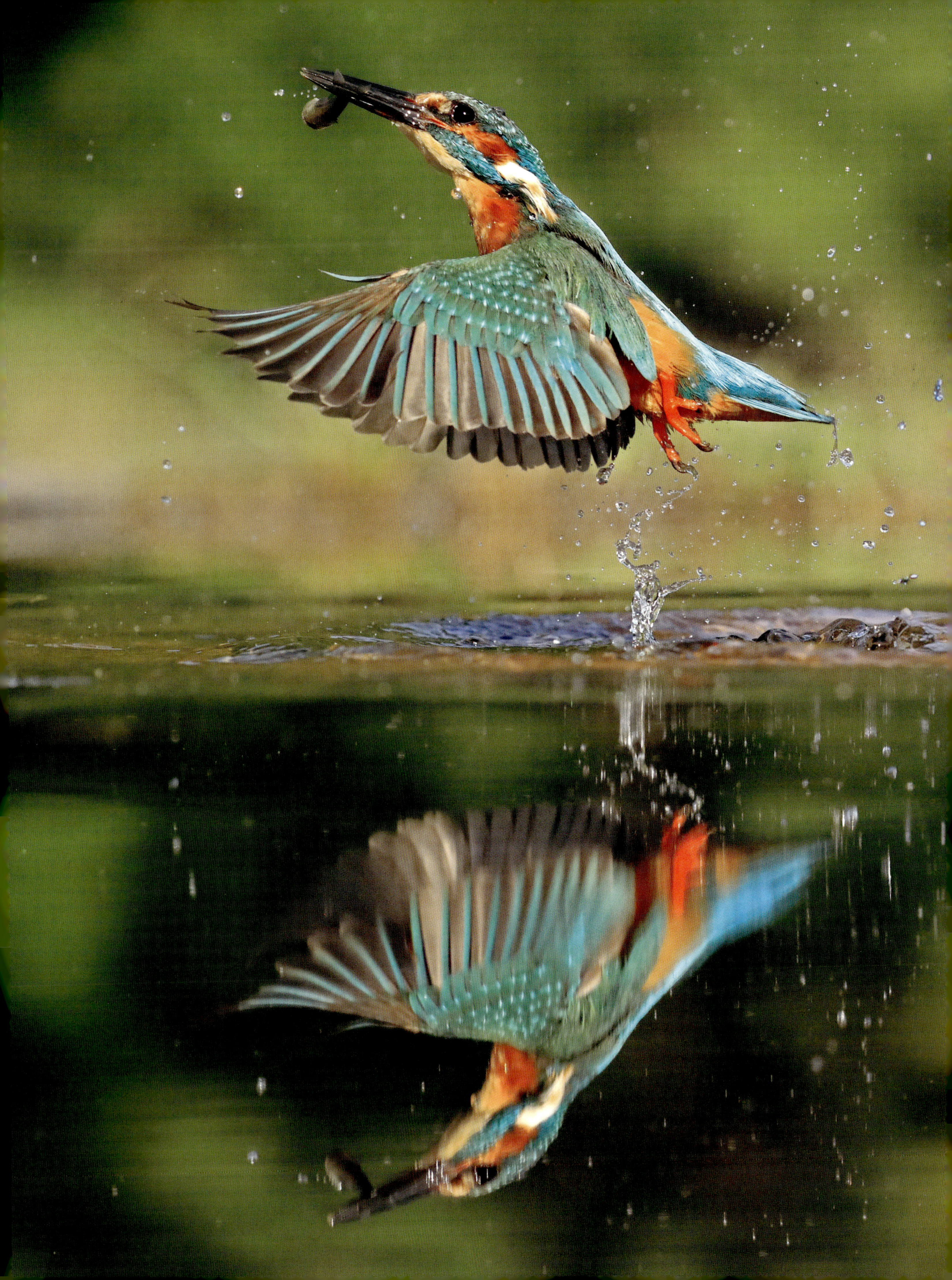

Like all the chalk that covers much of the south of England, the rock of the South Downs is around 90 million years old, formed when dinosaurs dominated the earth. The Cretaceous period left a legacy of so much chalk it was named after it – 'Creta' is the Latin word for the rock. The chalk of the South Downs was created from the lithified remains of dead sea creatures in calm tropical seas, forming a rock strata, which travelled across the world through continental drift before being thrust upwards and folded by the same era of tectonic upheaval that also created the Alps, the Atlas and the Apennines – albeit with gentler results in the South Downs. Subsequent millennia of weathering, erosion, freezing and thawing have sculpted these hills into the smooth shapes interrupted by steep, north-facing scarps that we see today.

The chalk is visible in stark white paths across the landscape, but most spectacularly at the enormous Seven Sisters, where close-cropped grassland abruptly meets a series of towering cliffs, which undulate like a rollercoaster along the edge of the English Channel, dazzling white.

Chalk is a porous rock, meaning that water sinks through it into underground cracks and cavities. In the South Downs this has created an aquifer that supplies water to more than a million people. The chalk's porousness also gives rise to distinctive landforms like Devil's Dyke, a V-shaped dry valley formed by glacial meltwater and a river that has since disappeared underground.

Elsewhere, water continues to flow through the South Downs in wonderful ways. The chalk stream of the Meon represents a rare kind of watercourse: it is fed entirely by springs, one of only 210 similar rivers in the world. It has remained relatively natural along its length, meandering through a series of lush marshes and water meadows and hosting wild brown trout, eel and a recently established population of otters. The Itchen is a larger chalk river, home to water voles and rare white-clawed crayfish, where dragonflies flit

The River Cuckmere undergoes a series of meanders across its floodplain as it approaches the English Channel near Seaford. With its water meadows, grazing marshes and grasslands, the valley around this part of the river is a nature reserve hosting overwintering wildfowl in winter, and wildflowers and butterflies in the warmer months.

Opposite:
The waterways of the South Downs and the Western Weald are home to kingfishers, which nest in riverbank burrows and hunt for small fish. Often seen flying fast and low over water, the streak of cyan down the back of the bird is one of British nature's most extraordinary colours; a laser-burst bolt of blue.

The South Downs is the most populous of Britain's national parks, with 117,000 people living within its boundaries. It is also extensively farmed, with a mix of livestock grazing and arable cultivation.

above mats of white water crowfoot and aquatic grasses wave gently in the clear waters.

This national park has a forgiving climate by British standards, enjoying similar weather to northern France. Indeed, the South Downs and the Weald are linked under the English Channel to the hills of North-East France via a geological structure known as the Weald–Artois Anticline. This landscape forms part of England's wine-growing heartland, and a plethora of vineyards are dotted across sunbathed southern slopes on the chalkland of the Downs and the sandstones of the Western Weald. Wineries open to the public include Rathfinny, Stopham and Hambledon.

Although it also forms part of this national park, the Western Weald, in the north-west of the park, is distinct from the South Downs. In part this is due to its underlying geology. Instead of chalk, the landscape of the Western Weald is largely made up of sandstone and clay formed from sediments laid down in huge Cretaceous rivers. This imparts a different ecology to the South Downs: calcareous grasslands and ash woods give way to wild acid heathlands like Iping and Shortheath Common, and an extensive patchwork of oak forest.

This is a mysterious-feeling landscape with a sense of quiet concealment. Centuries of footfall have eroded sunken lanes through the clays and sandstones, often deep enough to swallow a person; streams quietly work their way through wooded valleys. In early modern times this was a centre for the iron industry, when the sound of hammers beating upon anvils would have filled the region. This tumult is long gone now; the only sounds to be heard in the old hammer ponds are the clucking of moorhens or the soft splashes of hunting kingfishers.

'Weald' is derived from the Old English word for woodland, and the Western Weald lives up to the name. The underlying soils are relatively unproductive from an agricultural perspective and around a third of the area is forest, the majority being ancient and semi-natural broadleaved woodland, interlocked with heaths and farmland. The amount of tree cover in the Western Weald is rare for lowland England, creating a relatively intact forest ecosystem, which supports some significant wildlife communities; 14 of the UK's 16 bat species are found here, including Bechstein's and barbastelle bats. Looking out across the Weald from the high and steep northern escarpment of the South Downs, the canopy gives the illusion of being almost unbroken.

Calls for the South Downs to become a national park were made as early as the 1920s, and the eventual formation of the South Downs National Park in 2011 is a hopeful sign for the future. The Changing Chalk partnership – which is headed up by the National Trust and includes the South Downs National Park Authority, along with eight other organisations – has been working since 2022 with farmers and land managers on a four-year initiative to revive and restore various areas of chalk grassland totalling almost three times the size of the City of London. Past projects have already shown signs of progress: recent years, for example, have seen a revival in Duke of Burgundy butterflies, signifying the improving health of the grasslands.

The lost meadowlands of England may still be some way from returning to their prime, but the future looks brighter now: radiant with the colours of round-headed rampions, squinancywort, early spider orchids, hawksbeard, chalkhill blues, marble whites and many, many more.

Overleaf:
The underlying chalk geology of the South Downs is spectacularly exposed at the Seven Sisters, where the erosive power of the sea has sliced through the rolling hills like a cake knife. This chalk rock was 'born' around 100 million years ago when organisms called coccolithophores – phytoplankton cocooned in hard shells of calcium carbonate – died. Their tiny skeletons amassed and eventually solidified into a layer of rock up to a mile deep. These cliffs represent ancient marine life meeting and dissolving back into the sea. The iconic white cliffs of Dover are made from the same rock and enjoy more fame, but the Seven Sisters are bigger: Beachy Head, the tallest cliff, is 162 metres (530 feet) high.

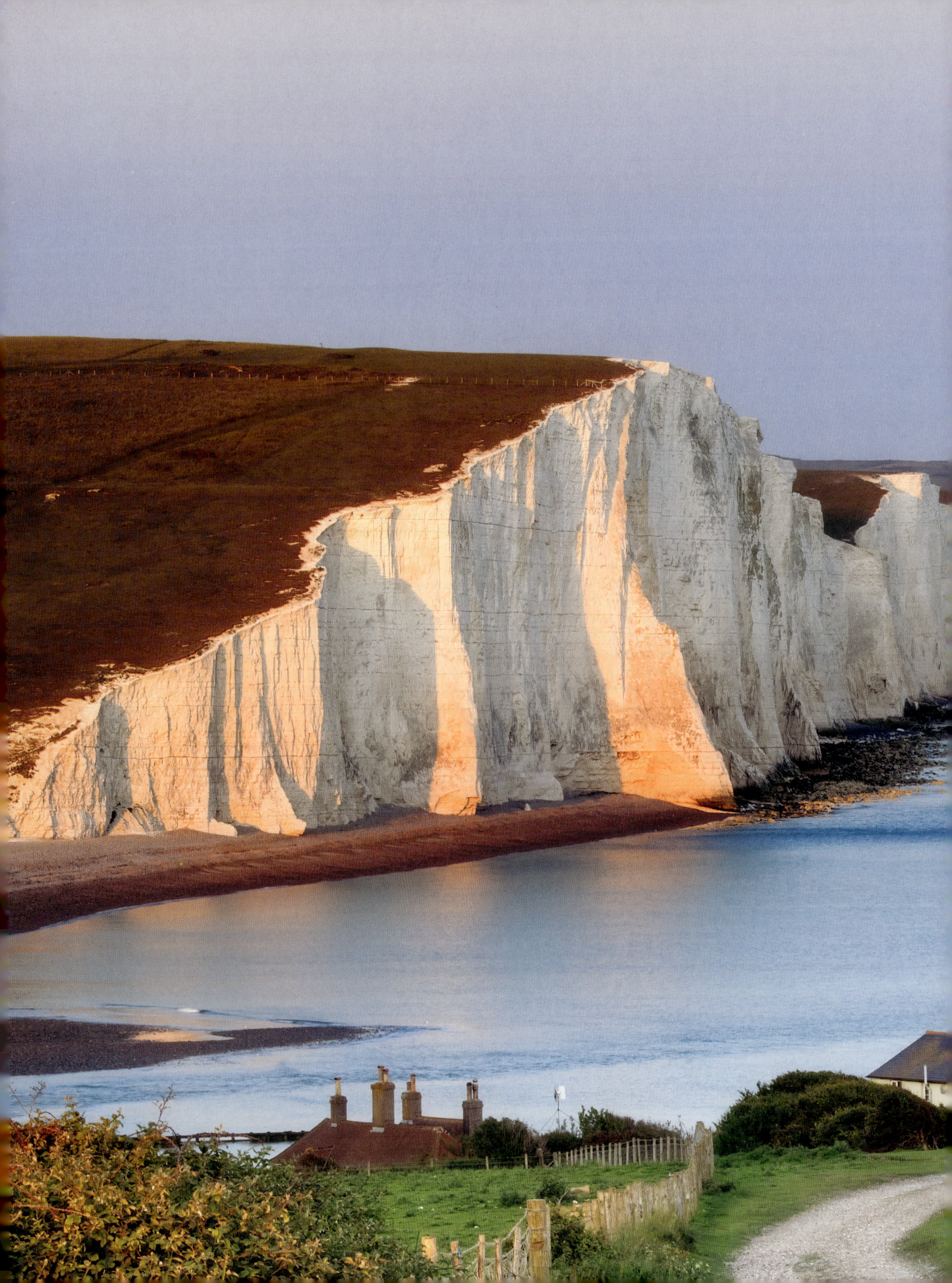

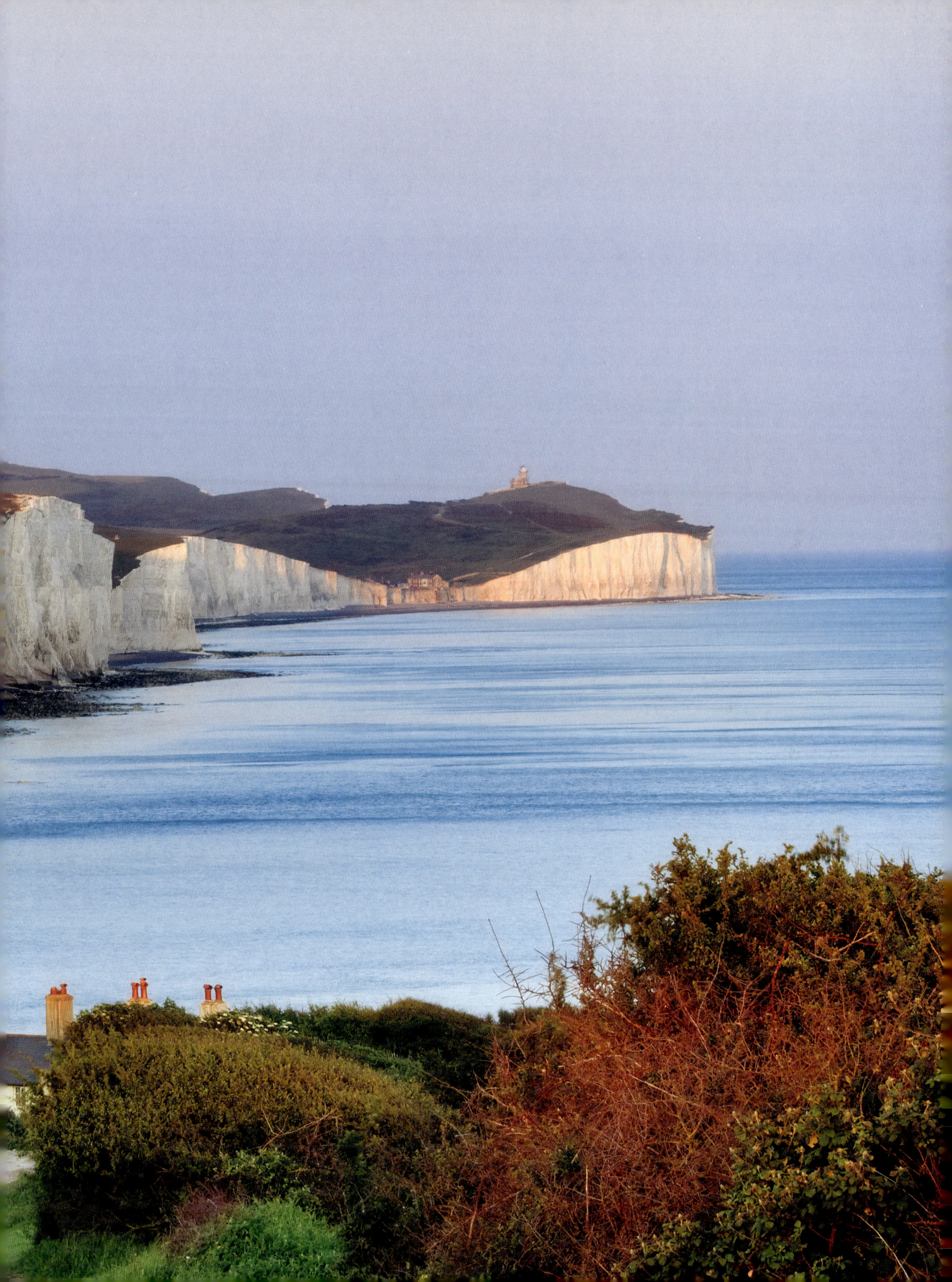

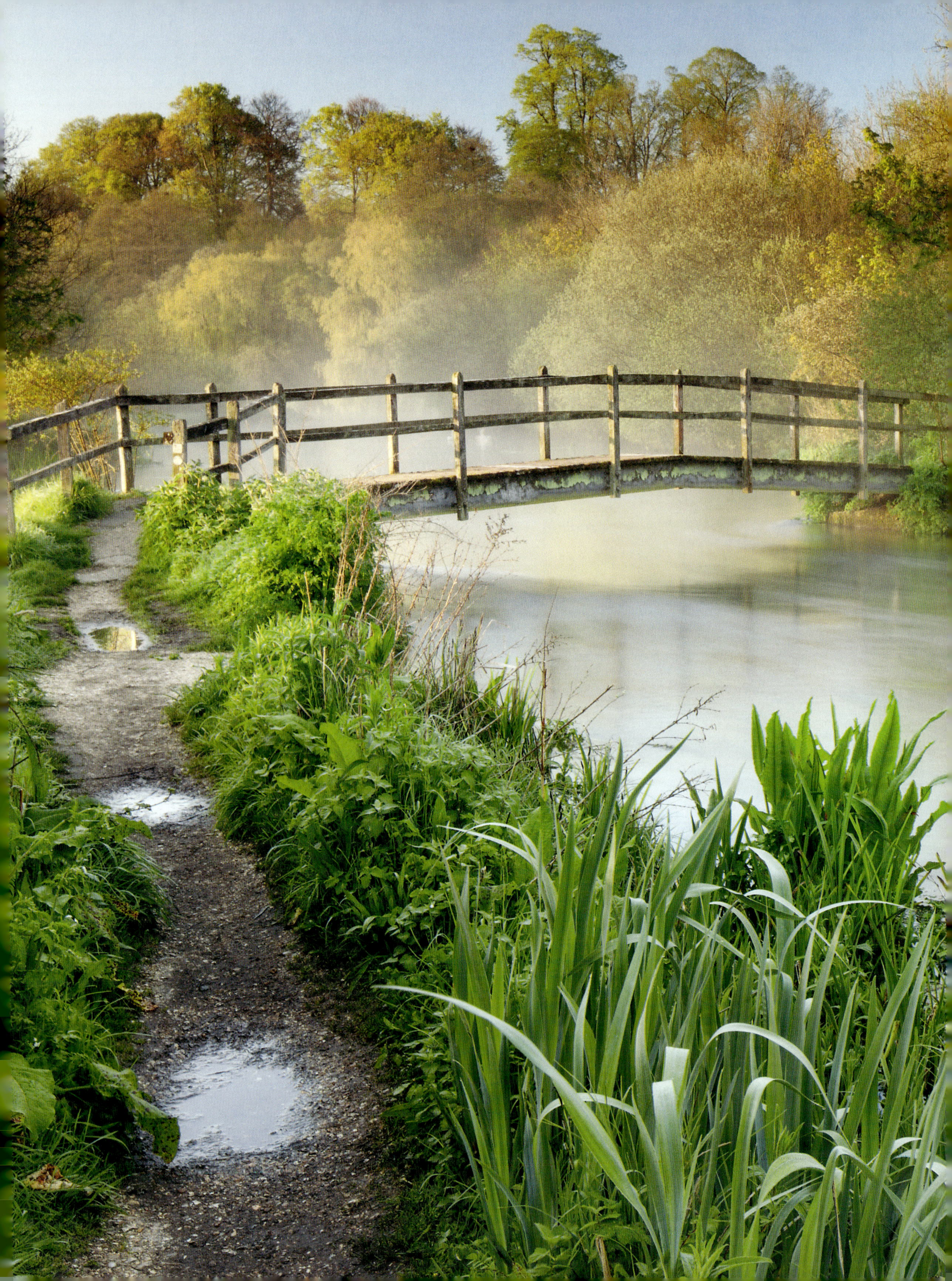

Dawn mists steam from the River Itchen on a spring morning. Flowing for more than 40km across the western boundary of the park and meeting the sea at Southampton, the Itchen is one of the most significant chalk rivers in England. Its clear waters spring from the natural filter of the chalk aquifer, and underwater plants wave gently in the current. Fens, flood meadows, wet woodlands and swamps fan out from the river in various places, supporting aquatic and riparian wildlife like white-clawed crayfish, southern damselfly, otters, water voles, Atlantic salmon and shoveler ducks. There are thought to be only 210 chalk rivers and streams across the world, 85 per cent of which are found in southern and eastern England.

Overleaf:
Warm sunset light bathes the slopes of Fulking Escarpment on the steep-sided northern side of the South Downs, near Edburton. The South Downs Way runs along the top of the escarpment, and offers dramatic views over the much lower-lying land to the north.

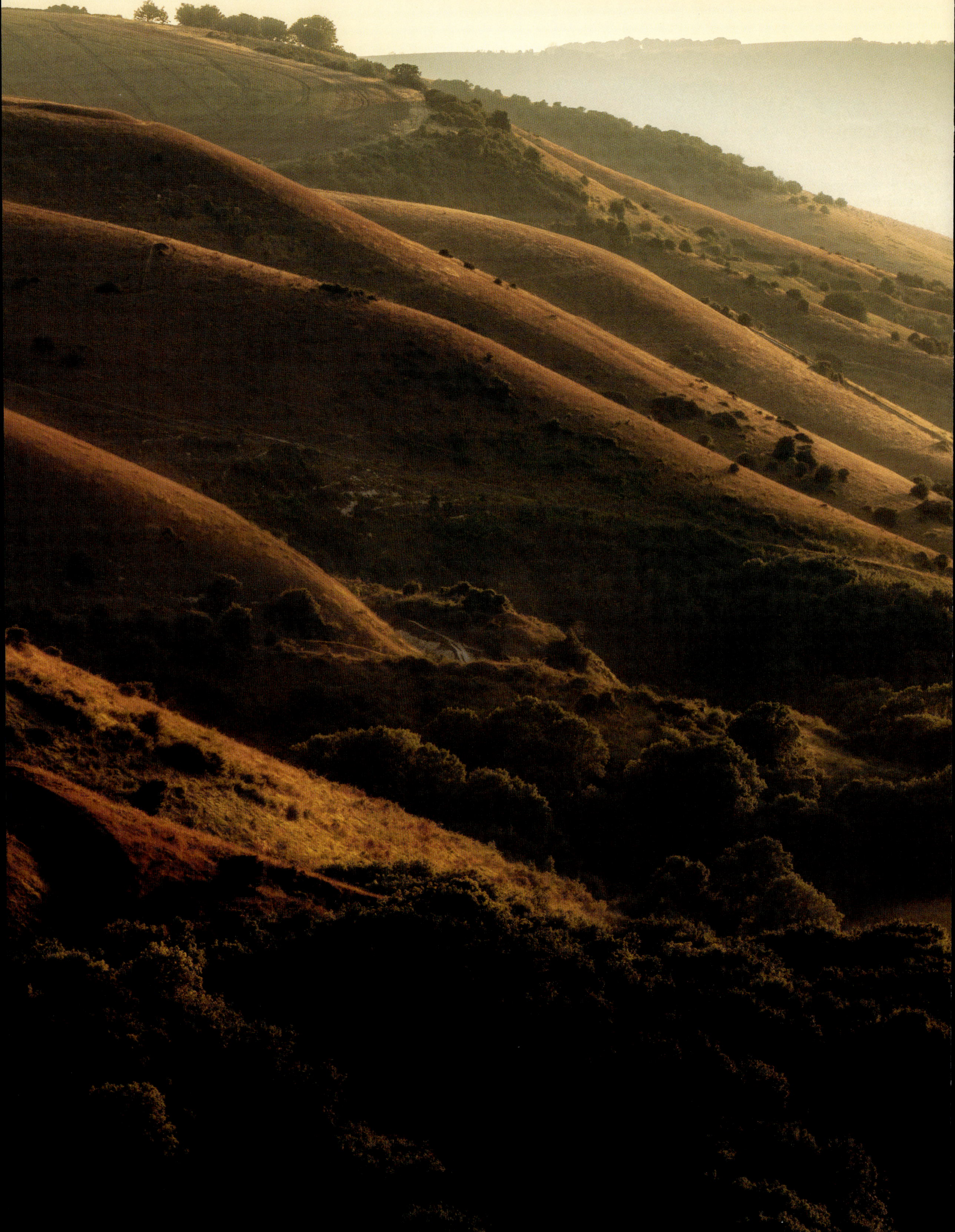

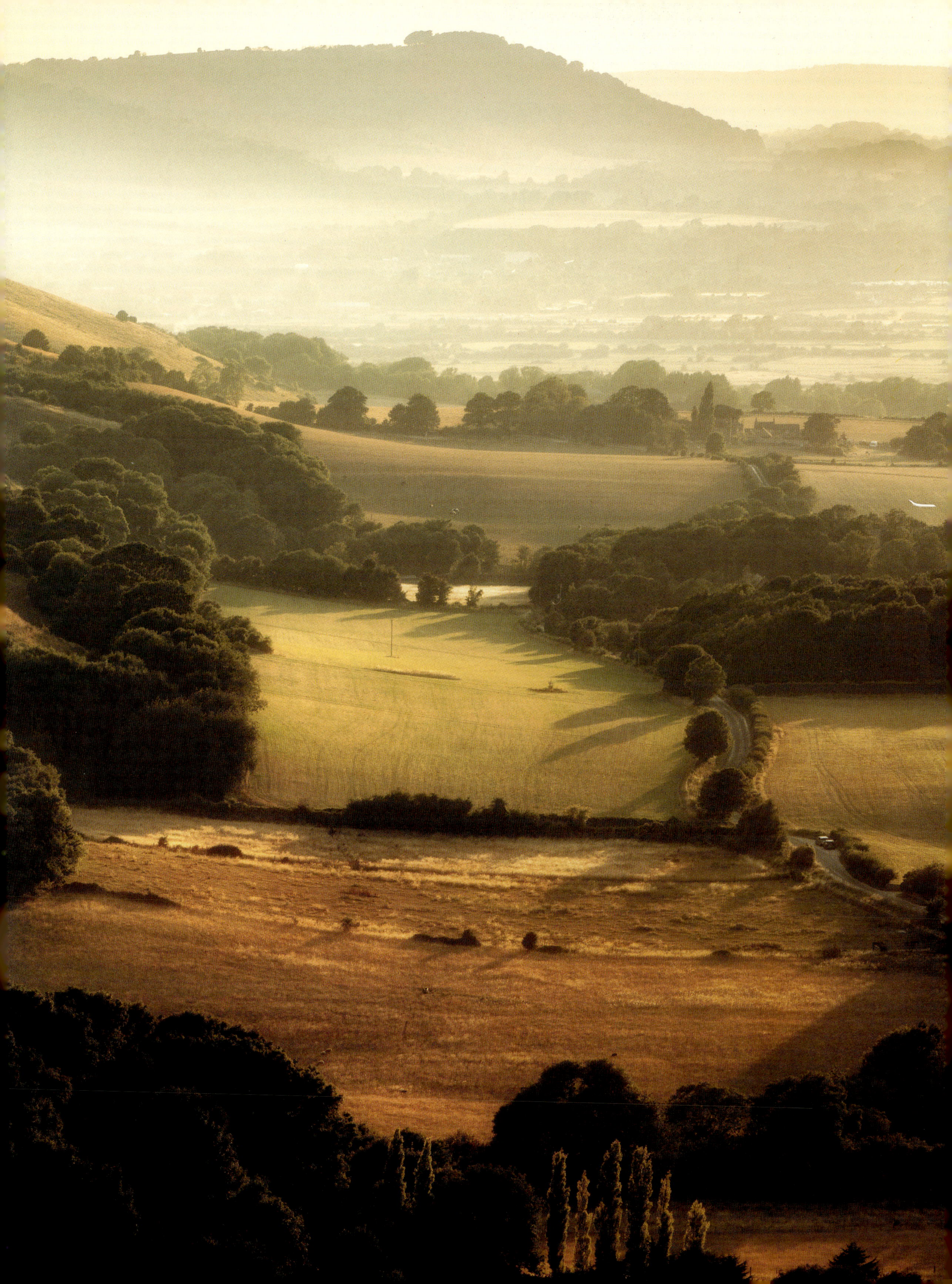

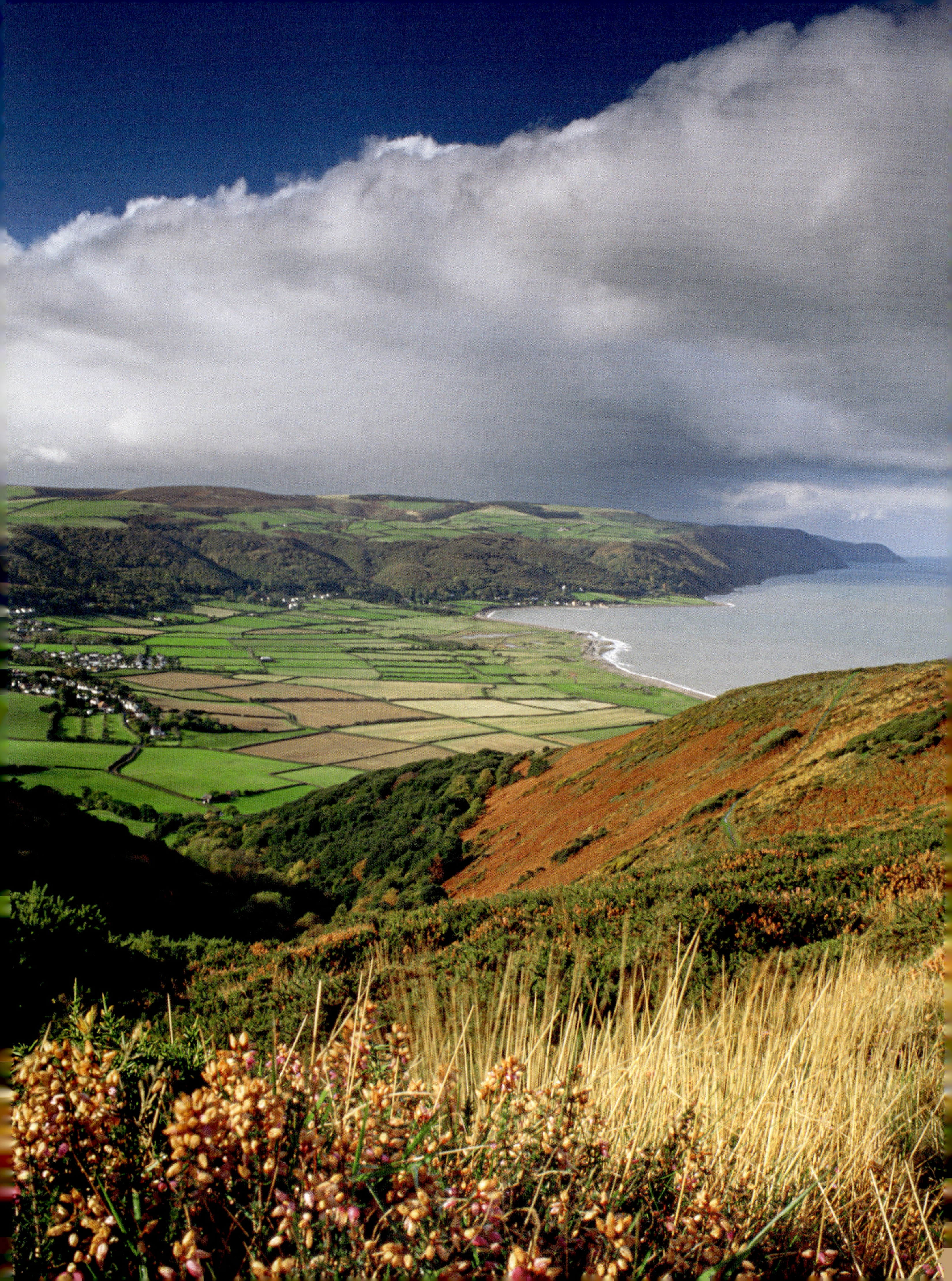

Exmoor

Few landscapes in England meet the sea as spectacularly as Exmoor. Sea cliffs as tall as London skyscrapers tower dizzyingly above the Bristol Channel, while peregrines hunt through the air below them. Waterfalls tumble from coastal crags into the foaming sea. Feral goats roam across precipitous rock formations with thousand-foot drops below them. Ancient oak forests plaster the sides of steep coastal slopes. Winding smugglers' trails descend through the woods, emerging into lush, secluded coves where beaches slope into clear waters and the rocky shoreline holds turquoise tidal pools. Villages with thatched-roof houses cling to the sides of combes and gorges at the mouths of fast-running rivers.

This 55-kilometre (34-mile) stretch of coastline is remarkable for a host of reasons – sheer spectacle is just one of them. This is the 'highest' coastline in England and Wales, with some of the most abrupt plunges from high ground to sea level on these islands. Take the 413-metre-high (1355 feet) Culbone Hill, for example, where the ground plunges rapidly to the shore in the space of a mile, and the ominously-named Great Hangman sea cliff which is a towering 244 metres (800 feet) high. But while most of Britain's coast, like its landscape as a whole, has been denuded of trees, the steepness and seclusion of the Exmoor coastline means that much of it is still covered in native forest, giving an unusually verdant dimension to the shoreline. The 16 kilometres (10 miles) between Foreland Point and Porlock contains the longest stretch of coastal woodland in Britain: an Atlantic oakwood – or temperate rainforest – where the clean and damp coastal air fosters a lush profusion of ferns, fungi, liverworts, lichens and mosses. These can often found garlanding the branches of sessile oak or hazel trees that have become gnarled and twisted from their exposure to the excoriating maritime winds.

Although many of Exmoor's coastal woods have been exploited for the likes of charcoal and tanning bark, there are fragments of woodland and shrubby vegetation clinging to cliffs that remain largely inaccessible to human beings and grazing animals. These are some of the few remaining fragments of 'wilderness' to be found in the British Isles. Seeing the huge cliffs from the sea on a boat tour reveals the true scale of this wild, vertical world, and the aerial life that inhabits it: peregrines, northern gannets, razorbills and guillemots all nest on these crags, sometimes in large numbers.

Vegetation and wildlife are not the only things to benefit from the remoteness of this craggy, complex coastline. In the 17th and 18th centuries Exmoor was

Looking down on Porlock Bay from the moorland of Bossington Hill. This seemingly timeless scene belies a story of change and transformation. On the coastal plain, between the farmland and sea, is a stretch of salt marsh created when the sea breached the shingle ridge of the beach during heavy storms in 1996. Nature has been allowed to take its course and new habitats have since developed, dominated by salt-tolerant plants like samphire and sea purslane. Native oakwoods can also be seen covering the steep slopes surrounding the bay and running along the coast – a distinctive feature of the Exmoor coastline.

Autumn foliage in its prime in the woods surrounding Webber's Post, a popular woodland area near Porlock made up of a mix of conifer plantations and temperate rainforest. Mist drifts through the Holnicote Estate, with the moorland of Selworthy Beacon beyond.

a hotspot for smuggling, with its coastal coves and caves serving as perfect refuges for the offloading of clandestine consumer goods like spirits, tea and tobacco, which would otherwise be subject to high tariffs in ports such as Bristol. One of Britain's most iconic long-distance trails, the South West Coast Path, which runs across Exmoor on its 1,000-kilometre (630-mile) loop around the edge of the south-west arm of England, has its origins as a coastguard patrol route used to combat underground commerce. The beautiful coastal villages of Combe Martin, Lynmouth and Porlock thrive on tourism now, but they were once known for what was euphemistically termed the 'free trade'.

Smugglers are not the only mariners who have taken advantage of the nooks and crannies of this coastline for secretive purposes. During World War Two, German U-boats are thought to have landed at isolated coves in the dead of night, where the chances of being discovered were minimal, to collect fresh water. According to one story, a former submarine captain returned to Exmoor in the 1950s as a visitor and chartered a boat to the Sherrycombe waterfall. During one of these furtive wartime landings, the sight of the waterfall, the coves and the cliffs in the moonlight had left a deep impression on the man, and with the war behind him he had returned to see it all in daylight.

Exmoor's exceptional coastline was one of the main reasons for its designation as a national park, but its name reveals the landscape of its interior: a roughly 690-square-kilometre (67-square-mile) swathe of high ground and moorland, dissected by sinuous, forest-filled river valleys and dotted with ancient villages and hamlets which reflect a long history of human habitation.

The underlying geology of Exmoor is mostly comprised of 400-million-year-old sedimentary sandstones and slates, laid down in shallow seas during the Devonian period, then uplifted during the Variscan orogeny, the period of continental collision that also created the Pyrenees and the Appalachians.

Exmoor moorlands, such as the sprawling whale backed hills of the Chains in the north-west part of the park, contain large areas of blanket peat bog, or mires – waterlogged, open expanses where the cool, damp conditions prevent the decay of vegetation and instead lead to the formation of peat. These moors are not strictly 'natural'. Their creation may have been significantly linked to ancient human activity. Neolithic and Bronze Age peoples are believed to have largely denuded the landscape of its once-extensive forest for agricultural and hunting purposes. More recently, blanket mires dried up due to expedient but ecologically harmful historic practices like harvesting peat for fuel. By contrast, healthy, wet peat moors help to lock up carbon, reduce flood risk, improve water quality and support a more complex array of vegetation and wildlife. In recent years the Exmoor Mires Partnership has sought to restore these boggy landscapes to better condition. Highlights of a healthy mire include sundews (carnivorous plants that devour small insects), sphagnum (peat-building wonder-mosses that can absorb up to twenty times their own weight in water) and bog asphodel (flowering plants that enliven the moors in early summer with starry, lemon-yellow spires).

If you take a walk over the moors, heaths and rough pastures of Exmoor, there is a good chance you will bump into some of their most beloved inhabitants: the Exmoor ponies. These beautiful horses are all privately owned, but they roam freely across the landscape and can live in the wild largely unaided. Their lineage is debated, but horses have been a part of the Exmoor landscape in some form for thousands of years – some have even argued these ponies are the nearest breed to the native wild ponies of Europe.

Exmoor's moors have produced other famous animal inhabitants, albeit with a questionable basis in reality. The Beast of Exmoor, a purported big black cat loose in and around the region, garnered publicity after locals blamed it for a spate of sheep mutilations in the 1980s. Despite extensive efforts – a team of

Exmoor ponies are all privately owned, but they roam freely across the landscape and can live in the wild largely unaided. Their lineage is debated, but horses have been present on Exmoor in some form for thousands of years. Despite revival efforts, the Exmoor pony is an endangered breed, with just a hundred or so left in Britain.

Opposite:
The huge-antlered red deer are Britain's largest wild animal species, and individuals can grow especially big on Exmoor due to their diet. The largest known red deer, the 'Emperor of Exmoor', was almost 3 metres (9 feet) tall, but was controversially killed in 2010 by a hunter.

Royal Marines was even deployed at one point to hunt it down – no compelling evidence of this feline has ever been found, but reported sightings and hastily captured photographs persist to this day.

Something that certainly does exist on these moors is the ghost of the past. Isolation coupled with the lack of extensive agriculture or development on Exmoor's high places has meant that the physical remnants of past inhabitants have been well-preserved for millennia, including Bronze Age burial barrows like those at Five Barrows Hill, standing stones like the Longstone menhir, which is around 3 metres (9 feet) tall, and stone circles at Porlock Common and Withypool Hill. We see these remnants now in their current context of windswept and chilly open moorland, but the world their builders knew would have been quite different: the climate was warmer then, and what is now the moorland would possibly still have been covered in large areas of forest.

Along with Dartmoor, Exmoor is one of the most extensive areas of high and hilly land in the southern half of England. These two landscapes could be thought of as national park 'siblings', or at least cousins as both encompass vast areas of open moorland, are filled with ancient artefacts and are populated by prowling folk phantoms. But geology underpins some important physical differences. Exmoor's 'softer' sedimentary rock is more susceptible to erosion by water than the granite of Dartmoor and, over the course of many millennia, the region's eight main rivers and tributaries have carved out a complex tracery of steep-sided valleys that snake through the moors, fed by the region's high levels of rainfall.

Many of these valleys are lined partly or entirely with oak forests, creating an atmosphere of verdant seclusion in their depths. The various gorges and contributing rivers, which eventually converge on the coastal village of Lynmouth, at the meeting of the East Lyn and West Lyn rivers, contain

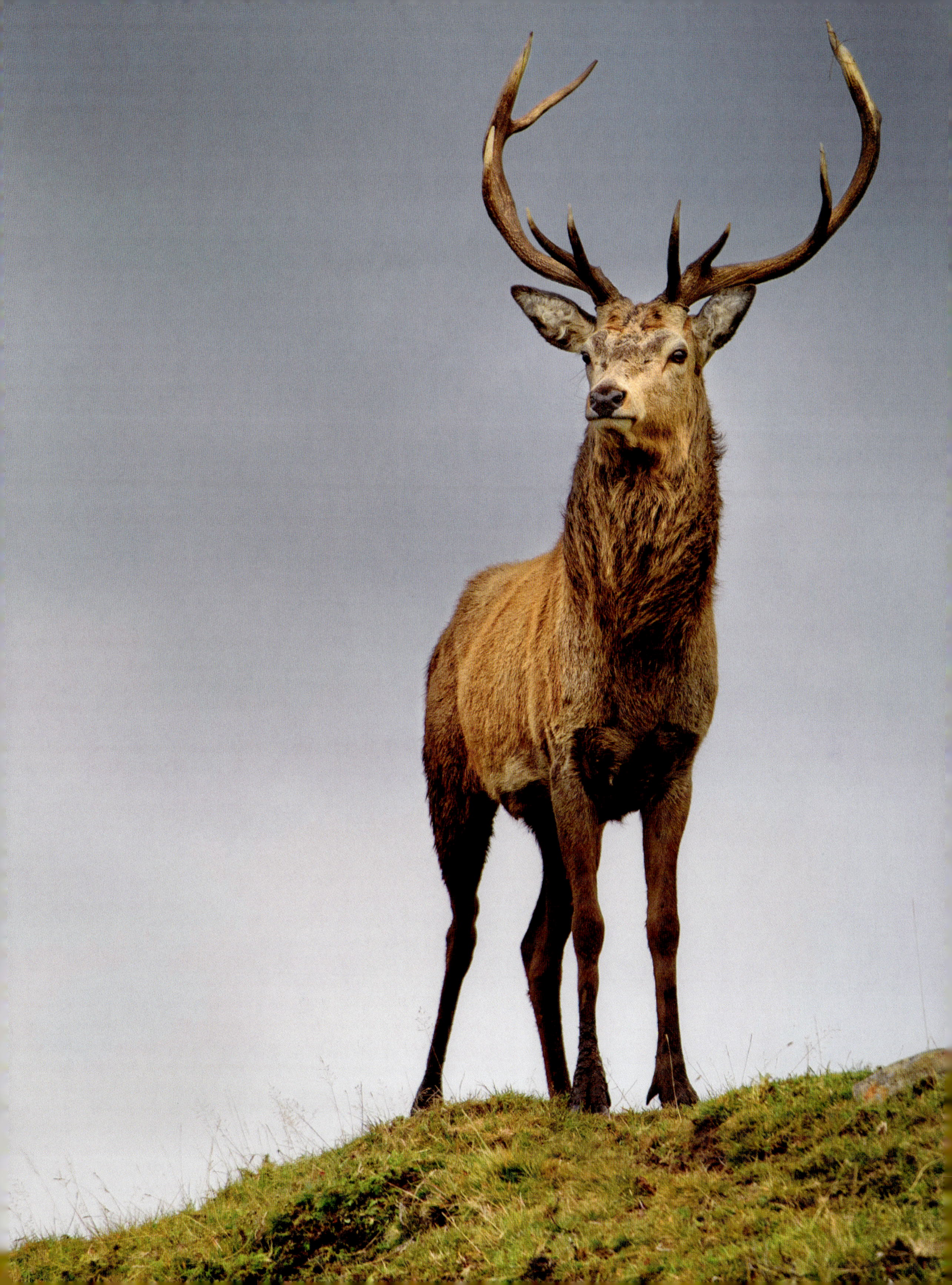

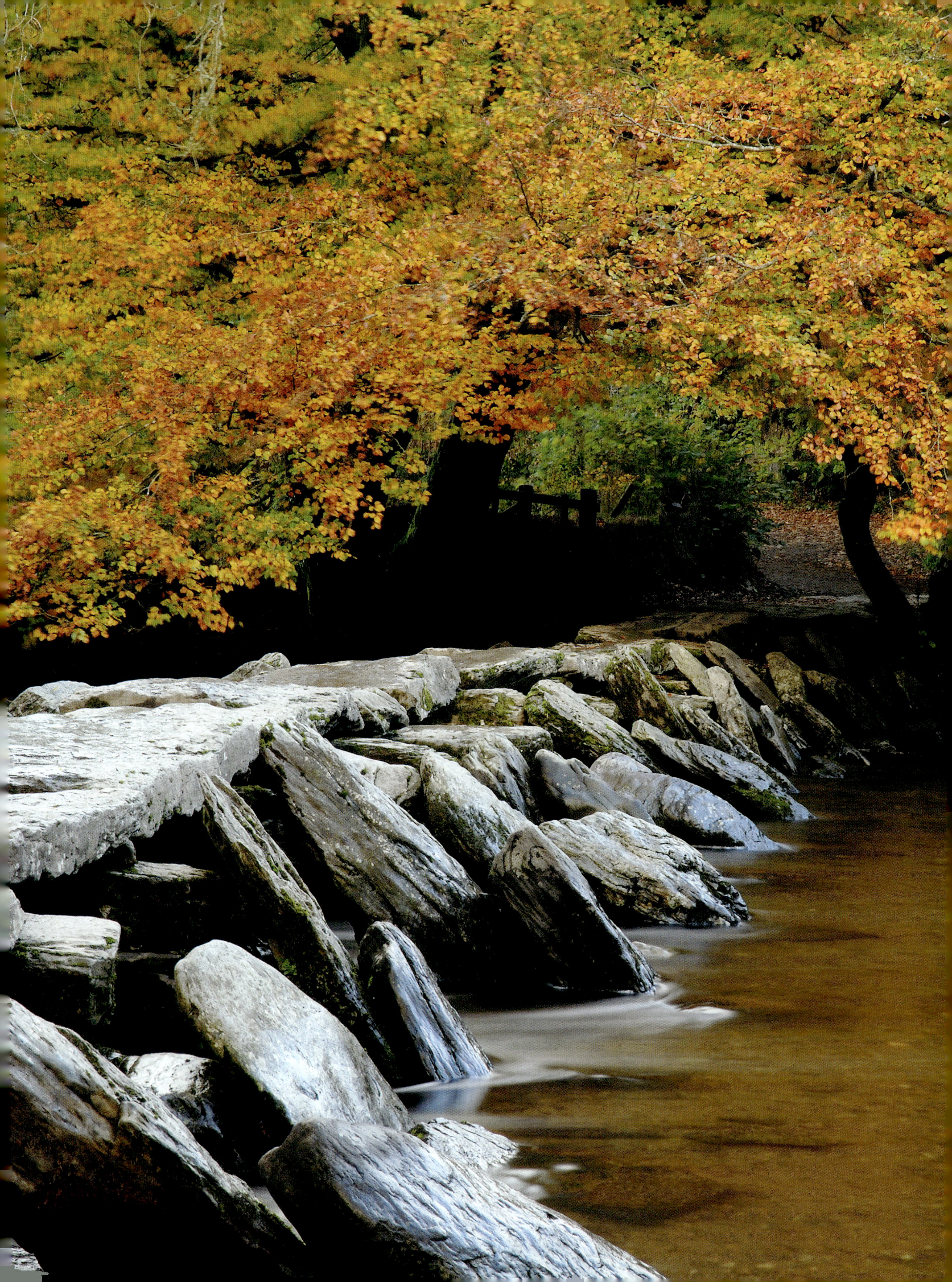

some of the most extensive continuous corridors of ancient or semi-natural woodland to be found in England. These valleys and gorges offer unbroken hours of sun-dappled streamside and woodland wandering, a particular joy in spring and autumn. Like the coastal woods, the valley forests of Exmoor are a stronghold for moisture-loving plants, including an array of large-leaved lungwort lichens.

Exmoor's rivers form a core part of the region's identity, interwoven through its history and culture. In the south of the park, the famous Tarr Steps – a stone clapper bridge spanning the River Barle, made from megaliths and surrounded by ancient woodland – is one of the national park's most celebrated landmarks. The river valleys are dotted with historic buildings that originated as fishing lodges, and responsible catch-and-release fishing is still a popular recreational activity. Many of the villages and landmarks take their name from rivers, as does the region itself: 'the moor of the Exe'. The Exe – whose name is thought to derive from a Brythonic root meaning 'abounding in fish' – rises on the Chains and lends its name to several other locations, such as Exeter and Exmouth, en route to the sea.

This is a place of sodden peat bogs covered in moorland flowers; sun glinting in rocky rivers; storms sweeping in from the Atlantic; leaves and lichens jewelled with rain; rocky beaches sloping into crystalline blue sea; and waterfalls tumbling into the ocean as it pounds at the base of huge coastal cliffs. Often, the images from Exmoor that leave the strongest impression, and linger the longest in the memory, are linked to water.

The Exmoor coastline is dotted with secluded sandy coves like Lee Bay. They can be idyllic places to visit today, but nooks and crannies in the coastline were often used for illicit landings during the heyday of the smuggling trade.

Opposite:
One of Exmoor's most famous landmarks, Tarr Steps is a clapper bridge spanning the River Barle, surrounded by lush oak woodland. At 55 metres (180 feet) long and made from stone slabs weighing up to 1.8 tonnes with no mortar, it is thought to be around 600 years old.

Overleaf:
The South West Coast Path runs across Hangman Point on its 1,000-kilometre (630-mile) loop around the edge of the south-west arm of England. The long-distance path has its origins as a coastguard patrol route used to combat smuggling.

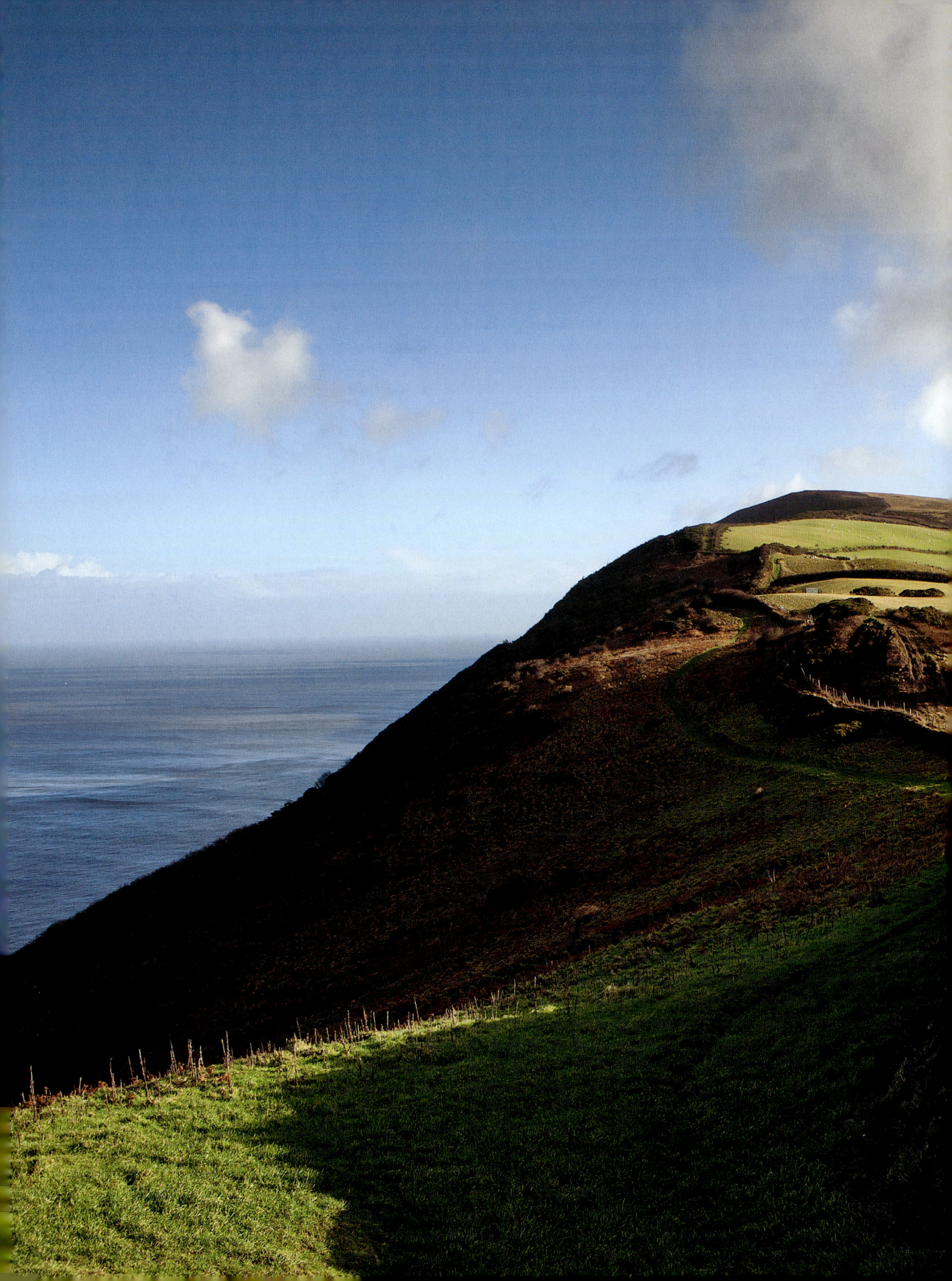

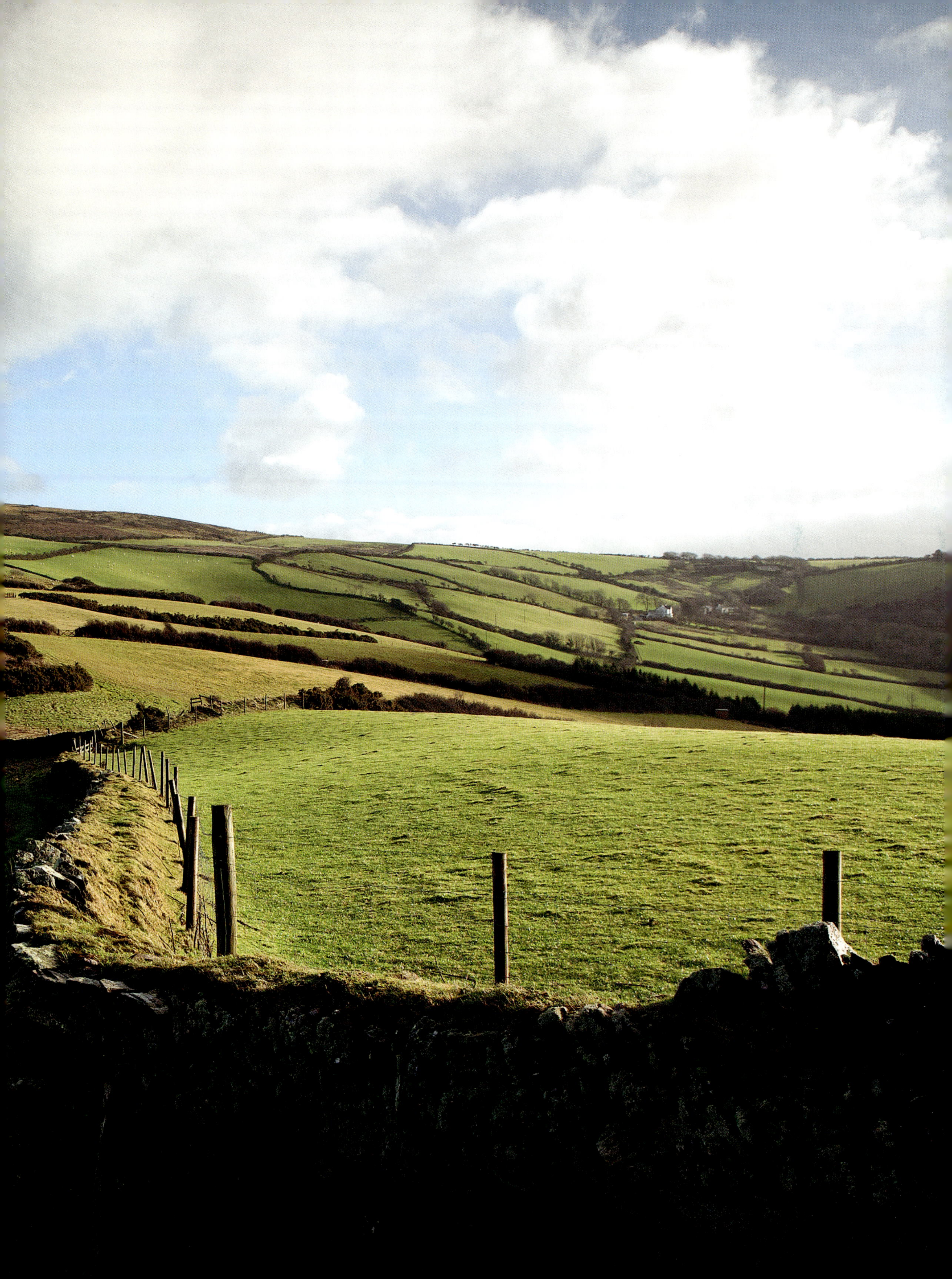

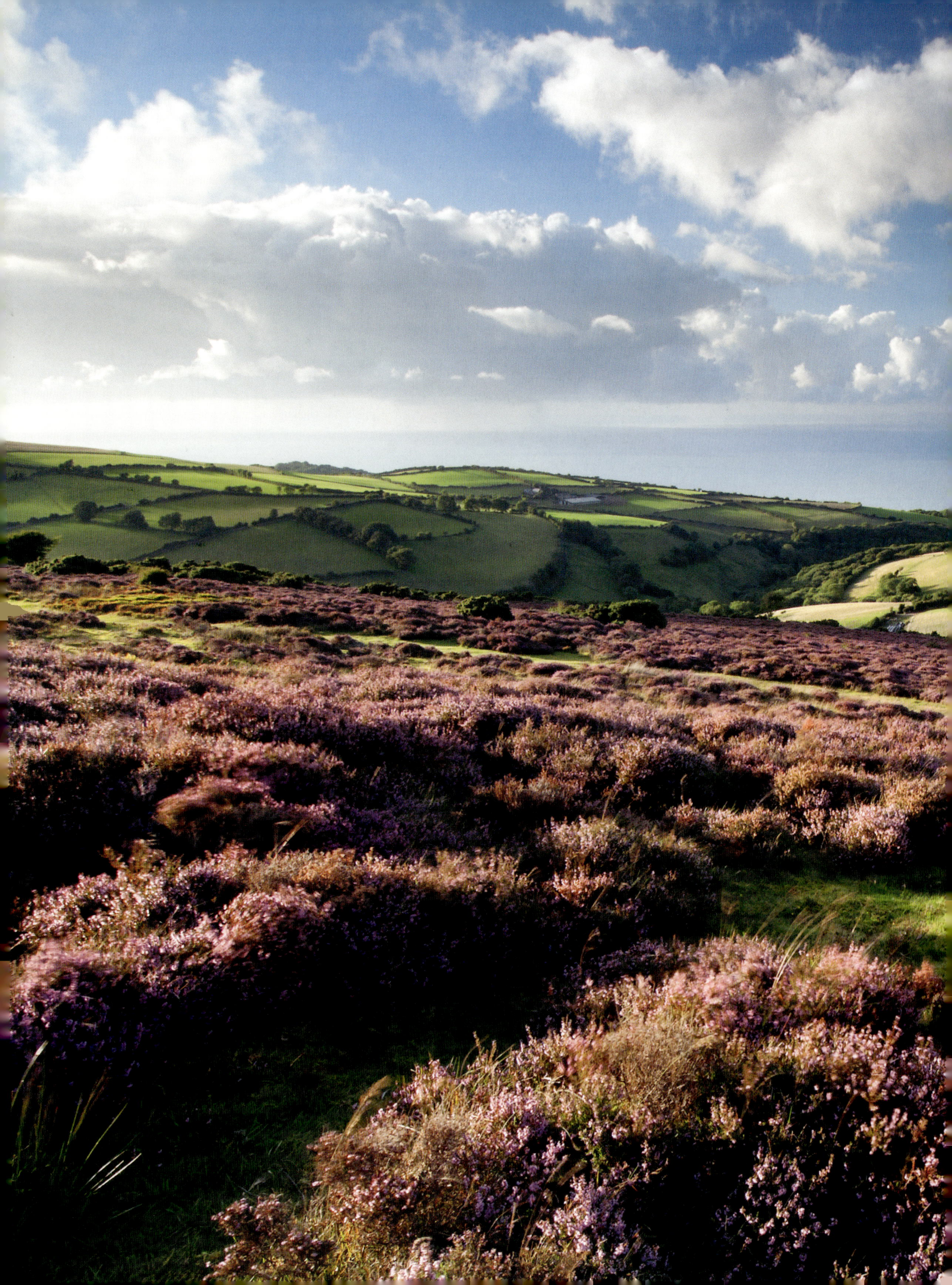

A typical Exmoor scene of flowering purple heather, farmland, woods and coastline, taken near Porlock.

Overleaf:
A dry valley running parallel to the sea, the dramatic Valley of Rocks is thought to have been formed when the route of the East Lyn river was blocked by the ice sheet during the last glacial maximum and got diverted westwards. Agile feral goats roam across the rocky ridge forming the wall of the valley, with a 100-metre (330-foot) drop to the sea below. Wordsworth and Coleridge visited the valley, and part of the famous Exmoor-set novel Lorna Doone *is based here. It is also home to what has to be one of England's most spectacularly situated cricket grounds, which can be seen in the foreground.*

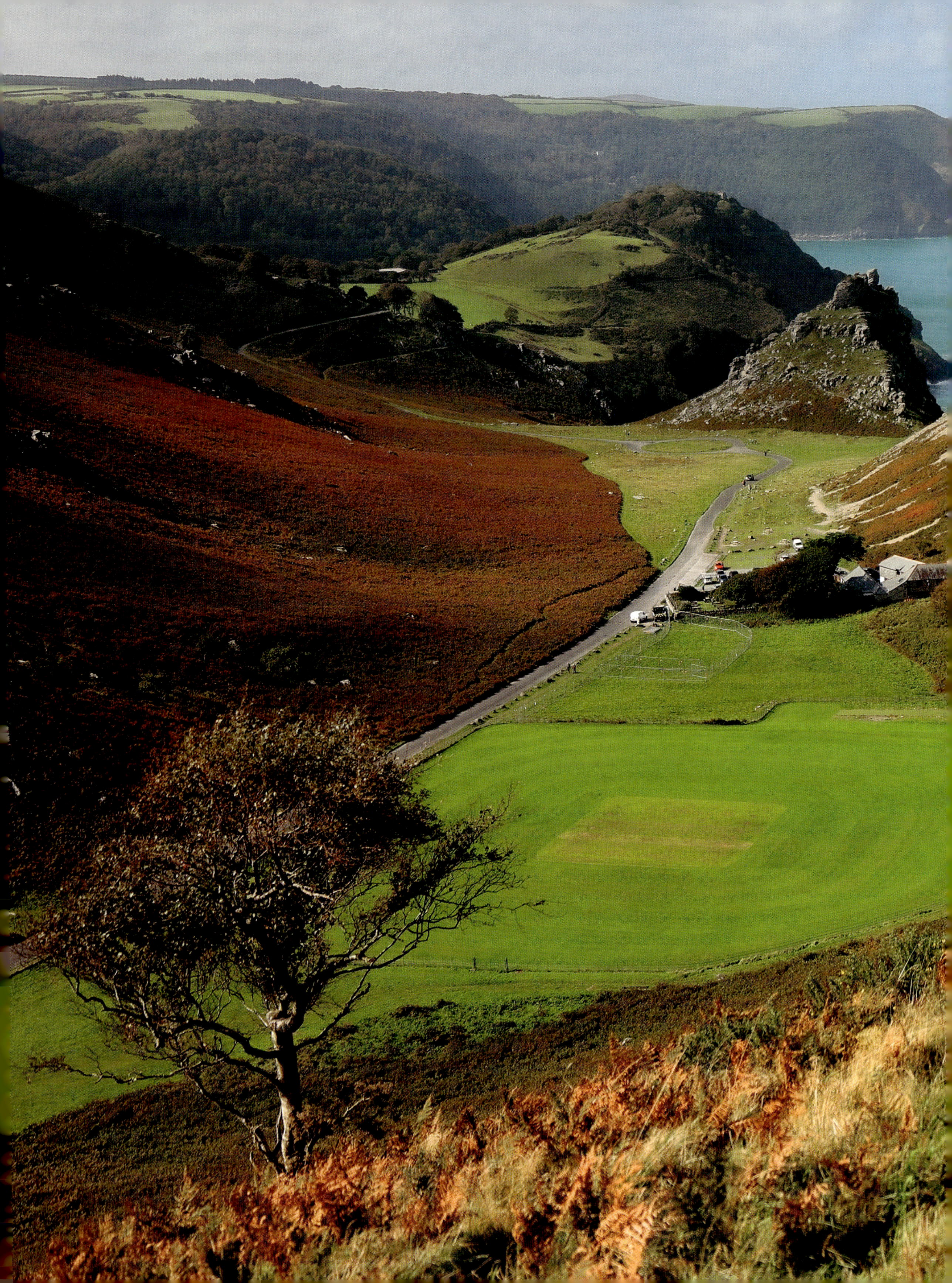

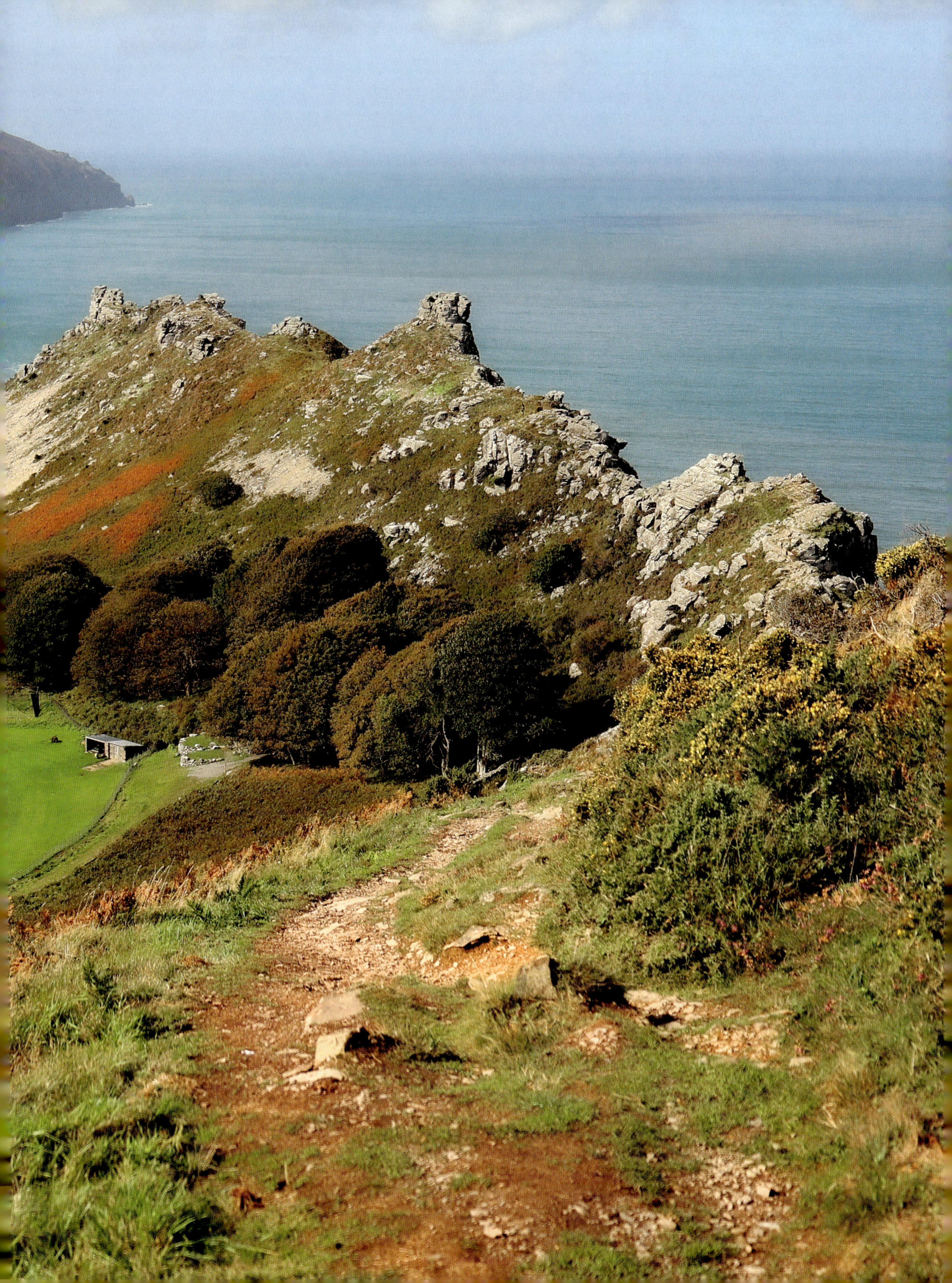

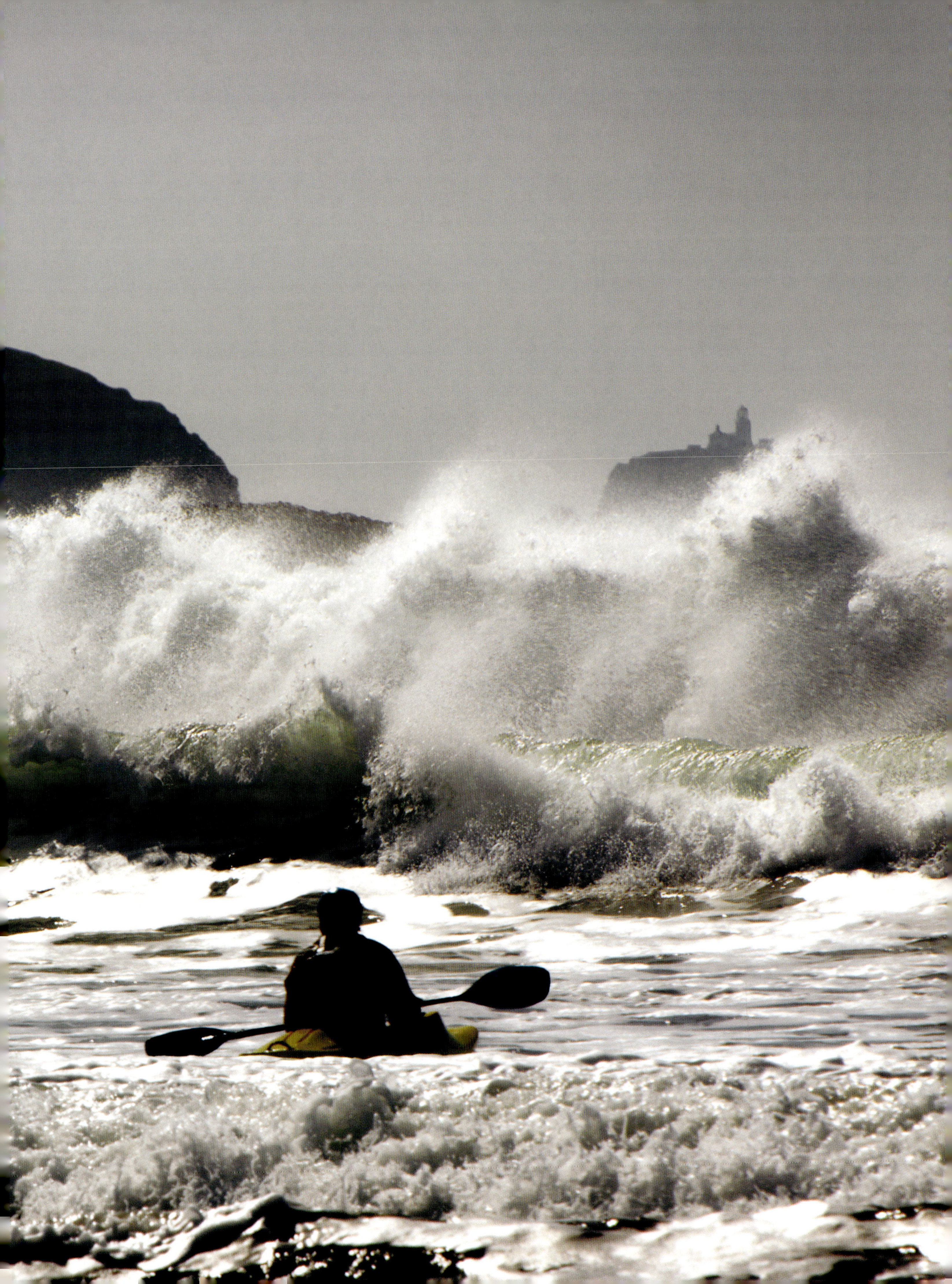

Pembrokeshire Coast

You don't need to travel to other continents to catch sight of some of the great wildlife spectacles of the world's oceans. The rich waters off West Wales – an area dubbed the 'Celtic Deep' – can prove to be just as rewarding.

Fin whales, the second-largest animals in the world, migrate through here every year to feed on shoals of herring. Bottlenose dolphins congregate in their hundreds and surf in the wake of boats. Minke whales live here all year round, gulping down mouthfuls of fish and krill, and can sometimes be seen leaping from the waters in spectacular breaches. Porbeagle sharks, blue sharks and basking sharks – some of the latter as long as a bus – swim through the depths. Vast flocks of diving gannets bombard shoals of mackerel like hails of white missiles. Puffins skim across the swells with sand eels dangling from their beaks.

All can be seen from within a boat-ride's reach of the Pembrokeshire Coast National Park, the only UK national park designated for the beauty and natural richness of its coastline. You don't even need to take to the waves here to see some of the most spectacular ocean megafauna. Humpback whales, a rare but not unheard of visitor, have been spotted less than a kilometre off the coast of Tenby. Leatherback turtles have been known to inundate the waters here in the summer months to feed on burgeoning numbers of jellyfish, coming so close to shore they have been spotted by coastal walkers.

We may often think of Britain as a tamed place, where several millennias' worth of cultivation has displaced the wildest and most charismatic natural creatures from our landscapes. But this is an island archipelago on the edge of the borderless ocean, and in the seas around us, a transformation seems to be underway. Following the worldwide whaling moratorium in the 1980s, whales are gradually returning to waters around Britain. Record numbers of grey seals and dolphins are also being spotted around the coasts; shark populations are growing. All this awesome aquatic life can be seen in the nutrient-rich waters off Pembrokeshire. The Atlantic-battered, rocky shoreline and its nearby islands also host extraordinary avian abundance, particularly evident in the teeming islands of Skomer and Grassholm, the pillars of Stack Rocks or Pencaer peninsula.

Beyond its wildlife, the landscape of this national park is simply beautiful. Every kind of coastal scenery is represented, from the rugged and rocky to the gentle and picturesque. Waves foam and crash beneath tectonically spectacular cliffs, gaping rock arches and towering sea stacks. Former fishing villages hunker in

A surf kayaker heads out into the tumult of Whitesands Bay, one of Pembrokeshire's best surf beaches. Directly exposed to the south-west swell channels and winds of the Atlantic, Pembrokeshire's rocky coastline experiences some dramatic waves and weather.

Whitesands beach and the headland of Pen Dal-aderyn – the westernmost point on the Welsh mainland – bathed in early morning light, with Ramsey Island beyond.

Opposite:
An Atlantic puffin couple on the seabird refuge of Skomer Island. This species of puffin forms monogamous bonds which usually last for life. They spend most of the year feeding in the open expanses of the North Atlantic, rejoining the same mate at the same burrow when they return to land for the spring breeding season. The pairs maintain their bond by rubbing bills together, as shown in this image. Hundreds of thousands of seabirds descend on Skomer Island every year to breed, including more than 40,000 puffins.

small coves and wooded inlets. Long lines of surf roll into sprawling, dune-backed beaches that would not look out of place in Australia or Portugal. Flower-lined clifftop paths run down to hidden bays where eggshell-coloured sands slope into turquoise waters.

Pembrokeshire National Park also encloses the salt flats, quiet woodlands and wetland marshes of the Cleddau river and the Daugleddau estuary, and the Preseli Hills (or Mynydd Preseli), a range of relic-dotted moors littered with monumental remnants from a prehistoric culture, and which supplied some of the stone for Stonehenge. Pembrokeshire as a whole is rich in relics, including a host of megalithic stone tombs, which have become some of the most iconic symbols of ancient Wales.

The Pembrokeshire coastline incorporates some of the finest swathes of sand in Britain, and many people are drawn here for this enticing array of world-class beaches. The pastel-coloured tourist hub of Tenby perches on a promontory surrounded by four gorgeous sands, their picturesqueness accentuated by the lush, wooded cliffs and limestone topography around them; Castle Beach is overlooked by a craggy island topped with a medieval fortress.

The surfing hotspot of Whitesands Bay cradles a wide sweep of sand overlooked by the beautiful mini-mountain of Carn Llidi, formed of an igneous rock called gabbro. At Barafundle Bay, woodland-dotted rocky headlands shelter a beach of fine soft sand where the Irish Sea does a convincing impression of the Caribbean. On the windswept, western edge of Pembrokeshire, wild Marloes Sands is studded with slanting rocky protrusions that dramatically echo the angle of the strata in the surrounding cliffs. Pembrokeshire's beaches have the most Blue Flag designations of any area in Wales – ten in total – and its coastal waters are some of the cleanest in the country; 27 of its 29 designated bathing areas were rated 'Excellent' in their latest annual classifications.

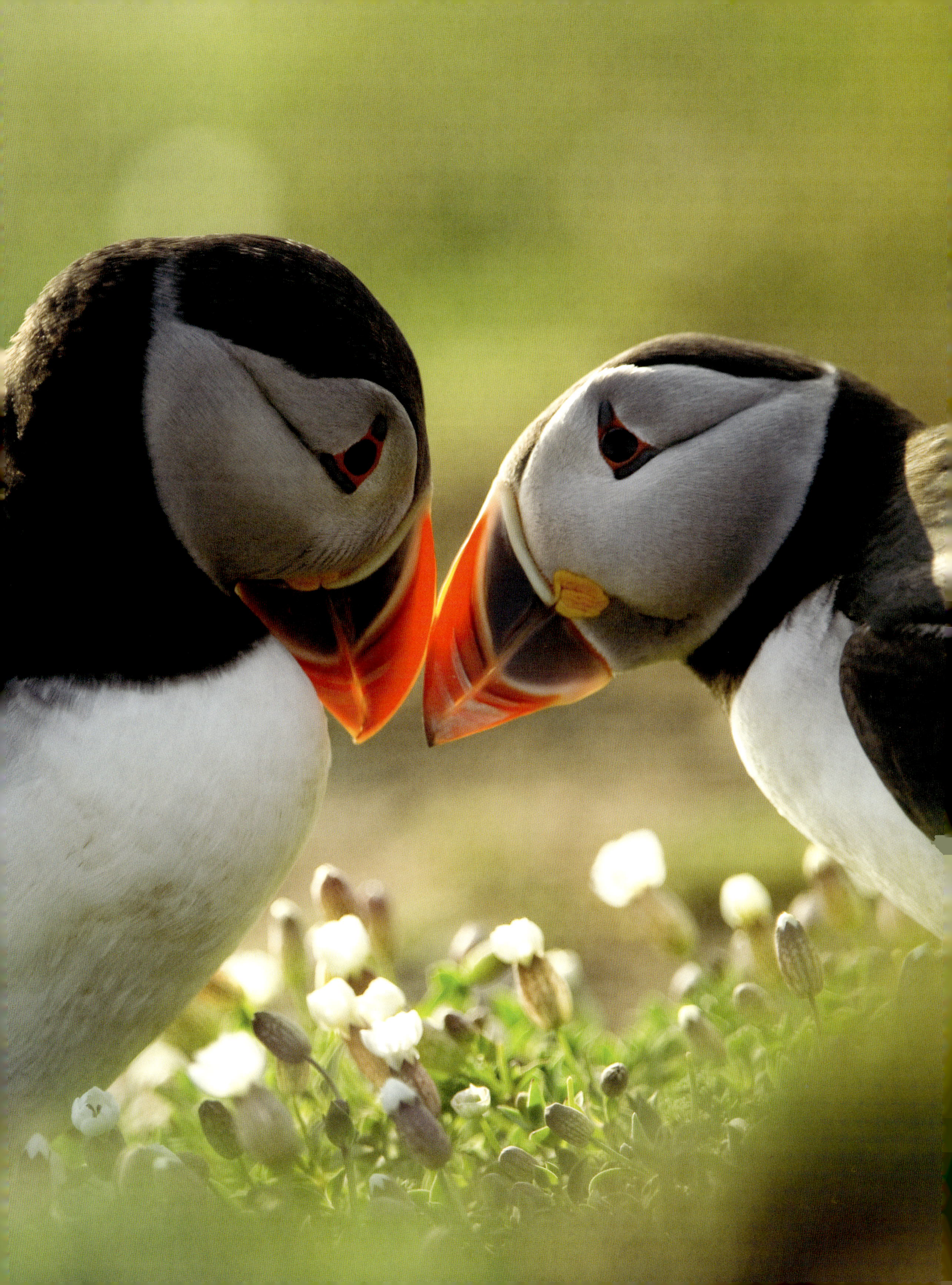

Constructed in 1908, the Strumble Head lighthouse – one of the last lighthouses to be built in the UK – is perched on a small island just offshore, reachable by a footbridge across the rocky strait.

The protected waters around Pembrokeshire are home to around 5,000 grey seals, which often feed in the fish-rich environments of kelp forests – underwater ecosystems dominated by large marine algae.

Stretching across the length of this coastline is the 300-kilometre (186-mile) Pembrokeshire Coast Path, one of Britain's longest-established national trails. Don't be fooled into thinking the coastal nature of this walk makes it easy: it takes in around 10,500 metres (35,000 feet) of ascent and descent, the equivalent of climbing up and down the height of Everest – albeit with more opportunities to stop for ice cream along the way. The rollercoaster nature of the path is testament to the craggy geological drama of the coastline, a smorgasbord of Carboniferous limestone and older Precambrian rocks, distorted into extraordinary, sometimes even grotesque, forms by tectonic forces and the pounding and pummelling of the sea. All along this coastline, the rocky guts of the earth are spectacularly visible.

Walking the whole path takes around 10 to 15 days, but it can readily be broken up into day hike-friendly sections. There are no dull stretches of this path, but highlights include the leg from St Non's to Whitesands, adding in a loop of St David's Head via Carn Llidi, or the challenging and remote section from Newport in Parrog, to Bae Ceredigion, which rises and falls along the top of high cliffs for a spectacular 30 kilometres (18 miles).

Although there is a great deal of enjoyment to be had on land, Pembrokeshire is one of Britain's water sports heartlands, and getting acquainted with the sea opens up new horizons of exploration and fun. Kayaking offers a way to discover this convoluted coastline from a porpoise's perspective, allowing you to reach secluded and otherwise inaccessible beaches, explore secret caves, tunnels and zawns (steep rocky inlets), or paddle out to rocky headlands with seals basking on the shore. Snorkelling in calmer coves reveals underwater kingdoms where pollock, wrasse and sea trout glide through waving kelp forests. Offshore snorkelling boat tours can even take you out into the Celtic Deep to offer an up-close glimpse of blue sharks.

For surfers, beaches like Whitesands and Newgale offer beginner-friendly swells, while the wilder waves of the likes of Freshwater West draw in the more experienced. Pembrokeshire is also the birthplace of coasteering, a hybrid sport often run in guided groups, which involves treating the rocky intertidal zone as a sort of aquatic adventure playground – think leaping into swells, exploring caves and making heart-in-mouth cliff jumps.

Pembrokeshire's hills and headlands contain some of the most striking and enigmatic prehistoric remnants in Britain. Built a thousand years before the construction of the Pyramids, Pentre Ifan is the site of the largest and best-preserved Neolithic monument in Wales. The heart of this megalithic monument is a huge dolmen, or portal tomb, generally thought to be the remnant of a larger structure. Today a 16-tonne capstone rests on the tapered tips of three upright stones, each as tall as an elephant. Similarly impressive Neolithic monuments include Carreg Samson, spectacularly situated on the coast, where a huge boulder rests on top of comparatively thin rock pillars, like the fingers of a hand carrying an overladen tray; or Carreg Coetan Arthur, often said to resemble a mushroom.

Neolithic remnants are widely distributed across Pembrokeshire, but one of the most significant focuses of attention seems to have been the Mynydd Preseli range and their surroundings. These hills are littered with relics, and Neolithic quarries along an outcrop here have even been identified as the source of the smaller 'bluestones' at Stonehenge, almost 325 kilometres (202 miles) away in Wiltshire. No written records remain from this time period, so the exact meaning, purpose and context for these monuments is a subject of archaeological debate. But despite being situated on the edges of the British landmass, these Neolithic cultures were not remote: they would have been connected via the seaways of the 'Atlantic network' to modern-day Cornwall, Iberia and France, which is how the practice of building megalithic monuments

Blue sharks migrate north from their breeding grounds and are often found in Welsh waters. Though usually only found in the deeper seas some distance from the coast, they can be spotted on 'sea safari' tours from Pembrokeshire.

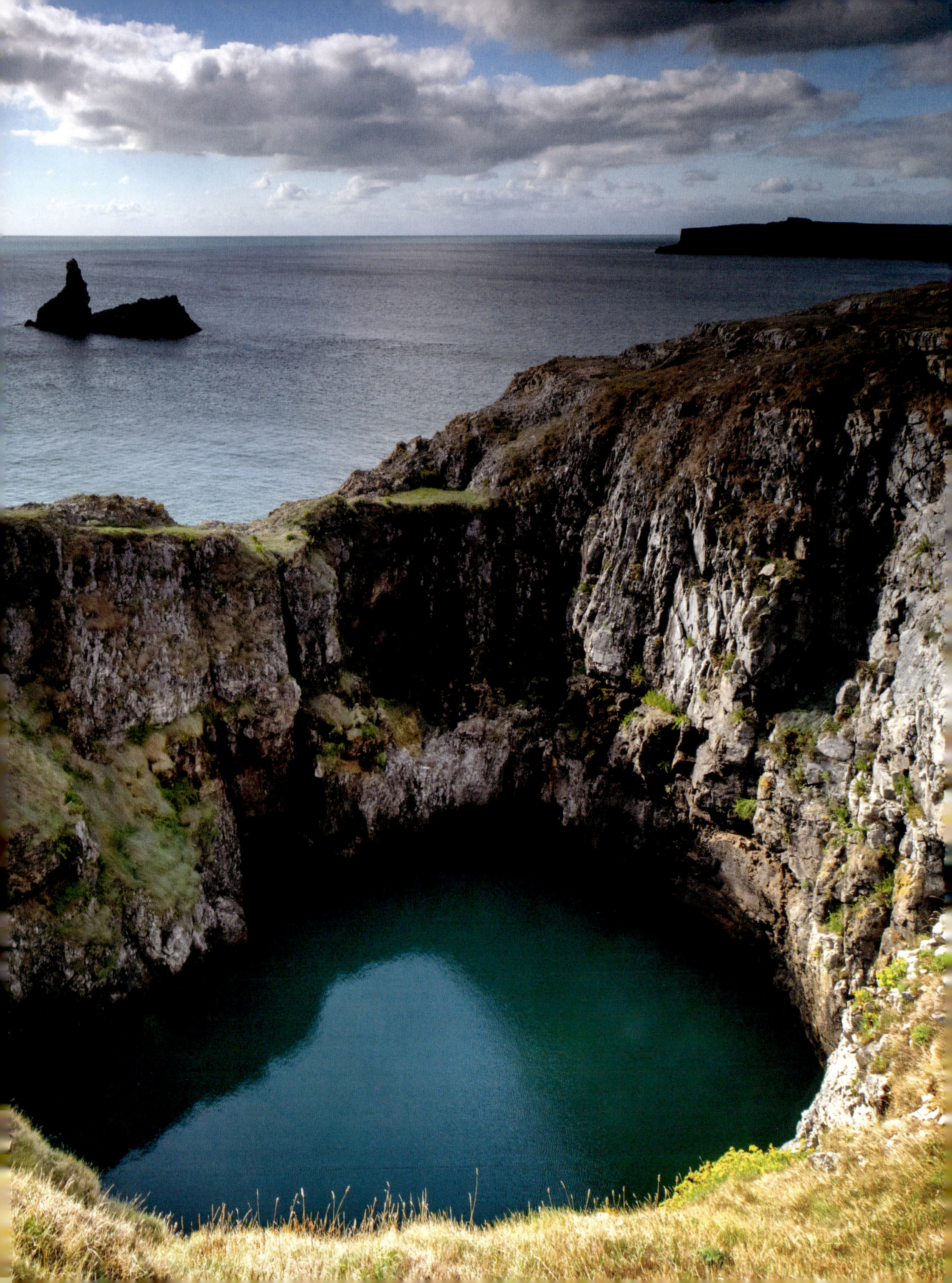

originally reached these shores. Far from being on the fringe of a bigger inland society, these were ocean-facing peoples, drawing on the sea for food, communication and wider cultural contact.

Pembrokeshire's significance as a sacred landscape connected to the sea has continued through subsequent millennia: the enormous Norman cathedral in St Davids – Britain's smallest official city, with a population of just a couple of thousand – is a legacy of a monastic community established in the 6th century by the Welsh patron saint, who is credited with helping to spread Christianity throughout Europe from his base in West Wales.

Humans are not the only ocean-faring species to have a long history in Pembrokeshire: the landscape and seascapes of this national park also contain some of the most important seabird habitats in both Britain and the world as a whole. In the spring breeding season, the islands and cliffs are transformed into enormous avian communities. On the island of Skomer, more than 350,000 Manx shearwaters – half the global population of the species – nest in a vast colony of burrows, and around 40,000 puffins fly in from thousands of miles across the North Atlantic to breed, a number that has more than doubled in the last ten years. A similar number of northern gannets squeeze on to the 200-metre-wide Grassholm Island, turning the grey rock white with a thick crust of guano. The towering limestone pillars of Stack Rocks and the nearby cliffs on the park's southern coastline teem with guillemots, razorbills, fulmars, kittiwakes and herring gulls. These great 'seabird cities' are among the most vibrant wildlife spectacles to be found in these islands, their cacophonous sounds, immense energy and overwhelming smells a reminder of the wild vitality that that still survives in the world's oceanic expanses.

Other parts of Pembrokeshire attract huge numbers of birds on their way to elsewhere. Strumble Head, or the Pencaer peninsula, juts out into the Irish Sea, attracting birds on their seasonal migrations along the coast. The autumn

The common guillemot breeds in large numbers on the Pembrokeshire coast, particularly on Skomer and other offshore islands. They are deep-diving seabirds, capable of reaching astonishing depths of up to 180 metres in search of prey. They are sometimes compared to penguins. Both are actually cousins of the great auk, a large flightless bird with white circles on its head, which inhabited the North Atlantic and was driven to extinction in the 19th century. The name northern hemisphere sailors gave to penguins may be derived from the Welsh words pen gwyn *– meaning white head.*

Opposite:
A spectacular limestone sinkhole near Broad Haven, with a narrow aperture leading to the sea. Beyond is the sea stack of Church Rock, so-named because of its, albeit faint, resemblance to a steepled chapel.

The village of Solva clusters around a harbour within a sheltered inlet. A local trading centre in medieval times, it is now a centre for leisure boating.

Opposite:
Whitesands Bay, near St Davids, is one of Pembrokeshire's most popular beaches, as well as one of the best for surfing. It is overlooked by Carn Llidi, an outcrop of 500-million-year-old volcanic gabbro rock, which is rich in Neolithic archaeology.

passage, between the end of July and mid-November, is the peak of activity. Arctic skuas and great skuas – birds of high latitudes, which in the UK only breed on the northernmost Scottish islands – are specialities of these locations; while national rarities like the high-arctic Sabine's gull and the Leach's petrel are comparatively common.

All these long-distance seabirds live their lives across vast expanses, with their migratory journeys sometimes spanning the length of the Atlantic, from Greenland to Patagonia. They only brush the edges of our land for short windows: most of their lives are spent hunting and feeding on the storm-swept, open ocean. When we spot them passing by, they give us glimpses of the huge wildness beyond – a world which, in Pembrokeshire, often feels thrillingly close.

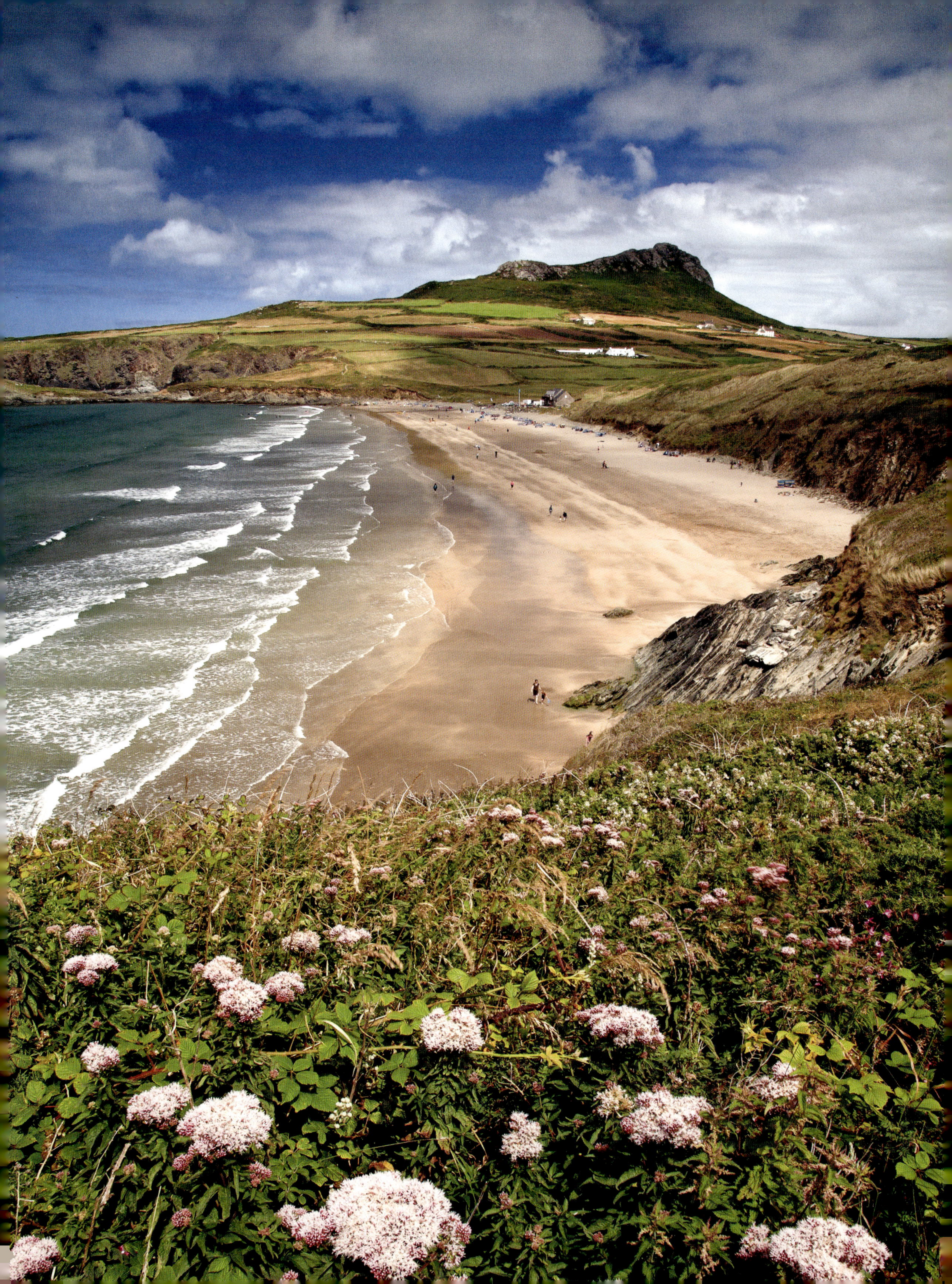

Wind, weather and waves have taken a spectacular toll on the Atlantic-battered Pembrokeshire coastline, where rock has been sculpted into fantastic forms by dynamic oceanic forces. The 'Green Bridge of Wales' is a natural rock arch, formed in part by erosion of the water-soluble Carboniferous limestone it is made from. Though usually open to visitors, this coastal landmark and others nearby form part of the Castlemartin military training area, and access can sometimes be restricted.

Overleaf:
Clinging to a headland in Carmarthen Bay, the pastel-coloured harbour town of Tenby is surrounded by four beautiful beaches. The town originated as a Norman outpost, and its impressive 13th-century walls and towers are some of the best-preserved medieval fortifications in Britain. Tenby boomed as a coastal resort during the Georgian and Victorian eras, and it remains one of Wales' most popular seaside towns; the stern walls now juxtaposed with vividly coloured shops selling ice creams and souvenirs.

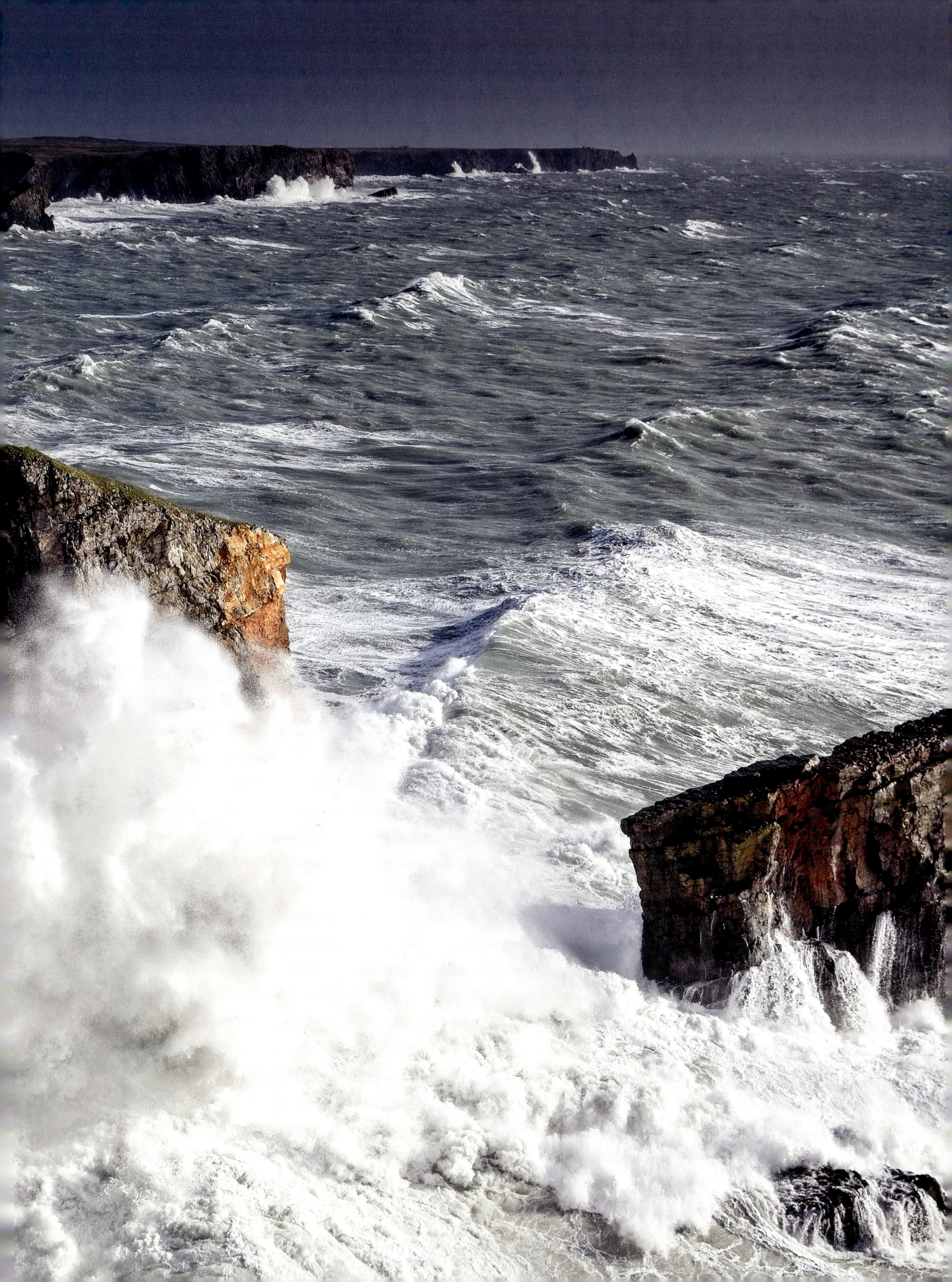

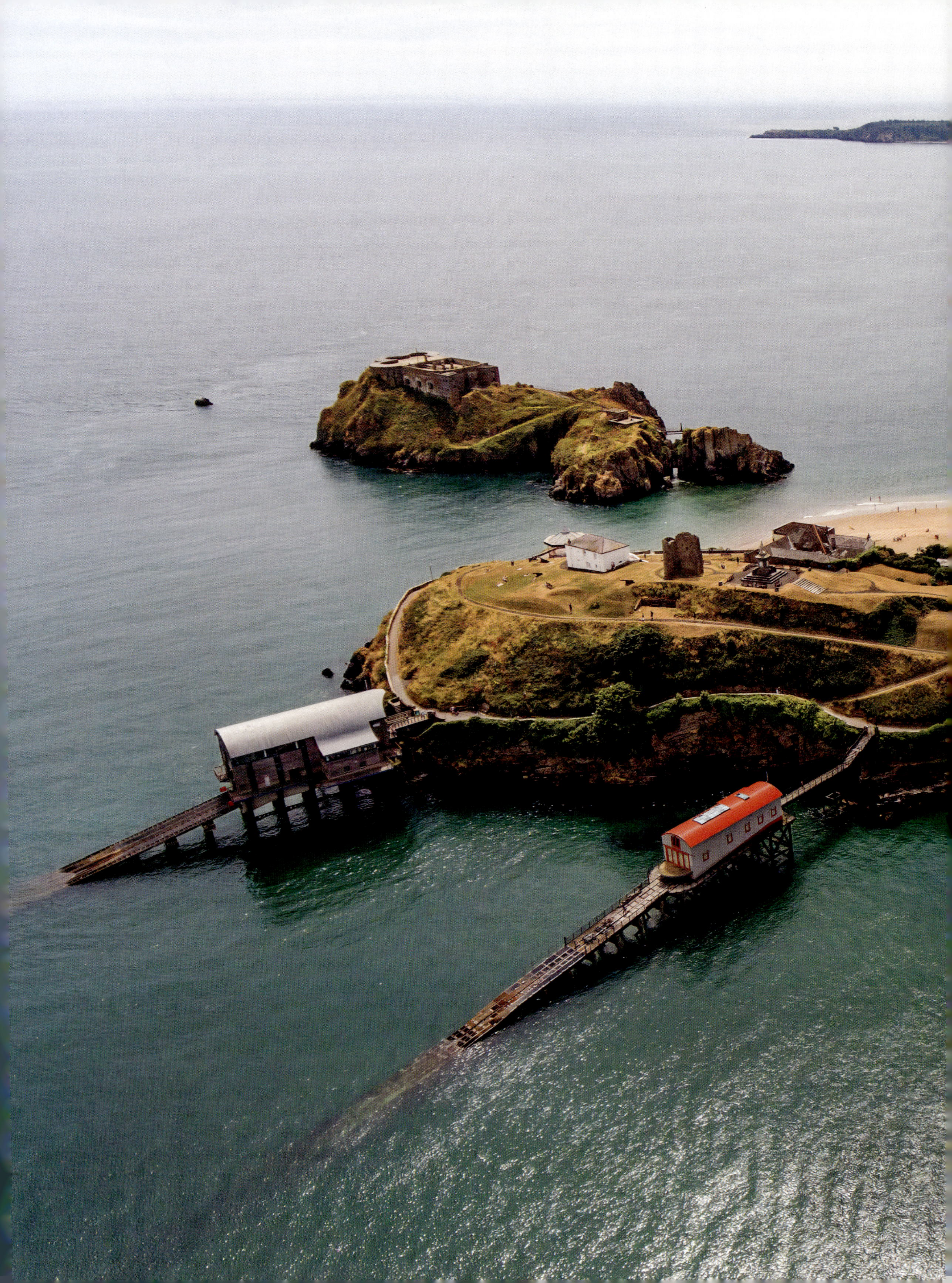

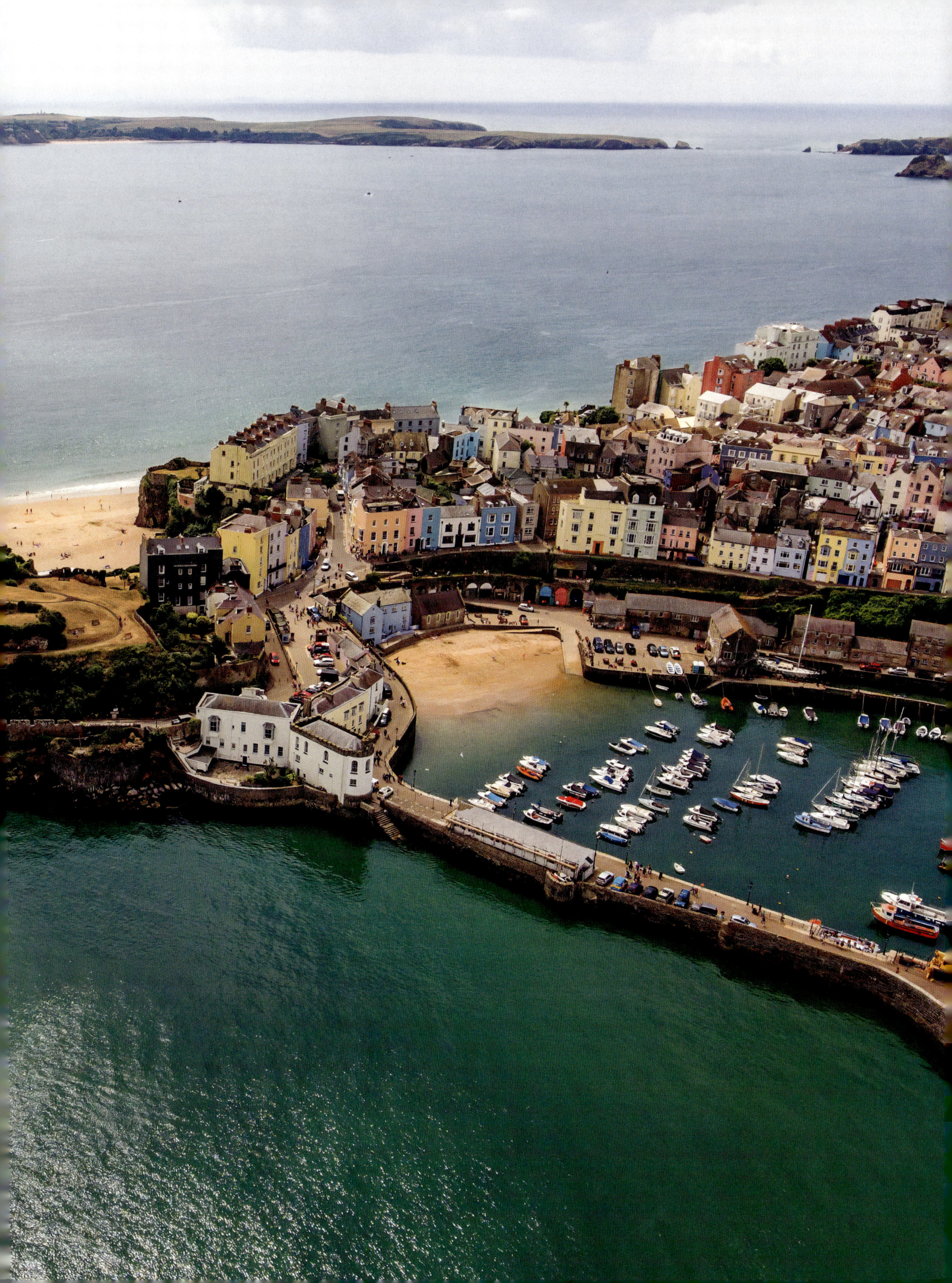

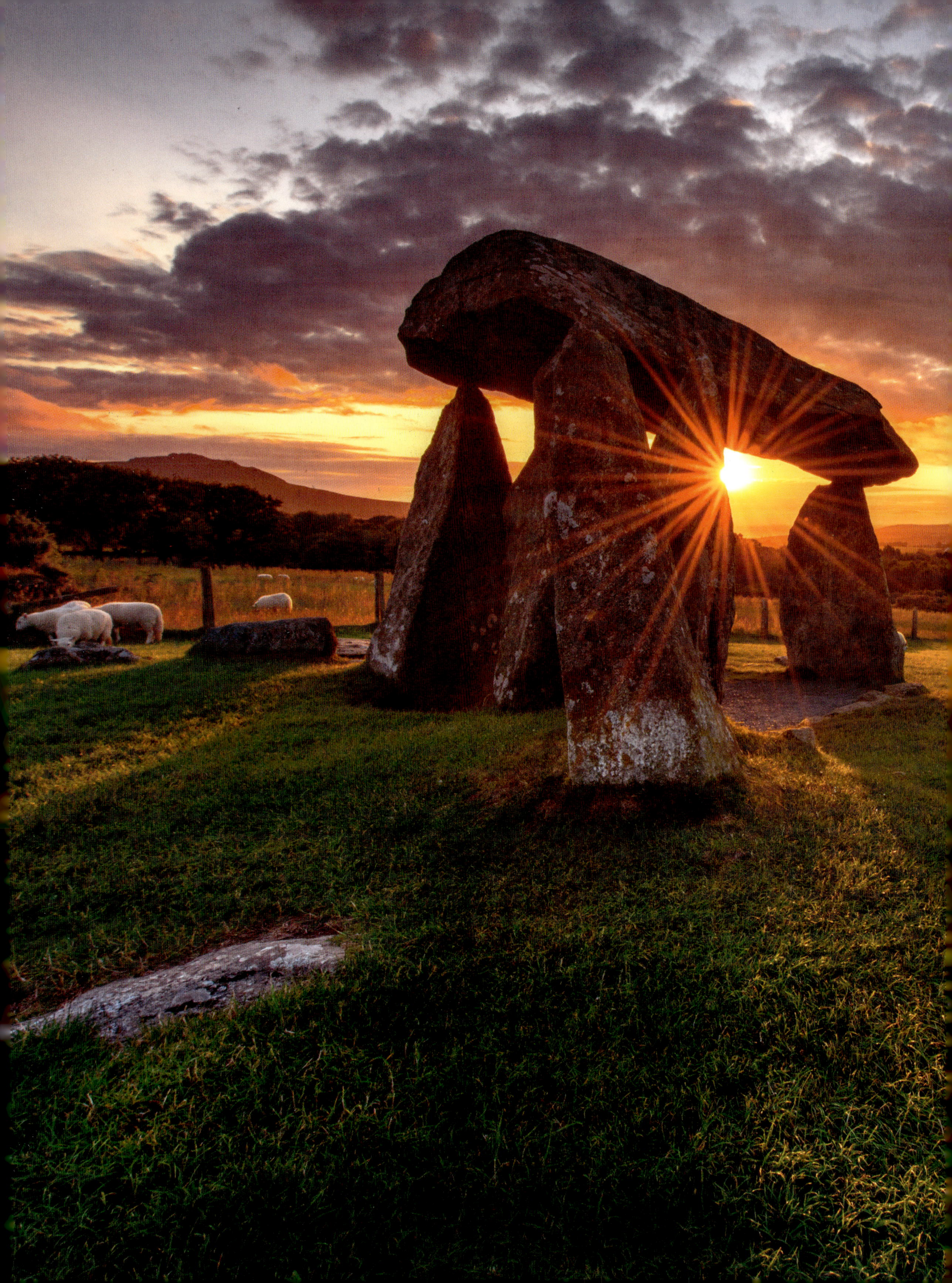

The monument at Pentre Ifan is thought to have been built around 5,500 years ago, about a millennia before the Pyramids. The capstone crowning the structure rests on three of the six upright stones and is estimated to weigh 16 tonnes. It is one of a host of Megalithic monuments found near the Pembrokeshire coast. Structures like this were built by small farming communities using stone tools and early farming methods, but they are thought to have been well connected by sea to a wider European culture, and achieved feats that experts still struggle to explain today. The 'bluestones' of Pentre Ifan were quarried from the nearby Mynydd Preseli range; stones from the same place, weighing up to 5 tonnes, were transported to Stonehenge, 325 kilometres (202 miles) away in modern-day Wiltshire.

Overleaf:
Looking over coastal sheep pastures, with the beach of Abermawr beyond.

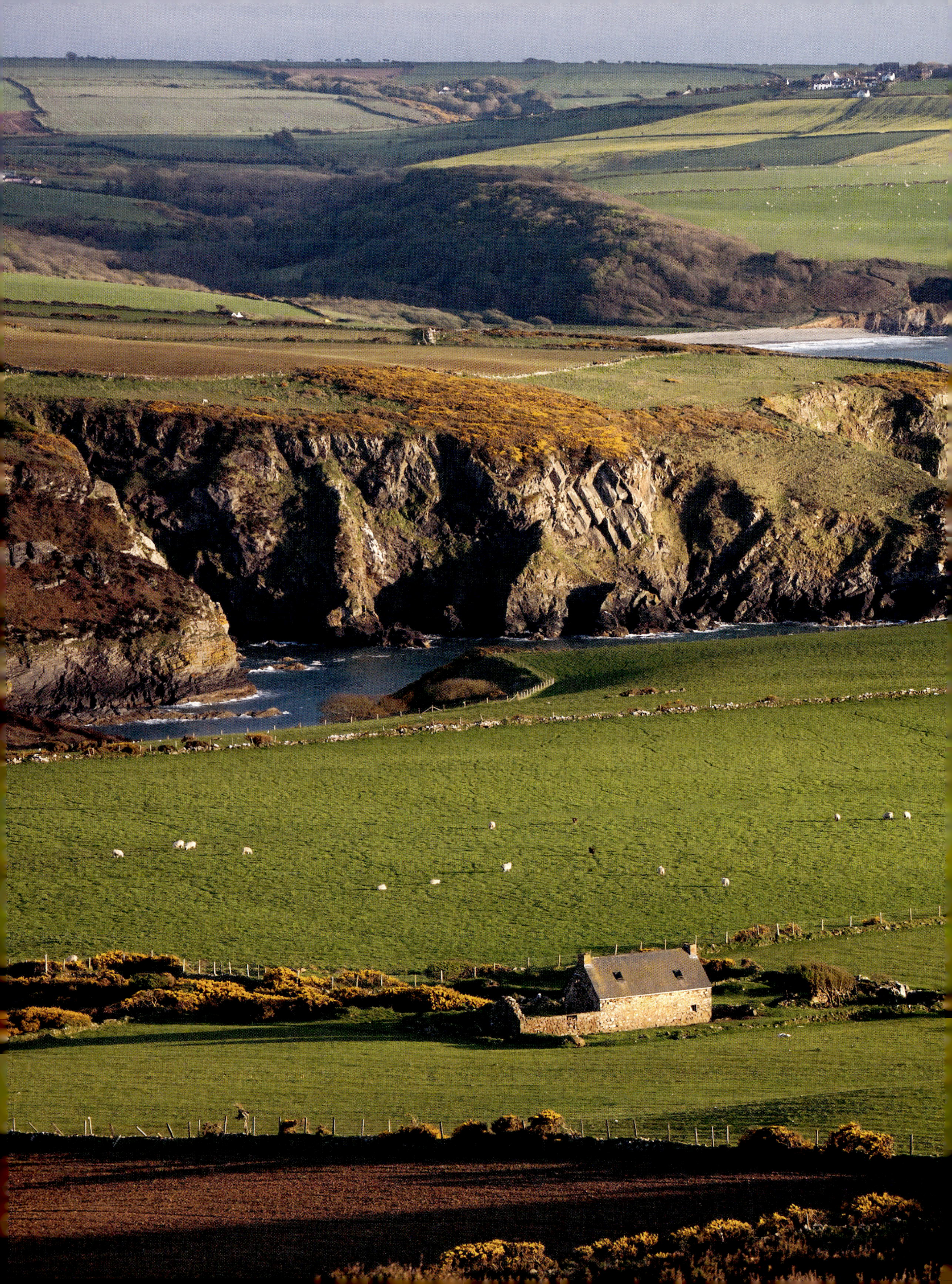

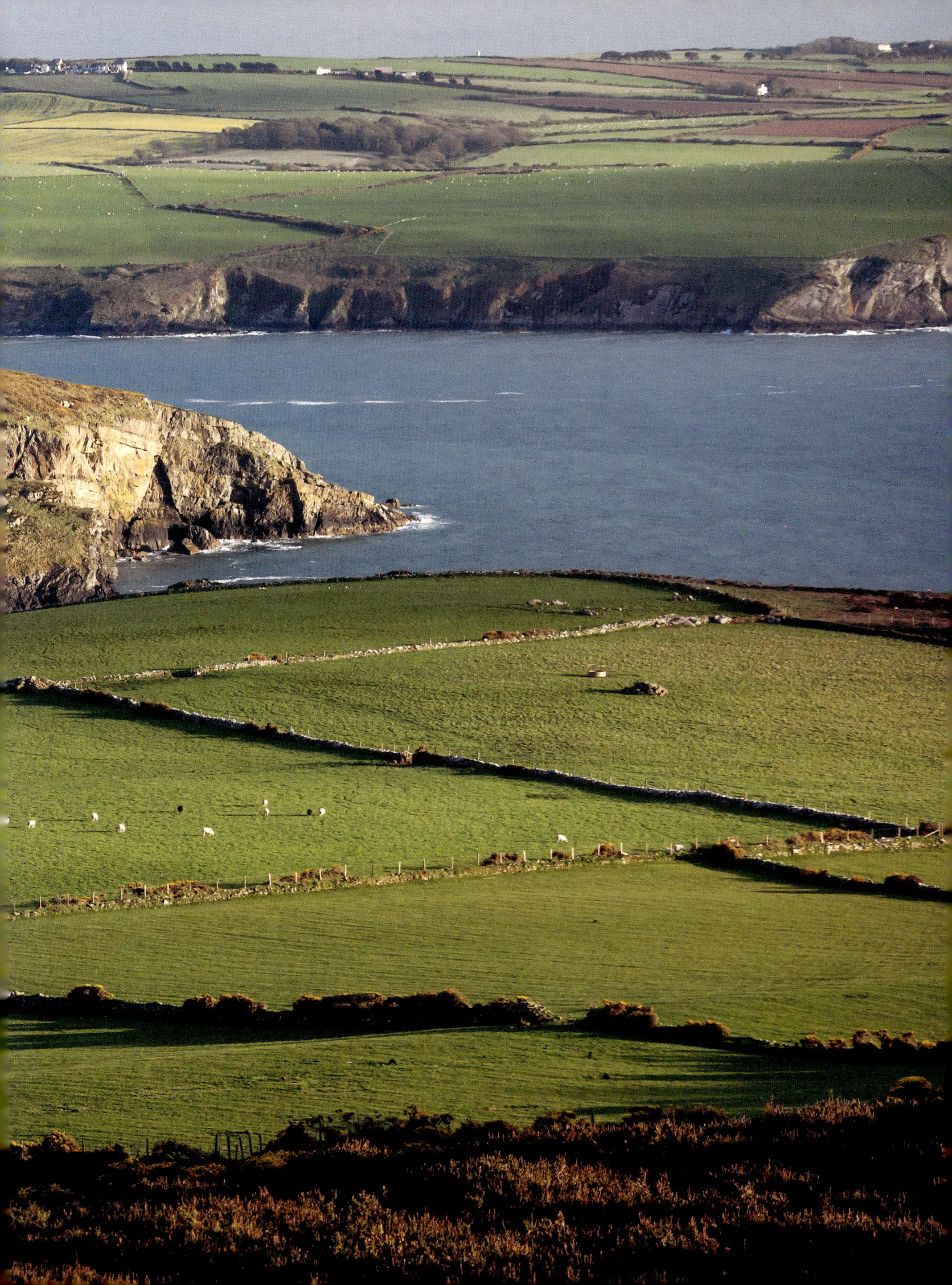

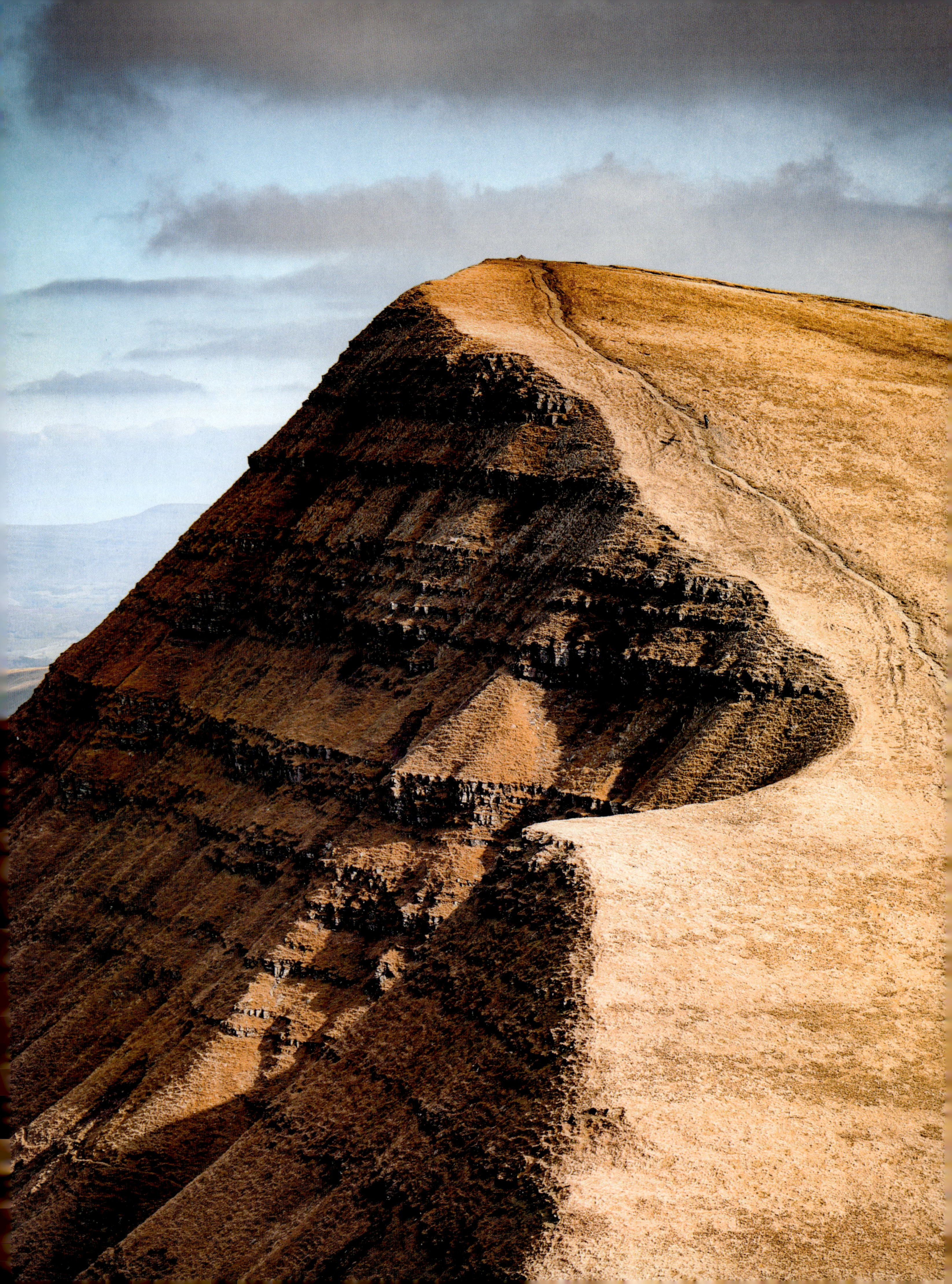

Bannau Brycheiniog

The rocks of Bannau Brycheiniog have stories to tell: of deserts, of tropical seas and of a world before flowers, where the first land plants radiated across the continents forming huge primitive forests, which would fuel an industrial revolution 300 million years later. They tell of ice sheets and glaciers. They tell of thousands years of human history; of ancient tribes repelling the Romans, of medieval rebellions in the name of Welsh independence, of worker uprisings. They tell of the freedom of the hills, the peace of the valleys, the quiet field.

Bannau Brycheiniog – known in English as the Brecon Beacons – is an atmospheric and richly resonant upland landscape between South and mid-Wales, stretching from the border with England in the east into Carmarthenshire, 70 kilometres (43 miles) or so to the west. Within this belt of mountainous terrain there are four distinct regional clusters and a host of different environments, ranging from wind-battered summits to lush woodland waterfalls; from secluded rural valleys to remote moorland expanses littered with relics.

Geology has indelibly shaped the history of Bannau Brycheiniog, sometimes shortened to 'the Bannau'. Around two-thirds of the national park lies within the Fforest Fawr Geopark, a designation that celebrates the region's geological heritage and its links to the tapestry of human and natural life that has arisen from it. A chain of dizzying escarpments runs across the northern edge of Bannau Brycheiniog's mountains, giving sandstone peaks like Twmpa, Pen y Fan and Fan Brycheiniog a dramatic profile, like towering waves about to break. They draw hikers and hillwalkers from far afield. In the other direction, travelling south, the underlying strata dips into a landscape of craggy limestone hills, wooded valleys and reservoirs, increasingly dotted with industrial relics as the national park approaches the coal country of South Wales.

Bannau Brycheiniog has had a rich and often tumultuous history. Successive waves of settlers, peoples, invaders and occupiers have come and gone, leaving castles, bastions and relics in their wake. This landscape lies between many different worlds, and contains many of its own, all of them coloured by the world beneath. 'Press your fingers close on this lichened sandstone,' wrote the local-born Welsh author Raymond Williams. 'With this stone and this grass, with this red earth, this place was received and made and remade. Its generations are distinct, but all suddenly present.'

Bannau Brycheiniog is known as the Brecon Beacons National Park in English but, strictly speaking, the latter term refers only to a single range of summits in the centre of the park. Strung together along a plunging escarpment of striated red sandstone, this range is crowned by Pen y Fan, which at 886 metres (2,900 feet) is the highest peak in southern Britain. The peak shown here is its neighbour, the smaller but distinctively pyramidal Cribyn.

Hay Bluff is the easternmost peak of the long escarpment that runs across the northern edge of Bannau Brycheiniog. The border with England, and the Offa's Dyke Path, both run across the ridge running south from its summit.

Opposite:
The Vale of Ewyas is one of several valleys that cut through the Black Mountains, the eastern part of Bannau Brycheiniog. The Afon Honddu runs through it, and the valley's impressive form – a classic U-shape – betrays the past presence of a glacier. A patchwork of hedgerows, villages, farmsteads, and old churches now fills the space where a flow of ice would once have ground its way through the landscape. The high walls of this long, winding valley help foster a powerful sense of shelter and seclusion.

At 886 metres (2,900 feet) high, Pen y Fan is the highest summit of the Bannau, and the highest peak in southern Britain. Although the whole national park is known in English as the Brecon Beacons, strictly speaking the term only refers to Pen y Fan and the massif it dominates, a chain of six main summits that also includes Corn Du, Cribyn and Fan y Big.

These hills – sometimes called the Central Beacons to avoid confusion – are the literal and figurative heart of the national park. They are made of Old Red Sandstone, a rock formed 400 million years ago in the Devonian period, with harder-wearing layers on their summits helping to create their distinctive crowning tops. These summits provide tremendous views and a sense of elevation far above their stature: on their north sides they plunge rapidly down via vertiginous cliffs, glacial cirques and narrow ridges into the rolling patchwork of mid-Wales, and on fine days these provide views stretching far into the heart of the country. As the monarch of Bannau Brycheiniog, Pen y Fan has an appropriately regal demeanour when viewed from the north, shaped as it is like a high-backed throne, with great arm-like ridges sweeping down from its summit.

The Central Beacons are one of Wales' biggest hubs for hiking and hillwalking, offering accessible adventure within easy reach of the great population centres of South Wales. Pen y Fan in particular is a crowd-magnet, thanks in large part to its approach from the A470 road, which allows walkers to start their climb at 450 metres (1,500 feet) from the Storey Arms and ascend the mountain via a wide and well-marked path. As with North Wales equivalent, Yr Wyddfa (Snowdon), long queues of people lining up for an obligatory summit selfie on Pen y Fan are a regular sight on summer weekends. Even so, these peaks should never be underestimated: like any mountain landscape, they can become hostile environments, particularly in poor visibility, or when the unimpeded winds blowing in from the Atlantic rake the mountains' streamlined contours.

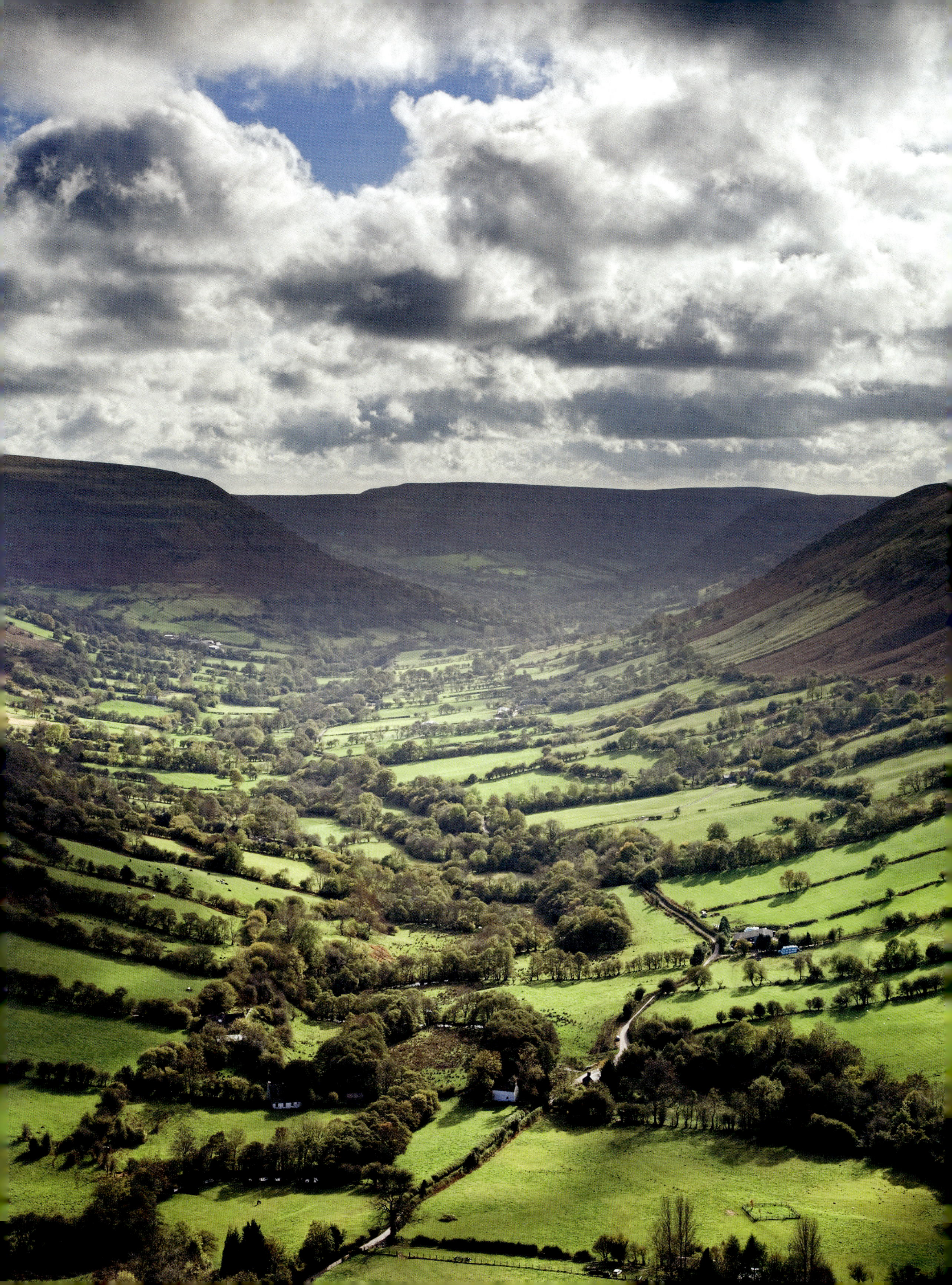

Much of the woodland cover of Bannau Brycheiniog is in the form of conifer plantations, like these covering the slopes of the Talybont reservoir. Many of these were created as a timber resource in the aftermath of World War One, but are now primarily managed for recreation.

If a quieter ambience is what you seek, the Black Mountains, in the eastern part of Bannau Brycheiniog, are a good place to look. Described by Williams as resembling the shape of an outspread hand, the Black Mountains are predominantly a range of long rounded ridges with wide river valleys running between them. Within the folds of these valleys there is an atmosphere of quiet, lived-in seclusion, and an uncanny sense that some sort of spell is at work, shielding the landscape from the attention of the wider world.

Arguably the loveliest of the Black Mountains valleys, the Vale of Ewyas is a snaking U-shaped corridor of hawthorn-edged pastures, high oak woodlands and secluded farms, where hawfinches flit through the trees and barn owls swoop on prey in the long dusks. Llanthony is home to the ruins of a beautiful Augustinian priory, while nestled within the pastoral patchwork of the valley, sequestered among the trees and villages, are several weird and wonderful little churches, like the owl faced Capel-y-ffin, or St Martin's Church in Cwmyoy, the latter of which is probably Britain's wonkiest place of worship. The hidden-away feel of the Black Mountains has often attracted and inspired writers, and the nearby town of Hay-on-Wye, which hosts a famous annual literature festival, is a well-known creative hub.

The eastern flank of the Vale of Ewyas is enclosed by the wide, whalebacked form of the Hatterall Ridge. Walking along this high-level frontier, you also follow the route of the Offa's Dyke path, a 285 kilometre (177 mile) long-distance trail, which roughly traces the route of an ancient linear earthwork marking the divide between what is now England and Wales. With the lightly rippling patchwork of Herefordshire fanning out below you to the east, and the dramatic hills of Wales filling the western horizon, it is a spectacular place to contemplate the often-contested history of this landscape. The Black Mountains, and the Bannau more generally, have been a border for at least 2,000 years. The Silure tribes who lived here fiercely resisted the Romans, leaving a legacy of Roman forts dotted around the region, while Norman castles like Tretower testify to centuries of medieval warfare aimed at subduing the Welsh. The sometimes-volatile industrial history of the nearby South Wales Valleys, with their underlying Carboniferous coal measures, is attested to in landmarks like the Chartist Cave on Mynydd Llangynidr, where pro-democracy rebels stored weapons before their, ultimately unsuccessful, march in Newport in 1839. On the western side of Bannau Brycheiniog lie the upland expanses of the Fforest Fawr range and, in the far west, the Black Mountain. Despite its singular name, the latter is actually a range of hills, the highest of which is Fan Brycheiniog (802 metres / 2,630 feet). These wild western ranges are also far less trodden than the central Brecon Beacons. In these places you are more likely to encounter the ghosts of the past than a living soul; yet despite their apparent remoteness, these landscapes are peppered with prehistoric remnants, including stone circles, menhirs and round barrows, as well as Roman roads and castras, or military encampments.

On the north-west fringes of the Black Mountain, the hilltop of Y Garn Goch hosts the remnants of one of the largest Iron Age hill fort complexes in Wales, Y Gaer Fawr and Y Gaer Fach. The former would have been a megacity of its day, with stone ramparts 10 metres (33 feet) high and at least six separate entrances. Not too far away is the spectacularly situated Norman castle of Carreg Cennen, which towers, Tolkienesque, atop a forest-fringed limestone cliff.

Much of Bannau Brycheiniog is high moorland. It is grazed by sheep and supports the relatively restricted range of flora and fauna typical of similar landscapes across these islands. Even so, heathery areas are home to red grouse; golden plover, skylark and curlew are common sights across the moors; and semi-wild Welsh mountain ponies roam across most high parts of the national park. Rockier areas provide nesting sites for migratory ring ouzels, the 'mountain blackbird', as well as raptors like peregrines and buzzards. This

Red kites were once an everyday sight in these islands, even mentioned in the writings of Shakespeare. Mistakenly blamed by farmers and gamekeepers for killing their animals, they were almost pushed to extinction in Britain. By 1990 there were just a few breeding pairs left in a region of Wales that included parts of Bannau Brycheiniog. An extensive reintroduction programme in a host of places has since bought them back from the brink.

An upland hill farm in the Black Mountains with woodland-cloaked valley walls leading to moorland heights beyond. Like much of Wales, the mountainous geography of Bannau Brycheiniog is unsuitable for arable cropping. Grazing livestock like sheep have historically been integral to the region's culture and economy, as well as creating the landscape as we know it. Family-run farmsteads with relatively small holdings are common. Hill farming faces a host of challenges and commercial pressures, leading to a decline in the number of people employed on the land. Various initiatives have been created to support hill farming while working with the community to foster more environmentally beneficial practices. Successes in recent years include a revival of the planting of traditional hedgerows.

part of the world also played an integral part in the survival and resurgence in Britain of the red kite, a large scavenging raptor, which in recent years has been widely reintroduced across the UK but which was once restricted to the western parts of Bannau Brycheiniog and nearby areas like Mynydd Mallaen.

Much of the woodland cover in this national park comes in the blocks of conifer plantations like those around the Talybont or Pontsticill reservoirs. Many of these were created as a timber resource in the aftermath of World War One, but are now primarily managed for recreation, offering accessible trails for walking, running, cycling and horse-riding. Goshawk, an elusive bird of prey, can be found in these coniferous areas, as can the nightjar, a bird whose plumage is dark and smoky, like the scales of a dragon, and whose mating call – an otherworldly 'churring' noise – falls somewhere between a bird call and the sound of an alien spacecraft.

Areas of broadleaved forest can be found in the southern parts of Bannau Brycheiniog, often lining the valleys or clinging to steep ridges. The Craig-y-Cilau nature reserve is a vast cliffed amphitheatre beneath the northern edge of Mynydd Llangatwg and now hosts some exceptionally rare flora, including the narrow-leaved and lesser whitebeam. In the 'Waterfall Country' between Ystradfellte and Pontneddfechan, in the south of the Fforest Fawr region, the Afon Mellte tumbles over a series of gritstone terraces in the midst of lavish temperate rainforest, producing some of the most photogenic cascades in Britain.

This national park briefly became the subject of a heated national debate in 2023, when the national park authority decided to prioritise the long-existing Welsh name for this landscape over its English counterpart. Bannau Brycheiniog means the 'peaks of Brychan's kingdom', Brychan being a legendary 5th century ruler. The town of Brecon and the 'beacons' – though there is no record of them ever actually being used as such – above it, got their names from Brychan. The decision to reclaim its Welsh name went alongside a plan designed to revive the natural vibrancy of the national park in the context of the climate and biodiversity crises. The park made an honest acknowledgement of the environmental challenges this landscape faces, including unsustainably managed uplands, polluted watercourses, wildfires and litter. The park pledged to restore 40,000 acres of peatland, clean up its rivers to bathing-water quality and improve wildlife corridors through the landscape. Bannau Brycheiniog is a place rooted in the past but, like all the UK's national parks and protected landscapes, it has a vital role to play in meeting the challenges of the future.

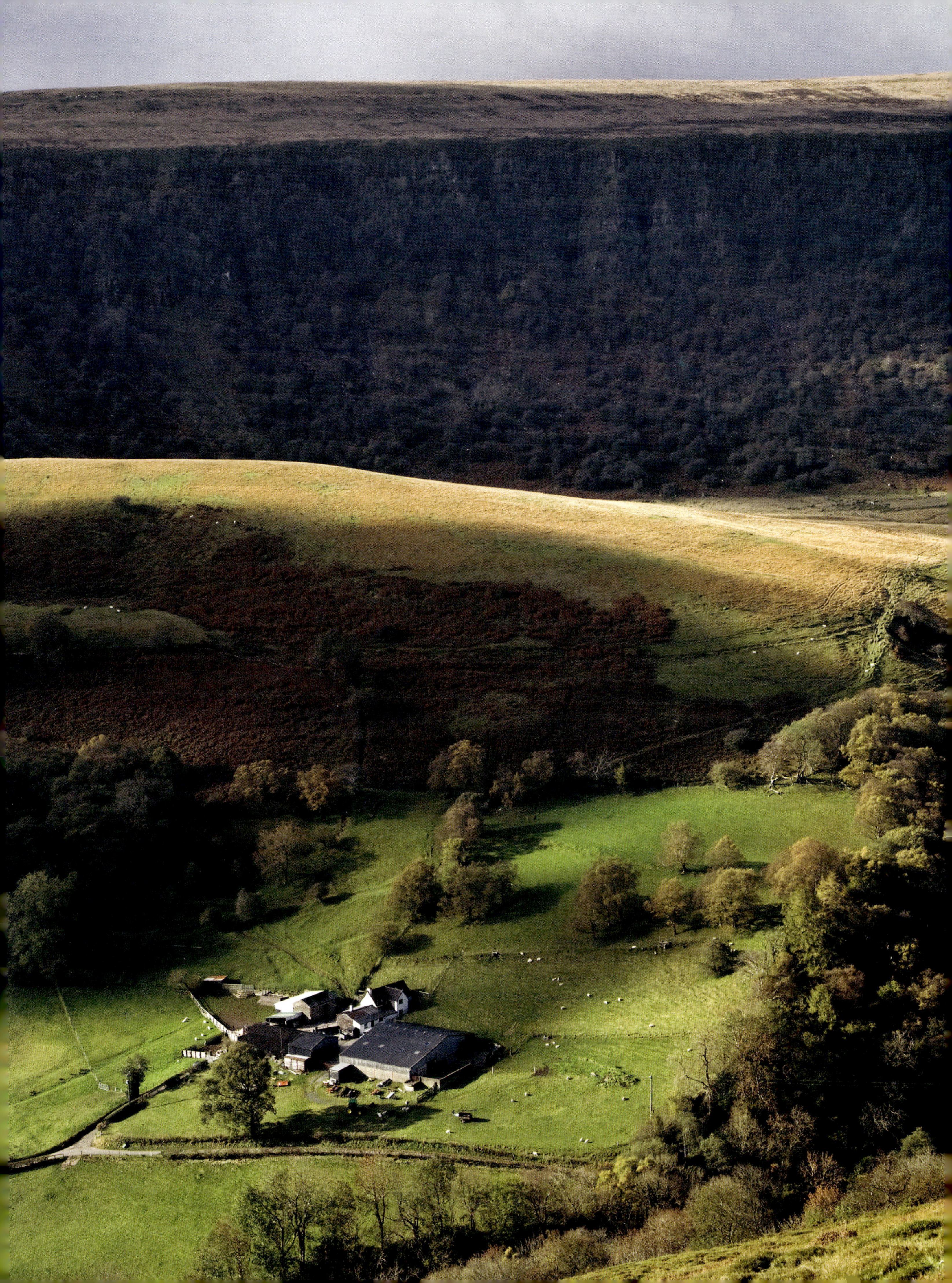

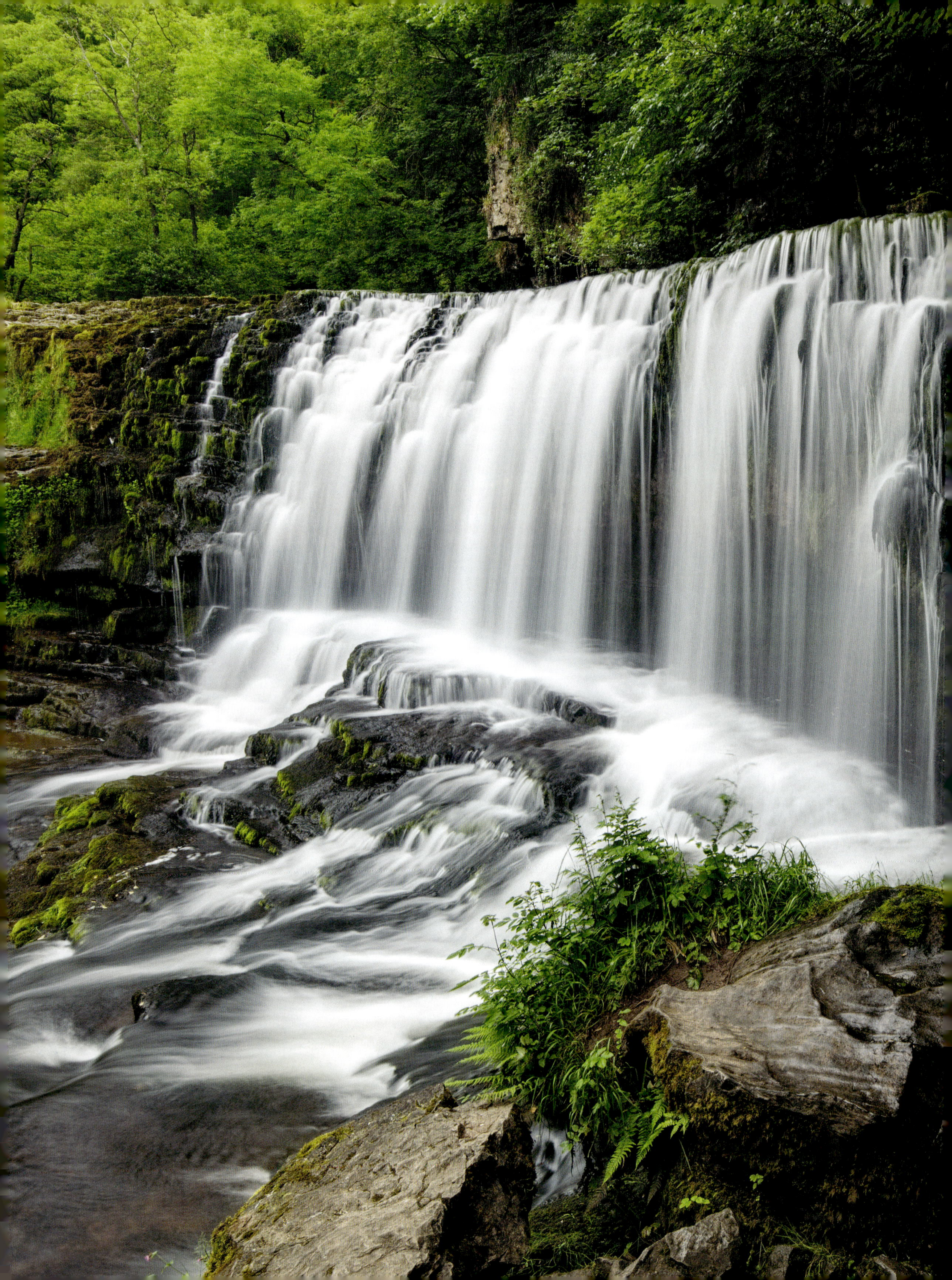

Sgwd Isaf Clun-Gwyn ('Lower Fall of the White Meadow') is one of a host of waterfalls that tumble through a lush corridor of temperate rainforest in the upper reaches of the Vale of Neath – a popular area known as 'Waterfall Country'. The falls are spread across several rivers that converge on the area, and are created by the erosion of soft mudstones, leaving harder sandstones that form the lips of the falls.

Overleaf:
Walkers enjoy the expansive upland landscapes in the high reaches of Bannau Brycheiniog.

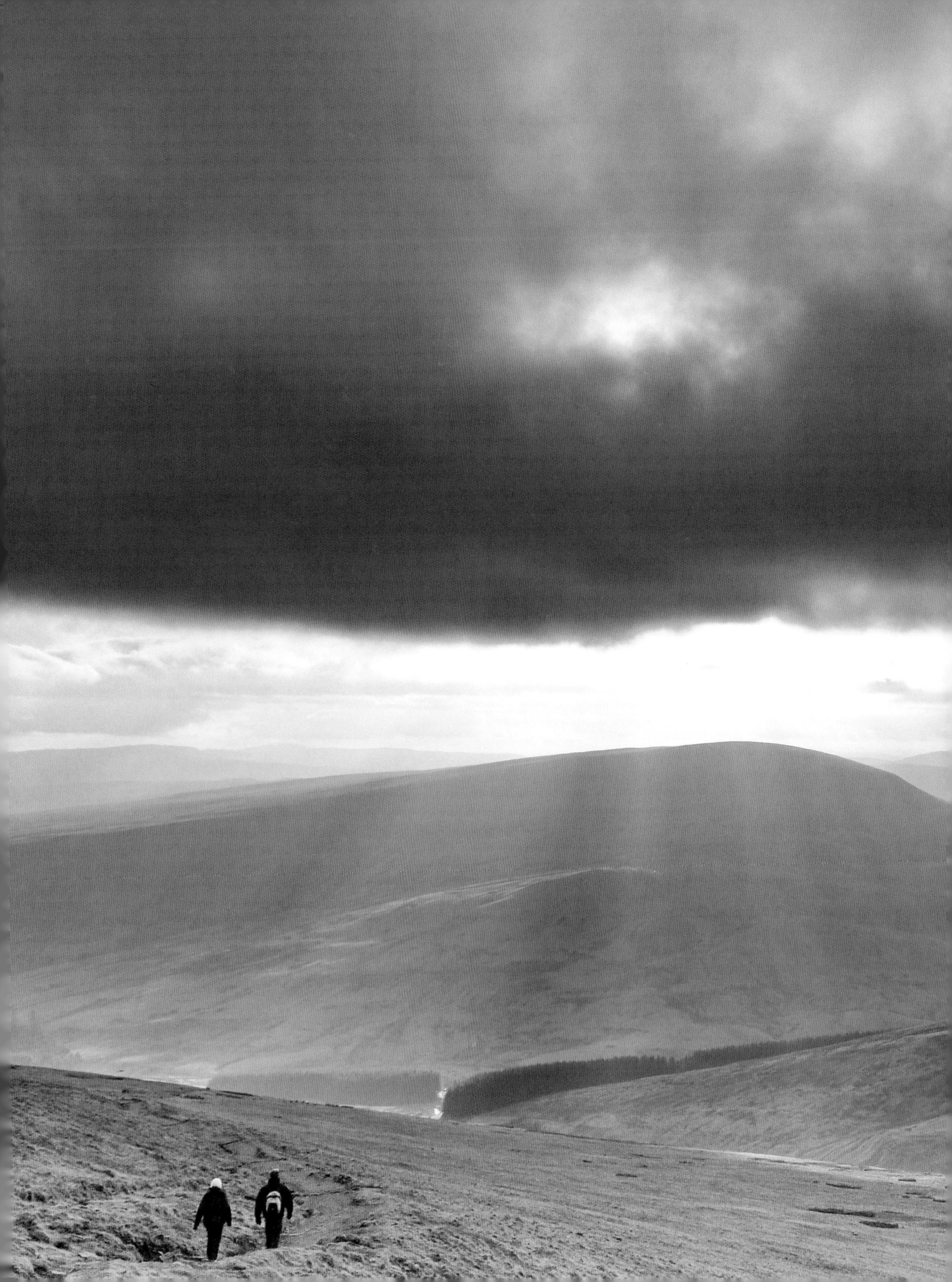

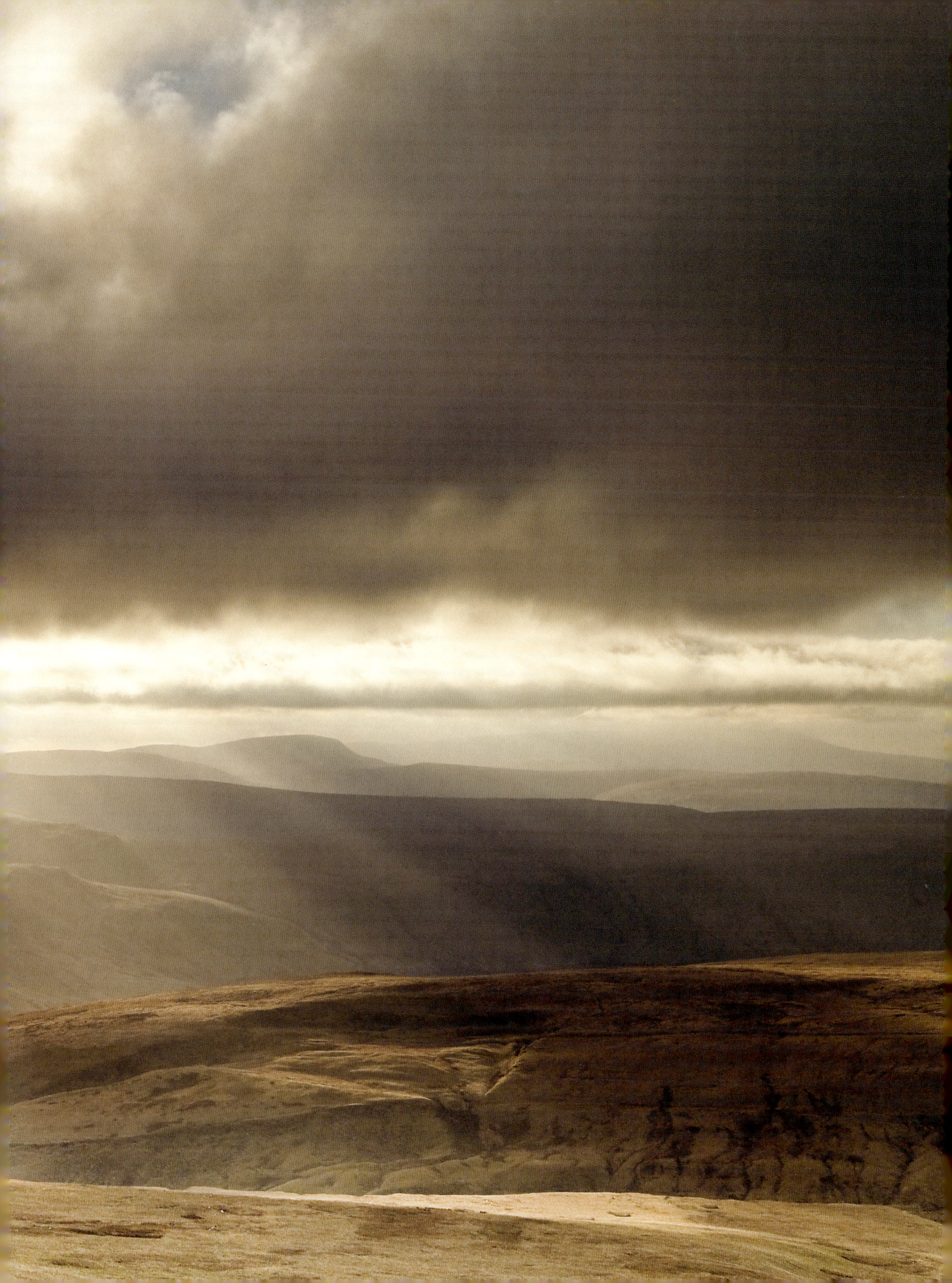

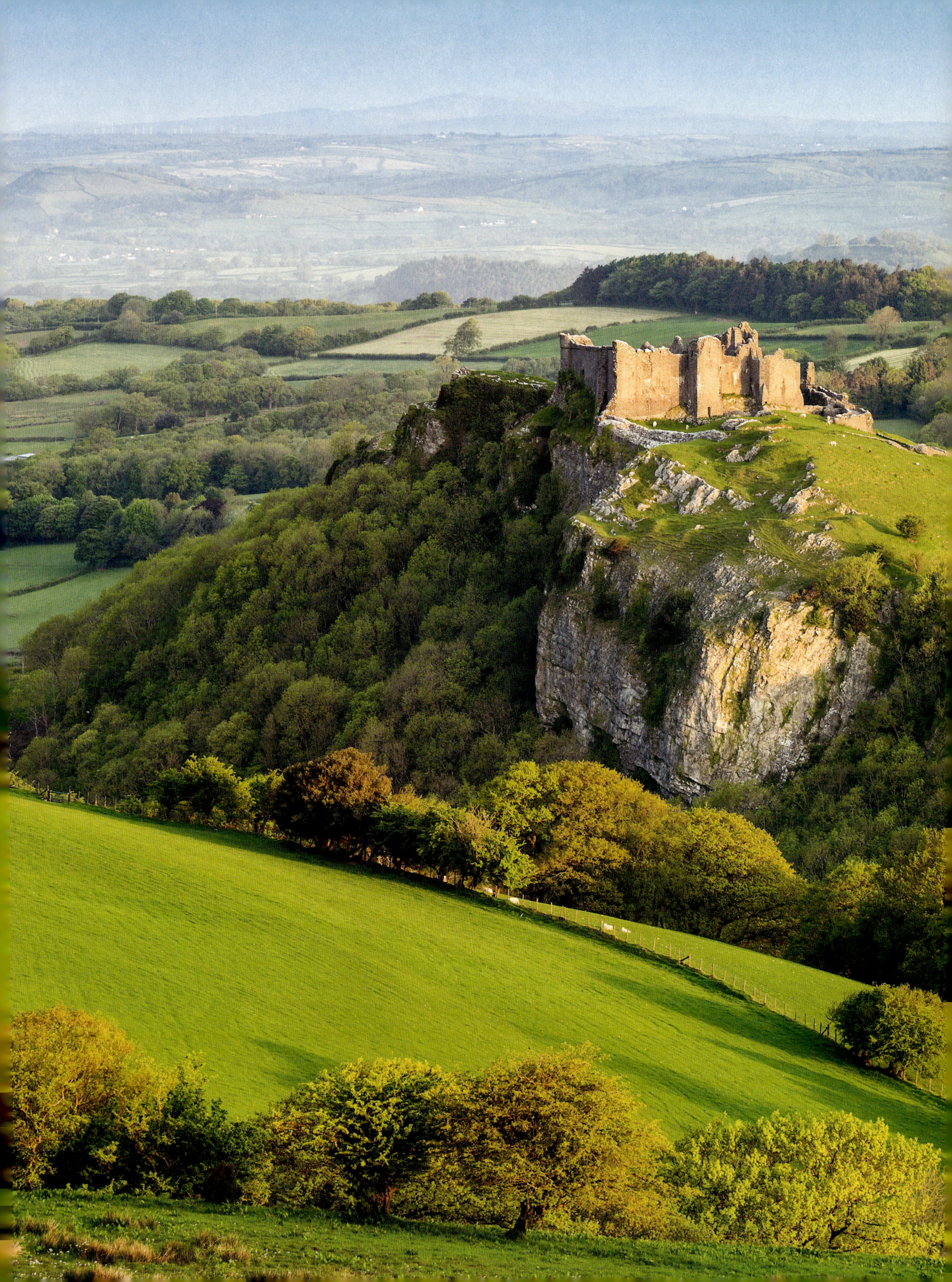

The ethereal-seeming castle of Carreg Cennen clings to an outcrop of Carboniferous limestone near the village of Trap. It was originally the site of a native Welsh castle, but was captured in 1277 during English king Edward I's conquest of Wales, and the castle we see today is largely English work. Owain Glyndŵr attempted to besiege the castle during his dramatic rebellion for Welsh independence in the early 15th century, but was unsuccessful.

Overleaf:
Early morning mists cloak the northern reaches of the Usk Valley.

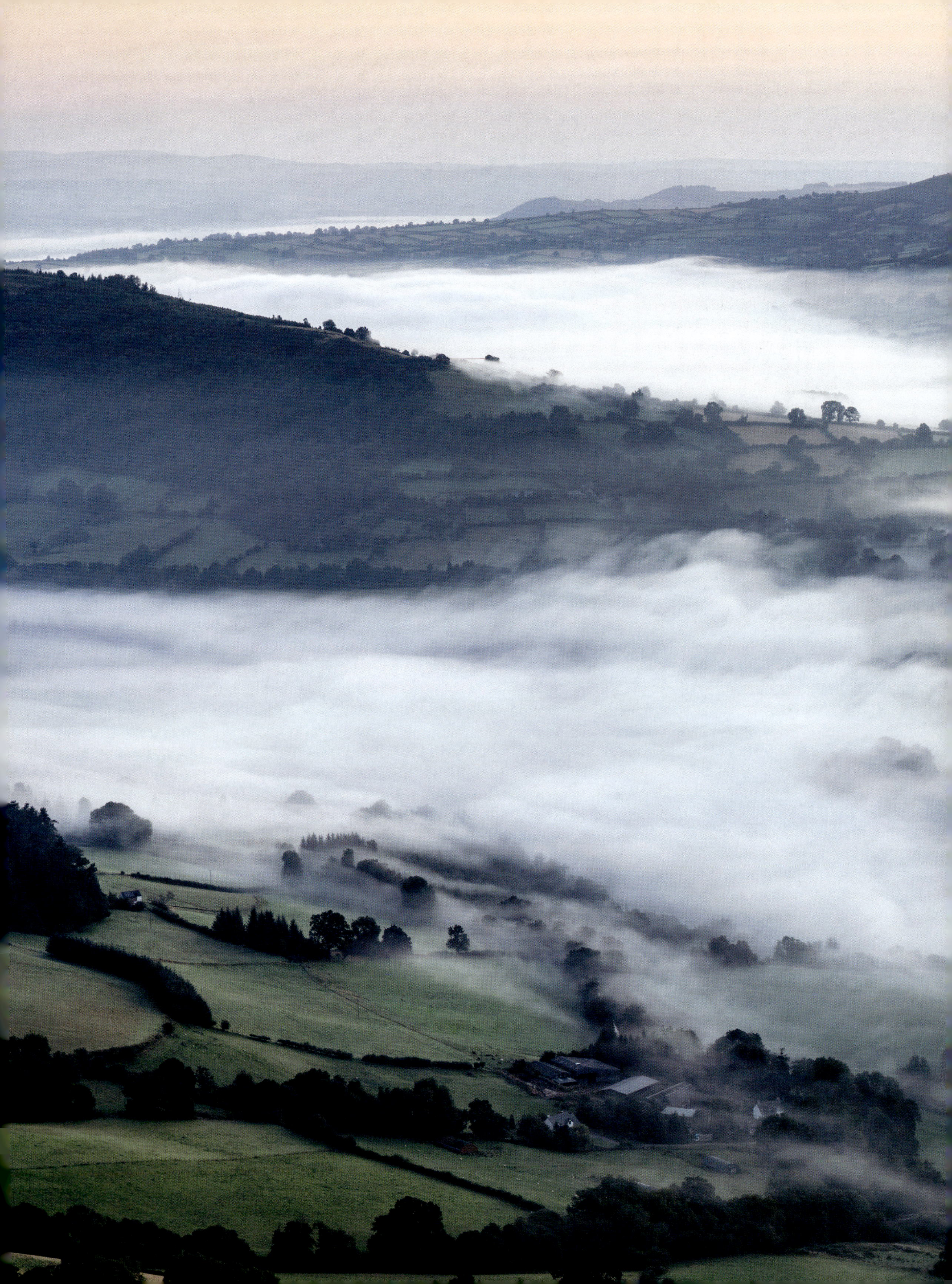

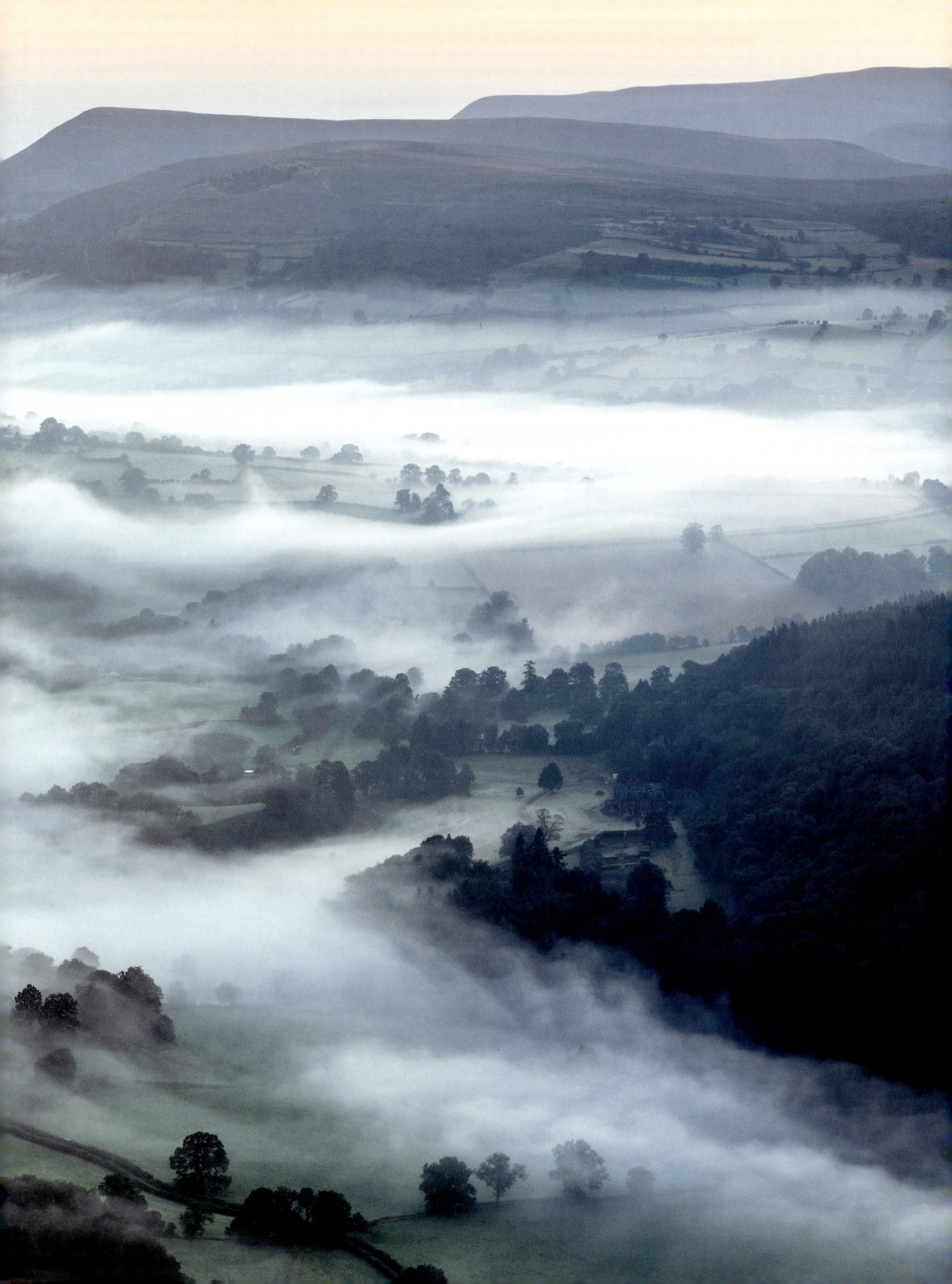

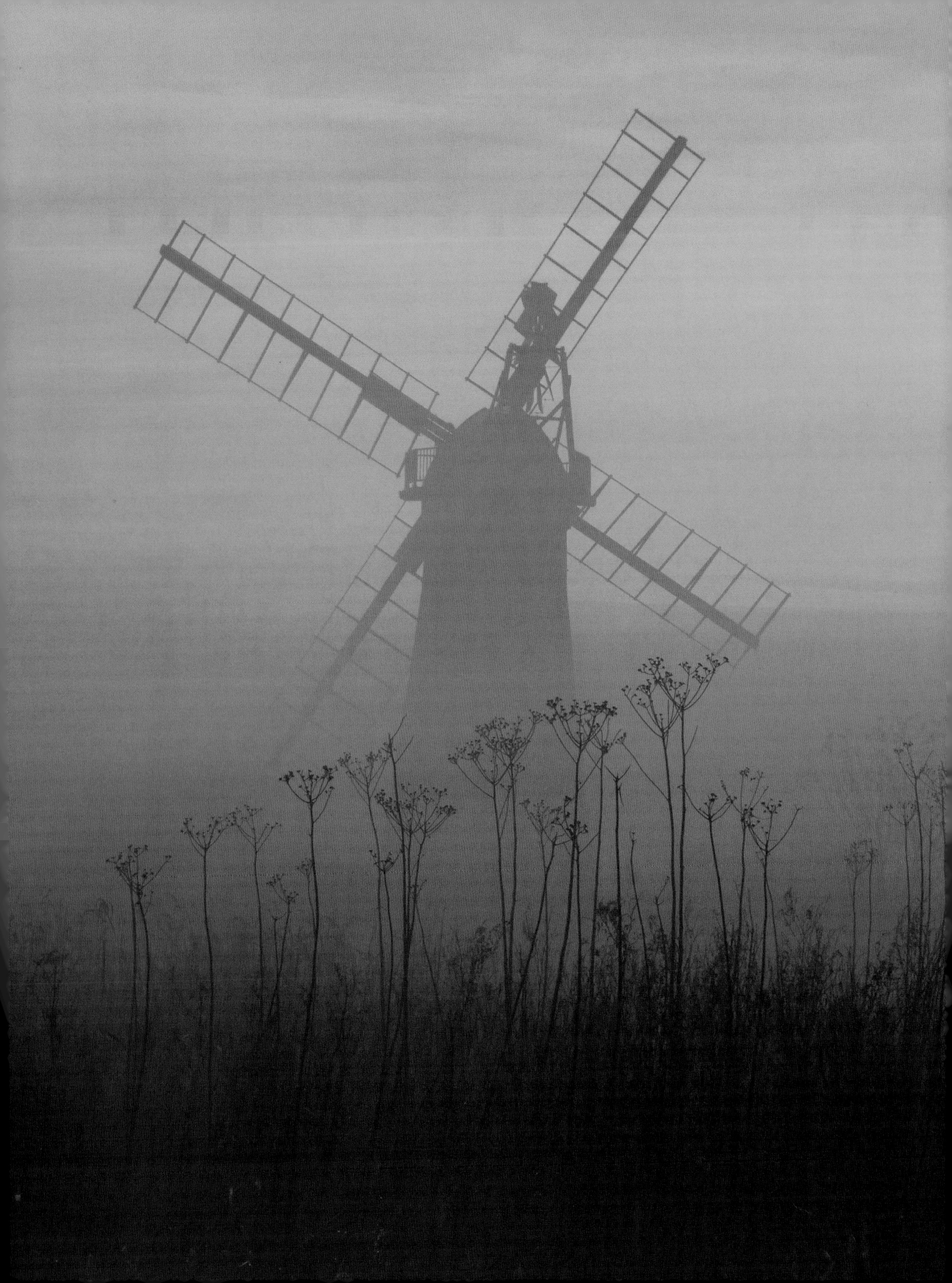

Broads

Wetlands are some of the world's most bountiful and biodiverse habitats, and as Britain's biggest protected wetland area, the Broads is no exception. Despite comprising just 0.1 per cent of the UK's surface area, the park provides a sanctuary for a quarter of our rarest species. Otters slink through the fens; the booms of bitterns reverberate for miles and vast flocks of starlings writhe over the marshes.

The landscape – or perhaps more accurately, waterscape – of the Broads has human origins. It was created when medieval peat diggings were flooded by rising water levels and abandoned, creating more than sixty shallow lakes, known as broads, scattered across a wide area veined with seven slow-winding rivers. Yet this industry of the Middle Ages has helped to give us one of our most naturally abundant national parks today: a labyrinthine water world composed of hundreds of miles of interconnected rivers, lakes and drainage dykes, buffered by a web of wet woodlands, fens, reedbeds and marshes.

Situated in Norfolk and Suffolk, no other UK landscape is like the Broads, Britain's only water-based national park. As well as a wildlife haven, the rivers and broads intertwine to comprise around 200 kilometres (125 miles) of navigable lock-free waterways. The Broads is administered by a body that has the same powers and responsibilities as other national parks but is also responsible for looking after the waterways and protecting the interests of navigation. You can make rewarding visits here on foot as a rambler or a birdwatcher, but taking to the water reveals the true dimensions of this realm. Boats, kayaks and canoes, all of which can easily be rented, are great ways to explore. Days can be spent on rivers flanked by corridors of lush water-woods with coots, cormorants and kingfishers diving and dipping through the current. Visitors can take a break from the sun-shimmered broads by mooring at riverside villages and heading to local pubs for refreshment.

The 63 broads vary widely in character, from comparatively large water sports centres like Oulton Broad on the outskirts of Lowestoft, to small and peaceful pools such as Upton Broad – a secluded lake set in the midst of sprawling fens and tangled carr woodland, swampy wet woods dominated by twisted alder and willow trees, entangled with hanging vegetation, tall herbs and tussock sedges, where the loudest sound is the chatter of waterbirds. Only 13 of the broads are fully navigable by boat, and a further 5 have channels or sections that enable navigation. Others can be explored by kayak or canoe.

The Broads landscape is dotted with more than 60 old drainage mills, like this one at St Benet's Level. They are the legacy of a 400-year struggle to drain the marshes for agriculture and prevent the low-lying landscape from being deluged by the sea. Water levels are now controlled by electric pumps, but one of the last wind-powered mills was operational as recently as 1953. The mill at St Benet's Level dates back to 1775.

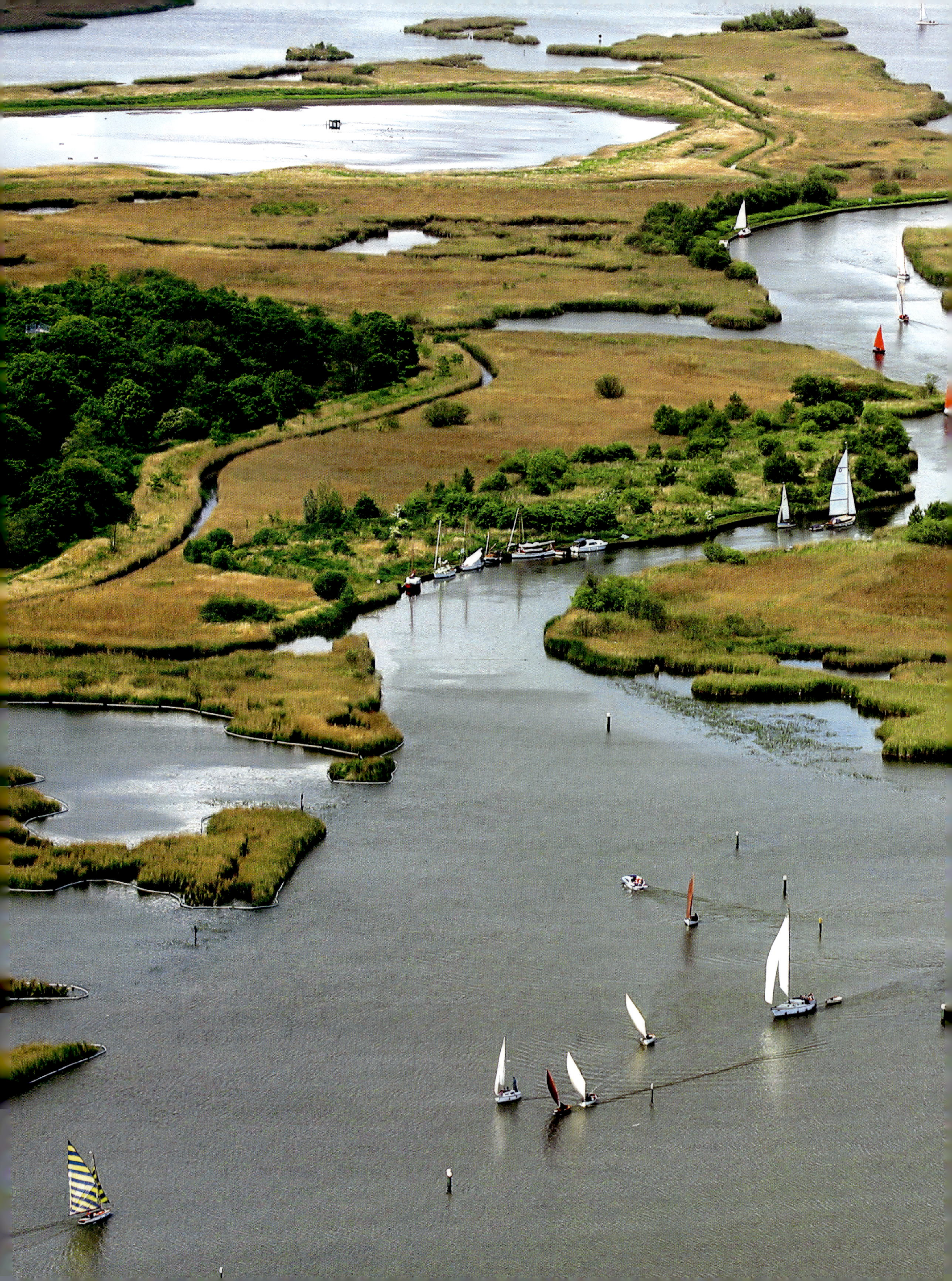

The Broads has a very distinctive outline compared to other UK national parks: a series of 'arms' that loosely encompass these river corridors and their wide marshy margins, where the distinction between land and water is often hazy. It meets the North Sea for a roughly 11-kilometre (7-mile) stretch of dune-backed beach between Sea Palling and Winterton-on-Sea, home to a colony of breeding grey seals in autumn.

Days in the Broads tend to unfold slowly. The speed of boats is restricted to jogging pace at most for conservation reasons, but to rush through these secluded aquatic arteries would be to defeat the point. If the rest of the world is a fast-flowing river, the Broads is a slow eddy away from the main current. Whether gliding through secretive backwaters or patiently waiting to catch sight of a rare bird, part of the appeal of visiting is to sink into a less hurried frame of mind; to go gently down the stream.

The rich natural dimension of the Broads is especially apparent in the avian kingdom. In terms of range, rarity and sheer numbers, this is arguably the best place in the national park family for bird enthusiasts. Although this is rightly known as a mecca for birdwatchers, you don't need high-powered binoculars to appreciate the richness of the birdlife – flying, flitting, flocking, dipping and diving birds form an organic backdrop to most activities here.

Birdlife in the Broads never has a 'low' season. Spring, always the height of activity in the bird world as the tide of life turns and the breeding season arrives, is especially vibrant. Migrant songbirds like the sedge, reed and willow warbler return from Africa, swelling the magnificent dawn chorus in the woods and fens. Breeding bitterns, locally known as butterbumps, are very difficult to see, but very easy to hear. They unleash deep booming calls from reedbeds, audible from as far away as 5 kilometres (3 miles). Marsh harriers perform their 'sky dance' courting displays, rising hundreds of feet before plunging to

Bitterns, or butterbumps, are Britain's loudest bird. Though well-camouflaged and hard to spot amid their reedbed habitat, their rumbling 'foghorn' calls can be heard from as far away as 5 kilometres (3 miles). Bitterns were driven to national extinction in the 1870s by drainage of their habitat for agriculture, but returned to Norfolk in the early 20th century. By 1997 they had almost been driven to extinction again, but habitat restoration work in recent years has seen numbers of breeding males swell from 11 to 228.

Opposite:
In the Broads, the line between water and land is blurred. Broads, rivers, drainage channels, wet woodlands, rough pastures and reedy marshes form a complex mosaic, much of which is navigable. Hickling Broad is notable for containing the largest expanse of reedbed in England – a transitional 'ecotone' habitat found between water and land, and a vital habitat for wildlife like bitterns.

Hunting and habitat destruction led to the common crane disappearing from Britain as a breeding bird around 400 years ago. In the late 20th century, they began recolonising these islands at a site in the Broads, at which there is now resident a population of around 20. They are Britain's tallest birds.

the ground in a sequence of athletic loop-the-loops. This is also one of the best places to see the newly hatched chicks of avocets, the return of which has been one of Britain's great conservation success stories.

Some of the most astonishing avian sounds and spectacles to be found in the Broads come with the arrival of autumn. As much of the rest of the country dies down for the cold months, this part of the world comes into spectacular life, as vast numbers of birds escape the Arctic winter or the chillier areas inland for the mild climate and abundant food of the Broads. Many either stay in the region or pass through, sometimes in migrations that are astonishing to witness. Tens of thousands of pink-footed geese descend on the marshes from Iceland and Greenland, arriving in endless waves that fill the sky with a vast cacophony of hoots and honking; Norfolk is thought to host a third of the worldwide population of these birds in winter. Bewick's swans and whooper swans lumber over the marshes. Great white egrets and little egrets hunt along the rivers. Wetlands are filled with great noisy flocks of wigeon, teal, lapwing and golden plover. Just before the cold weather and early nights set in, tens of thousands of starlings come together in vast flocks called murmurations, which twist and strobe in the reddening sky, moving like shoals of fish being hunted.

The last embers of the winter sunset can often be one of the best times to see the most special birdlife sights. On the grazing marshes and scrub next to Hickling Broad, against the backdrop of a skyline dotted with old windmills, up to a hundred marsh harriers drift in to roost on the hawthorns and other trees dotting the landscape, sometimes joined by hen harriers and merlin. The surroundings of Hickling Broad are also where, after an absence of several hundred years, the immense and beautiful common cranes, the UK's tallest bird, began recolonising Britain in the 1970s. Despite the name, these remain exceptionally rare as visitors, and even rarer as breeding birds, but there is a resident population of around 20 birds here.

A host of other rare flora and fauna thrive in the Broads, some of which are unique to it. It is usually the only place you are likely to catch sight of the magnificent British sub-species of swallowtail, a black-and-yellow patterned butterfly, which can be spotted flying over the summer fens, stopping to feed on plants like thistle and ragged robin. Eggs are laid on milk parsley – the food plant of the caterpillar – which is largely confined to the Broads as well. Another local speciality rarely found outside the Broads is the Norfolk hawker dragonfly. To survive it needs unpolluted freshwater dykes with a good population of water soldier – a rare aquatic plant that pops up from ponds and resembles the top of a pineapple – for its nymphs to shelter within.

With a high point just 38 metres (125 feet) above sea level, the Broads is a low-lying flatland, allowing for expansive skies and unobstructed views of dawns and dusks. In the reedy midst of a lush broad or the wooded riparian corridor of a river, with no human structures visible, it can feel like an untouched wilderness; some English version of Florida's Everglades. In reality, the Broads is surrounded by the farmland typical of the wider East Anglia landscape, England's most productive agricultural region. Farming also takes place within the Broads National Park itself, ranging from arable crops like sugar beet and barley to light-touch pasturing on grazing marshes.

It is impossible to disentangle the human and natural history of the Broads from this agricultural context. The drainage channels, which quarter swathes of the Broads landscape into marshes, run from the surrounding farmland. The use of artificial fertiliser – along with sewage discharge – has compounded the ongoing problem of eutrophication, where water becomes artificially enriched with minerals and nutrients, leading to the growth of harmful algal blooms and disrupting aquatic ecology. But farmers have also played their part in supporting the Broads ecology through initiatives like reducing pollution, improving water conservation and creating wildlife-friendly 'buffer strips'

The vast marshes of Halvergate fan out between the River Bure and the River Yare, crosshatched by a web of drainage dykes. Originally a tidal estuary, the area was drained 400 years ago to create a patchwork of grazing marshes, and it is still surrounded by a host of old drainage pumps, including Mutton's Mill, shown here. A scheme to encourage farmers to adopt more environmentally friendly methods was adopted in the 1980s, and has helped sustain important populations of Norfolk hawker dragonfly and Bewick's swan.

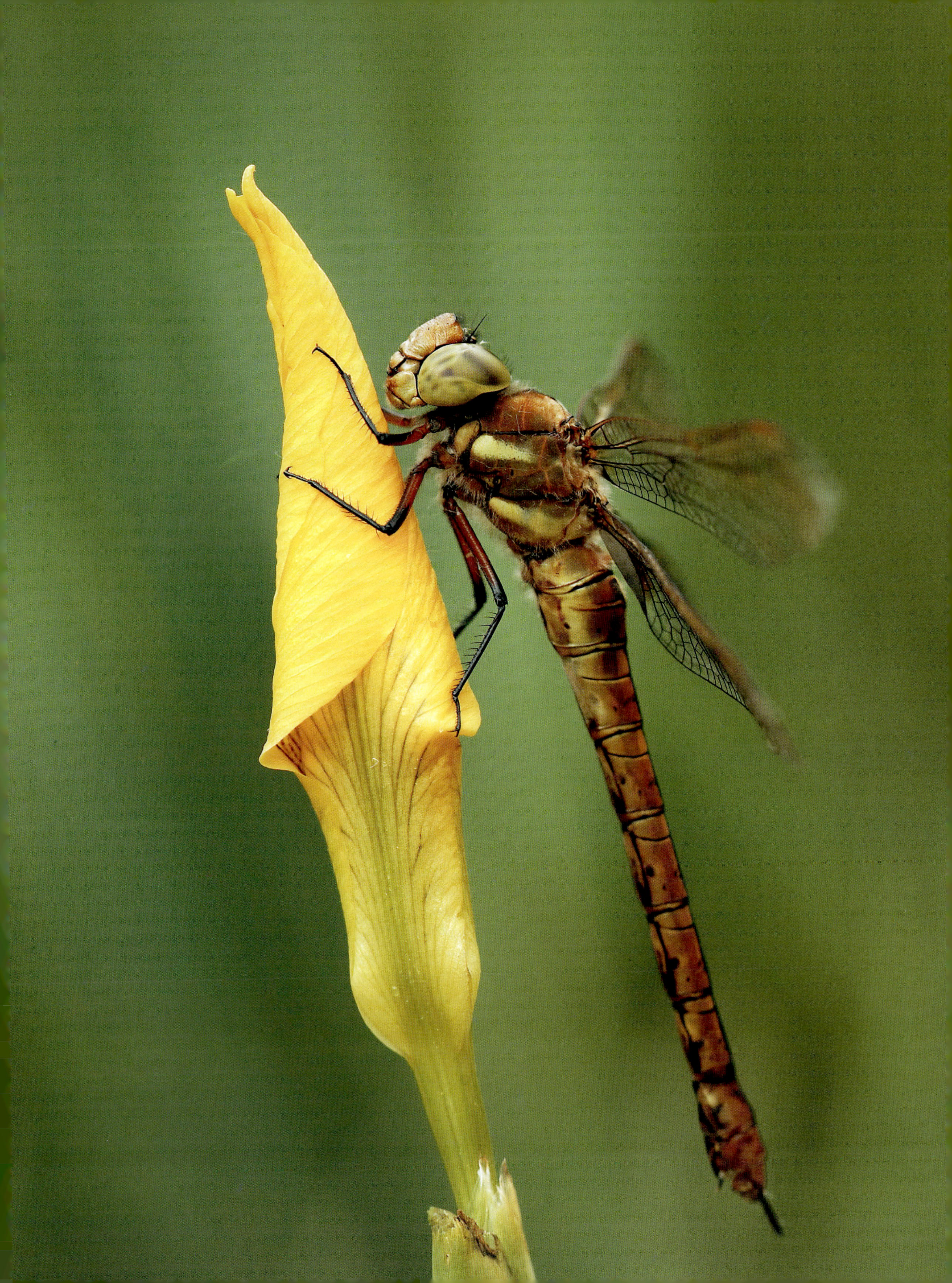

around fields. There is no doubt that if the natural richness of this fragile landscape is to be protected and enhanced in the future, the farming industry will have a vital role to play.

Although the national park itself has a relatively short coastline, the landscape has been indelibly shaped by its proximity to the North Sea. As in the Netherlands, which it faces across the water, for hundreds of years humans have been engaged in an ongoing battle to save the low-lying Broads landscape from the clutches of a rising ocean. In 1610, after a series of devastating storm surges, the parliament under King James I began building wind-powered pumps in an effort to control the 'rage of the sea'. These mills developed over subsequent centuries and, although with the advent of the Industrial Revolution some were replaced by coal-fired steam pumps, one of the last wind-powered mills remained operational until as recently as 1953. Water is now moved off the marshes through electric pumps, many powered by wind turbines off the shore of Great Yarmouth, but the Broads remains dotted with more than 60 old mills of widely varying types and in various states of repair. These structures, often visible for miles around, punctuate the landscape with history and are beloved fixtures of the Broads. Yet they also serve as poignant reminders of the uncertain future of this landscape, which is increasingly vulnerable to rising sea levels.

If we think of human and natural history as counterposed by each other, the Broads can seem like a paradox: this is a fundamentally anthropogenic, or human-made, landscape, yet by many measures it also supports the greatest natural riches of the whole national park family. It demonstrates the artificiality of this distinction. And as a place on the frontline of a world threatened by crises of biodiversity and climate, the Broads National Park is a microcosm of the future, in which 'natural' and 'human' fates flow together, inseparably intertwined.

Boating along the rivers and broads, then mooring up at a village pub for lunch, is a classic Broads day.

Opposite:
The Norfolk hawker dragonfly is found across Europe, particularly around the Mediterranean, but its range in Britain is largely confined to the Broads. To feed and breed, it needs unpolluted freshwater dykes with a good population of water soldier.

Overleaf:
Boat houses with thatched roofs at Hickling Broad. The use of local water reed for roofing – rather than the straw used elsewhere – was historically common in the Broads. As in the rest of the British Isles, thatching declined in the Broads following the Industrial Revolution, but recent decades have seen a revival in the use of this traditional technique.

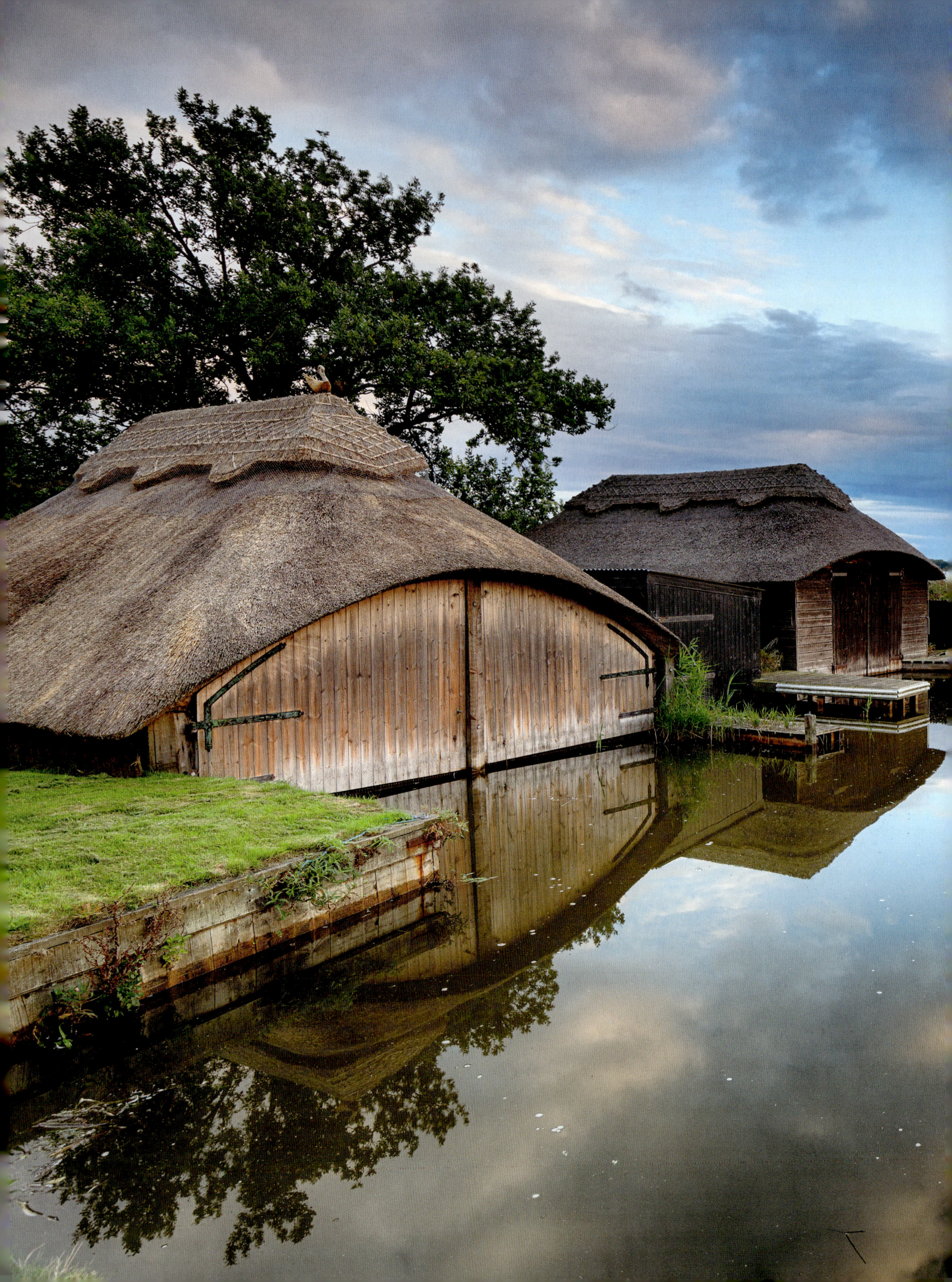

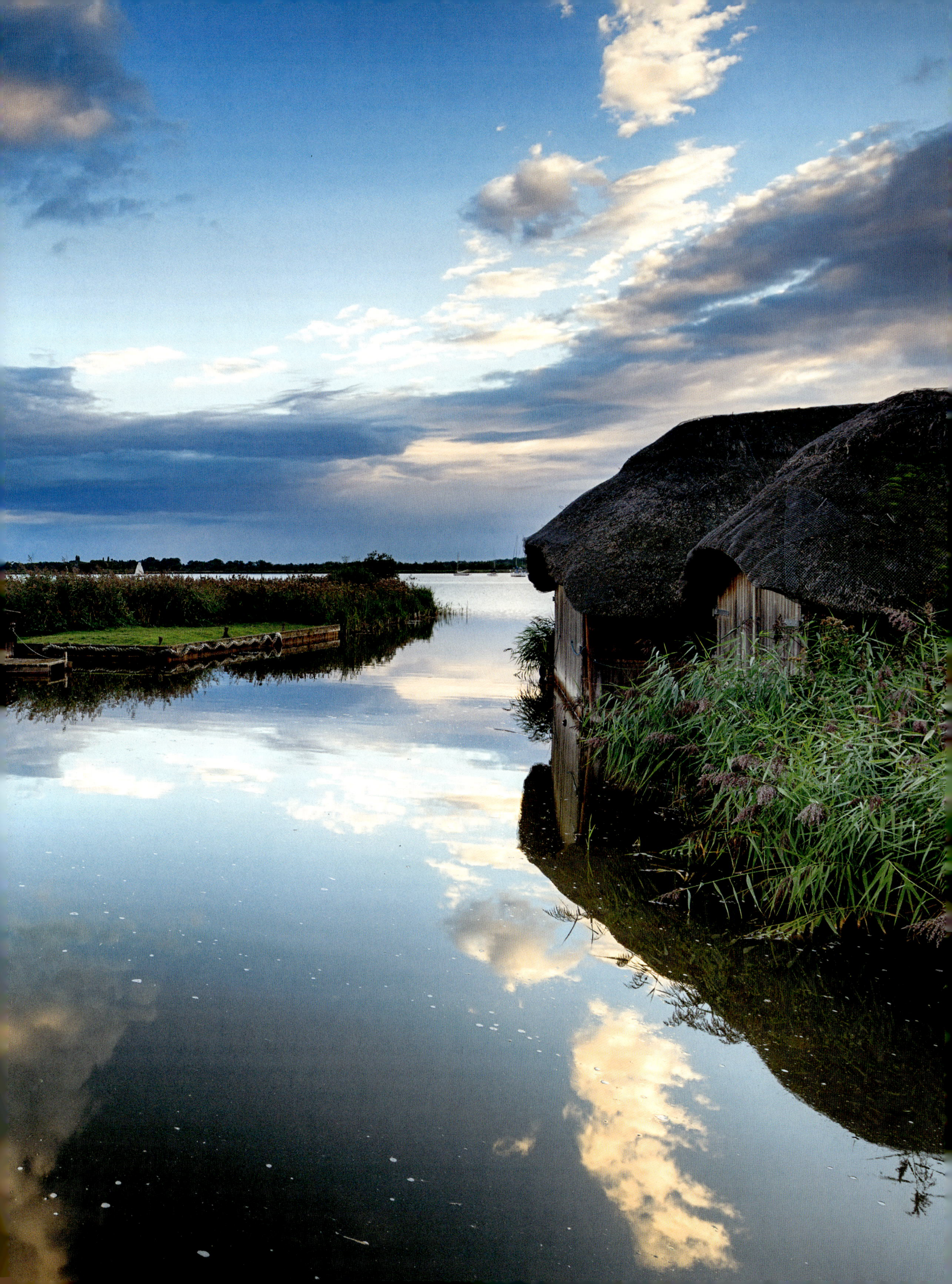

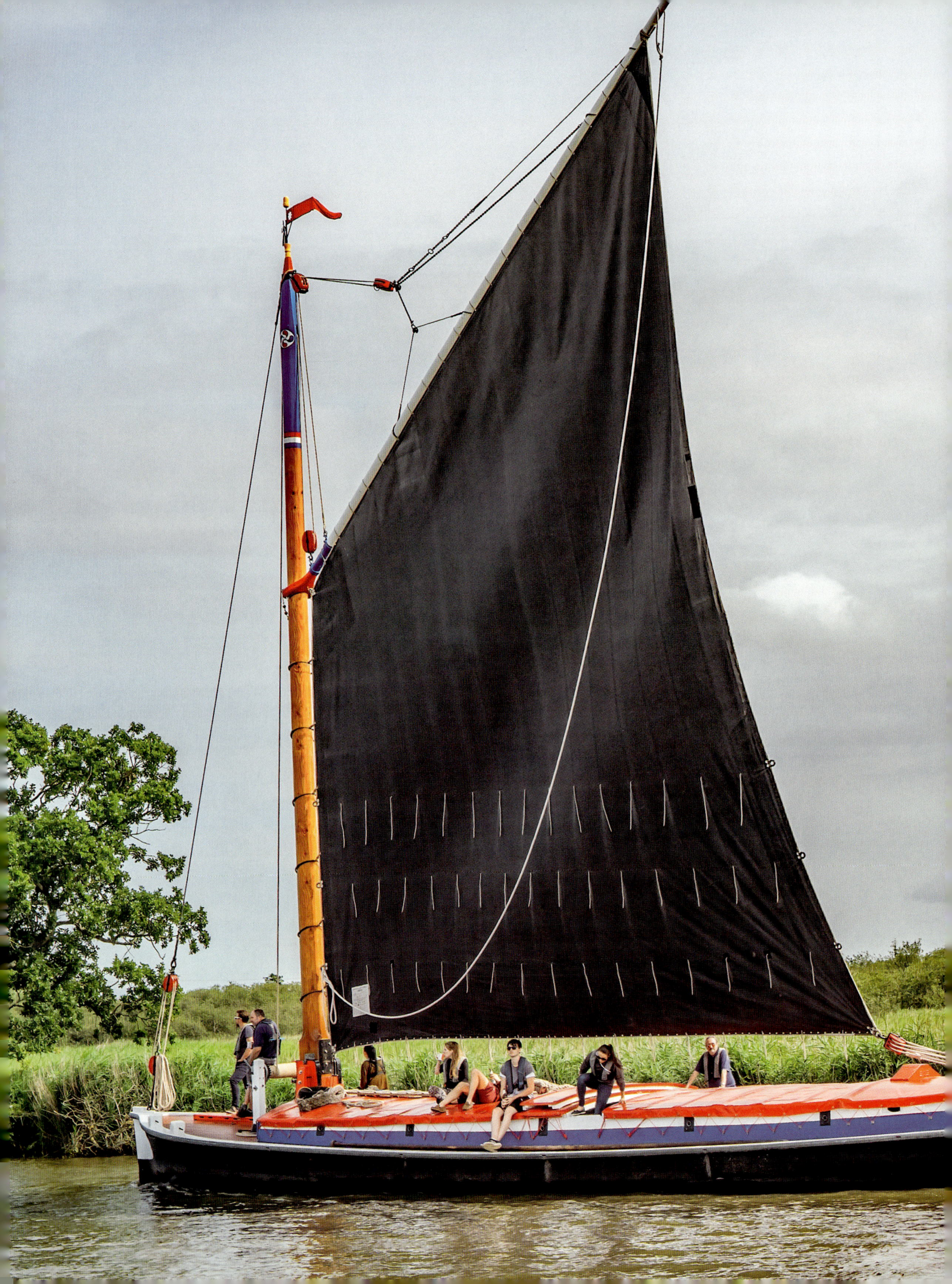

The Norfolk wherry is a traditional type of sailing boat used on the Broads, with origins stretching back to the early 17th century. Wherries were used to transport cargo along waterways of the Broads, including bringing cargo inland from larger boats moored at the ports of Great Yarmouth and Lowestoft. There are eight wherries today, either in private ownership or used as charter boats.

Overleaf:
Starlings migrate in large numbers to the relatively mild climate of the Broads in winter, and their swirling murmurations are a relatively common sight. These captivating phenomena can be seen in the last hour or so of winter days. Hundreds or even thousands of starlings coalesce together in hypnotic, writhing super-flocks, before suddenly descending to their roosts en masse. Winter can be a lively time on the Broads; overwintering wading birds and wildfowl also congregate in huge numbers.

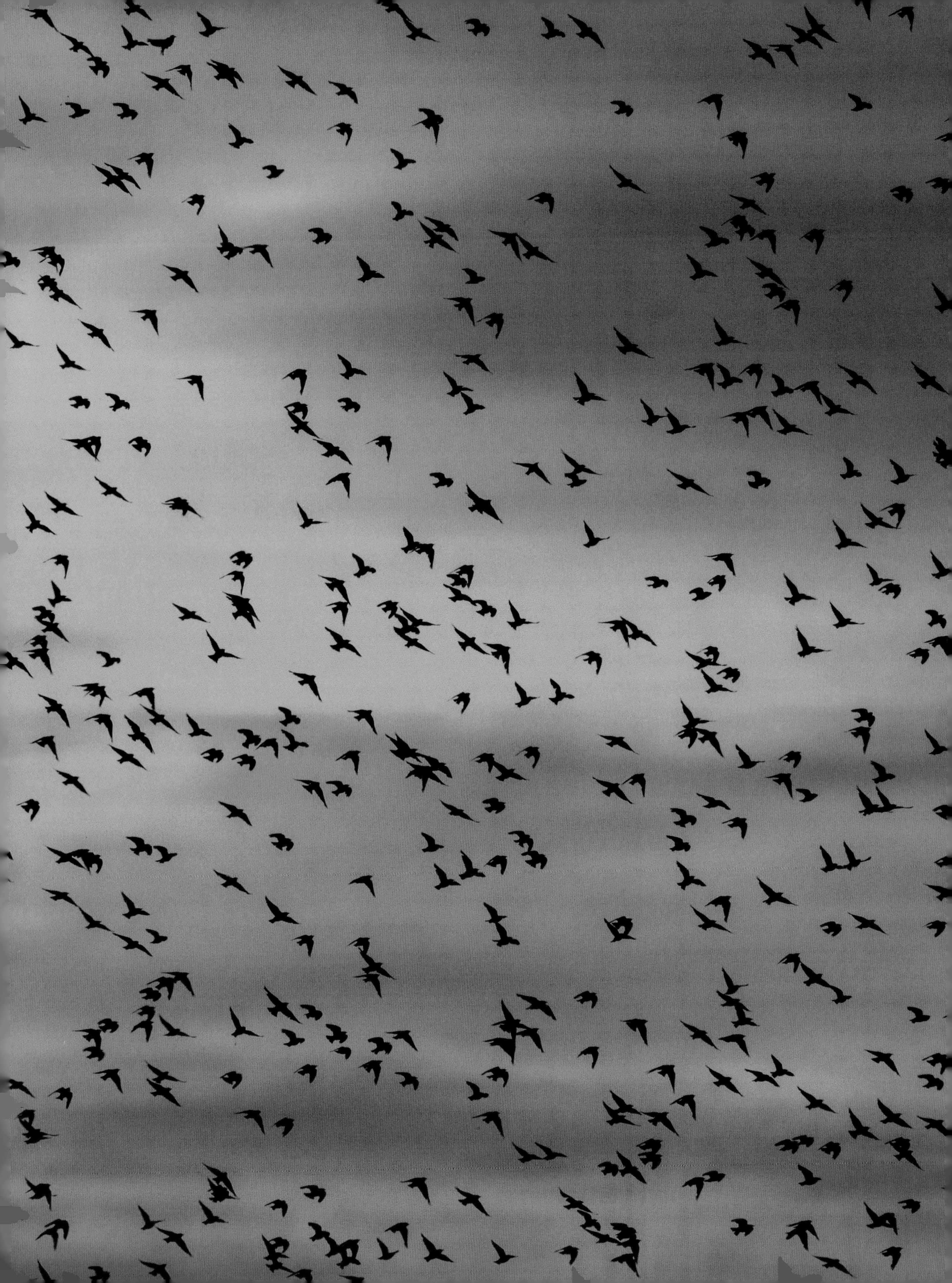

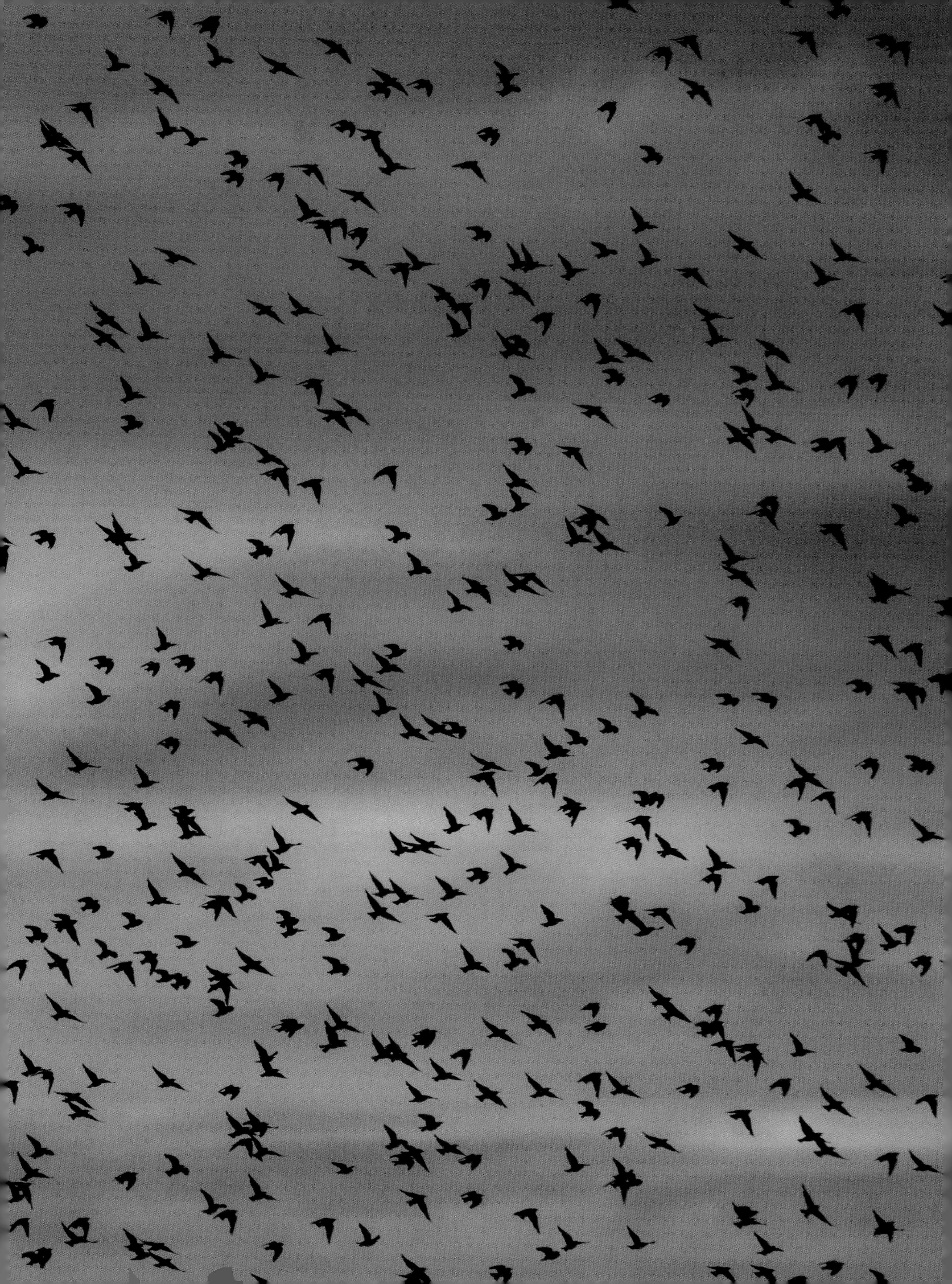

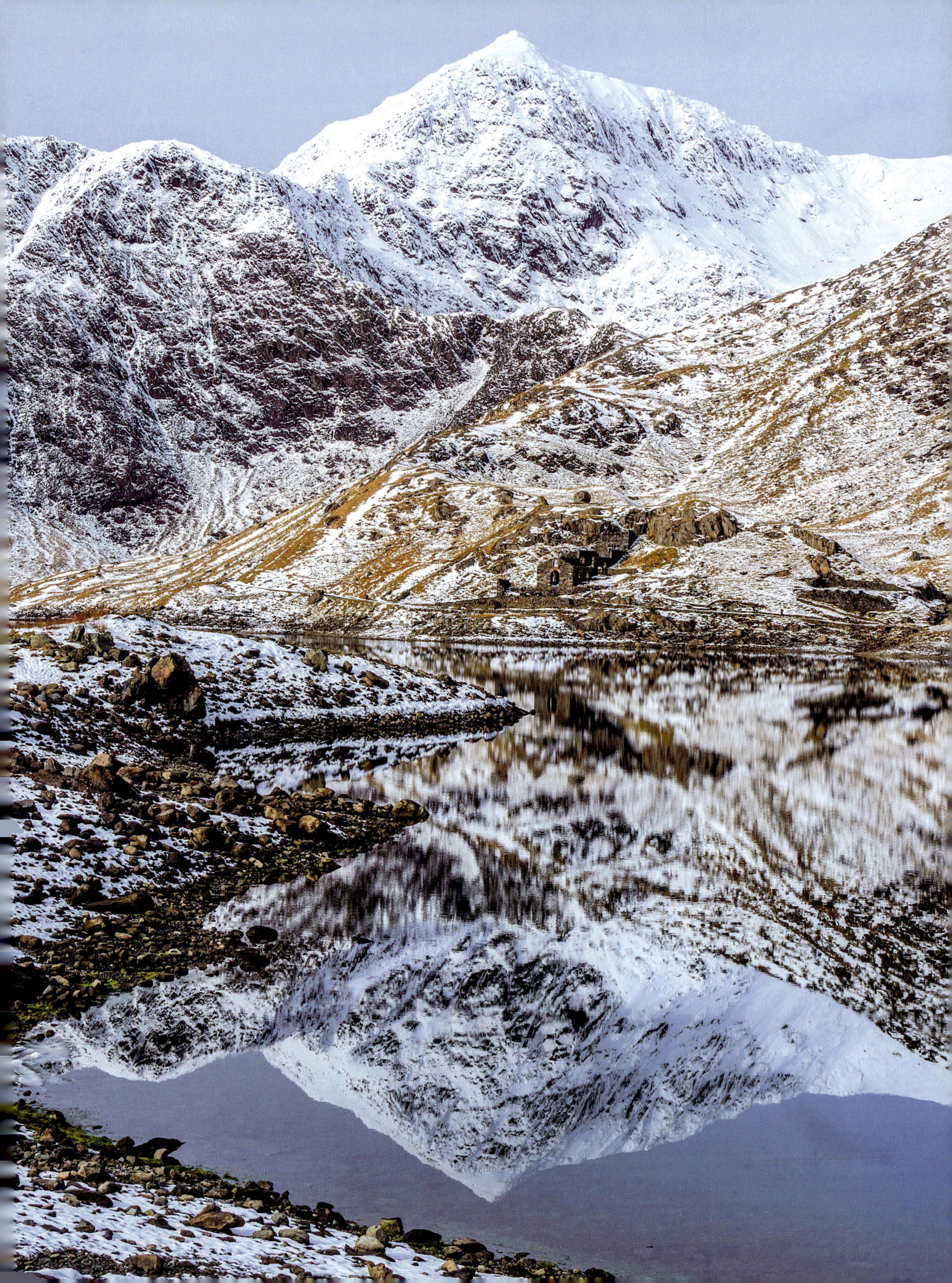

Eryri

Eryri, also known as Snowdonia, is a deeply storied landscape, strewn with relics from ancient legends, where literature is so embedded in the land that the mountains are said to be able turn you into a poet. It is a region of immense geological drama, rare flora and fauna and lush temperate rainforests. Beyond the tourist hotspots, much of it is also strikingly crowd-free; a timeworn place of quiet cwms, lonely llyns, rugged hillsides, hidden valleys and remote farmsteads.

Even so, much of the attention Eryri draws from the wider world is focused on just one mountain: Yr Wyddfa, or Snowdon. At 1,085 metres (3,560 feet), Yr Wyddfa is the highest mountain in Wales. With much of the land surrounding it sloping quickly down to the Irish Sea, the views from its summit across the ocean are unimpeded by any rival peaks, and on a perfectly clear day you can just about pick out the hills of southern Scotland – around 225 kilometres (140 miles) to the north – on the far horizon, or the Wicklow Mountains of Ireland, about 145 kilometres (90 miles) to the west. Eryri and Yr Wyddfa are close to the heart of the 'Celtic belt' spanning Britain and Ireland, and those connections across culture, language, history and sea are apparent from the top of this coastal mountain.

'Yr Wyddfa' refers to the mighty pyramid-shaped peak in the centre of a massif, which is actually made of multiple summits all strung together by an array of ridges radiating outwards from that central high point like the waving arms of a starfish. Some of the most impressive mountain architecture anywhere in Britain is found here. There is Crib Goch, where hikers must negotiate a rocky ridge lathed to a knife-edge sharpness by glaciers, less than a foot wide in places, with precipitous drops either side. There is Clogwyn Du'r Arddu, a tectonically spectacular crag hosting legendary climbing routes where life or death hinges on fingernail-thin holds. There is the similarly mighty face of Y Lliwedd, the highest inland rockface in England and Wales, that served as an important training venue for the 1953 British expedition that scaled Everest for the first time. In winter, when a cold blast coats the massif in snow, you can appreciate how this mountain could serve as an effective boot camp for the Himalayas.

Yet at the same time, if you're looking for a more leisurely route to the summit of Yr Wyddfa, it can be one of the easiest summits to reach anywhere in these islands. In good weather during the warmer months, the 100 year-old rack-and-pinion line of the Snowdon Mountain Railway will whisk you in comfort from Llanberis to within just a few metres of the mountain's crowning cairn. Then,

Yr Wyddfa, or Snowdon, the highest mountain in Wales, is the busiest mountain in Britain, attracting more than half a million hikers and visitors per year. On sunny summer weekends and bank holidays, it can feel like a congested place, with queues to climb the summit cairn sometimes stretching far back down the mountain. In winter, when the mountain railway closes, the crowds thin out significantly. Despite its popularity, Yr Wyddfa remains a formidable mountain that can present hazards when climbing via any route – especially when cloaked in snow and ice. This massif is also a bastion of rare flora and fauna, like the unique population of iridescent rainbow leaf beetles that lives on the western slopes of Yr Wyddfa, or the lili'r Wyddfa (Snowdon lily), an ice age relict plant, which clings on to Yr Wyddfa and a handful of other sites in Eryri at the very edge of its global range.

The effects of freeze-thaw weathering – when water expands as it freezes, widening fractures in the rock – can be spectacular in Eryri's mountains, particularly in the Glyderau range. The bristling Castell y Gwynt, on Glyder Fach, is an astonishing rock formation caused by the process.

Opposite:
Clogwyn Du'r Arddu, an architectonic beauty of a crag on the northern flank of Yr Wyddfa, is one of the great crucibles of British climbing. Some of the hardest and most dangerous traditional-style climbing routes ever created were put up here in the 1980s, including the legendary 'Indian Face', where a fall in the upper reaches would likely to be fatal due to the lack of places to place protective gear.

after taking the obligatory summit selfie, you can enjoy a coffee in the Hafod Eryri café, with views across the arc of Bae Ceredigion and the long arm of the Llŷn Peninsula reaching into the sea. The summit train, the proximity of Eryri to England's populous north-west and midlands, and the relative gentleness of hiking paths like the Llanberis or Miners' tracks, all combine to make this Britain's most popular mountaintop, visited by around 500,000 visitors a year. By comparison, Britain's highest mountain, Scotland's Ben Nevis, has only around 130,000 visitors. This is the paradox of Yr Wyddfa: on the one hand, a wild and challenging mountain stronghold; on the other, an accessible day out and one of Wales' biggest tourist attractions.

Eryri, Britain's third largest national park, occupies much of the north-west corner of Wales, stretching from the outskirts of Conwy on the north coast to the Dyfi estuary, around 110 kilometres south. The northern part of the park is where many of the region's mountain titans are concentrated. Yr Wyddfa's neighbouring massif, the Glyderau, is one of Britain's great hiking and climbing meccas. The heart of this range is the hulking, craggy pair of Glyder Fawr (1,001 metres / 3,283 feet) and Glyder Fach (994 metres / 3,261 feet), but few mountains anywhere are more visually arresting than the bristling stegosaurus-back shape of Tryfan (918 metres / 3,010 feet) – its summit is one of only a handful in these islands that can only be reached by laying hands on rock and employing scrambling skills. The volcanic rhyolitic rock of Eryri often erodes into angular, jagged forms, and nowhere is that more evident than in the Glyderau.

Moving south past a hole in the park created by the prolific historic slate mining around Blaenau Ffestiniog, the crowds thin out significantly through the Rhinogydd and Arenig ranges, which between them host some of Eryri's most rugged and intractable terrain, but also some of the greatest rewards for experienced hikers and solitude-seekers.

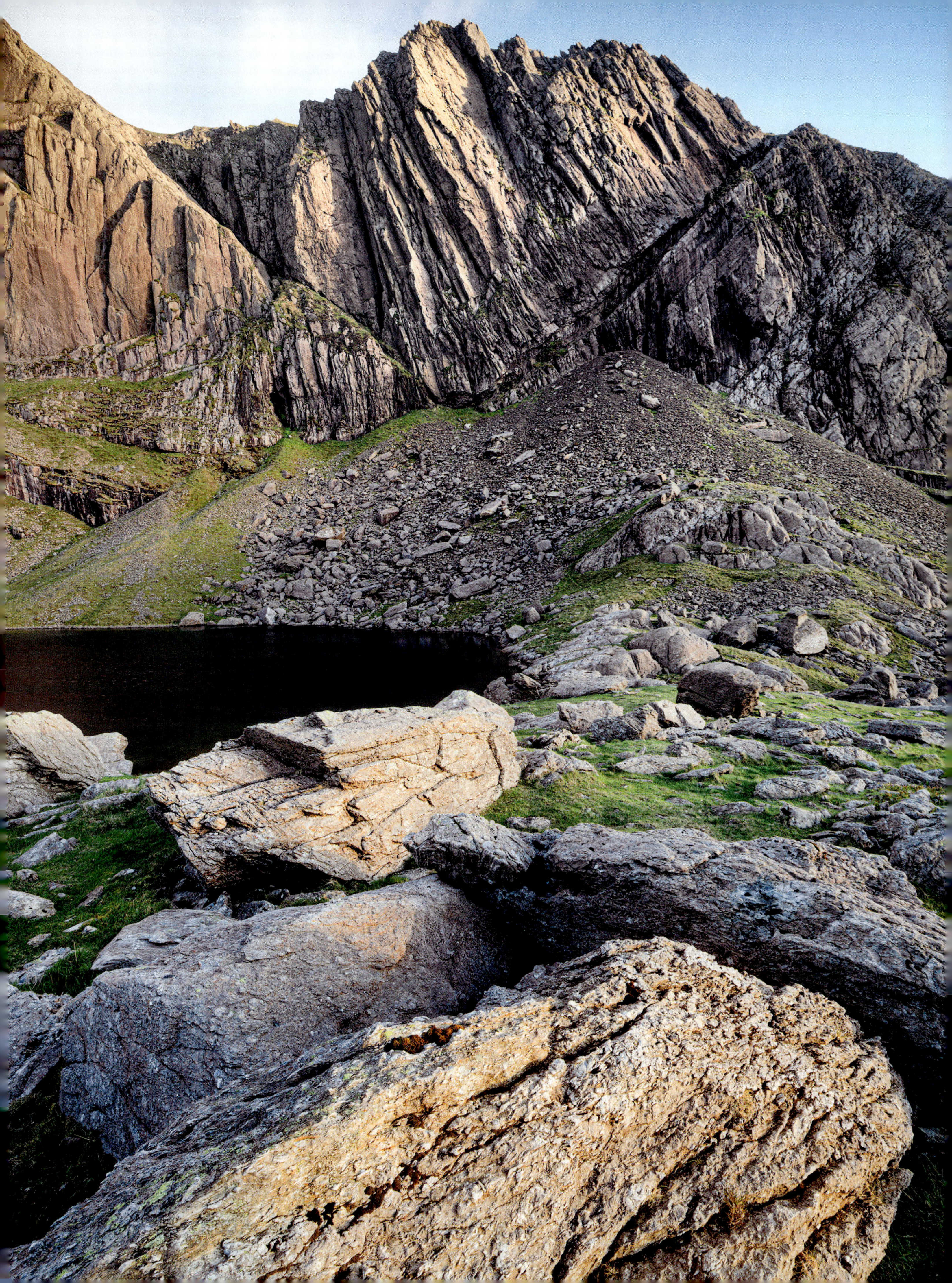

A panorama of the Glyderau, one of Wales' hiking and climbing heartlands, seen from Y Garn. To the left of the image, the busy A5 runs alongside Llyn Ogwen, with the stegosaurus-back shape of Tryfan towering above. The shadowed mountain in the centre is Glyder Fach, and the partially sunlit peak to the right is Glyder Fawr. Below Glyder Fawr, the upper reaches of the mighty ring of crags surrounding Cwm Idwal can be seen, with Llyn Idwal below and to left.

Cader Idris (893 metres / 2,930 feet) in the far south of Eryri is a rival to Yr Wyddfa in the drama stakes, with its imposing array of glacier-carved cwms and its own legendary giant: the mountain's name means 'Idris's Chair', after a cerebral colossus who was said to be a dab hand at philosophy and astronomy.

In the central and southern parts of Eryri there is often an evocative combination of summit and sea: mountains like the Rhinogydd and Cader Idris are within a stone's throw of the coast, and the boundaries of the park extend to the dunes, beaches and busy seaside towns of Bae Ceredigion. This national park is famed for its mountains and forests, but is also home to 119 kilometres (74 miles) of spectacular shoreline: highlights include Harlech Beach, a pristine sweep of sand backed by a sprawling dune system and cinematically overlooked by Harlech Castle, and the mouth of the Afon Mawddach, an estuary beautifully framed by wooded hills, where the sand and water ebbs and flows sinuously with the tide.

Like most of Britain's mountain areas, the landscape of Eryri was heavily sculpted by the extremes of the last Ice Age, and it still holds the shape of the ice flows that encased the earth 20,000 years ago in its cwms and contours. Cwm Idwal, a sublime amphitheatre in the Glyderau, is one of the best examples. Here, geological strata, having been bent and deformed by tectonic forces over millions of years, were further ground and gouged by a solid river of ice, which in the wake of its retreat has left an arc of almost-impregnable crags cradling the beautiful lake of Llyn Idwal and the bowl-shaped valley around it.

The cwm's geomorphological secrets were unlocked with the help of Charles Darwin, who first visited in 1831 and would later deduce the icy origins of this hanging valley's shape by identifying common features with glaciated landscapes he had studied in the Tierra del Fuego archipelago, at the far tip of South America. Darwin also noticed the fossils of marine seashells in boulders by Llyn Idwal, and realised that layers of the 400-million-year-old rock had formed underwater, between bouts of explosive volcanism. Like many of the older parts of these islands, the rock of Eryri has passed through lost worlds of water, fire and ice.

Although the glaciers are gone, relics of the Ice Age do still hang on in the upper reaches of Eryri. The Snowdon lily (*Gagea serotina*) is an arctic-alpine plant that is relatively common in cold, high, mountainous parts of the world, like the Alps and Siberia, and it would have flourished in the frigid conditions of Britain's last glacial era. Now its British range has retreated to just six elevated sites in Eryri where the plants cling to steep and shaded north-facing outcrops, beyond the reach of sheep who would otherwise gobble them up. Sadly, as the climate warms, the survival of this Ice Age vestige in the British Isles is in serious doubt, but Eryri remains a refuge for a range of other arctic-alpine and specialist plant species.

Rain falls on 200 days of the year in Eryri, and this abundance of precipitation is a defining feature of the region. As well as feeding booming, rocky rivers like the Afon Glaslyn, spectacular cascades like Aber Falls and deep lakes like Llyn Padarn, it also moulds the ecology of the landscape. Eryri is home to some of the best-surviving fragments of temperate rainforest – or Celtic rainforest – in Britain, woodlands so damp that plants grow on other plants, creating a riot of green growth. Ancient lower plants, plant groups that predate the dinosaurs, thrive in these primeval-seeming places. The twisted branches of sessile oaks are lushly festooned with mosses and fungi; ferns and liverworts sprout abundantly from soil and stone; unusual lichens like the leafy lungwort and the pongy 'Stingy Sticta' thrive on the gnarled barks of old trees. Evident in woods like Nant Gwynant, Coed Felenrhyd & Llennyrch, and Dolmelynllyn, these little lost worlds give a fascinating glimpse into an environment that would once have been prominent on the Atlantic edges of these islands.

Eryri's feral mountain goats have become a shaggy symbol of the region. Hardy and self-sufficient, they are part of a landrace known as 'British primitives', descended from breeds brought here by Neolithic nomadic pastoralists 5,000 years ago. They now roam freely, no longer used as livestock, but have been subject to culls when their numbers are deemed to be too large.

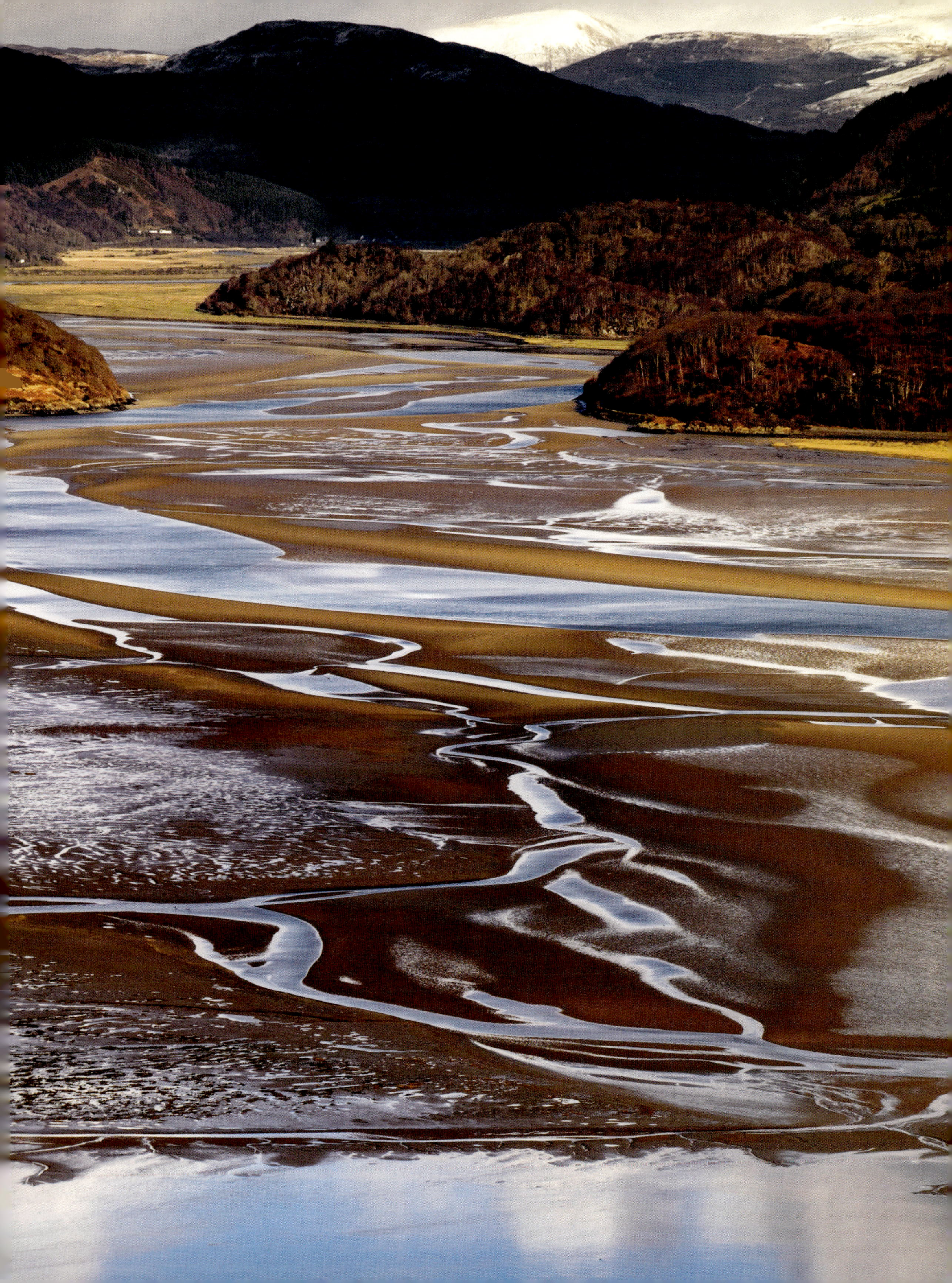

A popular myth holds that if you spend the night on the slopes of Cader Idris, you might wake up a poet. The catch? You might also go mad. In Eryri, it seems a risk worth taking; like all of Wales, this is a landscape steeped in poetry and literature.

Near the village of Trawsfynydd is Yr Ysgwrn, a stone farmhouse and family home of shepherd and poet Ellis Humphrey Evans. Born in 1887, he is better known by the bardic name of Hedd Wyn (Blessed Peace). Written in Welsh, Hedd Wyn's searching poetry, deeply influenced by his Christian pacifist beliefs, is steeped in natural imagery inspired by his home, and he even submitted an ode to Eryri as his first entry to his local eisteddfod, a traditional Welsh music and poetry competition. In 1917 he was enlisted to fight in World War One, but on a leave of absence back home he sent what many consider his finest work, 'Yr Arwr' ('The Hero'), to the National Eisteddfod of Wales under a pseudonym. The poem won the competition, but when the ritual trumpets were sounded for the winner to identify themselves, no one appeared: it was announced that the author had been killed at the Battle of Passchendaele. The ceremonial chair was draped in a black cloth and the event has since been referred to as the Eisteddfod of the Black Chair. This chair now sits in the parlour of Yr Ysgwrn, which has been carefully preserved by Hedd Wyn's descendants as a museum you can visit in the summer season.

Eryri is also the setting of some of the oldest surviving stories from these islands. *The Mabinogion* is a collection of stories written in medieval Welsh, but thought to have oral roots that stretch back much further. They follow the trials and tribulations of several royal families – thought to be personifications of ancient British gods – through a murderous, magical world of giants, shapeshifters, flower-women, enchanted cauldrons and supernatural mists. The influence of these stories has been far-reaching: tales connected to them form part of the mythology around King Arthur, and *Lord of the Rings*, *Game of Thrones* and other works of fantasy would not exist without their legacy.

Evening light over Llynnau Cregennen and the crags of Craig-las, with the steep northern flanks of Cader Idris behind.

Opposite:
Sinuous water channels vein the Mawddach estuary at low tide. The mudflats and marshes in and around the estuary provide important habitats for wetland and wading birds like redshank, rail, cormorant and merganser, while remnants of raised bog, like that of Arthog Bog, support distinctive flora, like St John's Wort and touch-me-not balsam.

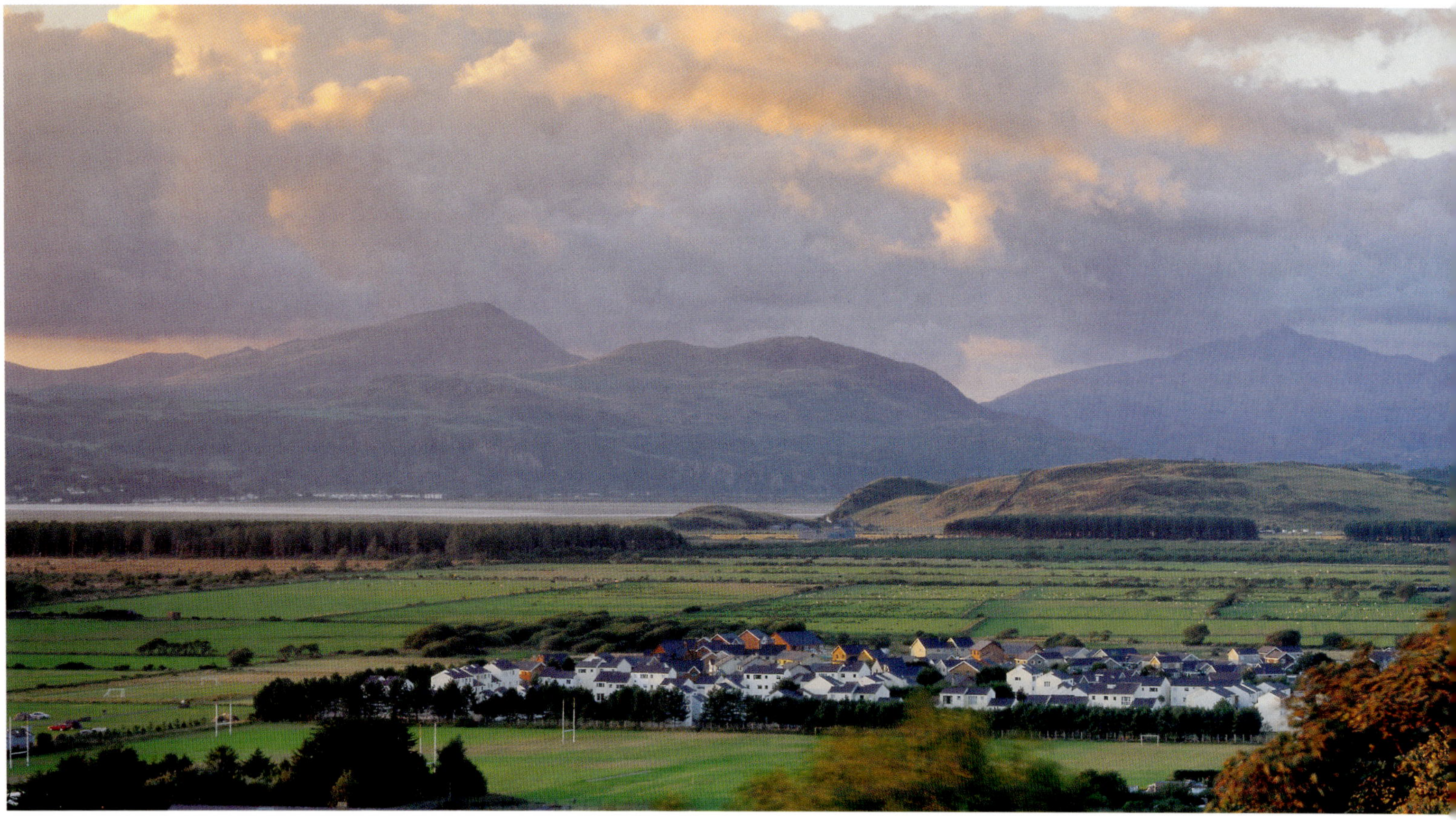

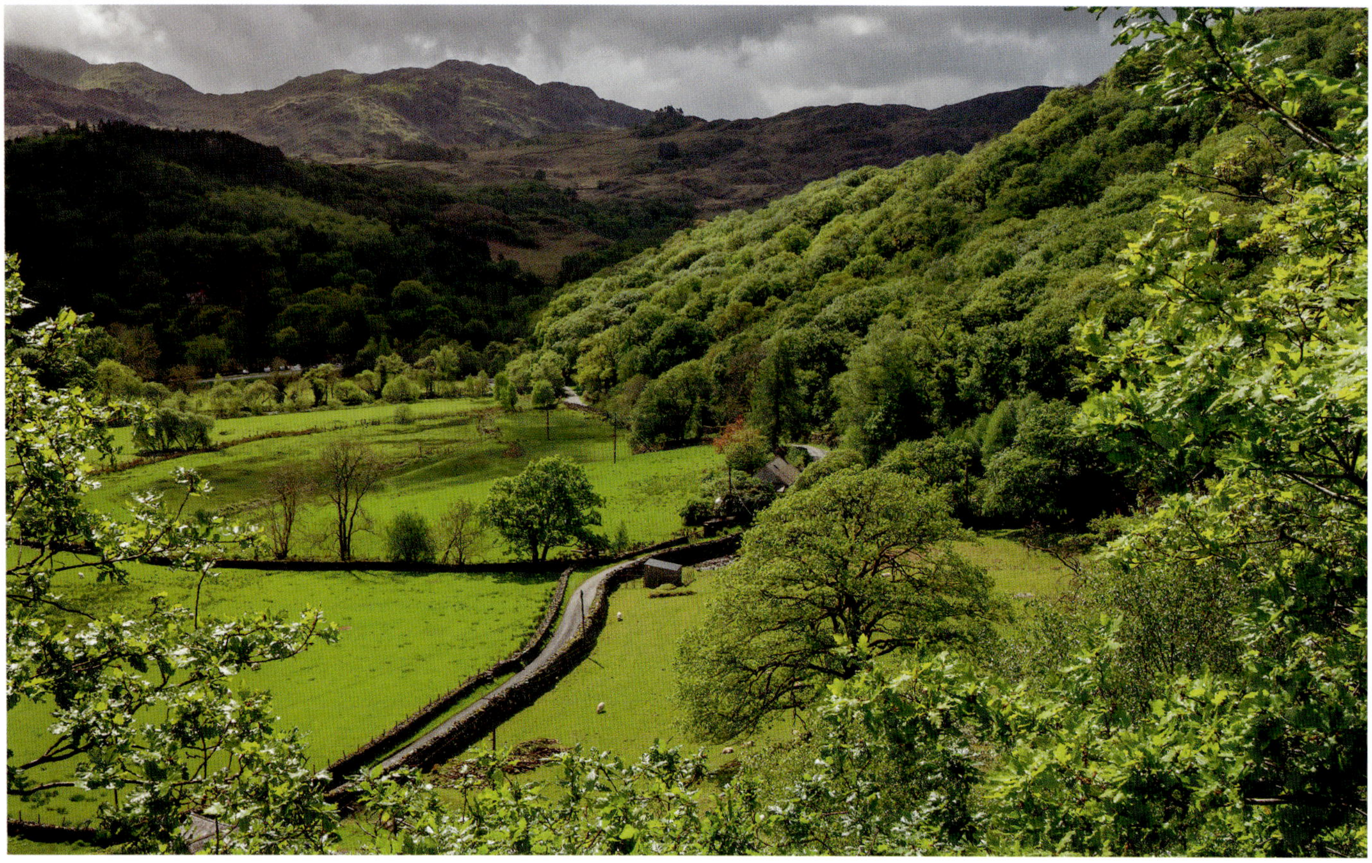

Many of the stories from *The Mabinogion* are set in or involve the landscape of Eryri, and landmarks from it appear throughout the tales. One of the stories sees a warrior, Gronw, make a botched attempt to kill a rival, Lleu. The two meet on opposite sides of the Afon Cynfal, a river tumbling through a gorge near modern-day Ffestiniog. In retaliation for the attempted murder, Lleu prepares to throw a spear at Gronw, but acquiesces to Gronw's plea to shield himself with a stone. It is to little avail: the force of Lleu's throw is so strong that the spear pierces through the rock, and Gronw is killed.

In 1934 an unusual stone – a slate around four feet high, with a perfectly circle-shaped hole in it – was found on the banks of Afon Cynfal. Locals connected it with this story and so 'Gronw's Stone', as it is known, now stands on a plinth near Bryn Saeth. It is an evocative symbol of Eryri, a place where myth and reality, legend and landscape, are all wonderfully intermingled.

Spectacularly situated on a rocky promontory overlooking a coastal plain is Harlech Castle, which was constructed under the orders of Edward I during his invasion of Wales in the late 13th century. Now a world heritage site, it is one of the most impressive and well-preserved medieval fortresses in Europe. In 1404, the castle fell to Owain Glyndŵr's forces during his campaign to restore Welsh independence. It became his military headquarters, and was held for four years.

Opposite:
Nant Gwynant flushed with the vivid green of young foliage in early spring.

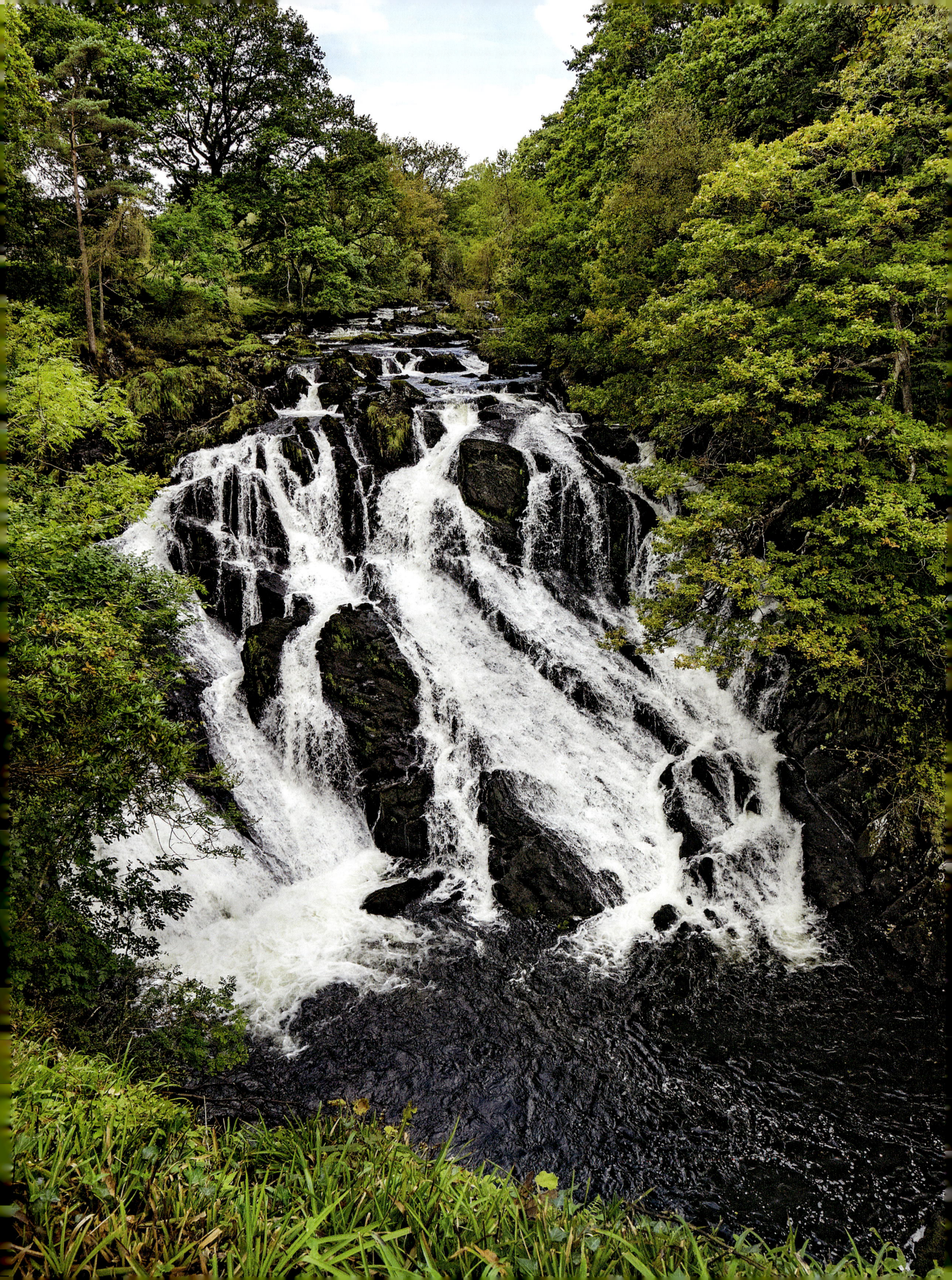

Hidden amid temperate rainforest, a Tolkienesque bridge at Penmachno is overgrown with vines and vegetation. The 'Roman Bridge' is actually thought to be around 400 years old. Further behind this bridge, obscured at certain angles, is a 19th century packhorse bridge.

Eryri's powerful mountain rivers have created impressive landforms. Sunlight catches in the mists of the Fairy Glen, a narrow forest-framed ravine carved through the rhyolite rock by the Afon Conwy.

Opposite:
The River Llugwy flows over the rocky cascades of Rhaeadr Ewynnol ('The Foaming Waterfall'), known in English as Swallow Falls.

Overleaf:
Remnants of farming activity in Llyn y Dywarchen ('Lake of the Floating Island') above Rhyd-Ddu, with the eastern flanks of Yr Wyddfa beyond.

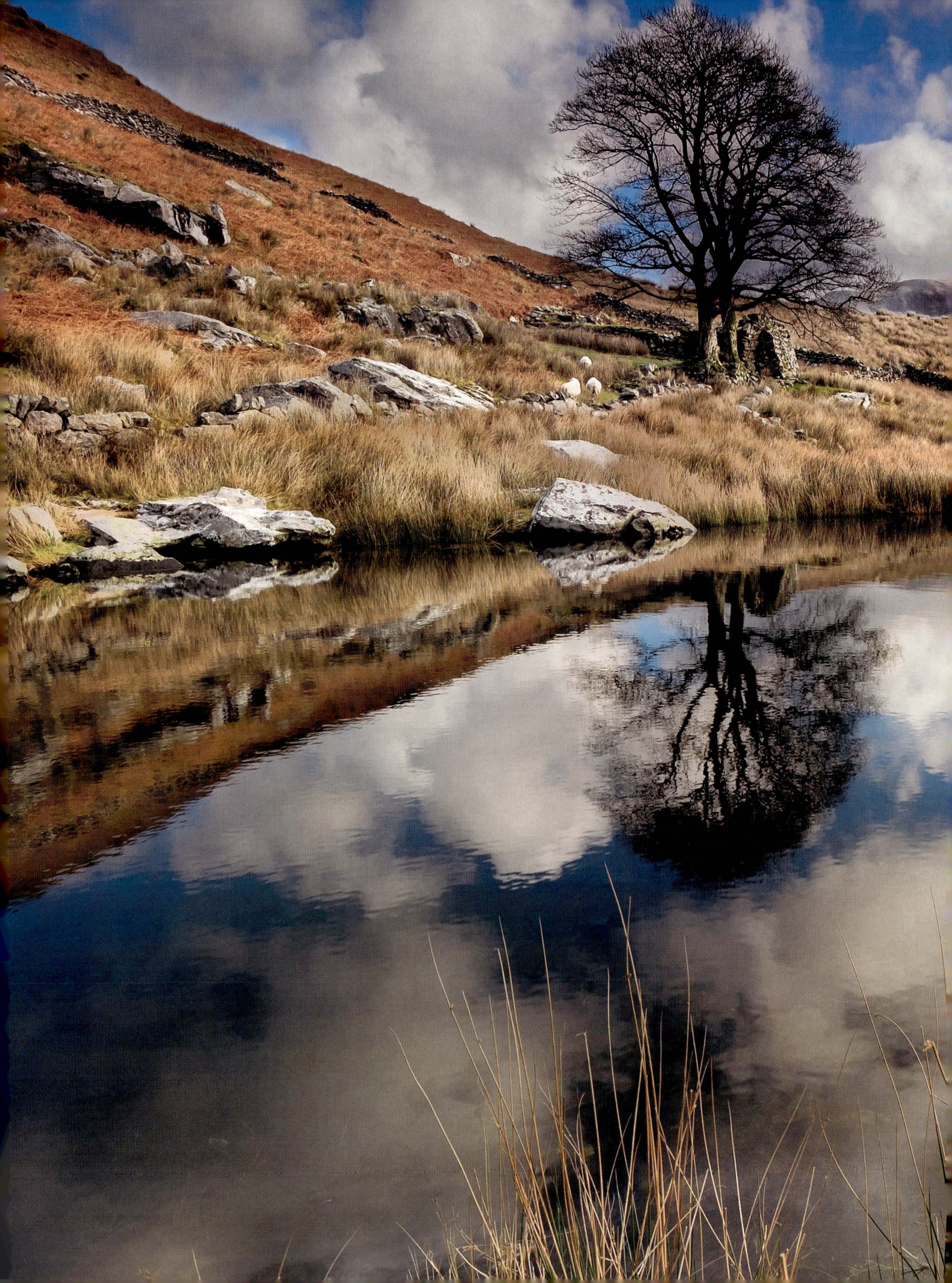

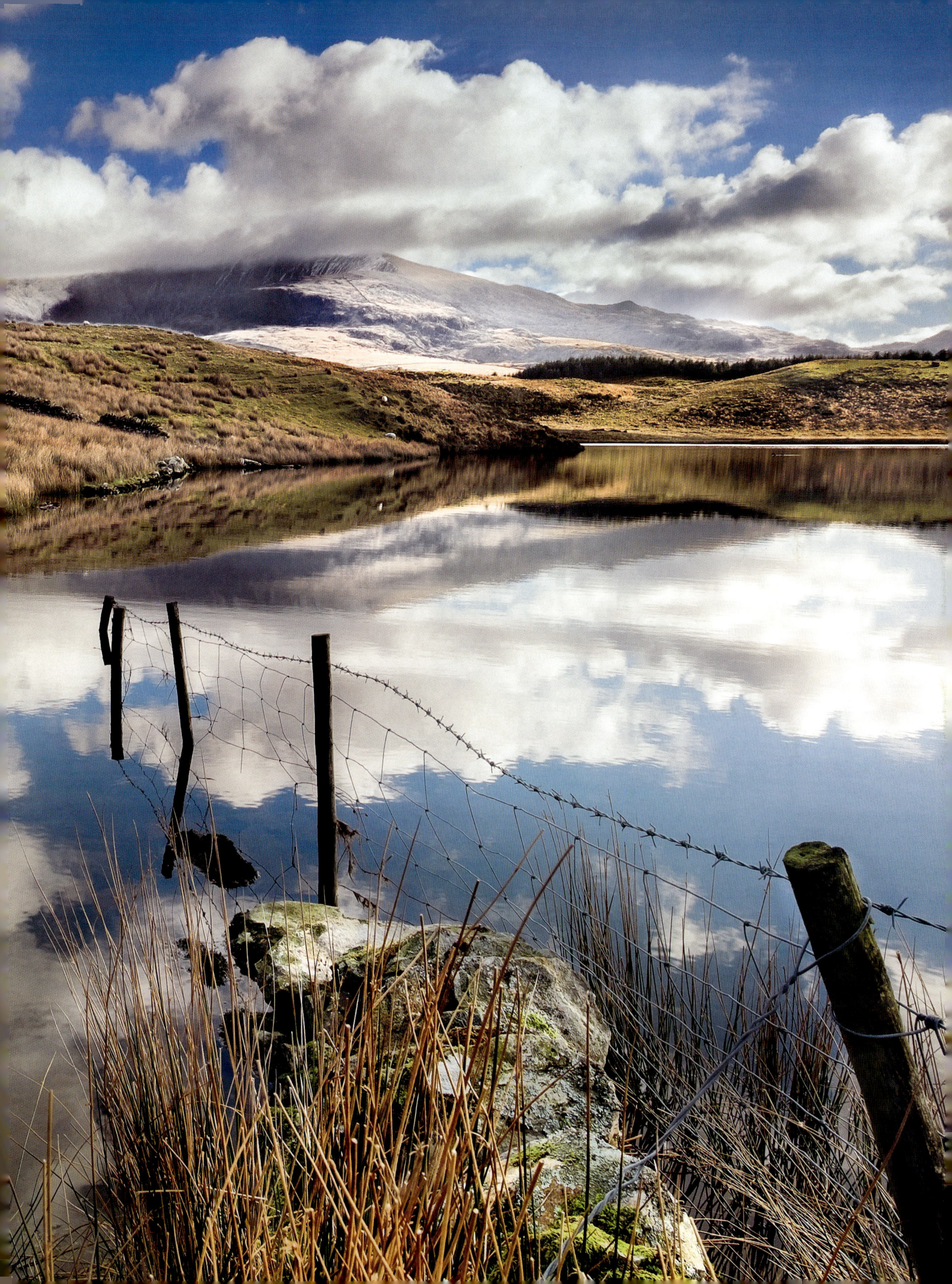

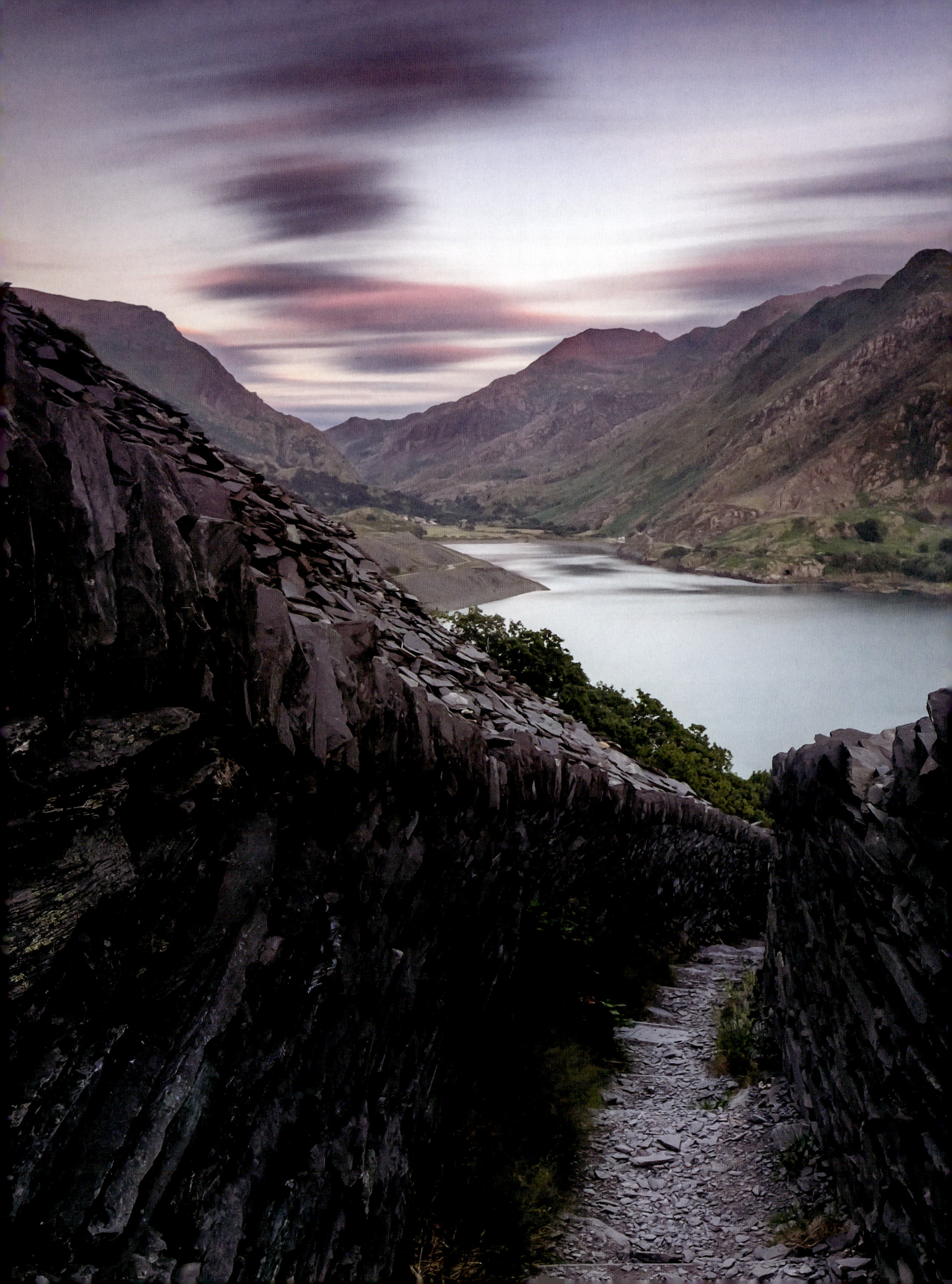

Slate is a rock made of mudstones that have been compressed through tectonic forces. Though a dark-looking rock at first glance, closer inspection reveals shimmering streaks of purple and green, like the iridescent wings of a raven. When struck in a certain way, it cleaves into smooth slabs of stone along uniform planes, making perfect roofing tiles. Slate has been mined in Eryri since Roman times, but in the 19th century it became one of the biggest slate quarrying regions in the world. Whole mountainsides were excavated, supplying slate to places as far away as Australasia and North America. The most cavernous ex-quarries, like Dinorwic or those around Blaenau Ffestiniog, lie just outside the national park boundary. This image of a path hemmed by drystone walls is taken at the Dinorwic site, looking towards Yr Wyddfa. Remnants of the industry can also be found across the national park itself, and many are linked together by the Snowdonia Slate Trail (134 kilometres / 83 miles long). The slate landscapes of North-West Wales are collectively designated a world heritage site. Some limited slate quarrying still takes place at Penrhyn, just outside the national park near Llanberis.

Overleaf:
The rugged hills of Craig Wen and Crimpiau reflected in the calm waters of Llyn Crafnant.

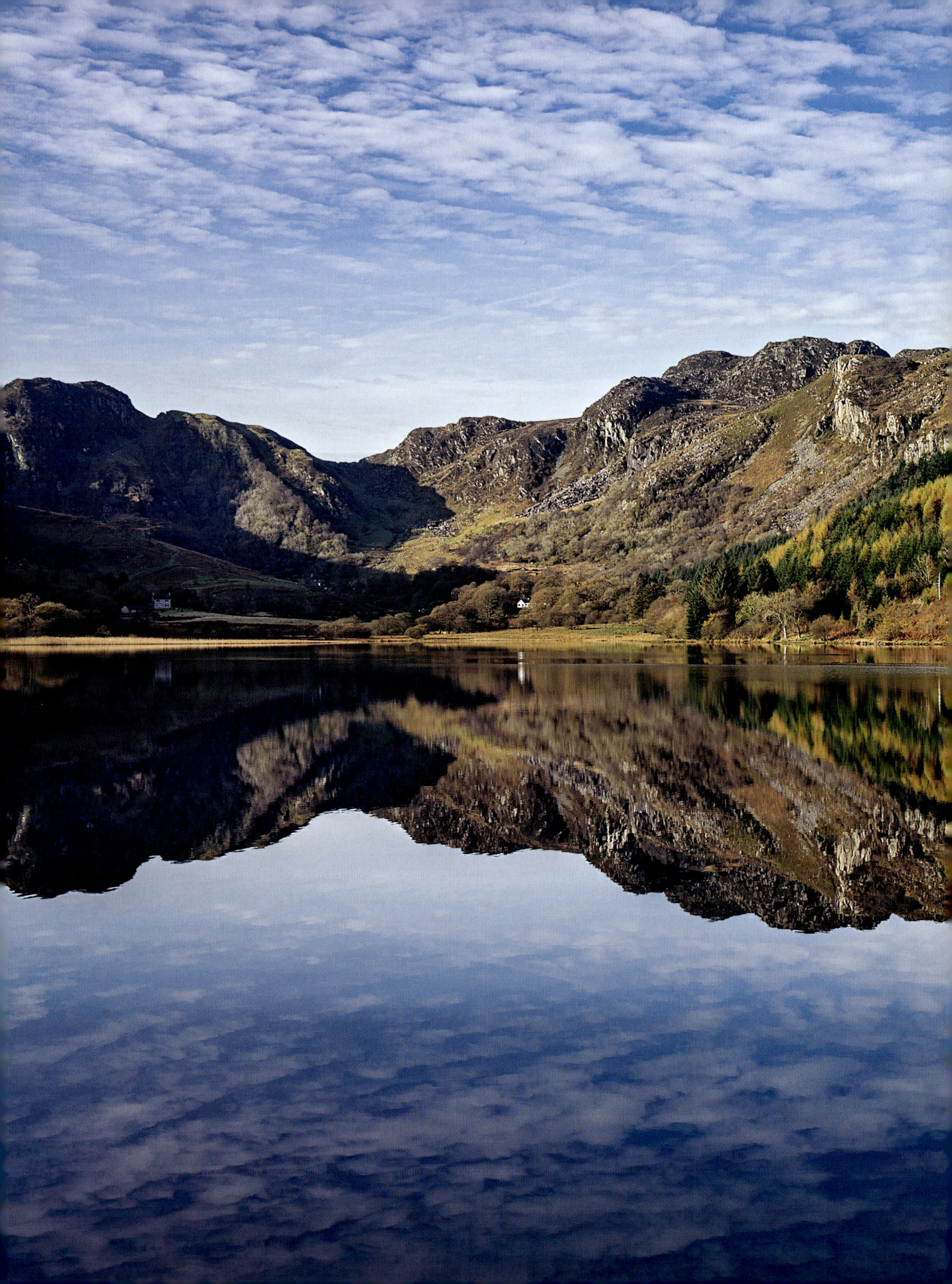

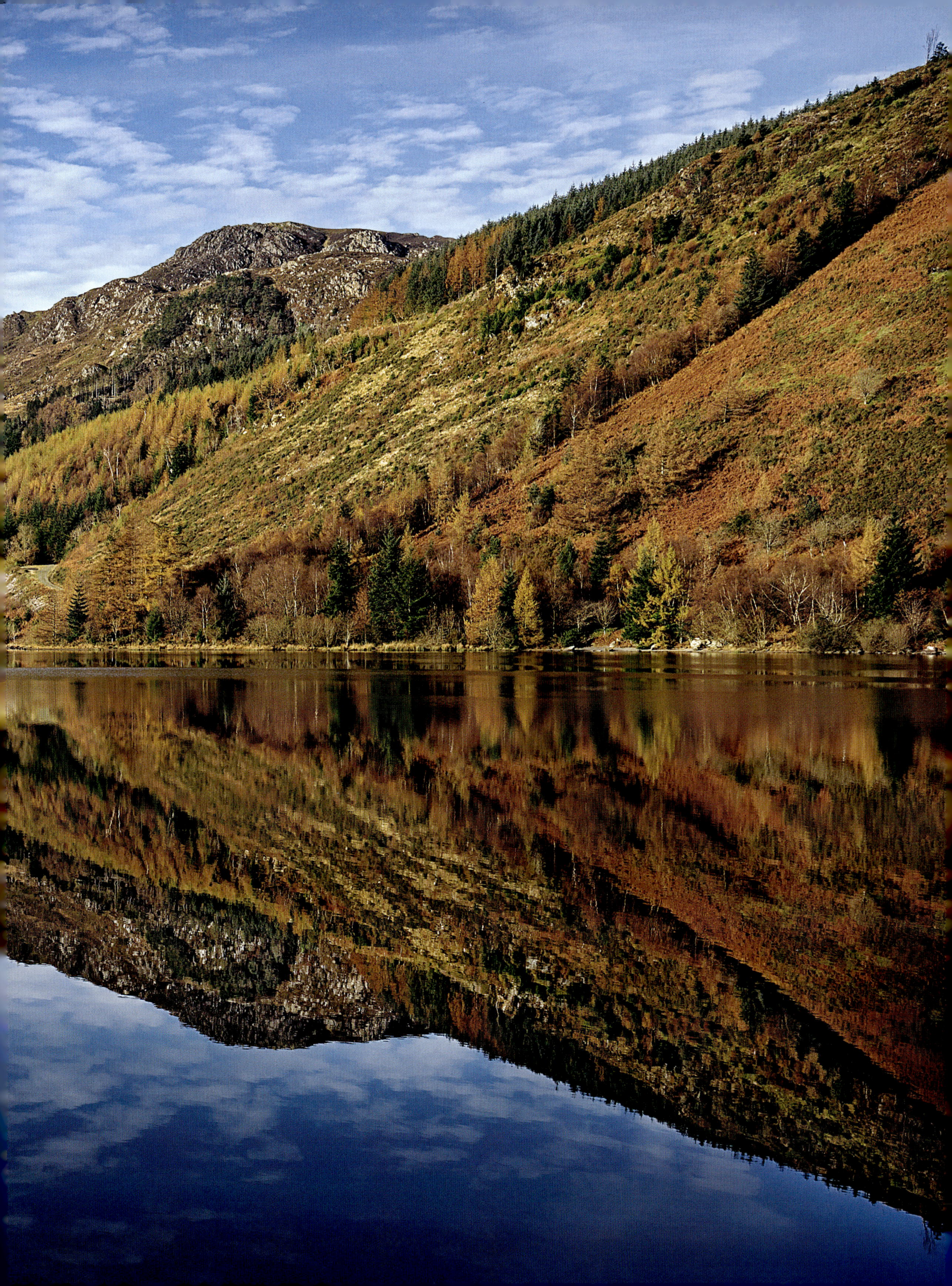

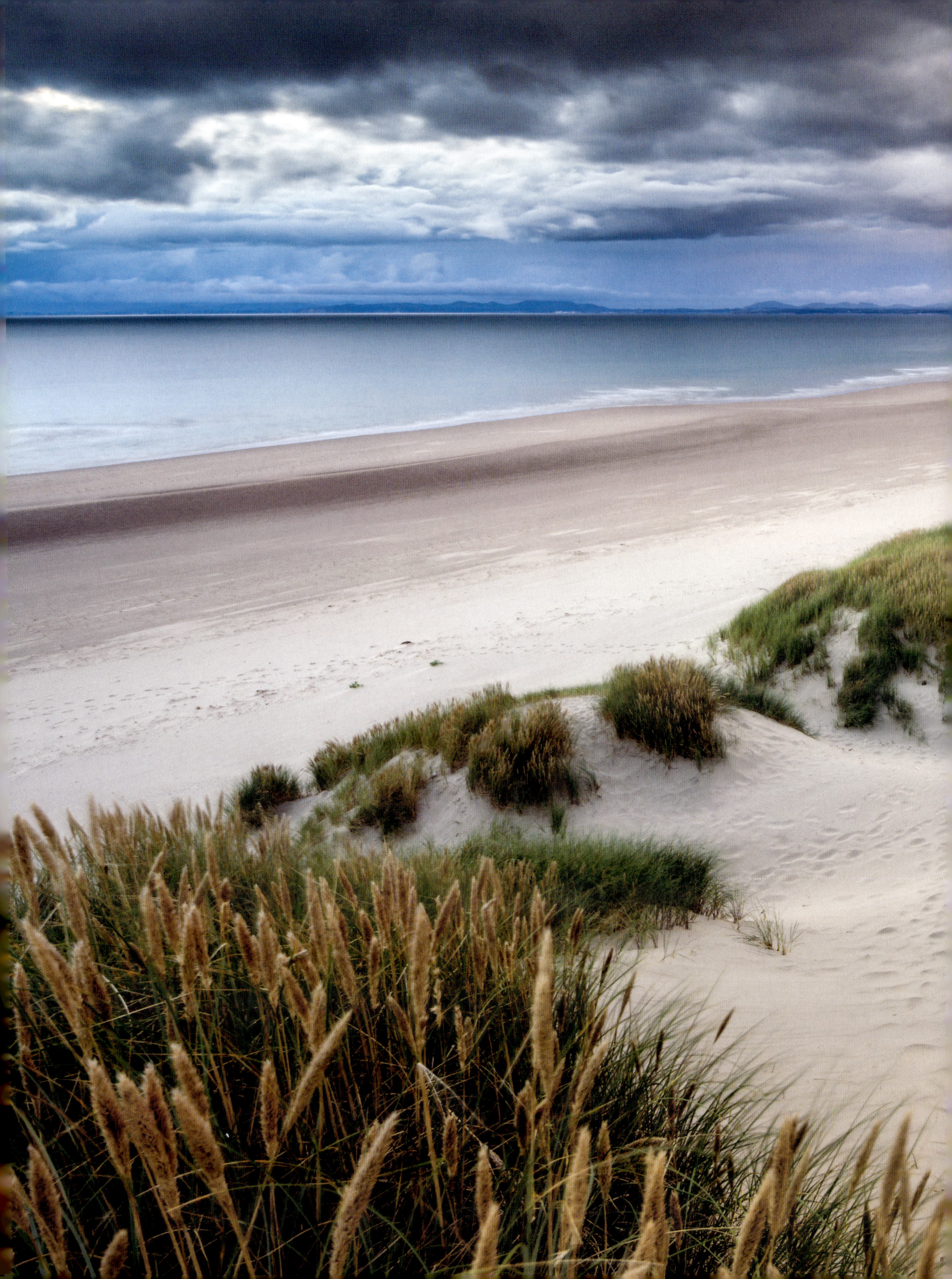

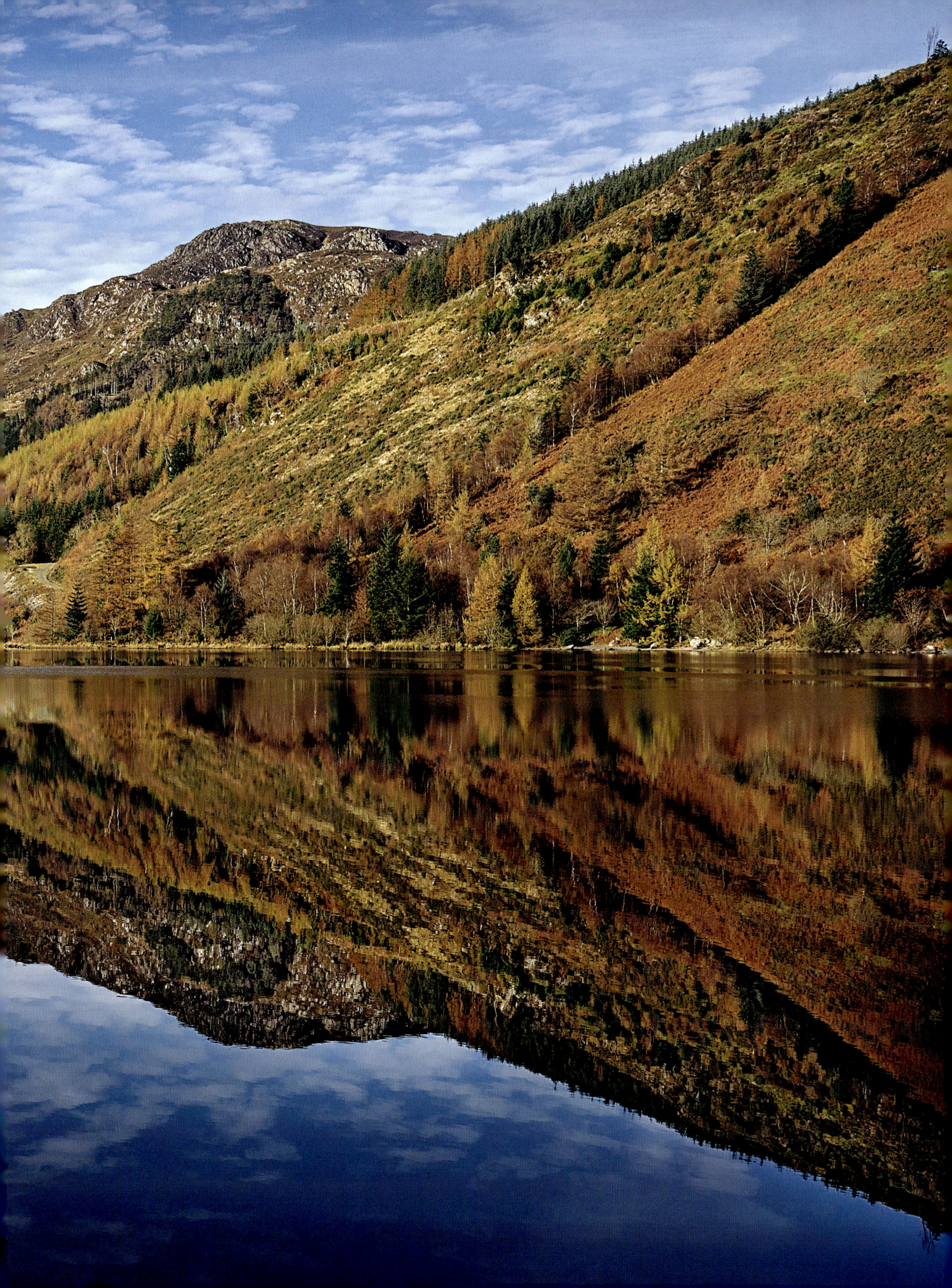

Morning mists drift through the pastures and oakwoods of Nant Gwynant. Sandwiched between the massifs of Yr Wyddfa and the Moelwynion, and flanked by woods, waterfalls and steep mountainsides, Nant Gwynant cuts through the mountainous heart of the northern part of Eryri, and cradles the beautiful lakes of Llyn Gwynant and Llyn Dinas.

Overleaf:
Beyond the village of Harlech, a swathe of grassy sand dunes fans out across the coastal plain, forming one of the few actively growing dune systems in Wales, before giving way to a 6-kilometre (3.5-mile) stretch of sandy beach. The dunes of Morfa Harlech are a national nature reserve, home to rare orchids and mining bees, as well as breeding birds like skylark and stonechat.

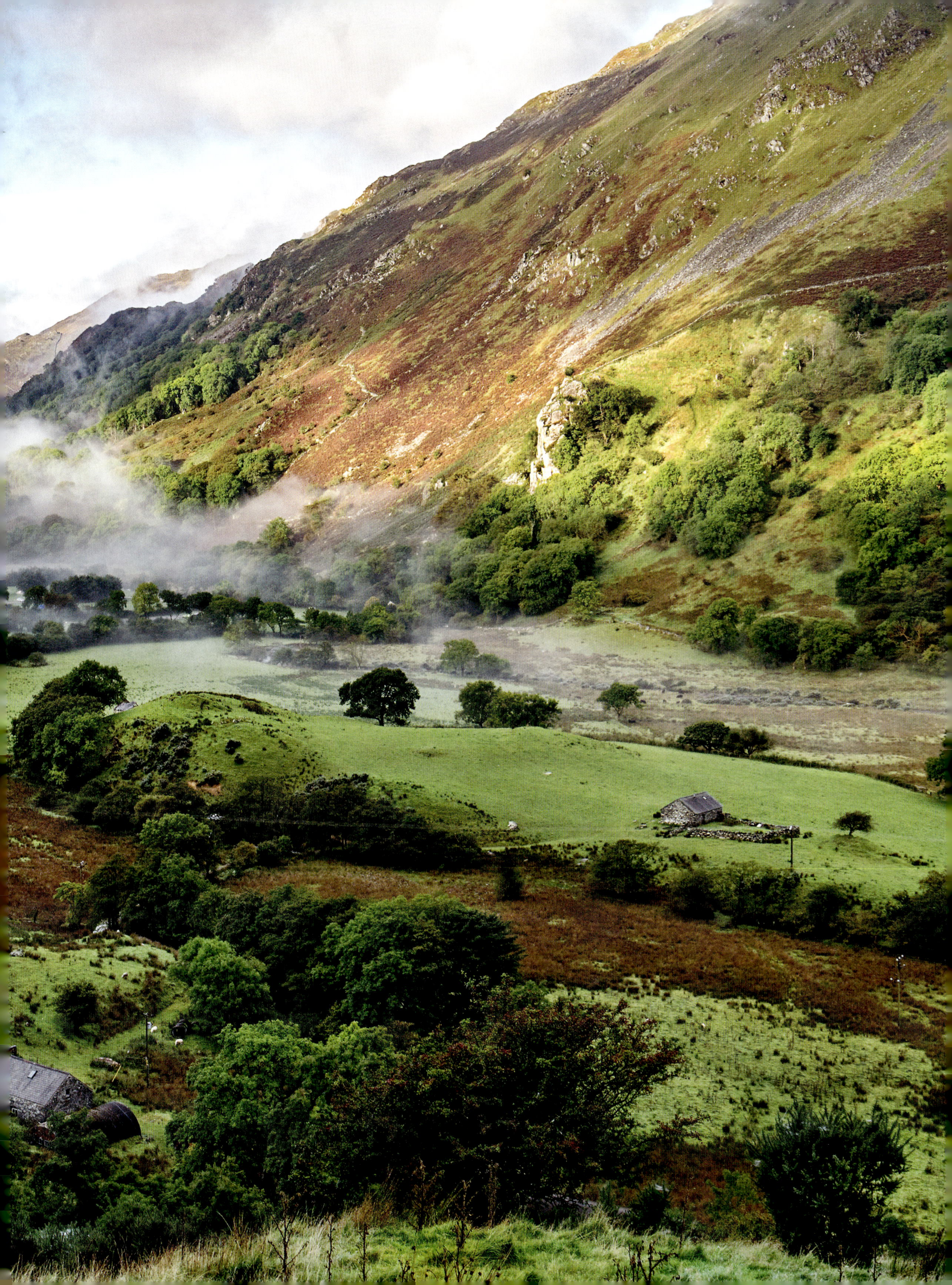

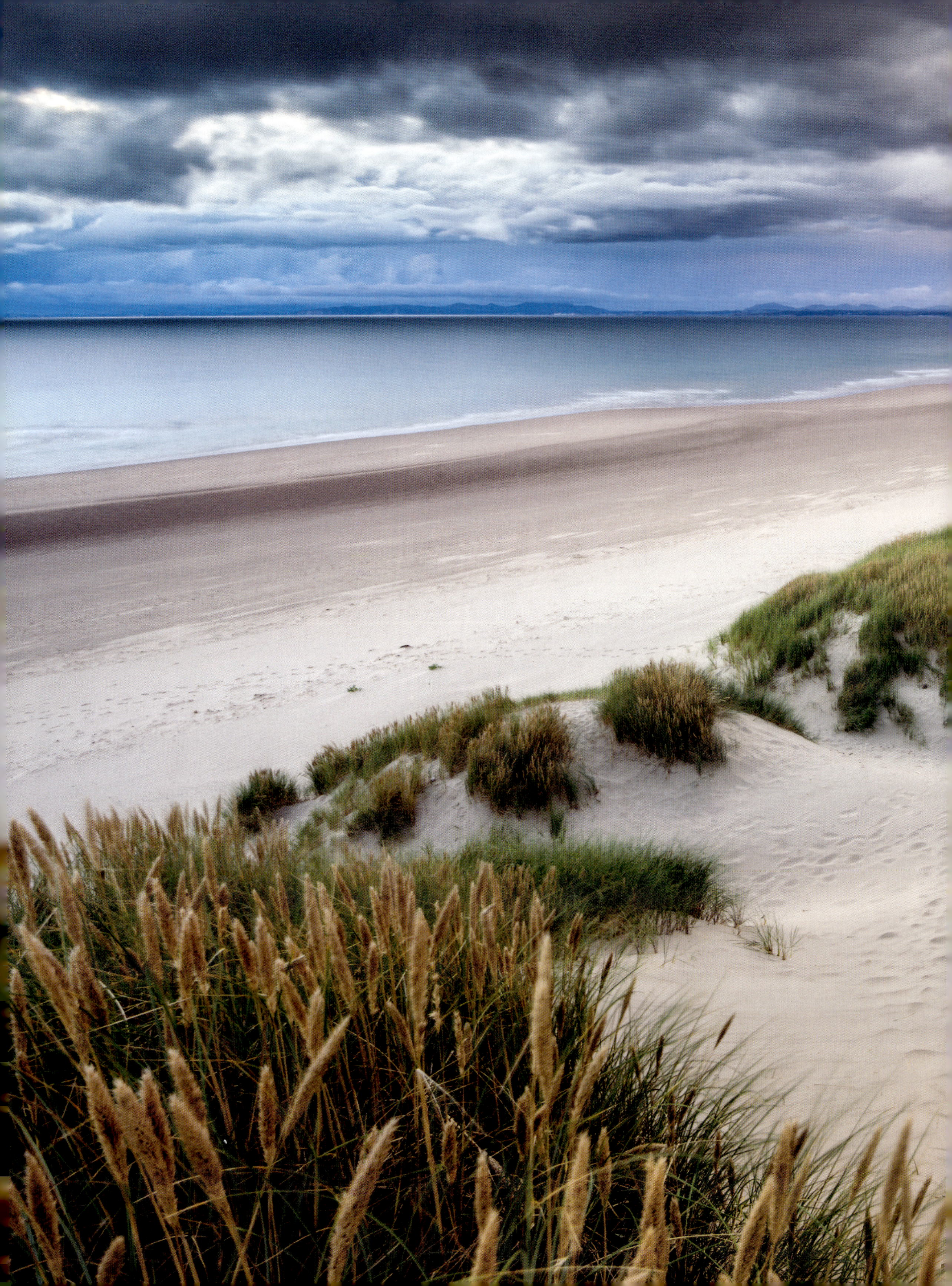

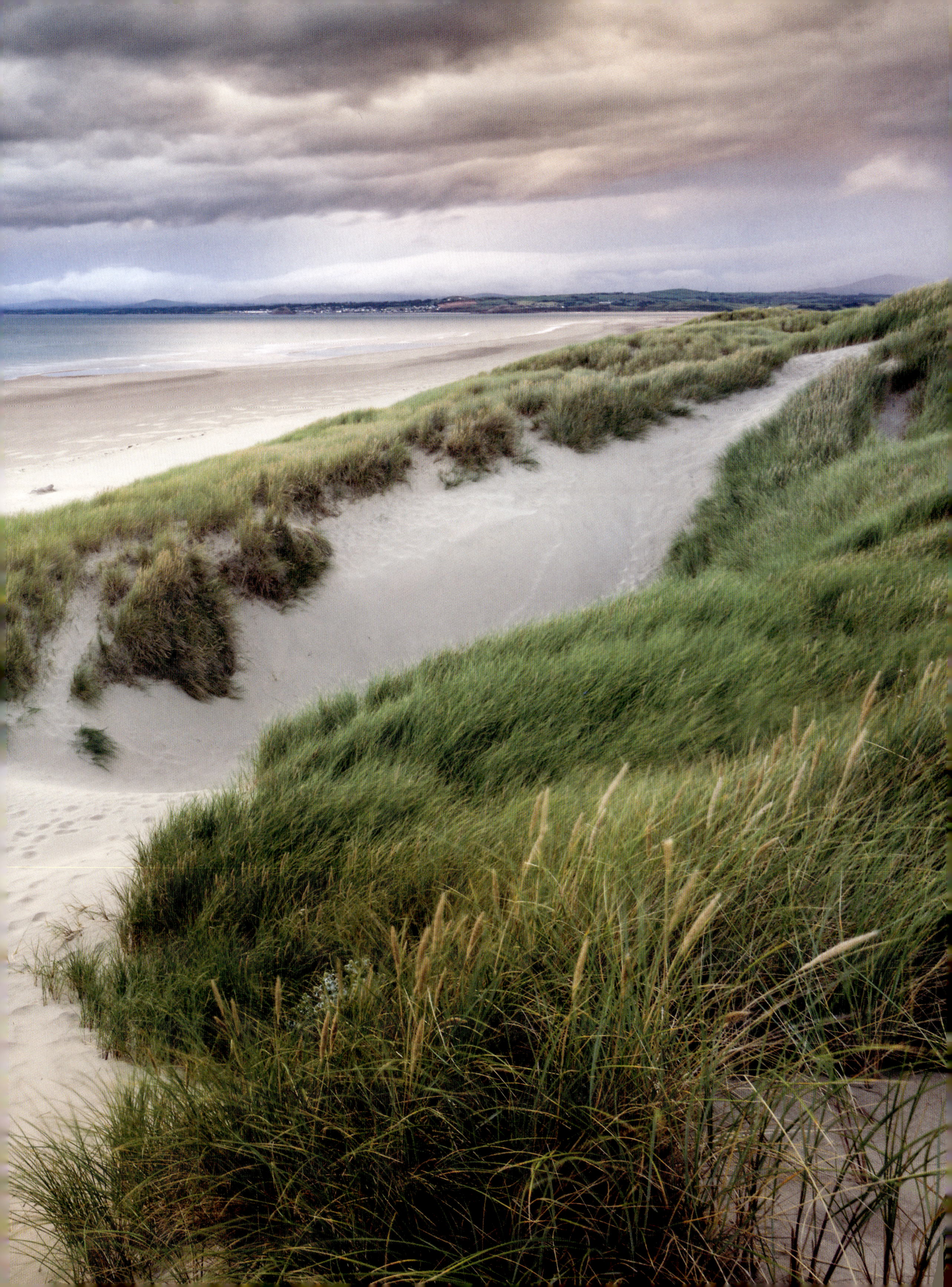

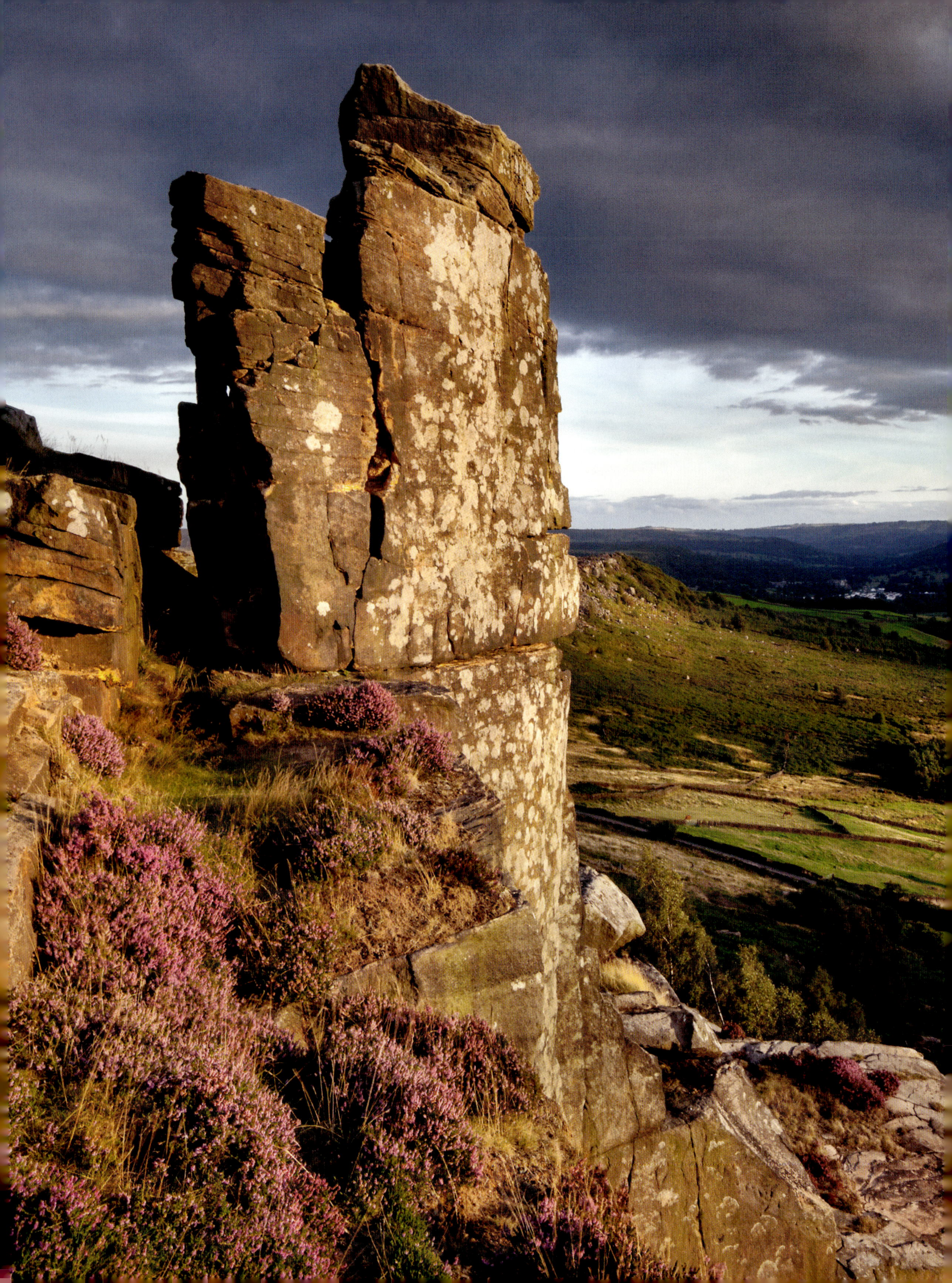

Peak District

Looking down from space on the British landmass at night reveals a ring of brightness that extends north from the heart of England, forming a huge, almost unbroken circle about 240 kilometres long. This lasso of light is home to about 20 million people: a constellation of cities and towns making up the historic heartland of England's industry. This loop includes Birmingham, Manchester, Bradford, Leeds, Nottingham, Derby, Sheffield and Stoke-on-Trent, cities that mushroomed during the Industrial Revolution as centres for textile, steel or pottery. They have continued to expand since, fusing together in places.

But no space traveller could fail to notice that in the middle of this circle of illumination is a mysterious patch of darkness. This oasis is the Peak District, the breathing space at the heart of England, where instead of towns and cities you'll find windswept high moorlands dotted with outlandish natural sculptures; secret limestone gorges full of lush meadows and lazy rivers; and villages where time seems to move at an altogether different pace.

This national park is really two landscapes in one – the Dark Peak and the White Peak. Both are distinctive and beautiful landscapes in their own right, but although there is plenty of craggy, hilly and even semi-mountainous terrain to be found in both, actual 'peaks' are thin on the ground. Rather than referring to mountains, the name is actually derived from the Pecsaetan, an Anglo-Saxon tribe who inhabited the region in early medieval times, and residents of the region were still referred to as 'Peakrills' as late as the 18th century.

The Peak District's landscapes have their origins in the Carboniferous era, more than 300 million years ago, when the earth was a warm, wet forest world dominated by amphibian life, and much of what is now land was inundated by seas and swamps. The Dark Peak, which makes up roughly the northern half of the national park, is underlain by a coarse sedimentary sandstone called Millstone Grit – often shortened to gritstone – which is essentially the solidified mud of an enormous ancient river delta, bigger than the mouth of the Nile is today. Due to a mix of natural processes and soot-staining from the industrial era, the rough surface patina of gritstone boulders and escarpments usually appears as a sombre shade of grey, which, coupled with the rich, dark soil of peatlands, is what makes the Dark Peak 'dark'. Here you'll find high moorland plateaus fringed with long crags, like Stanage Edge, and outlandish sky-sculpted rock formations, bisected by patchworked valleys containing fast-flowing rivers, Victorian-era reservoirs and charming mill villages.

The Pinnacle Stone on Curbar Edge, one of the 'Eastern Edges', a string of Millstone Grit escarpments that run along the eastern skyline of the Derwent Valley. Easily accessible from Sheffield, they are popular hiking destinations and some of England's best and busiest climbing venues.

Spectacular limestone caves and karstic landforms crowd around the head of the Hope Valley, including the dramatic canyon of Winnats Pass and the steep gorge of Cave Dale, where the remains of the 800-year-old Norman fortress of Peveril Castle perch atop the crags.

Opposite:
The Millstone Grit rock formation known as the Salt Cellar, on the northern flanks of Kinder Scout. Millennia's worth of storms, water and wind have sculpted gritstone outcrops into many fantastic shapes, which often punctuate the moorlands of the Dark Peak.

There are three species of heather in Britain – ling, bell and cross-leaved heath. Ling, shown here, is found in such quantities across the Peak District that it turns entire moorlands into huge swathes of purple-pink at its flowering peak in August.

The Dark Peak is where you'll find some of the region's most spectacular hillwalking. Kinder Scout, which contains the highest point in the Peak District, is a table mountain fringed by dramatic crags and topped by a high waterlogged world of deep peat bog, from which an array of torrents tumble down through rocky ghylls – a northern English term for ravine – waterfalls and plunge pools. With its summit at just 636 metres (2,087 feet), Kinder Scout is not a high mountain by any measure, but the atmosphere in its high reaches is unlike anywhere else; in the midst of its wild plateau, lost in the maze of groughs, or peat channels, you can feel very far from civilisation indeed, even though the edges of Greater Manchester are only a few miles away.

Up on the moors, Millstone Grit becomes a playful shapeshifter, having been sculpted by storms, water and wind into fantastic forms, tricking the imagination into seeing fish heads, sphinxes, salt cellars, seals, rabbit's ears, boxing gloves, baboon heads, cows, calves, coaches and horses. Although made from solid rock, the fluidity of these forms reflects the turbulence of the river currents of the Carboniferous; the ferocity of the sandstorms that followed the retreat of the glaciers after the end of the last Ice Age; and the volatility of Britain's Atlantic climate. An inspiration to countless artists, including Henry Moore and Barbara Hepworth, these rock forms are where we can see deep time in action on the edge of huge urban centres.

The White Peak is a landscape made of limestone, a rock that erodes in rainwater to produce a 'karst' landscape of sinkholes, springs, potholes, caves, caverns and gorges. If the Dark Peak is grand and expansive, the White Peak is a more intimate landscape, where the patchwork of sheep pastures is interrupted by steep-sided gorges like Miller's Dale and Dovedale, enchanting lost worlds where trout-filled rivers run through lush ash woodlands and wildflower meadows. The origins of the moniker 'White Peak' are not hard to spot as you walk around, with the bone-coloured carbonate rock outcropping in crags, limestone pavements and striking mini-mountains formed from

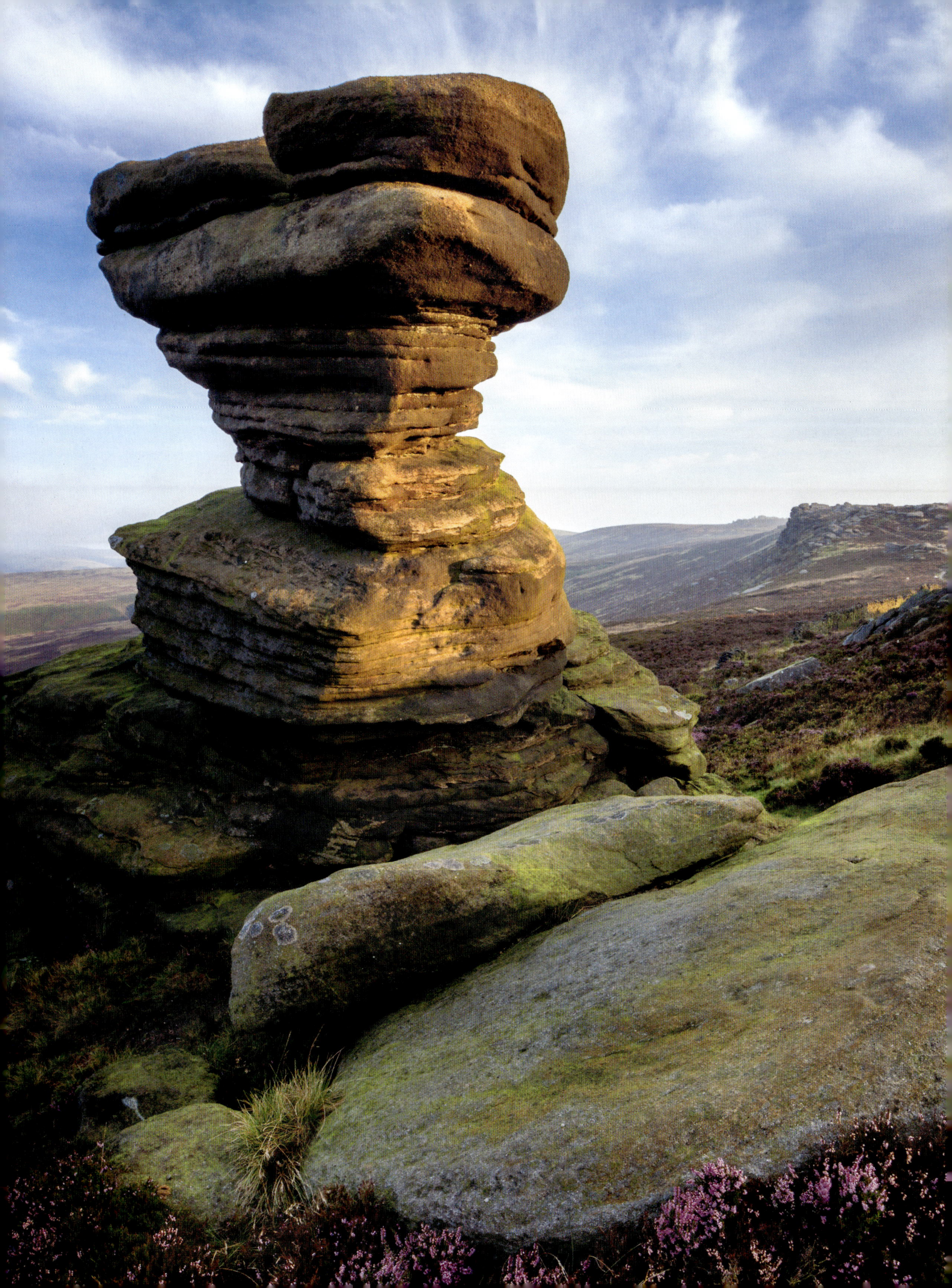

Adapted to high-altitude environments, mountain hares change the colour of their fur across the seasons. In their white winter coats they are seamlessly camouflaged when the land is snow-covered, but are otherwise conspicuous against the peaty-brown moorland. The small and vulnerable population of mountain hares in the Dark Peak is the only one in Britain outside Scotland.

ancient coral reefs, such as Chrome Hill and Parkhouse Hill – two of the most impressive peaks in the Peak District, despite their small size. The White Peak literally has hidden depths: the deepest cavern in England, Titan, lurks beneath the ground near the village of Castleton. It is only accessible to experienced cavers, but various other show caves are open to the public, giving glimpses of the scale and spectacle of the limestone underworld.

The underlying geology of the White Peak, and the distinctive role of water within it, is reflected in its culture. Villages in the White Peak have often developed around springs, which provide regular supplies of freshwater in the water-permeable karstic terrain. These founts of life are celebrated in the annual tradition of well dressing, or well flowering, where water sources are garlanded with elaborate decorations and designs made from flower petals.

All the UK's national parks are there to be enjoyed by everyone, but the Peak District holds a special symbolic significance among the national park family as the crucible of England's 'right to roam' movement. Today, it can be easy to take for granted our ability to freely enjoy open spaces like the moors and mountains, but this was not always the case. During the heyday of the industrial era, the big boggy moors, peaceful valleys and climbing crags of the Peak District were the closest sources of fresh air, natural beauty and adventure for workers from towns like Manchester or Sheffield. Though they were not the first to find freedom in the high places of the Pennines. The 'Brontë Country' around Haworth is to the north of the Peak District, but its moorland expanses share geological and atmospheric similarities with those of the Dark Peak. As Charlotte Brontë wrote about her sister Emily, author of *Wuthering Heights*, in 1850, 'My sister loved the moors. Flowers brighter than the rose bloomed in the blackest of the heath for her; out of a sullen hollow in a livid hill-side her mind could make an Eden. She found in the bleak solitude many and dear delights; and not the least and best loved was – liberty.'

Looking across Derwent Valley and the Ladybower Reservoir towards Win Hill, with the heather blooming at its vivid best.

But for urban visitors to the Peak District in the early 20th century, 'liberty' could be hard to find: landowners sought to manage the moors exclusively for grouse shooting, and employed men to literally beat back walkers. In April 1932 more than 400 walkers took part in a 'mass trespass' on Kinder Scout, which resulted in a brief scuffle with gamekeepers. Several of the trespassers were given jail sentences of up to six months. Speaking in his defence at his trial, trespass leader Benny Rothman said, 'We ramblers, after a hard week's work in smoky towns and cities, go out rambling for relaxation and fresh air. And we find the finest rambling country is closed to us … Our request, or demand, for access to all peaks and uncultivated moorland is nothing unreasonable.'

The imprisonment of the trespassers ultimately backfired, sparking a public outcry that galvanised the access movement. The decades that followed saw the creation of national parks, the protection of rights of way, and the major landmark of the Countryside and Rights of Way Act 2000, which allowed for the right to roam in open country.

The Kinder Trespass was by no means the first action of its kind in England, but it is the one that became the stuff of legend, inspiring campaigners to this day. For the 2022 anniversary of the Kinder Trespass, around 200 people climbed Kinder Scout in an event dubbed 'Kinder in Colour', designed to highlight the difficulties faced by people from underprivileged and minority ethnic backgrounds in accessing outdoor spaces.

The Peak District was also the birthplace of the Pennine Way. Officially opened in 1965, on another Kinder Trespass anniversary, it is Britain's first and arguably most iconic long-distance walk. The trail begins in the Peak District village of Edale and makes its way across Kinder Scout before heading north for 429 kilometres to the Scottish border. It was the brainchild of Tom Stephenson, a journalist and keen outdoor activist, who in 1935 dreamt of 'something akin to the Appalachian Trail' using the Pennines as its geographical

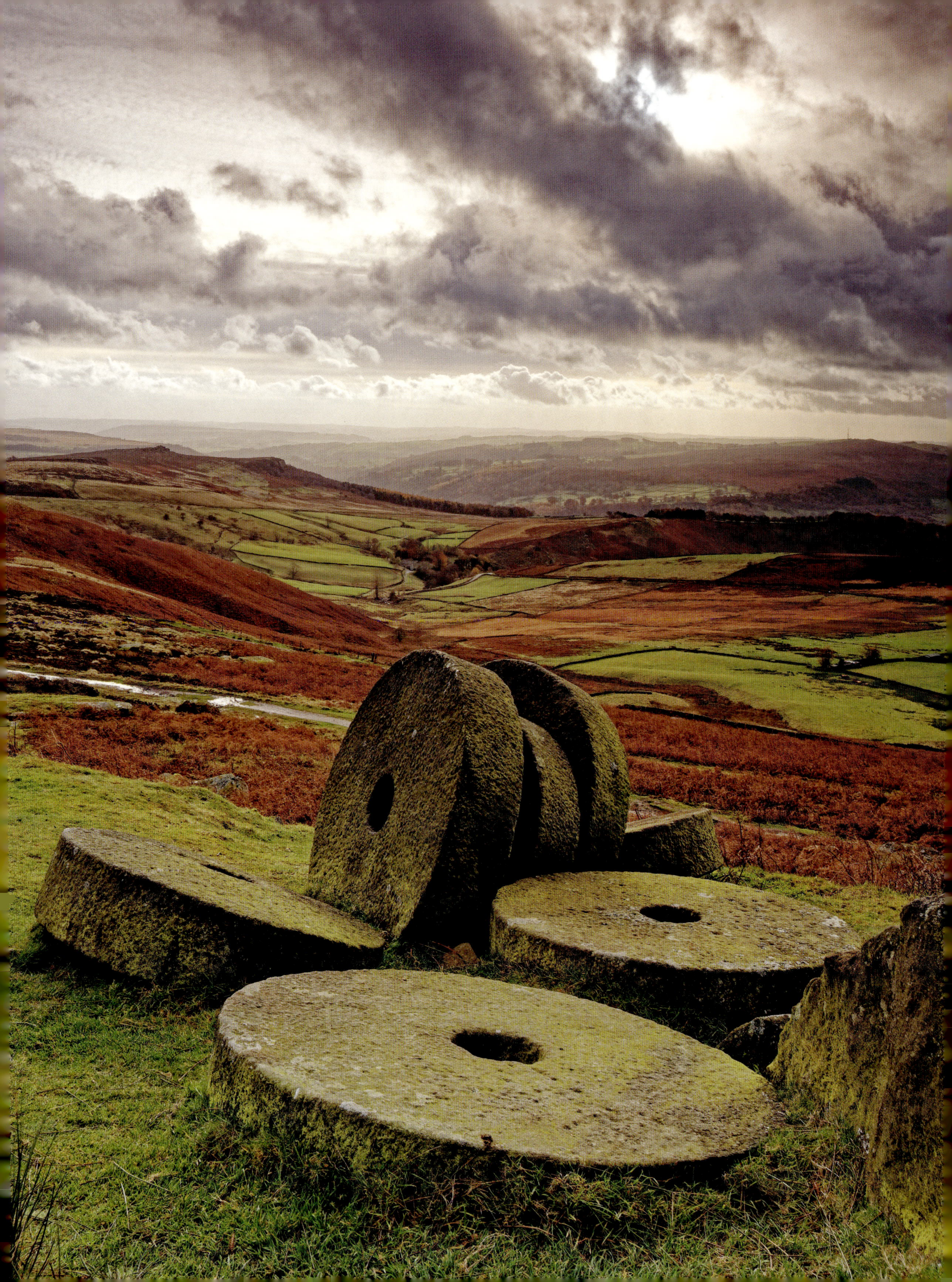

The ring ouzel ('mountain blackbird') is a member of the thrush family that breeds on crags, gullies and rocky places. Found breeding at altitudes of up to 1,200 metres (3,937 feet) in Scotland, they are generally a bird of Britain's high and remote areas and are sensitive to disturbance, but a population endures on the busy gritstone escarpments of the Peak District, thanks in no small part to a monitoring and conservation effort led by climbers.

Opposite:
For around a millennia, coarse Millstone Grit was quarried and used to grind grains like oats, rye and wheat. This economic purpose became so closely associated with the rock that its name derived from it. During the 18th and nineteenth centuries, distinctive wheel-shaped stones were used, and the rock was also used to make grindstones for sharpening metal. But swift economic changes in the late 19th century made these millstones obsolete, and many were simply abandoned where they lay, like these near Stanage Edge, despite having already been quarried and cut.

canvas – 'a Pennine Way stretching from the Peak to the Cheviots'. The trail would inscribe the right of walkers to be in the landscape through the steady drip-drip of hiking boots: Stephenson envisaged it being 'a faint line on the Ordnance Survey maps which the feet of grateful pilgrims would, with the passing years, engrave on the face of the land'.

The Peak District's location at the heart of industrial England exacted a toll on the natural fabric of the landscape. Coal-burning in the surrounding cities and atmospheric pollution from the factories, forges, potteries and mills fell as acid rain on deep peat moorlands like Kinder Scout, Bleaklow and Black Hill, denuding them of vegetation and creating bare, black morasses where the soil was as acidic as orange juice. This pollution, coupled with practices like moorland burning and draining – thought to be beneficial for agriculture and grouse production – meant that, by the latter half of the 20th century these moors became the most degraded habitat in Europe, and were infamous among walkers as arduous bog-trots, sometimes offering an experience more akin to snorkelling than walking. The celebrated guidebook author Alfred Wainwright once sank deep into peat on the appropriately named Black Hill, a moment he described as 'my most frightening experience in a long lifetime of fellwalking'.

Recent decades, though, have seen an extraordinary transformation. Thanks to extensive restoration work by the Moors for the Future Partnership, in many places where there were once desolate expanses of bare peat, now you can find thriving prairies. The likes of Black Hill are now vibrant with purple heather, yellow bog asphodel, white cotton grass and lime-bright sphagnum moss. Bilberries grow abundantly, while rarer fruiting plants like cloudberries, cranberries and cowberries are gaining a foothold. Short-eared owls hunt through the labyrinths of peat groughs; kestrels hang in updrafts; golden plovers swoop through rowdy winds in close formations; mountain hares scurry through the mossy understory; and dragonflies chase their prey above newly created

Spring scenes in the White Peak. Cow parsley, red campion and other wildflowers bloom in the meadows surrounding a limestone drystone wall near the village of Youlgreave.

Opposite:
A path descending into the Derwent Valley from Curbar Edge on a bright summer day. The Peak District contains around 3,000 kilometres (almost 1,900 miles) of paths.

Overleaf:
The Upper Derwent Valley contains a sequence of three imposing reservoirs: Howden, Derwent and Ladybower. This image shows the neo-Gothic dam wall of the first of these, which along with the neighbouring Derwent Reservoir, was built to supply water to Sheffield and to the industrial cities of the East Midlands. It was completed in 1912.

mires and pools. This thickening of natural texture makes moors like Kinder Scout enchanting places to be, but healthy moors benefit humanity in very concrete ways too: they lock up huge amounts of carbon, ameliorate the impacts of floods, improve water quality and potentially lessen the spread of wildfires.

The spirit of custodianship is evident elsewhere in the Peak District. Ring ouzels (also known as mountain blackbirds) migrate every spring from Africa to upland landscapes across Britain, including gritstone escarpments in the Peak District like Stanage Edge and Froggatt Edge. These are some of the most popular climbing venues in the world – the former alone contains 2,000 routes across its mile-long length. Yet with careful monitoring and a conservation effort led by the climbing community itself, the birds continue to breed successfully in these crowded environments.

Regeneration efforts on the moors have also been helped by path-restoration work, often supported by walkers and the outdoor community, which have sometimes seen Millstone Grit flagstones from the floors of disused mills and factories repurposed as trails. These provide a robust surface to walk across the bogs, helping to prevent erosion and allowing the moors to continue to regenerate. There is a wonderful circular symbolism in the journey of Millstone Grit from the hills to the mills and back again; from its use in the manufacturing industries, which contributed to damaging the moors, to its new vocation in service of those very places.

As with most of Britain's landscapes, there is still a long way to go along the road of natural renewal in the Peak District, but the revival of some of the most heavily damaged landscapes in the world serves as a testament to the ability of nature to rejuvenate itself, and the power of guardianship, stewardship and care.

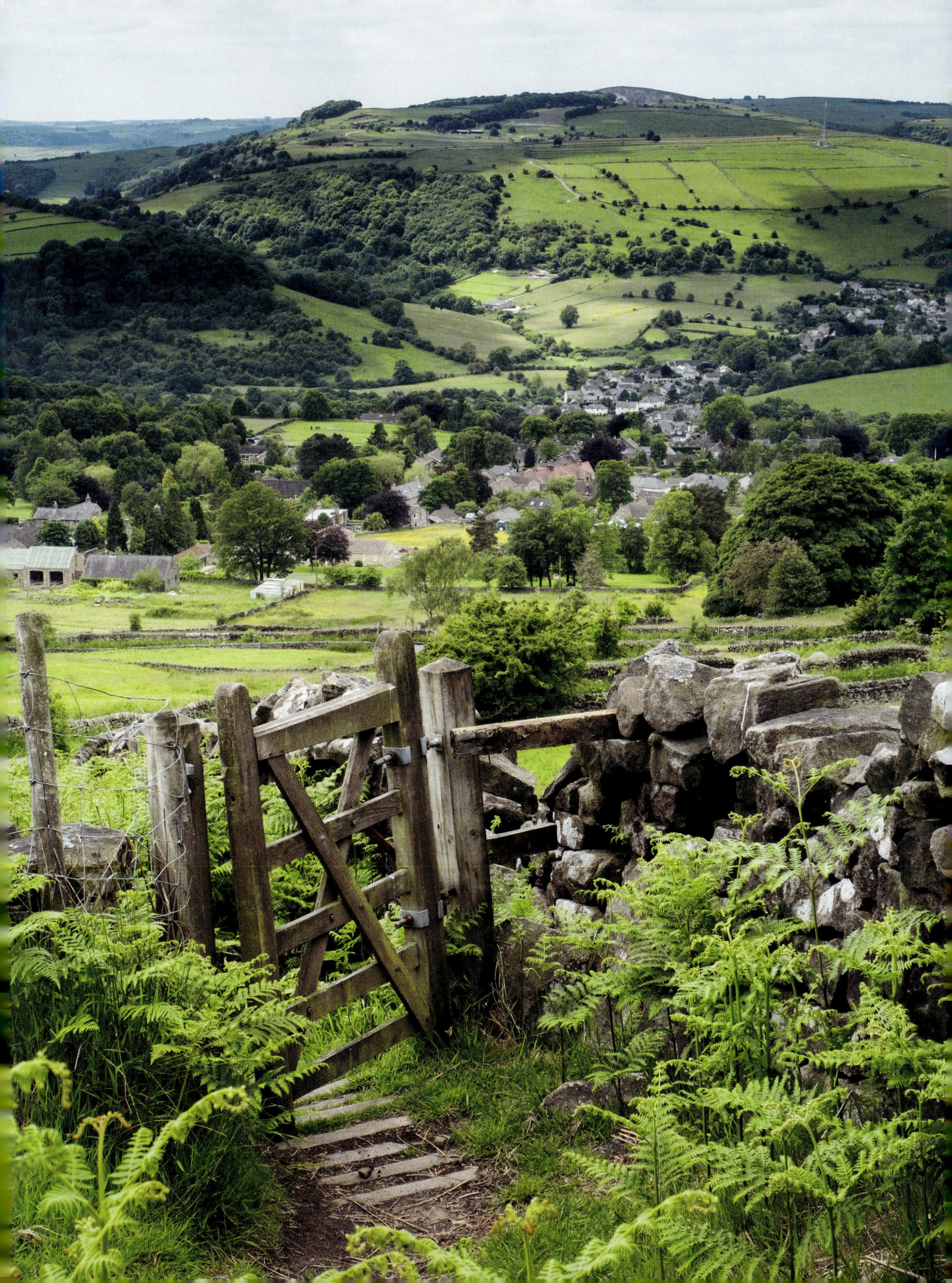

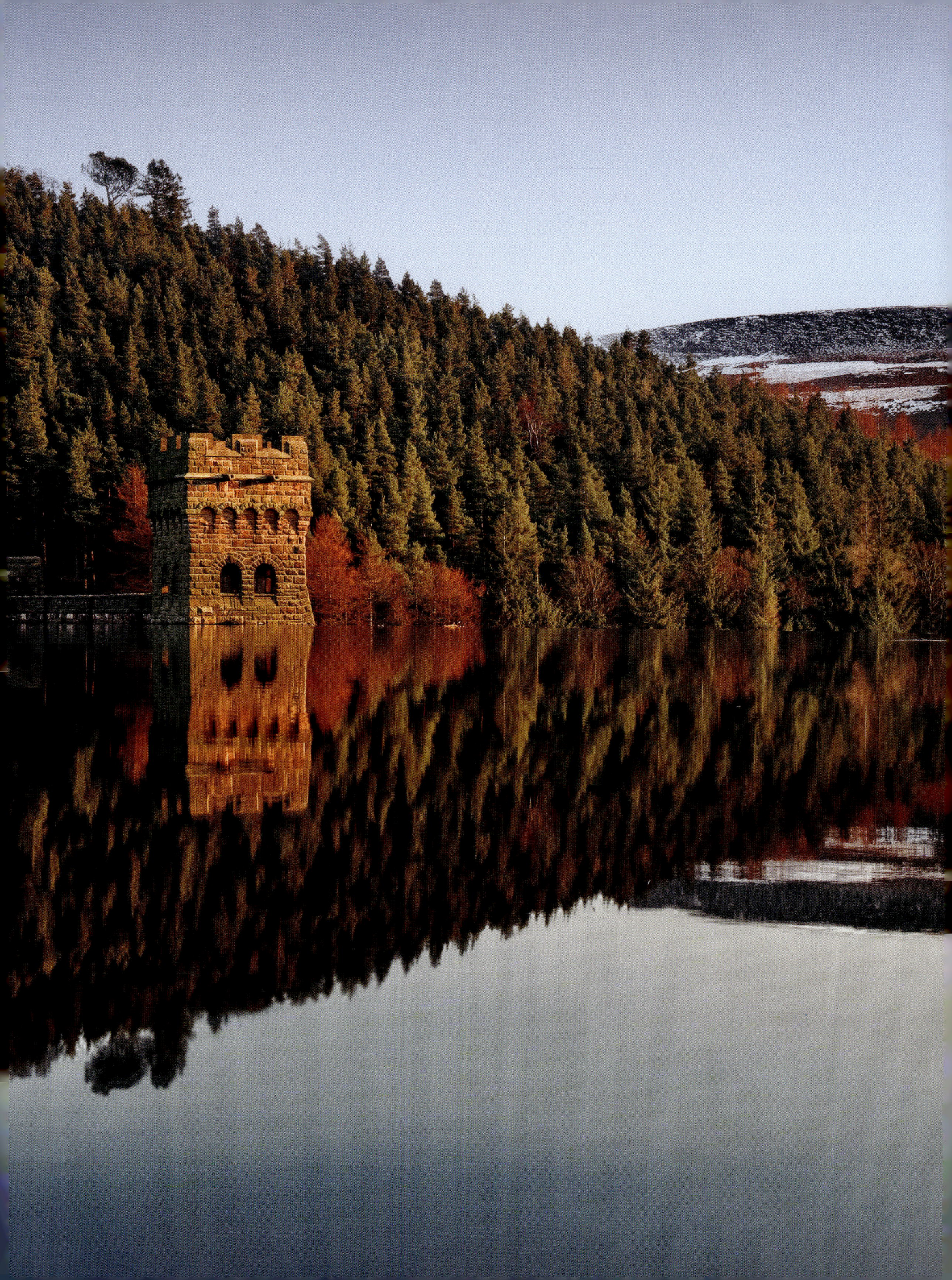

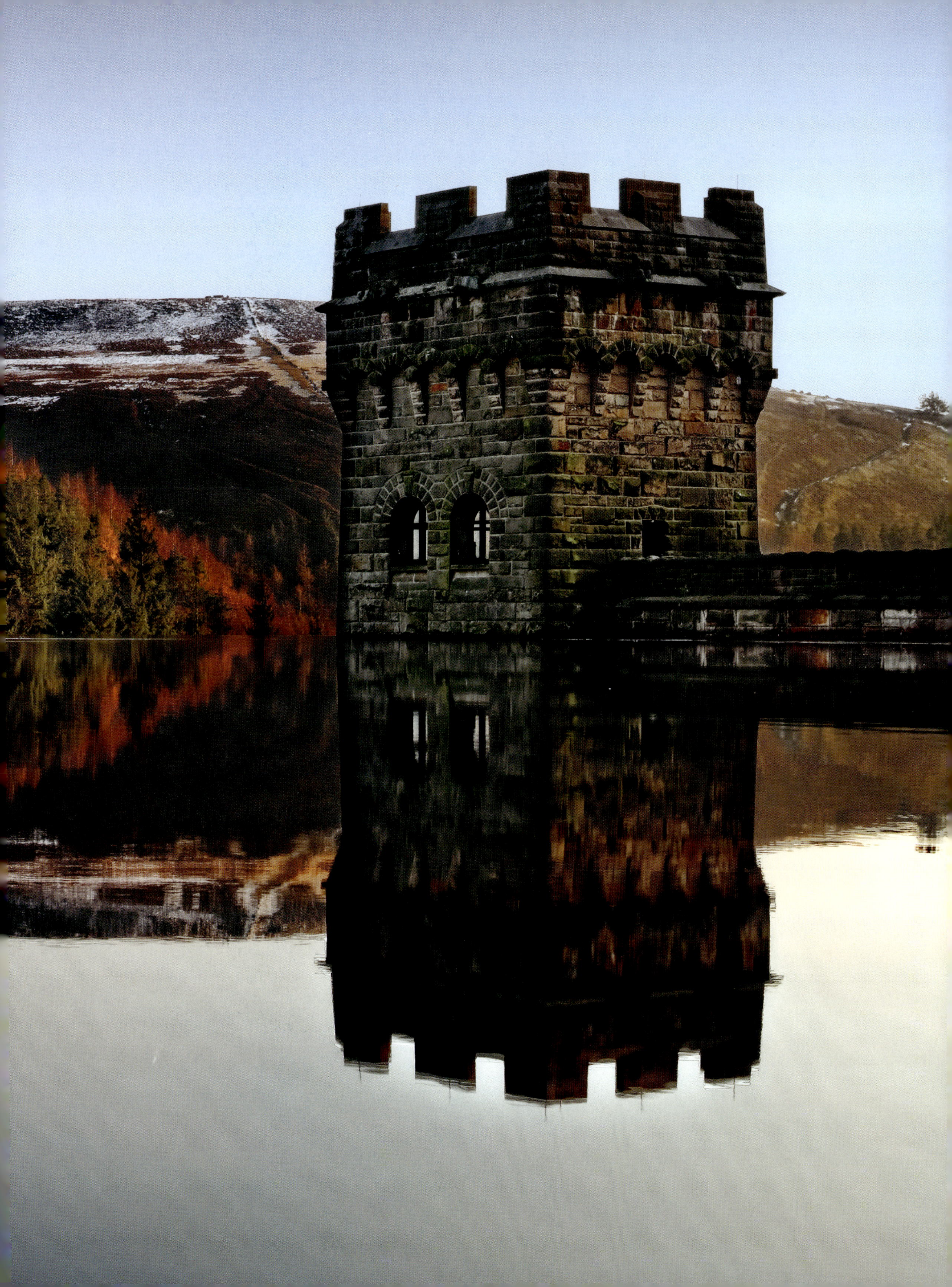

Nine Stones Close, also known as the Grey Ladies, a prehistoric stone circle in the south of the Peak District, thought to date from the late Neolithic or early Bronze Age. As with all megalithic monuments, the original function or meaning of the stone circle is unknown, but archaeologists have put forward various theories, including that it was linked to the nearby Millstone Grit rock formation known as Robin Hood's Stride.

Overleaf:
The fog of a cloud inversion fills the floors of the valleys, as seen from Curbar Edge on a winter dawn.

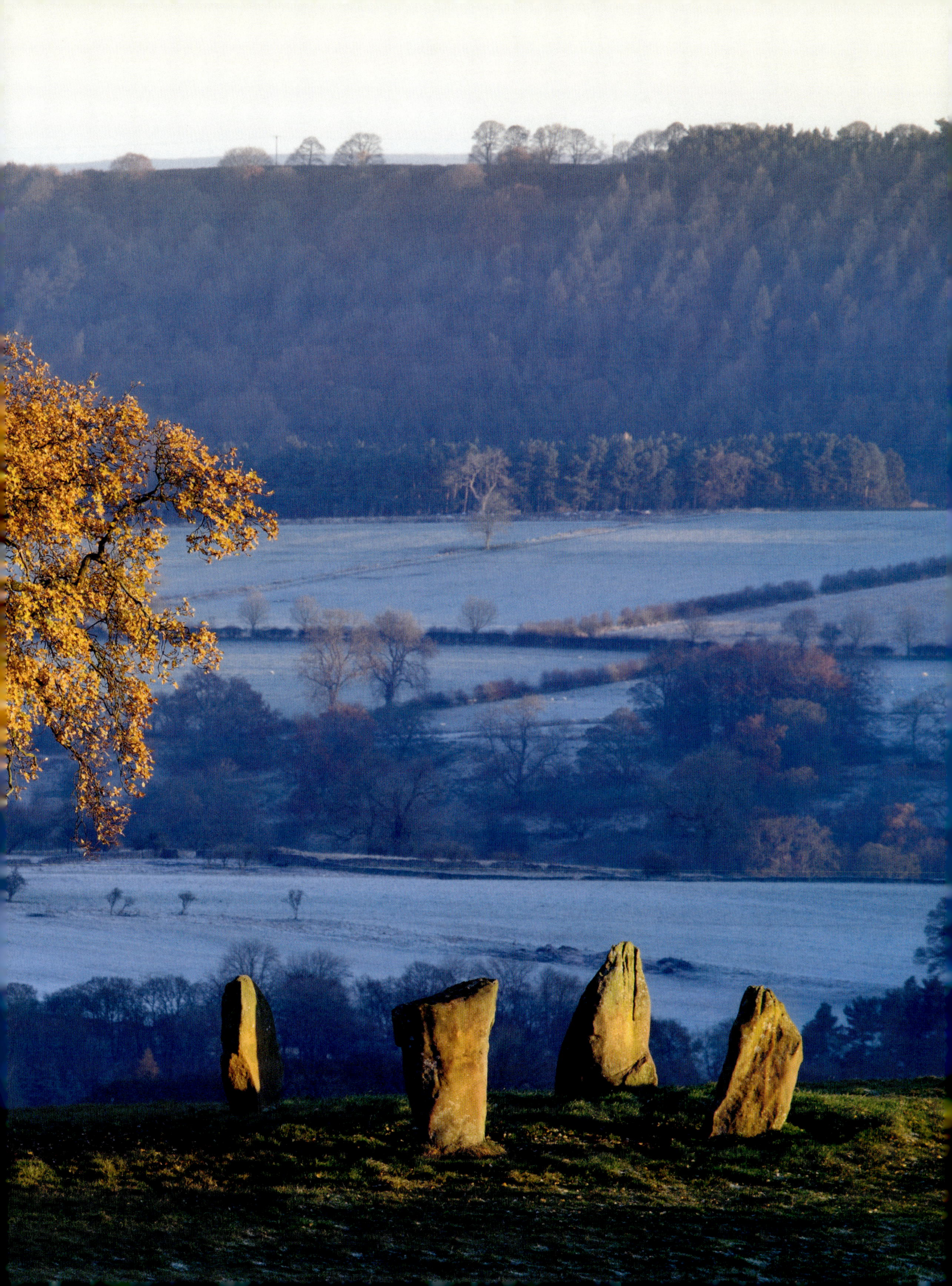

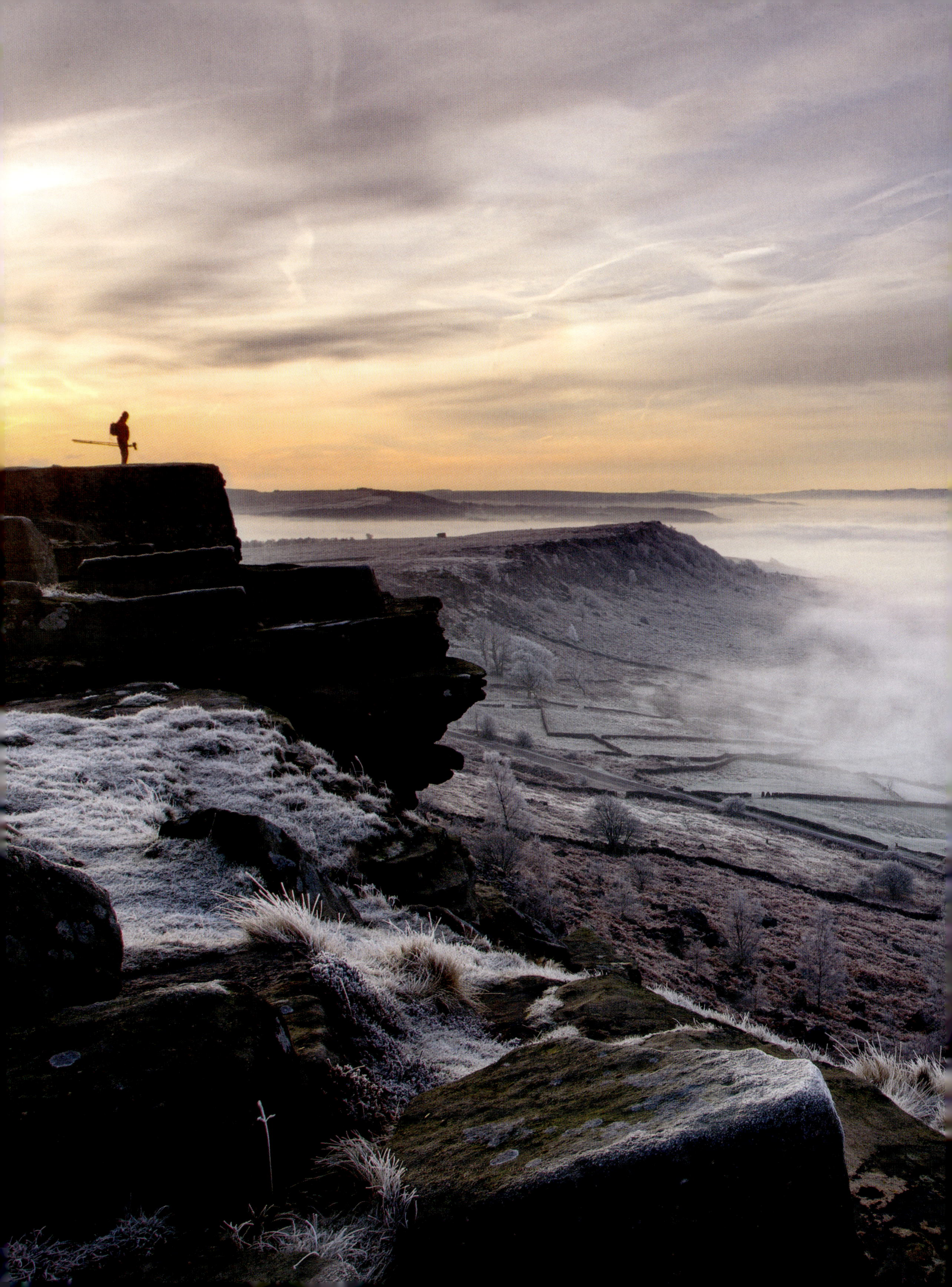

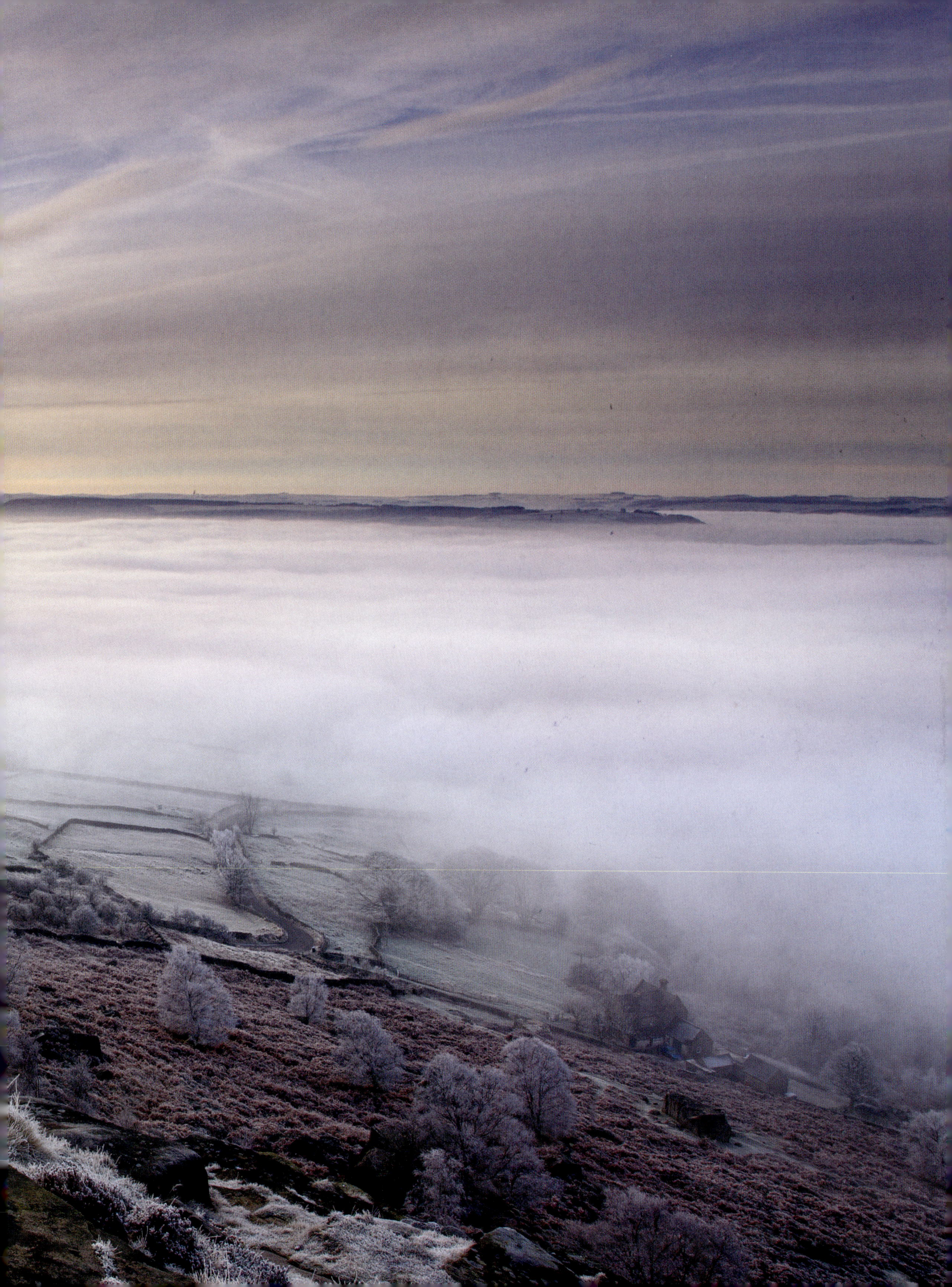

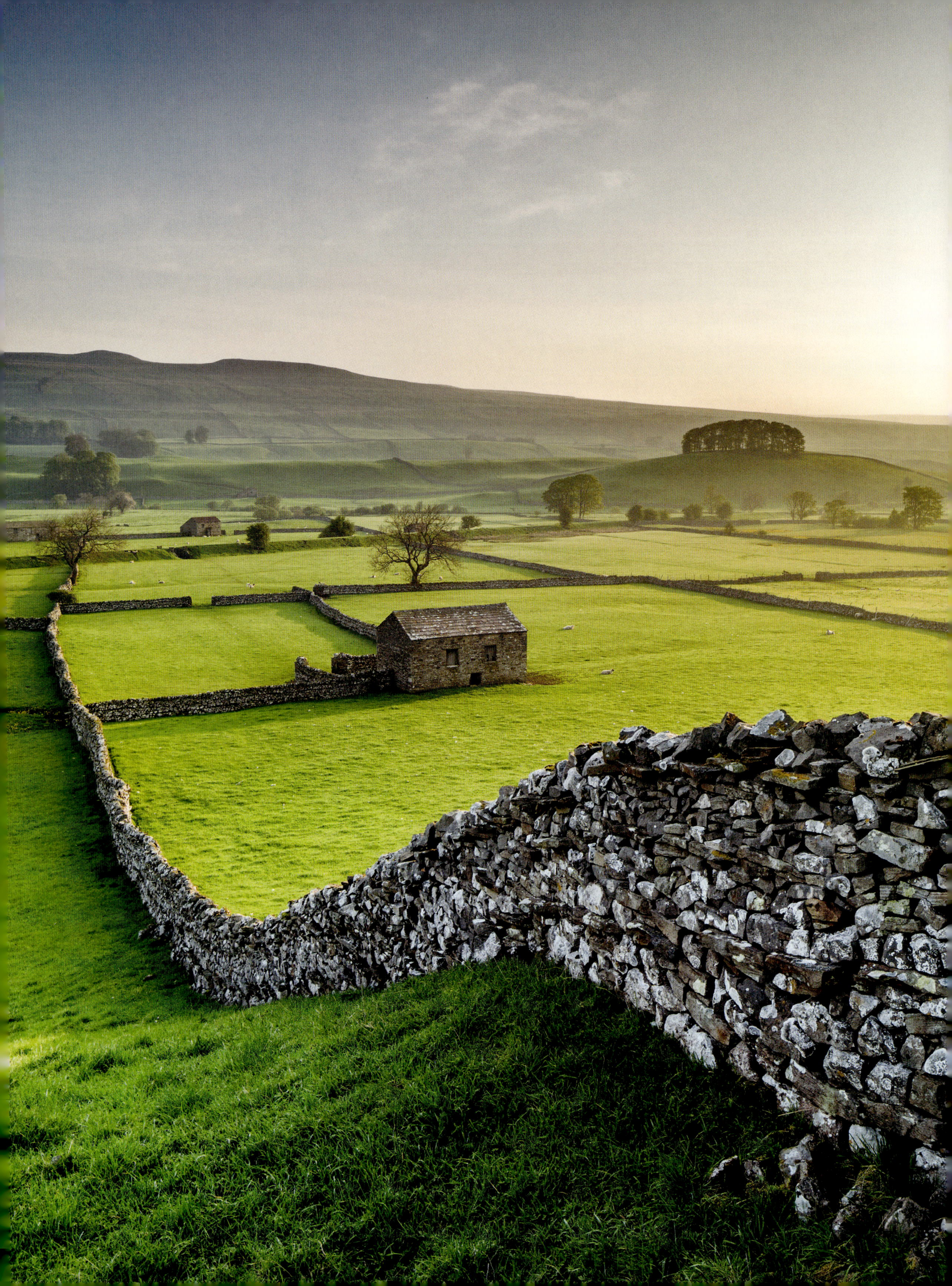

Yorkshire Dales

The story of the Great Scar limestone, the landscape-forming rock at the heart of the Yorkshire Dales National Park, is a remarkable one. Around 350 million years ago a warm tropical sea lay on a shallow ocean shelf near the equator, teeming with life, full of ocean creatures. Reefs of coral grew high, long stems of sea lilies swayed in the gentle currents and hard-shelled brachiopods thrived on the seabed.

When these shelly sea creatures died, their skeletal remains fell to the bottom of the sea and piled up in deep layers. These remains were subjected to huge pressure until they eventually lithified into rock. Bone became stone. Over many millions of years the tectonic movement of the earth caused this strata to drift around 6,500 kilometres north, and pushed it upwards. Now exposed to the earth's surface, rain and rivers carved the rock into scars, coves, gorges, ghylls and vast underground caves and conduits. Ice ages came and went; glaciers chewed out broad valleys and left fissured expanses of rock behind them. Eventually, human beings arrived, settling the land, turning its forests into pastures, and lifting the rock from the fields to use in boundaries, barns, farms and villages. The 'memory' of this rock extends through many lost worlds, from tropical seas to hostile icy wildernesses.

Despite the long migration, echoes of the life of that ancient sea are still visible in this landscape in the form of fossils, rippling beds of limestone and 'reef knolls' – hills formed from those mountains of ancient coral. Millions of years of natural processes have turned the deceased life of a tropical sea into a living landscape where trees grow and flowers bloom. When you hike across the stony expanses of the Yorkshire Dales, you are walking across a sea of bones.

The Yorkshire Dales is a region within the wider Pennine chain, but it is a world in itself. The national park is named after the glacier-gouged dales, a Norse-derived term that betrays the influence of Viking settlers on the north of England. These dales, like Wharfedale and Wensleydale, are bastions of rural Englishness with a distinctly Yorkshire flair: U-shaped valleys patchworked with drystone walls, ash woodlands, wildflower meadows and stone-built villages with rocky rivers running through them.

Here, a distinct pastoral flavour, influenced by geology, industry and sheep farming, has evolved over centuries. Although they have features in common, each dale has its own character, developed through their comparative isolation. Deep in the folds of one of these dales, supping a pint outside an isolated pub

Drystone walls are a ubiquitous feature of the Yorkshire Dales landscape, with roughly 8,000 kilometres (5,000 miles) of these painstakingly created boundaries etching the landscape into sheep pastures. Usually assembled from local rock, they are constructed purely by intelligent layering of stone, without the use of mortar, which can be challenging with irregularly shaped Carboniferous limestone. Many Dales walls are as old as 200 years, and some have origins dating back to medieval times. They can be home to some distinctive flora, like the Nowell's limestone moss, which is found at just seven sites, all in the Dales, and many on drystone walls.

A track leading from Horton-in-Ribblesdale to Pen-y-ghent, one of the famous 'Three Peaks', the others being Whernside and Ingleborough. The famous Three Peaks challenge walk is a rite of passage for hikers and hillwalkers that lassos the trio of summits together in one roughly 38-kilometre (24-mile) undertaking, with around 1,500 metres (5,000 feet) of ascent.

Native red squirrel numbers have been in drastic decline across Britain since the introduction of the grey squirrel in the early 20th century, but populations cling on in places. A protected community lives in conifer plantations in the north-west of the national park, in the Cumbrian area and around Hawes.

next to a sun-glimmered beck, you might only be an hour's drive or less from the edges of Leeds or Bradford, but it can feel much further than that.

Separating the dales are broad-backed and sometimes formidable fells, which either come in the form of long, windswept ridges like those above Wharfedale, or standalone sentinels like the Three Peaks of Pen-y-ghent (694 metres / 2,277 feet), Whernside (736 metres / 2,415 feet) and Ingleborough (723 metres / 2,372 feet). The boundaries of the national park also encompass the distinct hill groups of the Howgills – a compact range of rounded hills memorably described by author Alfred Wainwright as resembling a 'herd of sleeping elephants' – and the Orton Fells, both of which actually lie in the county of Cumbria.

What really sets this landscape apart is the underlying geology at the core of the region. Although a strong rock, limestone is soluble in water, particularly the mild acid of rainfall, and millennia of exposure to Britain's oceanic climate has sculpted the Great Scar limestone into some of the most extraordinary karstic landforms to be found in these islands. Malham Cove is an 80-metre (260-foot) overhanging crag; an echoing, upside-down amphitheatre created by an ancient waterfall that was taller than Niagara Falls. Today the cove is dry, but on extremely rare occasions a waterfall reappears over the lip of the cliff – most recently during the record-breaking rainfall of 2015's Storm Desmond. It is one of the national park's biggest tourist draws, a home for nesting peregrine falcons, and a world-class climbing venue.

The nearby Gordale Scar enjoys slightly less fame but is no less impressive: the Gordale Beck river booms through a precipitously overhung chasm via a series spectacular waterfalls tumbling over pillars of tufa (bulging, baroque limestone sculptures formed from minerals that have been deposited by the water). But some of the most immense karstic landforms in the Yorkshire Dales lurk below the surface: the cave of Gaping Gill, below Ingleborough, is one of the largest underground chambers in Britain, big enough to accommodate York Minster. With more than 2,500 known caves across the Dales, including the longest system in Britain, this is one of Britain's caving heartlands.

Back above ground, the bone-coloured limestone is ubiquitously visible in outcrops, escarpments, and most elements of the built environment, from barns to boundaries. It affects the colour palette of the landscape, lending the Yorkshire Dales a 'lighter' feel than other parts of the Pennines. In the full glare of the sun, the exposed scars of rock, weathered to a shinbone-smoothness by water and weather, shine like pearly teeth. Outside of sublime spectacles like Malham Cove and Gordale Scar, the limestone generally lends the Dales a certain sense of intimacy, a feeling of cosy seclusion created by the ghylls, gorges, hidden waterfalls, and often gentle valley topography.

The influence of limestone on the landscape goes far deeper than aesthetics and atmosphere: it also creates some of the most distinctive ecology in Britain. A particularly striking legacy of the glaciers that once scraped their long way across the land are the Yorkshire Dales' many limestone pavements. These are expanses of rock, originally exposed by the scouring action of the ice, then carved by rainwater into a criss-cross pattern of slabs and fissures – known as 'clints' and 'grykes' – which create patterns of striking uniformity, as if they were scored by a knife. Naturally out of the reach of grazing animals, these cracks and crevices create shady, sheltered nooks, sunken green mini-worlds providing a niche for a host of lime-loving plants with excellent names like green spleenwort, dog's mercury, bloody cranesbill, lily of the valley, rigid buckler fern, frog orchids and wall lettuce. Some limestone pavements with nature reserves have been entirely closed off to sheep, uncorking the habitat's full potential and giving rise to rich, rocky woodlands. In Europe, limestone pavements are only found in great quantity in Britain, Ireland and Scandinavia, and the Yorkshire Dales National Park hosts half of those in Britain.

With their 'space invader' calls and barrelling mating displays in the breeding season, northern lapwings are one of Britain's most eccentric and entertaining birds. Lapwings have experienced drastic declines with the rise of intensive farming, but the Yorkshire Dales holds internationally important populations of this wading bird, and they are often seen on high rough pastures and moors.

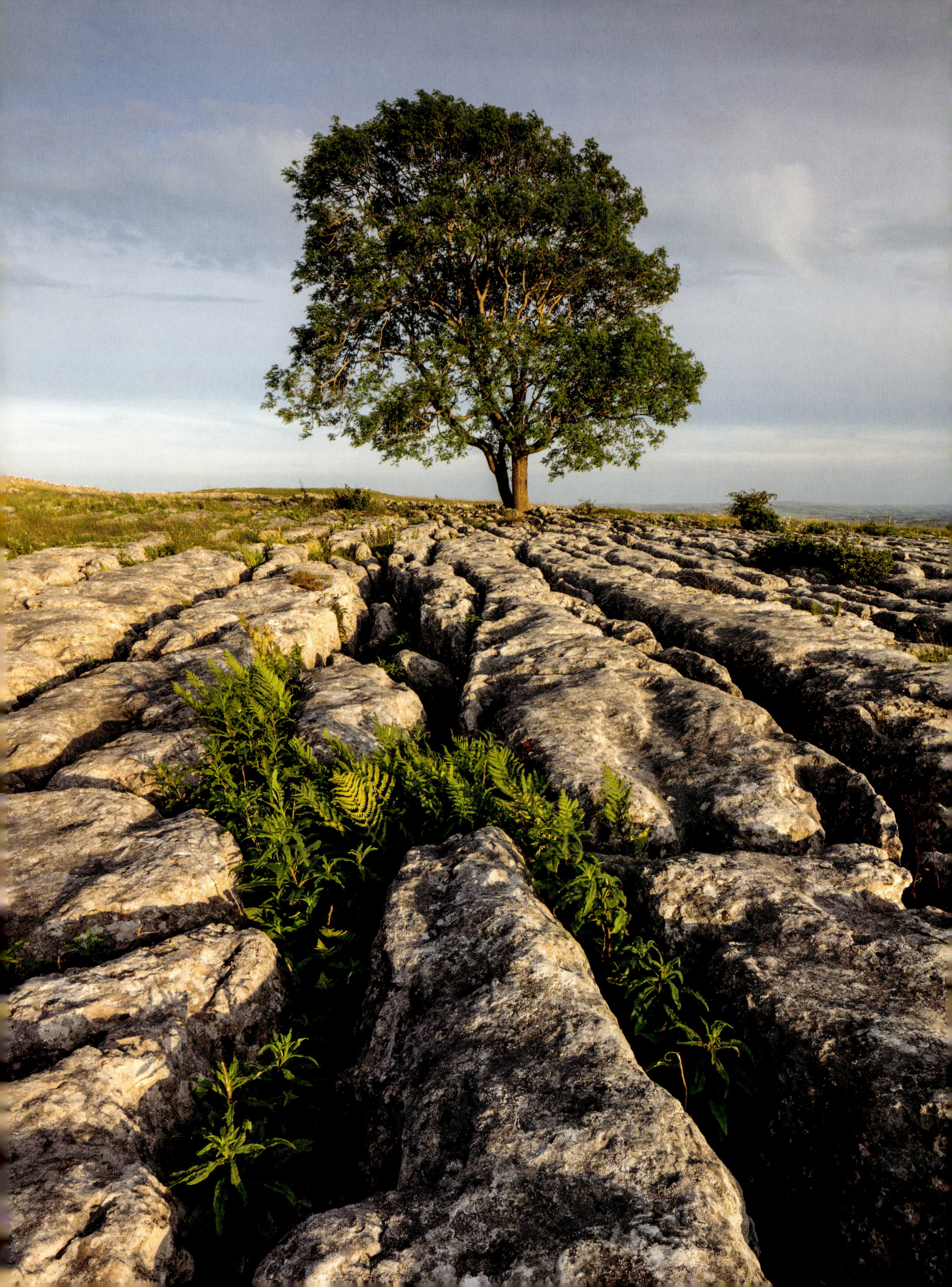

More botanical riches can be found in the pockets of ancient ash woodland across the Dales, like the woods of Bastow and Oxenber. The lime-rich soils, coupled with the local climate, give them a very different feel to the oak woods typical of the English countryside. Ash is the climax vegetation here, and its tendency to come into leaf late in the season, coupled with the higher altitude, allows for long-lasting and spectacular displays of ground flora in spring, when these exquisite woods can have the feel of wild gardens. The rocky, mossy forest floors become confettied with the flowering colours of purple thyme, wild white strawberries, pink campion, blue bugle flowers and the maroon blooms of water avens, all flooded with the particular lemon-and-lime light produced by sunlight diffusing through an ash canopy. Sadly, however, the spread of ash dieback disease has taken its toll on these high ash woods, and their future is uncertain.

With contours carved by a glacier, the classic U-shaped valley of Upper Wharfedale is dotted with ash woodlands and striated with drystone walls.

Opposite:
Lime-loving plants sprout from the clints and grykes of limestone pavement near Malham.

As beautiful as the woodlands of the Yorkshire Dales are, they are not typical of the wider landscape. Like much of Britain's highlands, the moors and fells were denuded of their original forest cover thousands of years ago, creating the conditions for the formation of deep peat bogs – in places 6 metres (20 feet) deep – and providing the foundation for a typical upland habitat that is home to quintessential birds of the moor such as the golden plover, curlew, snipe, skylark and – if you are lucky – the merlin, Britain's smallest bird of prey.

Primrose flowers carpet the ground in an ash woodland.

Grouse shooting is extensively practised on some moorland areas, entailing controversial practices like heather burning. Walking on the moors, you are also likely to encounter relics of the region's industrial past: abandoned haulage, disused mine workings and crumbling chimneys, the wreckage of a lead-mining industry that was once a significant part of the local economy. Yarnbury in Wharfedale and Gunnerside Gill in Swaledale are particularly vivid examples. Above all, though, the Yorkshire Dales are defined by sheep farming. The ancestors of the black-faced Swaledale sheep were originally brought over by the Vikings, but sheep became the mainstay of Yorkshire's economy during

The market town of Hawes is a tourist hub, and a major producer of the much-loved Wensleydale cheese.

The exquisite lady's slipper orchid was declared nationally extinct in 1917, but 13 years later a single survivor was found in in the Yorkshire Dales. The secret site has been guarded or monitored since, and the plant has been reintroduced to various locations in northern England.

Opposite:
Formed by a waterfall that would have been higher than Niagara, the echoing crag of Malham Cove is a major natural attraction and a world-class climbing venue.

Overleaf:
The Yorkshire Dales landscape is scattered with more than 6,000 traditional field barns, like those shown here amid the wildflower-rich hay meadows of Swaledale. They were used to store hay and shelter cows over winter, with muck from the cows then being used to fertilise the surrounding meadows.

the medieval heyday of the Cistercian and Augustinian monasteries. Within the national park, the beautiful remains of one of these, Bolton Priory, stand picturesquely on the bend of a curve in the River Wharfe.

The Industrial Revolution and the demand for wool to feed the textile industry in Yorkshire's towns and cities helped to sustain and expand sheep farming in the Dales, but in more recent times, changes in agriculture and the economy have undermined the viability of the industry. Even so, it remains alive, and the ways in which it has shaped the region are immediately apparent to any visitor. There are around 600,000 sheep in the Dales; roughly 8,000 kilometres (5,000 miles) of drystone walls crosshatch the valleys into pastures; and farmsteads and field barns cover the landscape. The traditional architecture associated with sheep farming is a spectacle in itself; Carboniferous limestone comes from the ground in irregular chunks, which cannot easily be chipped into regular shapes by a hammer, and the resulting drystone walls are completed puzzles that testify to the skill and creativity of the builder.

The farming heritage of the Yorkshire Dales is also connected with some of its most important botanical treasures: its wildflower-rich, traditionally-managed hay meadows, a host of which have been restored in recent years with the help of agri-environment schemes. In places like Swaledale and Langstrothdale, many thousands of wildflowers fill the fields with dense constellations of colour in spring and early summer – as many as 50 different species can be found in a single square metre in some places.

In the poem 'In Praise of Limestone', Yorkshire-born W. H. Auden implies that he imagines heaven to be a limestone landscape. The Yorkshire Dales at it's beautiful flowering best serves as a vivid reminder of the cyclical essence of life, and the strangeness and wonder of nature.

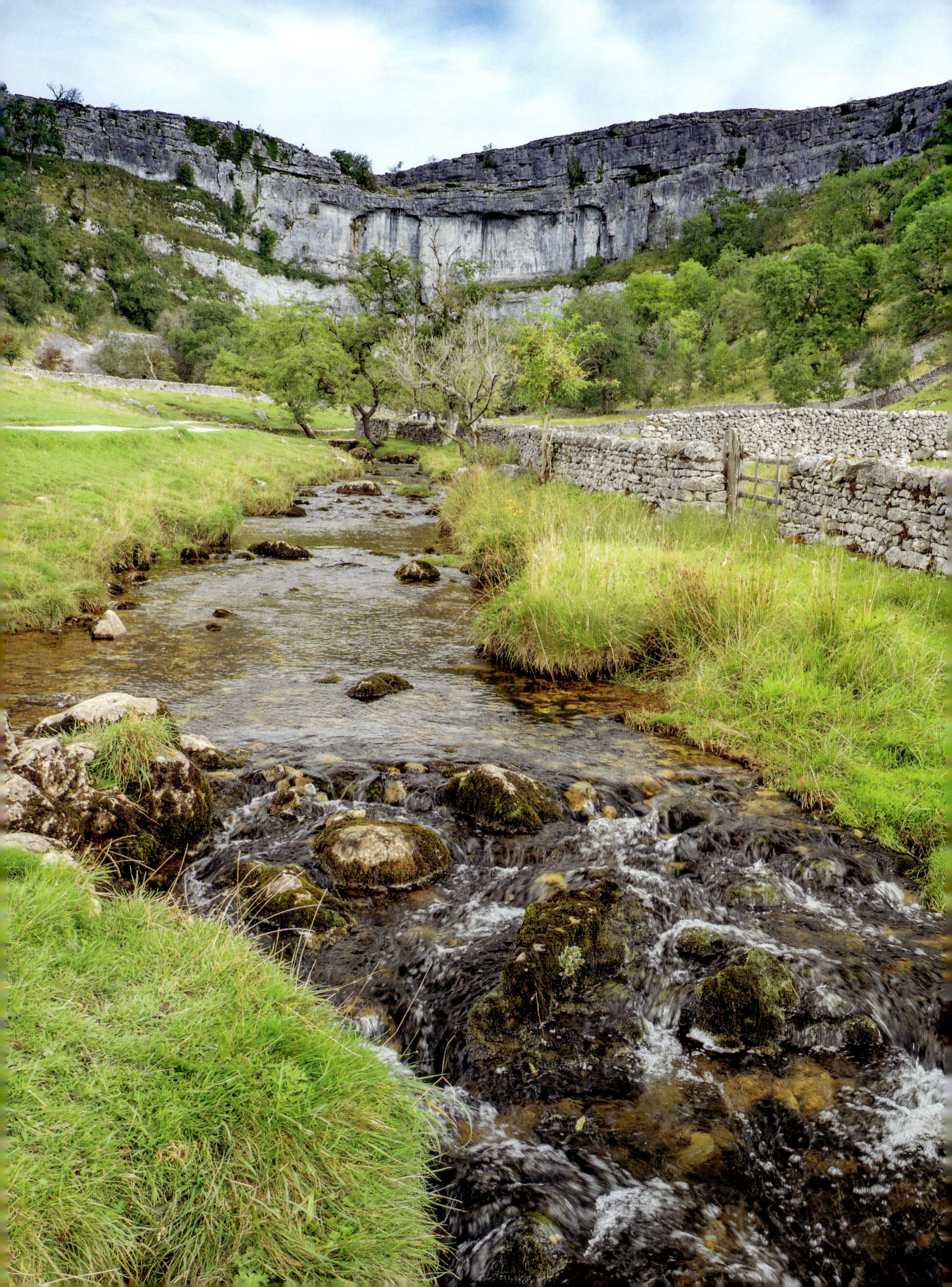

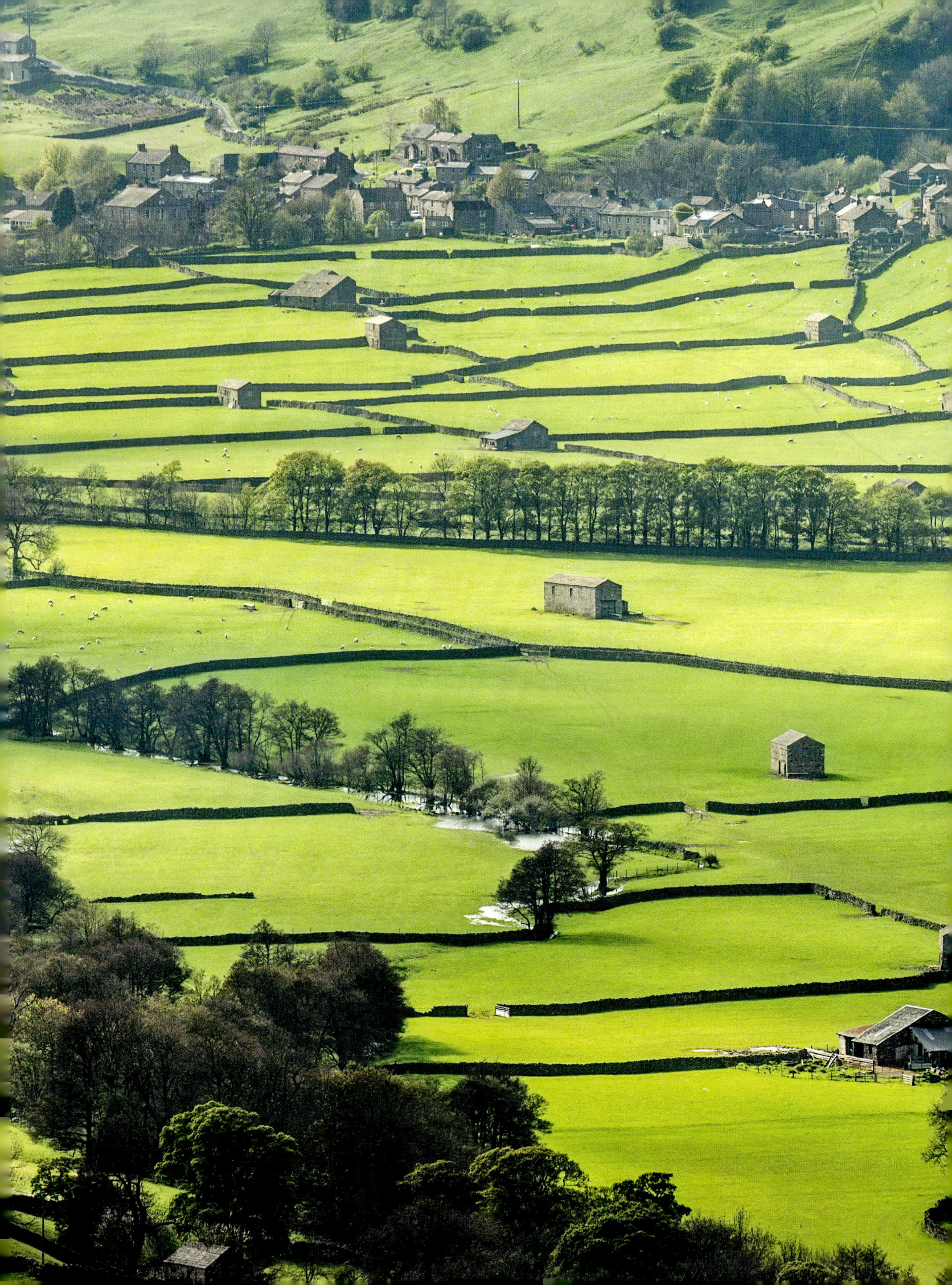

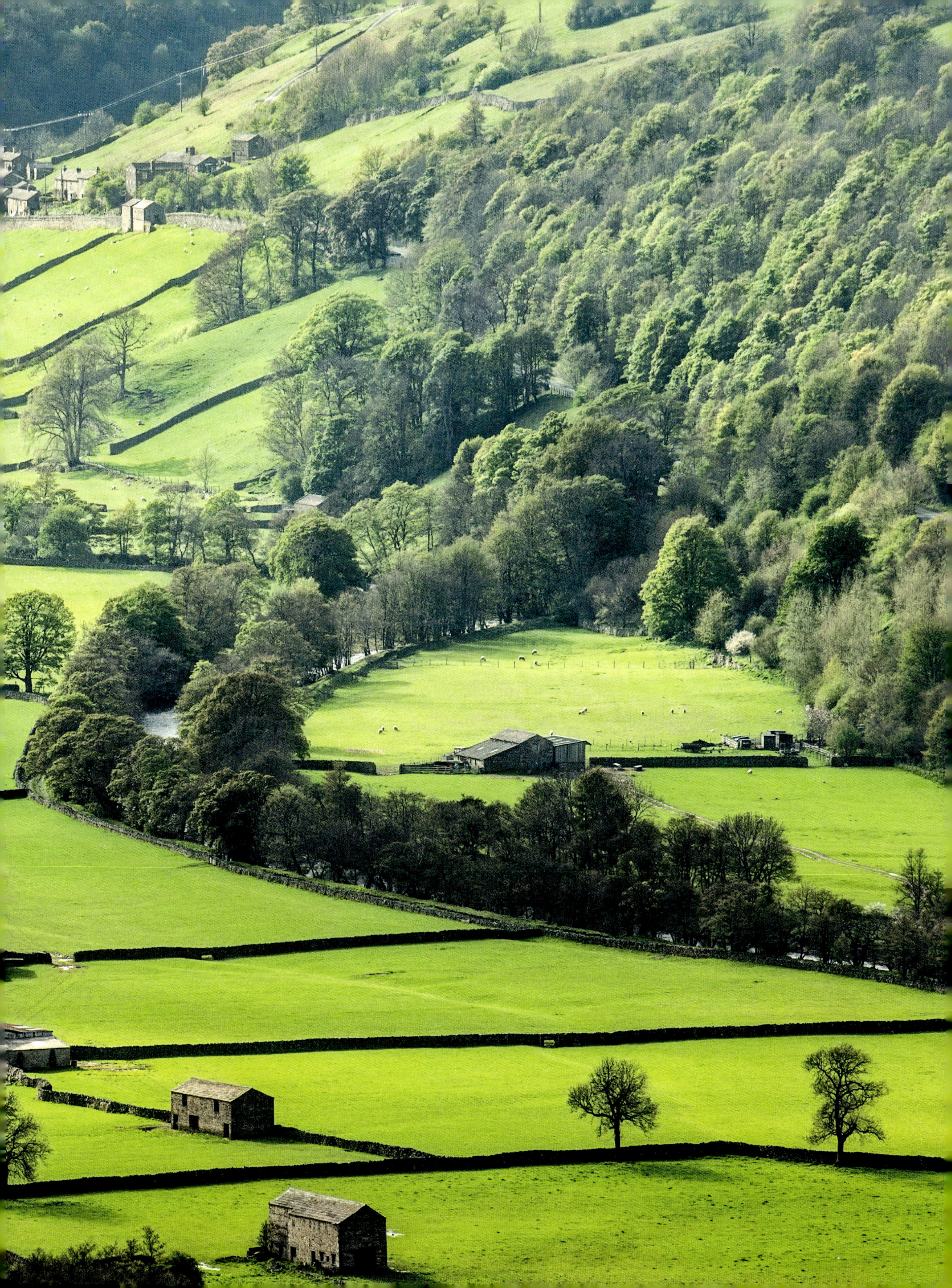

The River Ure cascades over a series of limestone steps at Aysgarth Falls in Wensleydale, a sequence of three waterfalls spread over two kilometres. Rhapsodised over by Romantics and featured in films, they are a popular visitor attraction.

Overleaf:
Situated in the sparse upper reaches of Ribblesdale, spanning the valley between Ingleborough and Whernside, the Ribblehead Viaduct is one of the most impressive Victorian artefacts of England's north. Finished in 1874, it was constructed by the Midland Railway as part of the 117-kilometre (73-mile) Settle to Carlisle line, which cuts through some of the most imposing terrain of the Dales and is still an active railway. The viaduct was built over four years by a workforce of thousands of navvies, hundreds of whom lost their lives to accidents, fights and smallpox outbreaks in the shanty towns that sprung up at the viaduct's base.

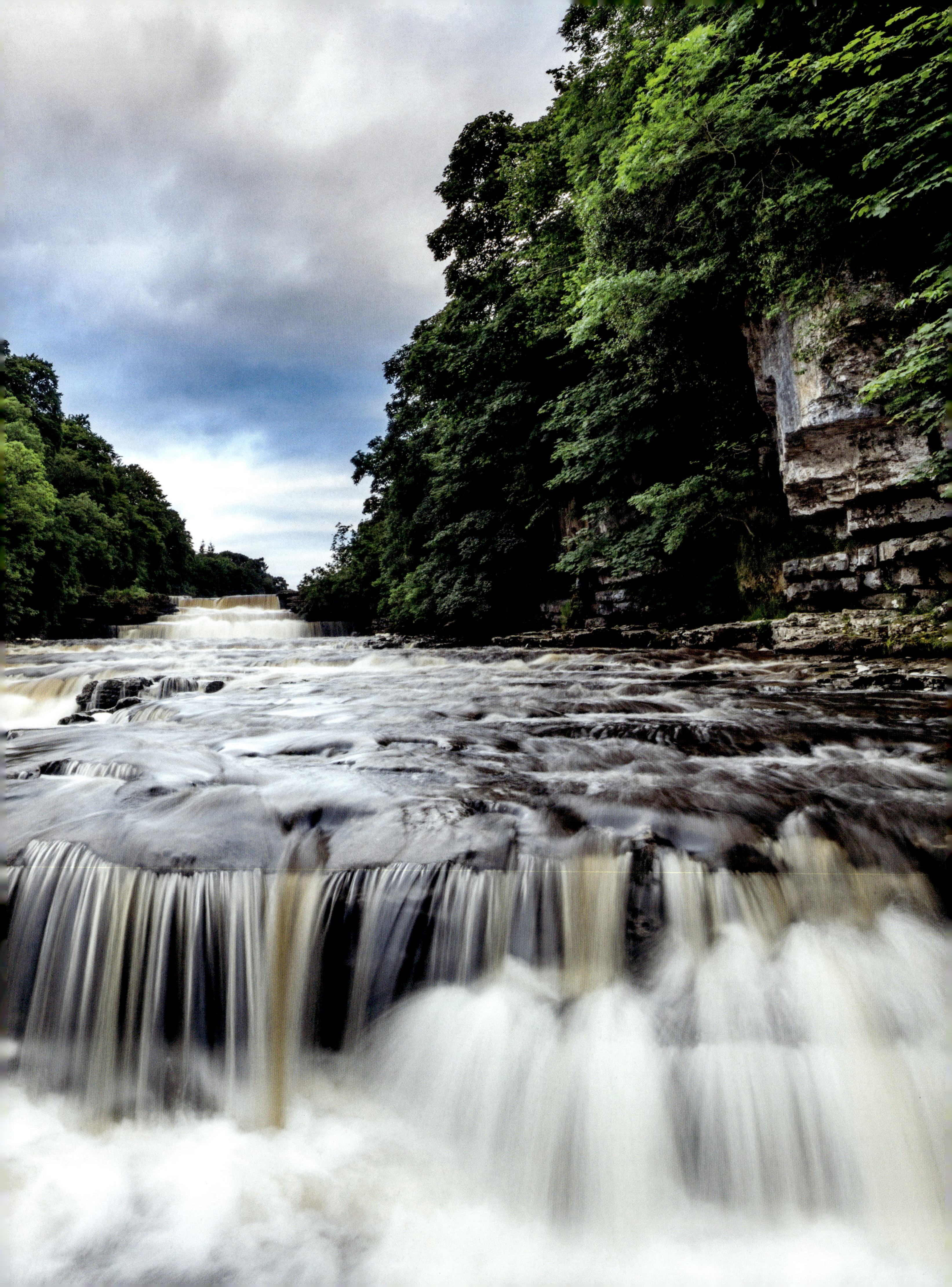

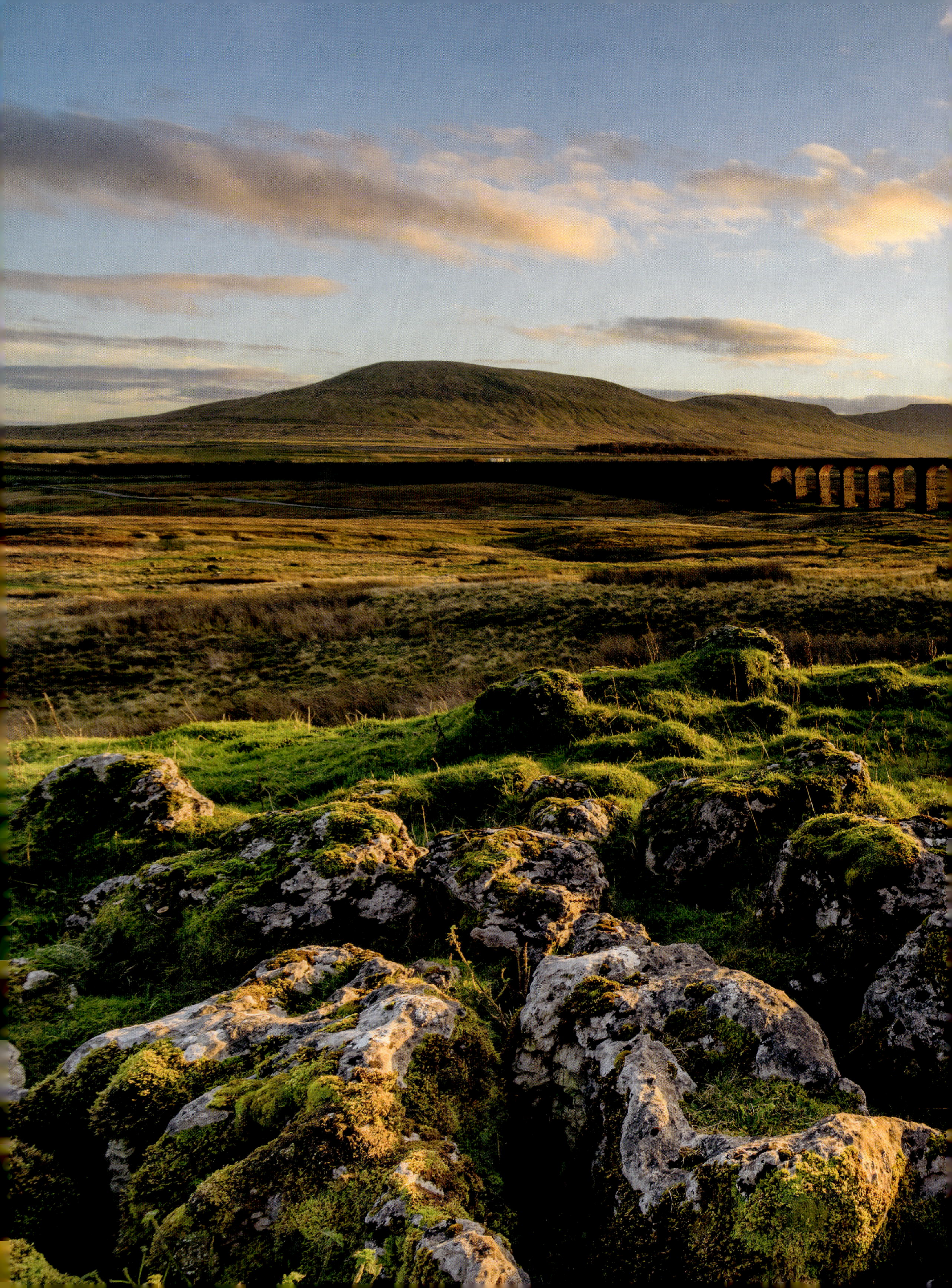

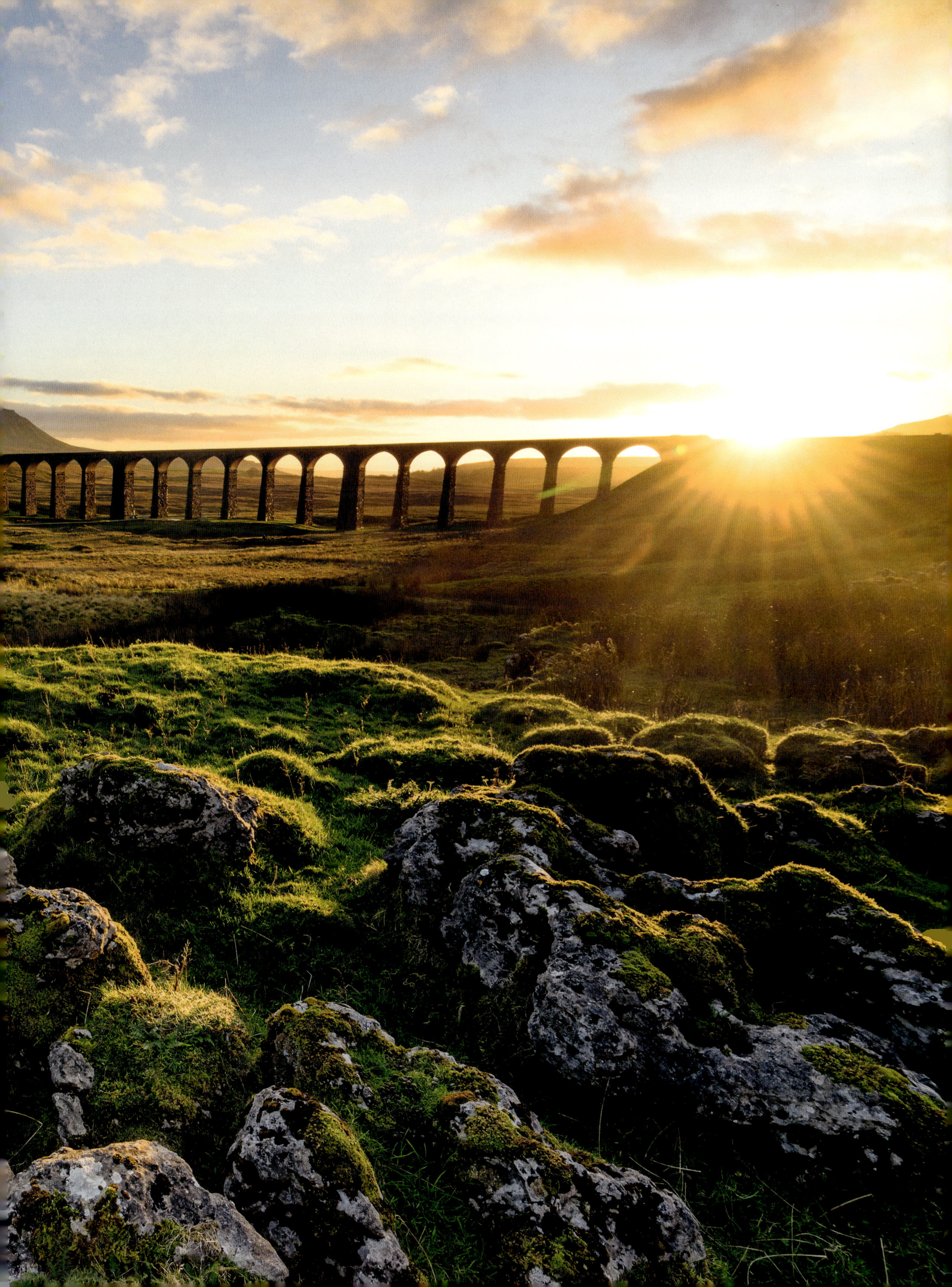

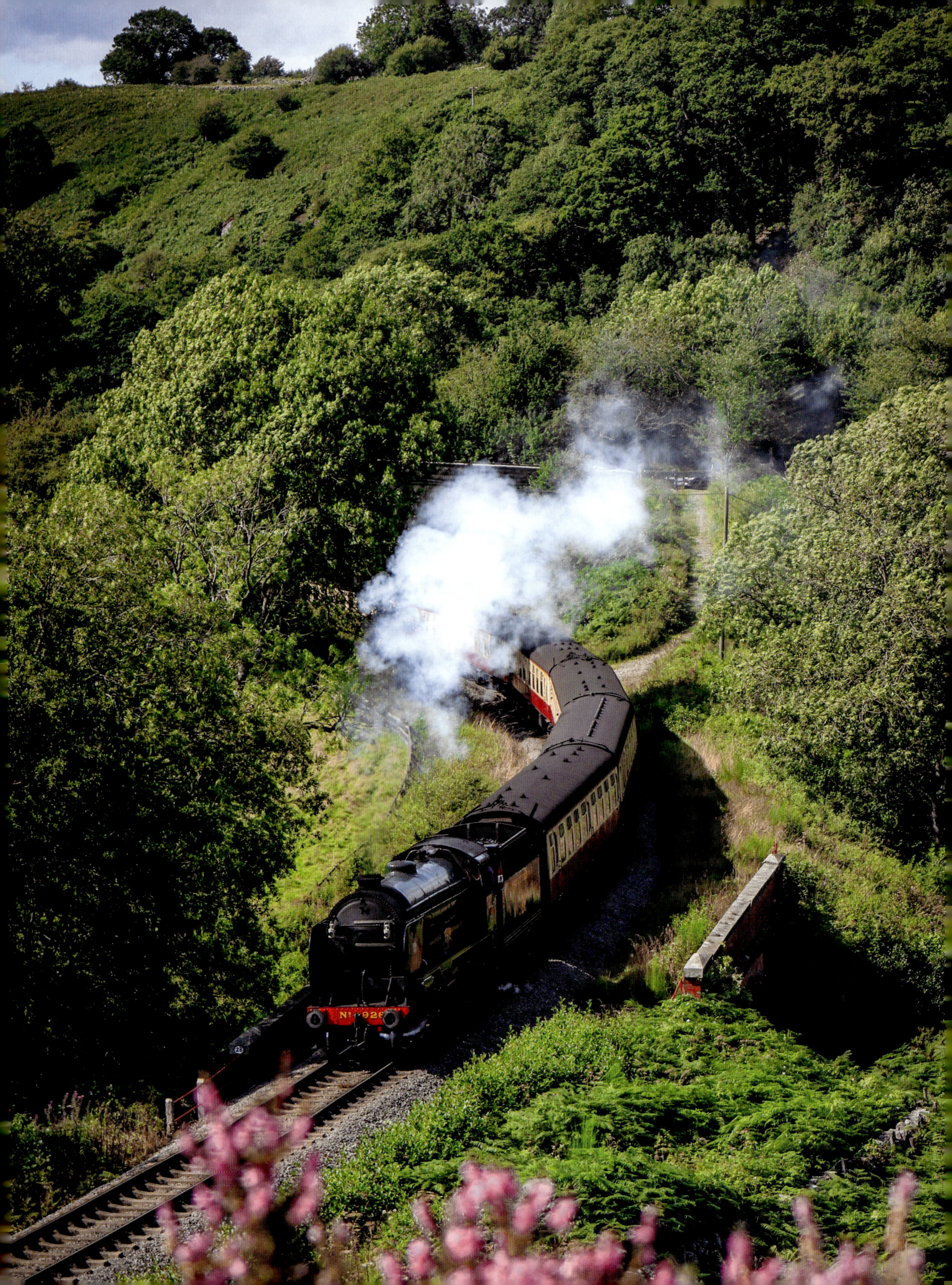

North York Moors

The sound of the approaching beast comes rolling and ricocheting through the quiet valley, bouncing around the sinuous walls of the gorge. The noise builds, until finally its source powers around the bend in all its glory: an old-fashioned steam-powered train with pistons pumping, drive rods churning and a chimney billowing steam, a living relic of the Industrial Revolution chuntering through the otherwise gentle countryside of the North York Moors.

Past and present can become blurred together in the North York Moors, as can the worlds of reality and fiction. Take a visit to the immaculate 1920s-style train station of Goathland on a sunny Saturday in summer, for instance, and you will find the platform guards of the North Yorkshire Moors Railway wearing waistcoats and pocket whistles, and *Harry Potter* fans enjoying guided tours of the place used as the filming location for Hogsmeade Station, the last stop on the line for the *Hogwarts Express*. When darkness descends and the day-trippers have gone, the lack of glaring street lighting means you can see the Milky Way vaulting across the night sky, a rare sight in most of England. It is easy to imagine you have slipped through a portal into a place that is not quite on the same timeline as the rest of the world.

It is not hard to see what draws film crews from the big and small screen to the North York Moors. Here you will find an antique, chocolate-box version of England, with a distinctly Yorkshire flavour: immaculately preserved red-roofed hamlets huddled around well-kept greens; picturesque remnants of monasteries and castles nestled next to winding rivers; and coastal villages impressively shoehorned into cliffs and coves, with the vinegary tang of fish and chips filling their narrow streets. If you're looking for a dose of cosy nostalgia, there are few better places to find it.

But this landscape has its fair share of ruggedness too, particularly on the upland expanses from which the national park takes its name. Heather moorland covers one-third of the national park, one of the largest single areas of this habitat in England and Wales. Those sprawling moors offer miles and miles of bracing hiking or biking under big open skies, and in August or early September, when the heather blooms, they become a rolling sea of purple stretching from horizon to horizon. Becks and streams burble up from the moorland, tumble down into the dales and spill over waterfalls as they cascade through ancient woodlands, finally becoming wildlife-rich rivers before eventually meeting the North Sea.

A stream locomotive puffs along the North Yorkshire Moors Railway near Goathland. The line was originally built in the 1830s to open trade routes inland to the then-significant seaport of Whitby. It was rescued from complete closure in the 1970s by a charitable trust and is now Britain's most popular heritage railway, carrying 350,000 passengers a year. The line follows a route from Whitby to Pickering through the sinuous curves of Newtondale, a valley carved by glacial meltwater as the last ice age ended.

There are 161 standing stones dotted across the North York Moors, 129 of which are thought to have been erected by prehistoric peoples. The significance of these mini-monuments is debated: they may have been memorials, territory markers or simply orientating landmarks.

The antique-looking Goathland railway station serves as the fictional stations of Aidensfield in the Heartbeat *TV series and Hogsmeade in the* Harry Potter *movies.*

The origins of this landscape lie between about 200 to 150 million years ago, in the Jurassic era. What would become the rock strata forming the landscape today were deposited as layers of sediment in subtropical oceans. This created several distinct rock types, which were tilted on their side about 30 million years ago by tectonic forces. Each now outcrops at the surface in roughly chronological order, from north to south. This makes the North York Moors a good example of how the underlying geology of a place shapes its landscape, its life, its agriculture and industry, and even its culture.

If you were to walk over a few days from north to south across this national park, which is about the size of Greater London, you would cross distinctly different landscapes as the geology underfoot changes. In the northern and central part of the region, sandstones, shales and ironstones dominate, creating a landscape of high, largely heather-covered boggy moors, such as the Cleveland Hills, incised by valleys covered in a patchwork of sheep pasture and woodland.

Although much of the high expanses of the North York Moors are managed for grouse shooting, the moors and their margins can support a variety of birdlife besides the ubiquitous red grouse. On Rosedale Moor, in the spring breeding season, the bubbling calls of curlew will float on the air, lapwings will barrel around performing mating displays, tight formations of golden plover will swing through the sky, and ring ouzels fresh from their migratory journeys from North Africa will be nesting in the rocky escarpments fringing the moorland edges. If you're lucky, you might also spot wheatear or merlin, or hear the increasingly rare but unmistakeable sound of a cuckoo.

The geology here has also played its role in Britain's Industrial Revolution: Rosedale is home to the remnants of a once-extensive ironstone mining industry, which at its height in the mid-19th century produced more than 2,000 tonnes of iron ore a week and supported a community of almost 3,000 people.

Production ceased in 1926, but the imprint of the industry remains in the form of atmospheric ruins and legacies that have come to benefit people and wildlife: the route of the old Rosedale railway is now an accessible, stile-free trail around the valley, while disused quarries, cuttings and other remnants of the iron industry provide more than half of the locations chosen as nesting sites by the local population of ring ouzels.

The southern part of the national park is underlain by a belt of limestone, which lends a different topography, texture and atmosphere to the landscape. There is a sense of lushness which is often a feature of limestone landscapes: rich alkaline soils allow for arable as well as livestock farming, while the woodland floors, grasslands and field margins can be vibrant in spring with characteristic limestone flora – including 21 species of orchid – and support rare butterflies.

The Tabular Hills, as the name suggests, are broad, almost flat-topped plateaus, split by winding, often beautifully verdant river valleys. Some of these, like Newtondale, which the North Yorkshire Moors Railway runs through, and the Forge Valley, are the spectacular legacy of the last ice age, created when torrents of glacial meltwater had their way to the North Sea blocked by ice sheets, and instead surged south, gouging through the permeable rock to create steep-sided gorges that twist through the landscape for around 32 kilometres (20 miles). The view from the wooded inland cliff of Sutton Bank, with endless miles of English countryside stretching out into the far distance, was described by James Herriot, veterinarian and author of the memoir *All Creatures Great and Small*, as the finest view in England. Looking out from here on a sunny afternoon in August, with the landscape maturing into its late summer palette of deep green and straw-coloured yellow, it certainly is impressive.

Despite its title, the North York Moors National Park is one of the most sylvan of all Britain's national parks – around 23 per cent of the landscape is

A red grouse among flowering heather. Although a native bird, red grouse numbers are maximised for grouse shooting on parts of the North York Moors, which entails habitat engineering like moorland burning and predator control. The environmental impact of the grouse shooting industry has been the subject of heated debate in recent years.

In March and April the fields and woods of Farndale are carpeted with the yellow blooms of wild daffodils. These wild plants are typically smaller than cultivated varieties of daffodil, and the 'trumpets' of their flowers are darker than the surrounding petals. Once abundant in these islands, they can now be found in only a handful of places across the British Isles.

Opposite:
The tallest waterfall in the North York Moors, the 20 metre-high (66 feet-high) Mallyan Spout tumbles into a steep-sided sandstone ravine lined with lush mixed broadleaf woods near Goathland. It has been a popular tourist attraction since at least Victorian times.

woodland, and while much of this is comprised of conifer plantations created as a timber resource in the 20th century, the park contains one of northern England's largest concentrations of veteran trees. This is perhaps particularly evident in and around Eskdale, where corridors of ancient woodland often line the sides of rivers and streams. Wander through these woods in spring and early summer and you will find bluebells, yellow archangel and wild daffodils carpeting the ground. Beautiful woodland waterfalls like Thomason Foss, Falling Foss and Mallyan Spout feel like something from a lush and secretive lost world. These rivers and watercourses are also important environments for aquatic life, including Atlantic salmon, which migrate from the open Atlantic to the Esk every autumn, returning to breed in the same spawning grounds where they were born in one of nature's most extraordinary journeys. These fish are also integral to the river's population of freshwater pearl mussels, who, as larvae, hitch a lift upstream on the gills of the salmon, dropping off once they reach the gravel beds where the fish spawn.

For all the North York Moors has to offer in its interior, though, one of the most crowd-pleasing parts of this landscape is where it ends: the roughly 42-kilometre (26-mile) stretch of salt-sprayed, craggy coastline where North Yorkshire meets the North Sea. The moorland and fields abruptly give way to an almost continuous march of high cliffs, which rise up to around 200 metres (660 feet) tall at the high point of Boulby. It is as if the land had been sliced straight through with a lathe; often there is little margin between the pastures on one side and the cliffs plunging down to the rolling breakers on the other. All of this is linked by the Cleveland Way national trail, which skirts the western and northern boundary of the national park before running down the whole length of the North York Moors coastline to reach the seaside town of Filey.

Partly because of the precipitous geography, settlements are far less numerous along this stretch of shore than many other parts of England, but when they do

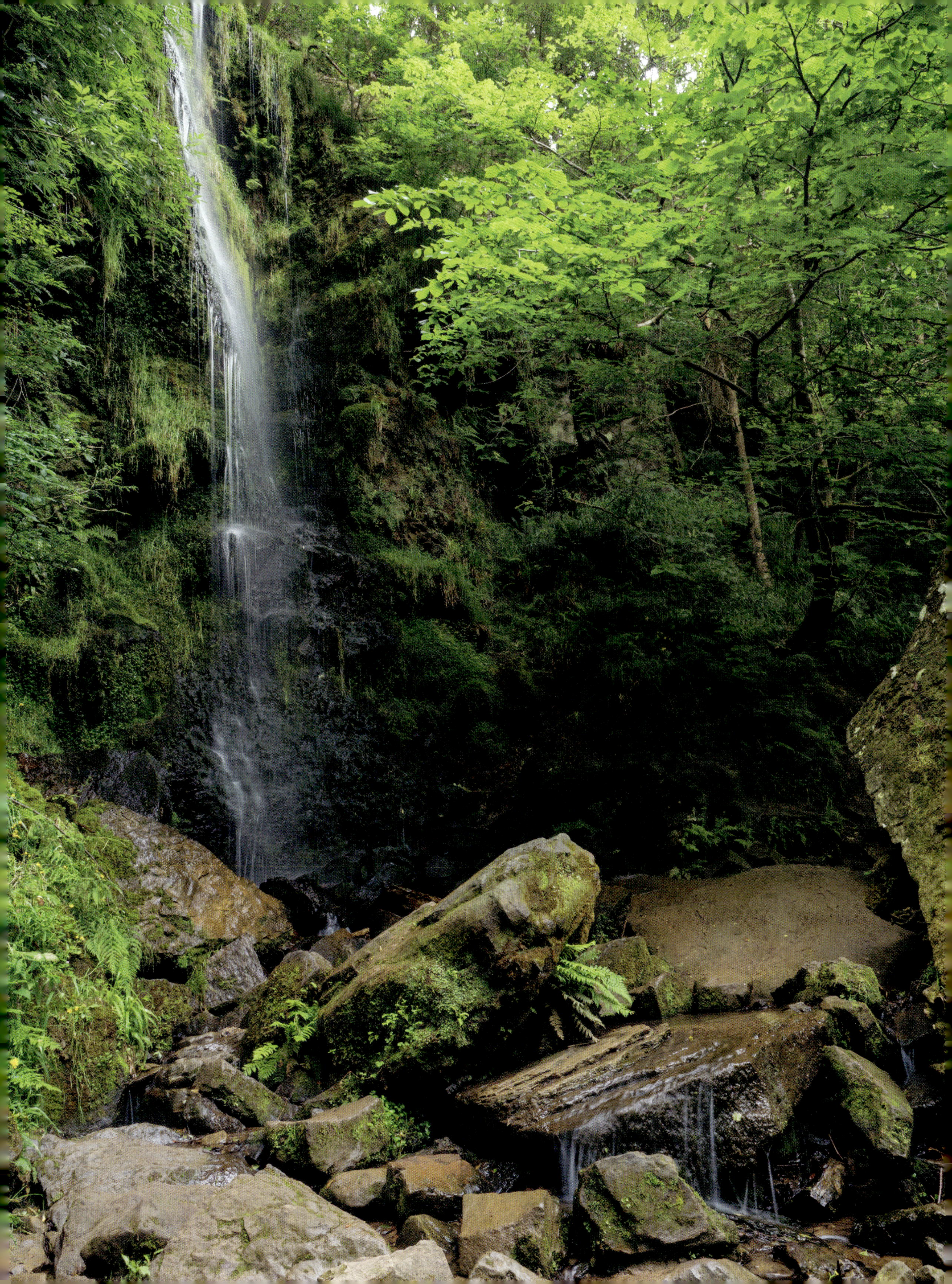

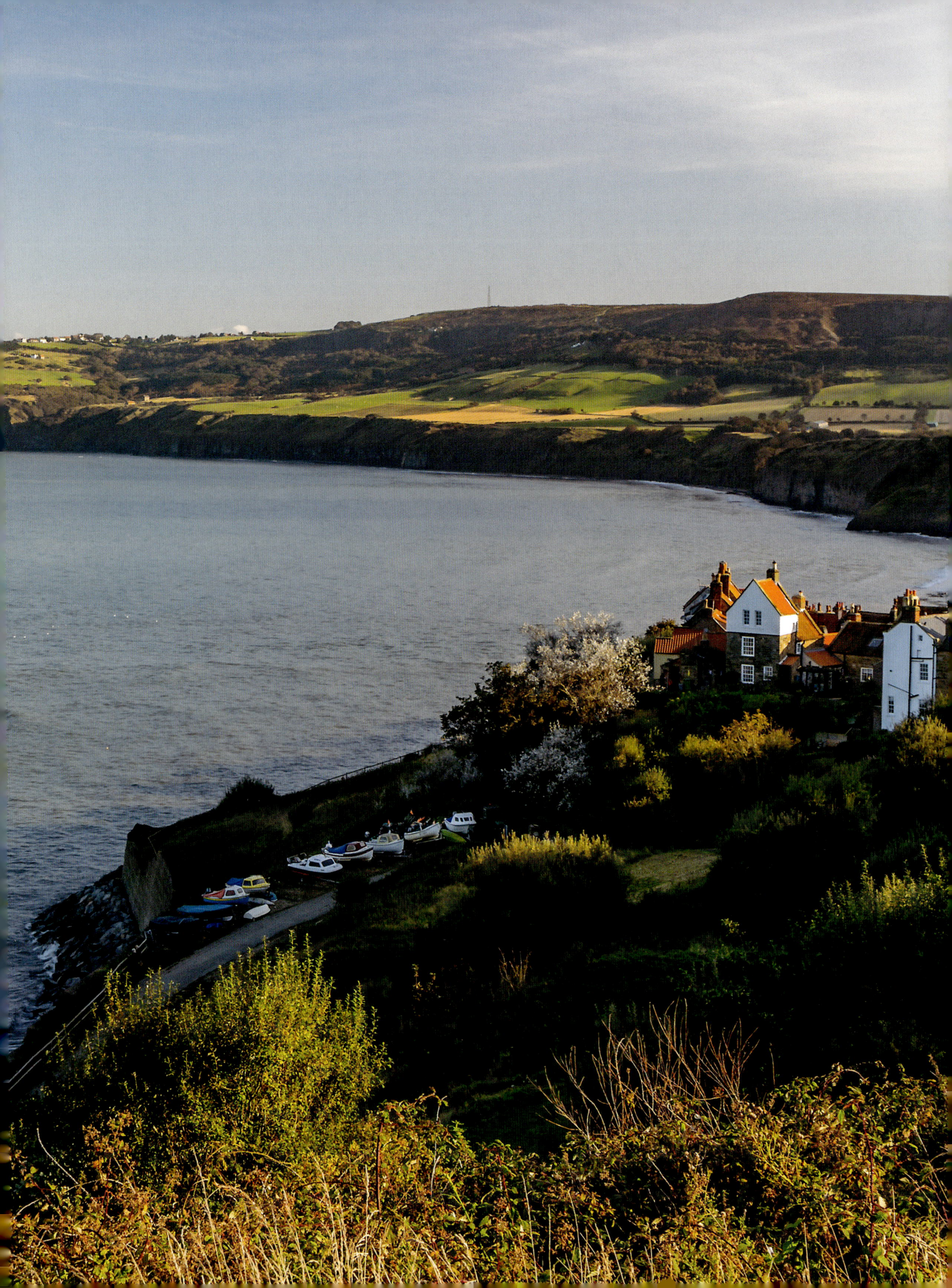

A quintessential cross-section of a North York Moors dale: a patchwork of hedgerow-bounded pastures and farm buildings gives way to high heather moorland.

Opposite:
The picturesque coastal village of Robin Hood's Bay, a maze of red-roofed cottages and winding cobbled alleys tumbling down to a rocky cove, is a popular tourist draw. Although it developed as a fishing village, in the 18th century it was a hotspot for smuggling, aided by a subterranean network of tunnels connected to the tightly packed warren of houses. The Bay Hotel, on the edge of the dock, is one end of the 309 kilometre (192 mile) coast to coast long-distance walk.

appear, they are some of the most photogenic and delightful coastal villages to be found in Britain. Former fishing villages like Robin Hood's Bay and Staithes nestle snugly into the narrow spaces where the cliffs are breached by river gorges or rocky coves, resulting in a jumble of tightly furled streets and narrow cobbled alleys flanked by stone cottages, tearooms and pubs. There are also a handful of beaches: the village at Runswick Bay overlooks perhaps one of the most beautiful sweeps of sand on the entire English coastline, enclosed by a wide amphitheatre of woodland-clad slopes.

Perhaps the most famous 'son' of this coast is Captain James Cook, who would go on to chart huge areas of the Pacific and make the first European contact with several Oceanic civilisations, but who as a young man apprenticed in Staithes and entered the merchant navy in Whitby. It was here on this cloudy North Sea coastline, working on coal barges, that Cook got his first taste of maritime life and began to learn the skills that would lead him to dream of going, as he later wrote, 'as far as I think it is possible for a man to go'.

On the rocky coves and intertidal scars of this coastline you can find the fossils of ancient monkey-puzzle trees, ammonites and, perhaps most remarkably of all, the astonishingly well-preserved footprints of the dinosaurs who walked and hunted across this region 160 million years ago. This is a landscape with many lost worlds, all of which can feel vividly present.

The watery calls of the curlew form an unmistakeable soundtrack to the moorland areas of Britain throughout spring and summer. Even so, their numbers are in rapid decline, dropping by almost 50 per cent between 1995 and 2015. An urgent conservation effort is underway to halt this fall, although the North York Moors still have a good number.

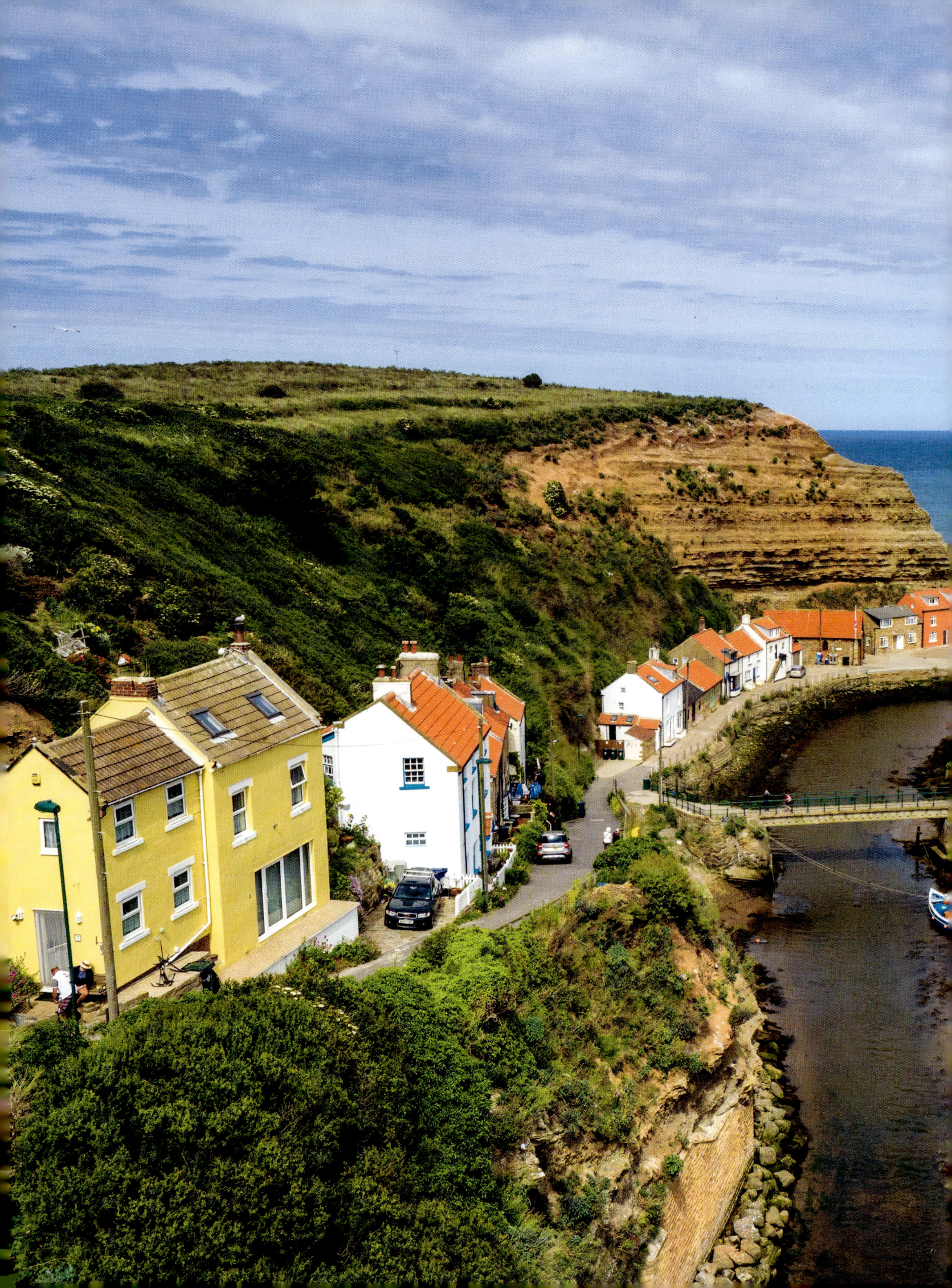

A popular tourist hub, the former fishing village of Staithes nestles picturesquely into a coastal cove, enclosing a sheltered harbour. Once home to a teenage Captain Cook, the streets of the tightly packed village are winding and narrow; one of them, Dog Loup, is under 50cm wide, and is claimed to be the narrowest street in England. The surrounding cliffs are rich in fossils like ammonites, while a rockfall in the 1990s revealed the remnants of an oceangoing dinosaur.

Overleaf:
Heather moorland is usually associated with the high uplands, but near Ravenscar it runs almost right to the edge of the land, nearly touching the coastal clifftops. The site of a large alum processing works for 200 years, Victorian developers planned to create a large seaside resort at Ravenscar, but the plan never came to fruition. The small hamlet there has since been known as 'the town that never was'.

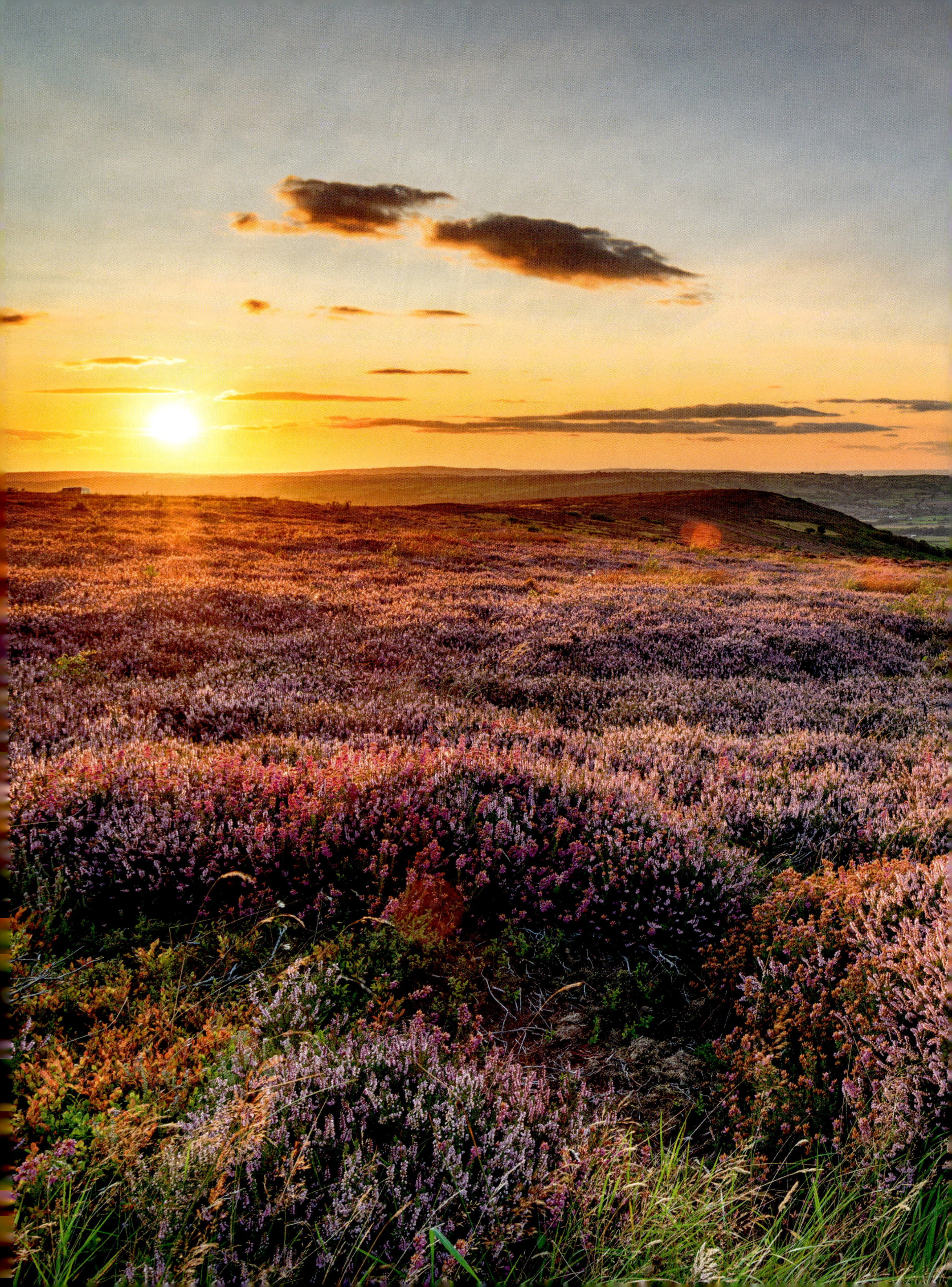

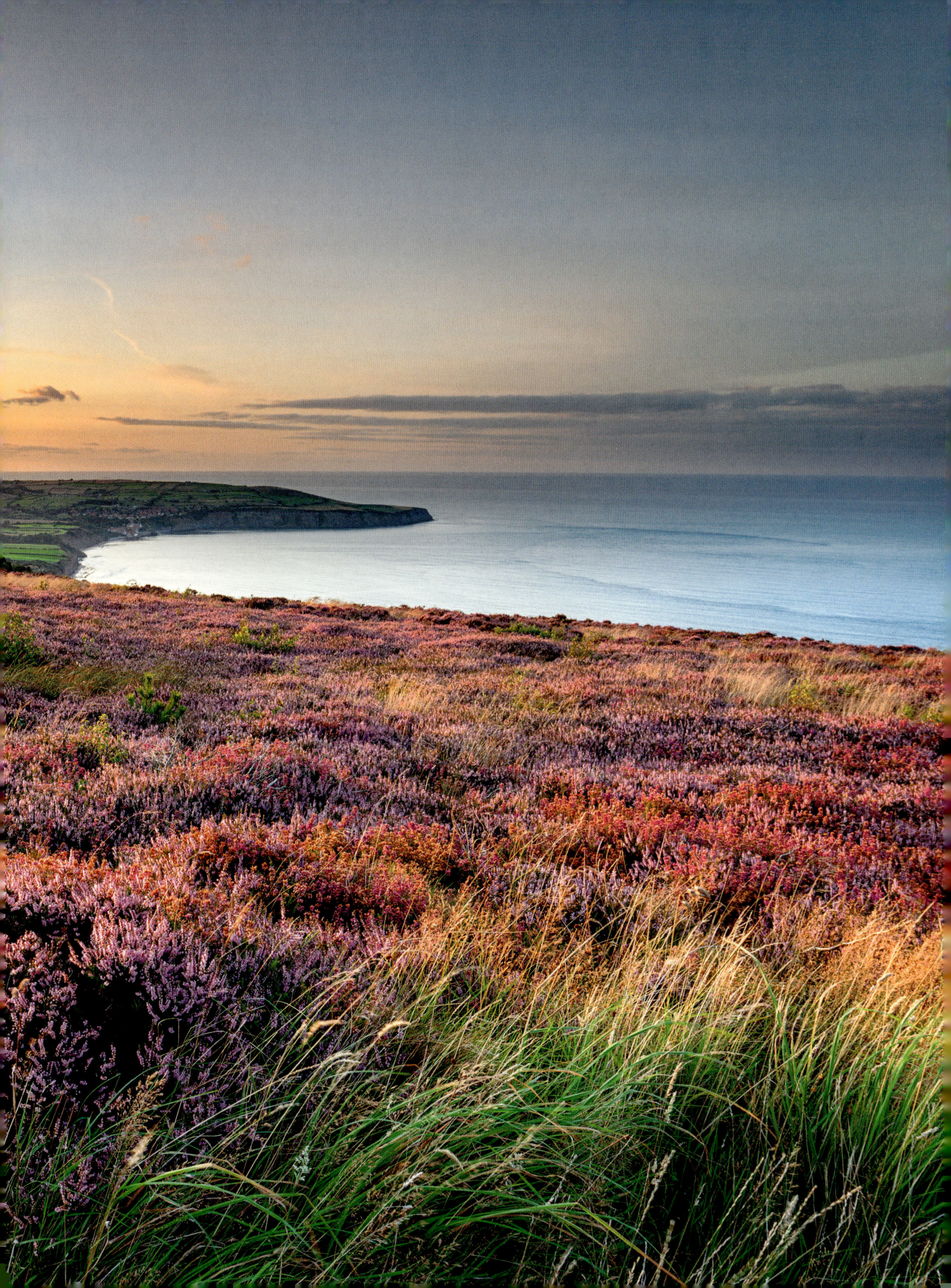

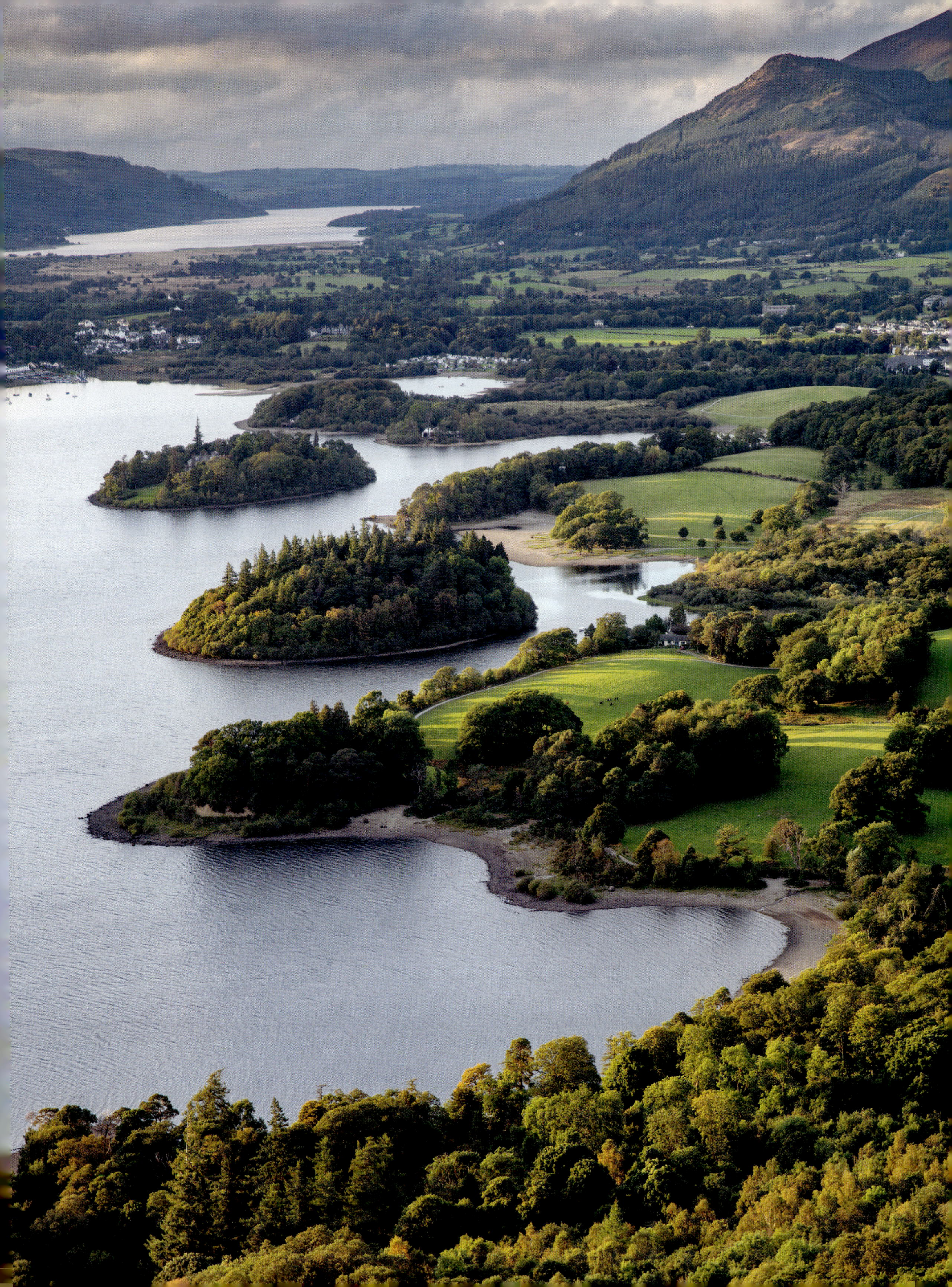

Lake District

In the early 18th century, passing through what would later become known as the Lake District, *Robinson Crusoe*'s author, Daniel Defoe, was unimpressed. He described it as 'a country eminent only for being the wildest, most barren and frightful of any that I have passed over in England'. The region's hills and mountains, he complained, had 'kind of an unhospitable terror in them' and were 'no use or advantage either to man or beast'.

Today, however, the Lake District is one of the UK's most adored landscapes. It attracts around 18 million visitors a year, draws in tourists from all over the world, and is a designated UNESCO world heritage due to its distinctive blend of rural culture and natural history. In the centuries since Defoe wrote his dour assessment, this landscape has inspired generations of artists, writers and poets, creating a cultural imprint that spans the globe. It has fed the spirits of ramblers, hikers, scramblers, bikers, botanists, birdwatchers, day-trippers, climbers, and mountaineers, all of whom flock to the Lake District seeking rejuvenation, relaxation, inspiration or adventure. It is no exaggeration to say that billions of happy days have been spent here. Author Alfred Wainwright's Pictorial Guides to the Lakeland Fells – a series of seven beautiful hand-drawn volumes, covering 214 Lakeland fells – is considered by many to be the definitive walking guide to the region, selling more than 2 million copies since the first volume was published in 1955. As he put it, 'Surely there is no other place in this whole wonderful world quite like Lakeland… no other so exquisitely lovely, no other so charming, no other than calls so insistently across a gulf of distance. All who truly love Lakeland are exiles when away from it.'

Clearly, things have changed since the 1700s. Is it that the landscape is very different? Not particularly – this grand tapestry of mountains, lakes and pastoral dales in the far north-west corner of England has retained the same essential character. There are dales covered in a patchwork of farms, fields, woods and walls, enclosed by mountains with evocative Celtic or Norse names like Blencathra, Helvellyn, Scafell or Skiddaw. There are hefted sheep herds (which means that they have been taught to stay on their territory without the need for shepherding, knowledge that is passed on from ewe to lamb) grazing on the fells in much the same way as they have done for centuries. There are huge crags, home to rare arctic-alpine plant communities and nesting birds of prey; mountain rivers tumbling into plunge pools and slaloming through rocky cataracts; lush, cavernous gills full of vegetation; and tarns set into the rugged mountain landscape like jewels.

Ringed by mountains, fringed by oakwoods and dotted with islands, Derwentwater is one of the most popular and accessible lakes in the Lake District. The nearby town of Keswick, one of the national park's biggest towns and tourist hubs, sits at the northern shore of Derwentwater, and a host of marinas around the 18 kilometre (10 mile) shore of the lake are connected by passenger ferries. Derwentwater's verdant beauty has often made it the focus of artistic attention, and it continues to fire imaginations today – the lake served as an alien planet in the movie Star Wars: The Force Awakens, *and as a backdrop in the* Silent Hill *and* Forza Horizon *video games.*

A classic view of the head of Wasdale, with mountain giants crowded around it. Yewbarrow is the arch-backed peak on the left; Great Gable is the cloud-topped mountain in the middle; and the sunbathed slopes of the Scafells rise up to the right, culminating in England's highest ground.

If the landscape itself hasn't changed much, why do we now find it beautiful, rather than 'frightful'? The answer to this question is closely linked to how European attitudes towards mountains, nature and conservation have changed over the last three centuries – a shift that has been inspired in no small part by the Lake District itself.

The mountainous heartland of the Lake District was born in the depths of an ocean lying south of the equator 450 million years ago during a period of volcanic uproar, and then flung out of the sea by tectonic forces to form a mountain range the size of the Himalayas. Over subsequent eons these mountains were gradually eroded down to their current size, with their dales and corries still holding the shape of the glaciers that ground through them until as recently as 15,000 years ago.

The most noticeable relics of those retreated glaciers are the lakes, where water has filled the gouges left in the landscape by the sheer force of those rivers of ice. The dales and lakes radiate outwards from the centre of the region – the 'hub' being roughly around Grasmere – like the spokes on a wheel. There are hundreds of bodies of water in the Lake District. These range from big valley lakes studded with forested islands and often thronged with boats and sightseers – like the Windermere, which at 18 kilometres (10.5 miles) long is the biggest lake in the region and England as a whole; or the achingly beautiful Ullswater – to quiet and nameless mountain tarns nestled in the folds of the high fells. The larger lakes and their shores make idyllic places for family recreation, scenic strolling and leisurely boat cruising.

Most of the region's 'lakes' are referred to as meres (like Buttermere), tarns (like Blea Tarn) or waters (like Wastwater); and only one body of water has 'lake' in its name (Bassenthwaite Lake), so by that criteria, there is only one lake in the Lake District! In reality, this terminology simply reflects the different cultures that have called Cumbria home over the course of the last two millennia. Although now thought of as quintessentially 'English', this landscape was once part of the Brittonic kingdom of Strathclyde, which originated in Scotland, and like much of northern England, it still carries the echoes of Celtic, Scandinavian, German and even Roman influences in the names of its mountains, waters and settlements.

The Lakeland's fells may be small as mountains go. At just 978 metres (3,209 feet), for example, Scafell Pike, the highest summit of both Lakeland and England, would barely qualify as a foothill in the Alps, while many peaks of the Scottish and Welsh mountains are higher. But the tumultuous natural processes that built the Lake District mountains are the same as much bigger ranges, and the fells still carry the drama of their creation in their crags and contours. You can see this in the spectacle of the Wasdale Screes plunging into the depths of Wastwater; the majesty of Great Gable with its summit bathed in sunset light; the alpine grandeur of Helvellyn's ridges on a snowy winter day; or the view across the churning sea of the Lakeland fells from High Street, so-named for the Roman road that once ran across it.

Mountains are not simply measured in size, but in the atmosphere and emotions they evoke. And these hills and mountains have left an outsized imprint on the imagination of England and the wider world. This influence is the result of the Lake District's role in the emergence of the Romantic movement in the late-18th century, in particular the Lake Poets, most famously, William Wordsworth and Samuel Taylor Coleridge.

In contrast to the classical view of the wild – typified by Defoe's attitude – as a savage realm in need of taming and 'civilising', the Romantics celebrated untrammelled nature as a source of spiritual vitality and wonder. Mountain landscapes held a particular fascination for Romantic painters and poets as places where the forces of nature were at their most unbridled and powerful.

Arctic charr are often called a 'relic of the Ice Age'; they are much more numerous in colder Scandinavian waters, but fragmented populations were left behind in some parts of Britain as the glaciers retreated. These individuals were photographed in Ennerdale, where the last breeding population of these fish in England is found. In recent years, a conservation initiative linked to the Wild Ennerdale project has helped to boost their numbers.

Hill farming in the Lake District is indelibly associated with Herdwick sheep, a hardy breed whose ancestors are thought to have been brought to Britain by Norse settlers 1,000 years ago. Herdwick husbandry has profoundly shaped the culture and landscape of the Lake District. The network of drystone walls covering the valleys and pushing into the mountains is a physical legacy of sheep farming, and local customs, events and even speech patterns reflect its importance. The impact of sheep grazing also keeps the fells largely lacking in trees and montane vegetation.

Opposite:
The Langdale Pikes look down on the glacier-gouged valley of Great Langdale. A magnet for hikers and hillwalkers today, the Langdale Pikes were the site of an ancient industry: Neolithic peoples quarried their slopes and foraged in their screes to produce stone axe tools.

Wordsworth was born in the vicinity of the Lake District and his Lakeland-inspired works include some of the most famous lines of poetry in the English language, including 'I wandered lonely as a cloud …' from a poem inspired by the sight of daffodils waving in the wind on the shores of Ullswater. Coleridge's most famous work, 'Rime of the Ancient Mariner', sees a ship adrift in the vastness of an unforgiving ocean, but he also experienced his fair share of terrors in the mountains. During a nine-day walking tour of the Lakeland fells in 1802, he attempted to descend from Scafell via a precipitous crag now known as Broad Stand, above the valley of Wasdale. Before long, the poet realised he had bitten off more than he could chew. He came to a narrow ledge, was unable to retrace his steps upwards, and was faced with a perilous downclimb to reach safety: 'I shook all over … and the ledge at the bottom was so exceedingly narrow, that if I dropped down upon it I must of necessity have fallen backwards and of course killed myself.' After making it down to safe ground, Coleridge laughed at himself for being 'a madman' and 'lay in a state of almost prophetic trance and delight'.

This white-knuckle descent has been held up as the first description of a recreational rock climb, and in his account of the same 1802 tour, Coleridge is also thought to have coined the first use of a new word: 'mountaineering'. The idea of scaling mountains for no reason other than challenge and adventure is thought to have been relatively novel in Coleridge's time, but as the 19th century progressed, it grew in popularity among the upper classes of Europe. Victorian gentlemen based themselves in the Wasdale Head Inn to pioneer new athletic routes up the ghylls, gullies, crags and chimneys of the surrounding fells. The iconic pub is still a sight for sore eyes after a long day in the fells.

It is in no small part due to the change in thinking brought about by the Romantics and related movements that we now see mountains as beautiful, rejuvenating places rather than hostile, unproductive wastelands. As leading members of this movement, the Lake Poets went on to influence generations of

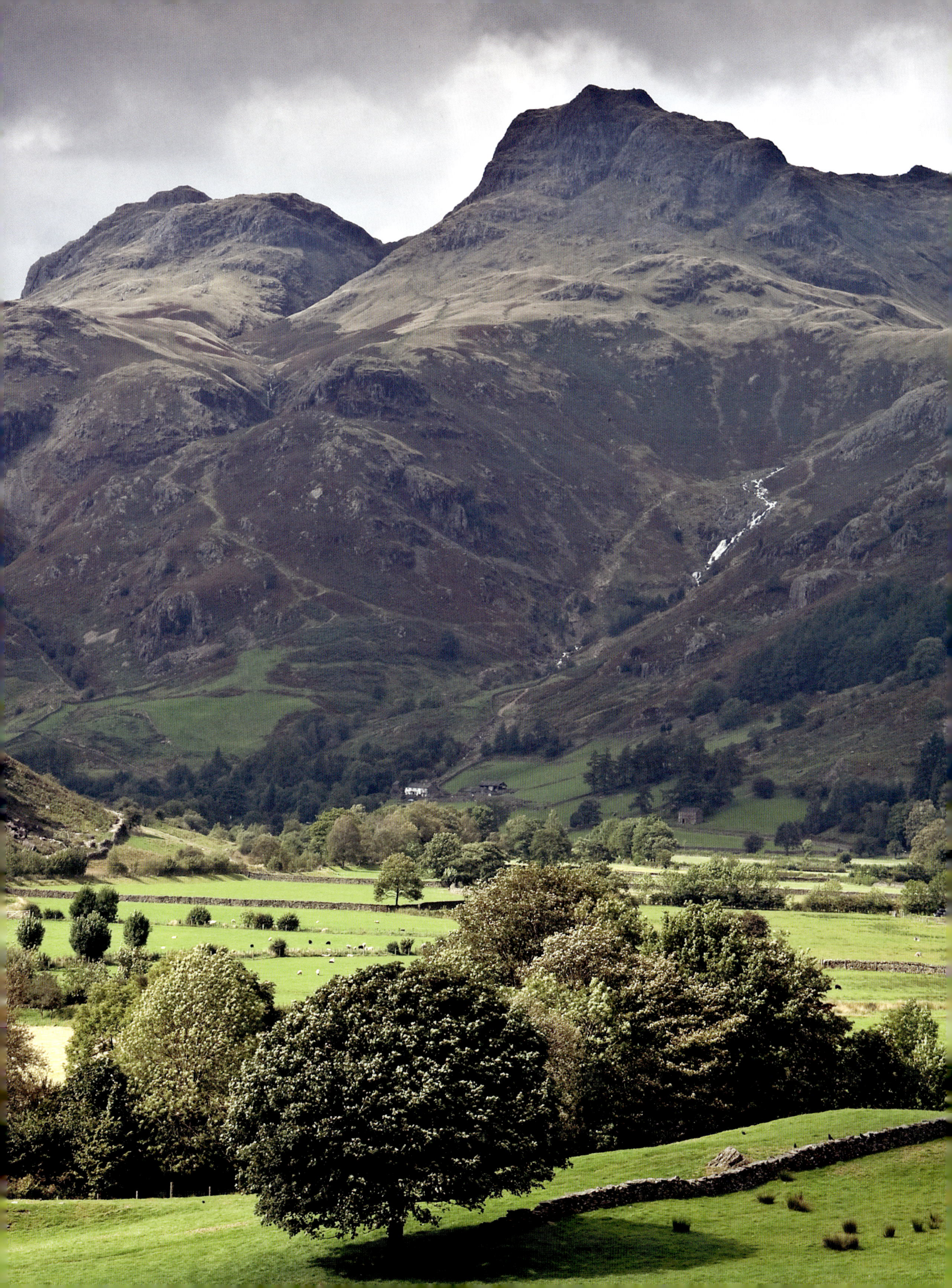

A walker makes their way across Red Screes on a hazy mountain morning. The Lake District is one of the places that gave birth to the idea of climbing mountains for fun in its modern form, and today it is one of Britain's most popular places for outdoor recreation – particularly hiking and hillwalking. The sheer number of hikers can make popular routes on 'honeypot' mountains like Scafell Pike, Helvellyn and Skiddaw feel crowded, but the Lake District fells are expansive and quieter corners can always be found.

artists, inspire conservationists, and blaze a trail for the mountain sports that millions of people enjoy today.

But the Lake District is not all about sublime spectacle and daring mountain exploits. The essential appeal of this landscape is found in the juxtaposition of rugged high fells set alongside the cosy intimacy of valleys and lakesides. Stone-built villages smell of woodsmoke, and pubs with low wooden beams and crackling fires offer sanctuary after hours of rainswept hiking. The valleys are deeply lived-in places, typically carpeted in a patchwork reflecting the human and natural influences on the landscape: including drystone-wall-bounded sheep pastures like the wiggling field boundaries of Wasdale Head; waterfall-filled woodlands hosting some of England's few surviving remnants of lichen-rich 'temperate rainforest'; and pretty villages with excellent old pubs where you can sit with a pint of golden ale and be fairly convinced there is nowhere more beautiful on the planet. Almost everywhere you go in this compact landscape, there are artefacts and excavations testifying to past cultures, rhythms of life and industries.

The pastoral side of the Lake District was of huge importance to another of the region's world-renowned artists, Beatrix Potter. The celebrated author and illustrator of innovative, pastel-coloured children's stories – most famously, *The Tale of Peter Rabbit* – spent childhood holidays in Lakeland, and her love of the region's flora and fauna was one of the chief influences on her work, particularly after her midlife move to Hill Top Farm in the village of Near Sawrey, close to Windermere. Her outwardly quaint but subtly subversive work became a staple in the upbringings of generations of children.

This is the most popular holiday destination of all the UK's national parks, and while it's always possible to find quieter corners, particularly in the fells, the spectre of overtourism and development has always hung over Lakeland.

But this concern has also made the Lake District a conservation heartland, fostering pioneering ideas and initiatives to preserve and enhance the landscape. Wordsworth himself described the Lake District as 'a sort of national property in which every man has a right and interest who has an eye to perceive and a heart to enjoy', an early forerunner of the idea of national parks. Artist John Ruskin, who was based in the Lake District for much of his life, was a key early supporter of the National Trust, while Beatrix Potter was one of the Trust's most significant sponsors, buying and donating 4,000 acres of land and 15 farms in the Lake District to the care of the organisation.

Today, the Lake District remains at the forefront of debates around conservation, the impact of tourism and the future of upland farming. Recent decades have seen sheep farming in the region come under scrutiny for its ecological impact, but the Lake District has also witnessed ambitious restoration projects like the 'rewilding' of Ennerdale and Haweswater, 'rewiggling' of rivers, restoration of hay meadows and the rise of 'nature first' farming.

Few landscapes can lay claim to as many hearts as the Lake District: if it stirs passions, it is because it is loved by so many.

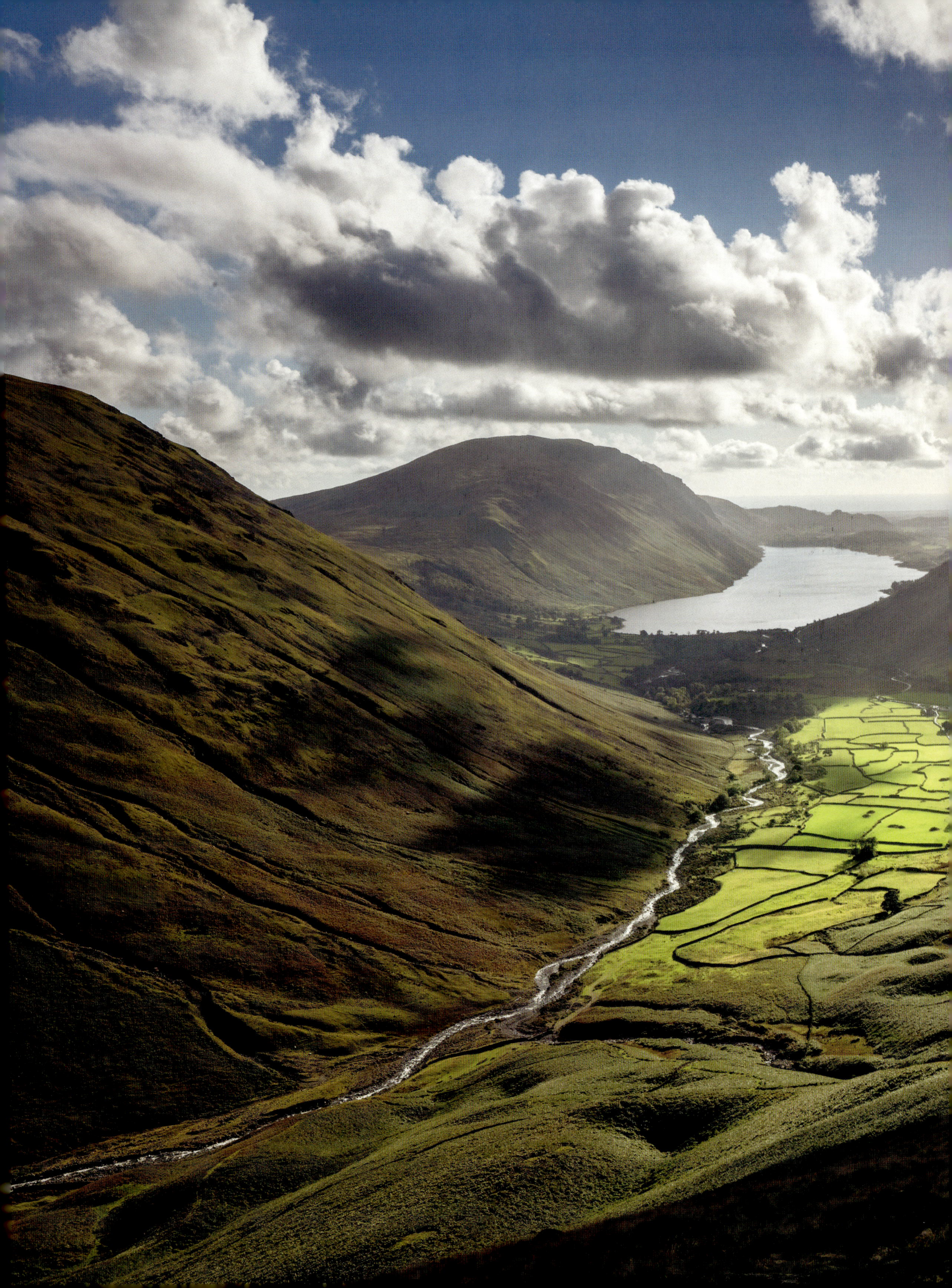

Looking out to the Irish Sea along the length of Wasdale, one of Lakeland's most dramatic and storied valleys, from the flanks of Kirk Fell. The distinctive pattern created by the fields of Wasdale Head is the legacy of traditional sheep farming. Further along the valley, the Wasdale Screes plunge into Wastwater, England's deepest lake, evoking some of the trench-like feel of a Norwegian fjord. Indeed, Wastwater and its screes were created by glacial 'overdeepening', the same process that created the fjord landscapes of Scandinavia and elsewhere.

Overleaf:
The climb to the 451 metre-high (1479 feet) peak of Cat Bells is one of the most popular and accessible hikes in Lakeland. The pronounced line of the path ascending its ridgeline is testament to this popularity. Heavy footfall on the Lake District's paths means that constant maintenance is needed control the spread of erosion.

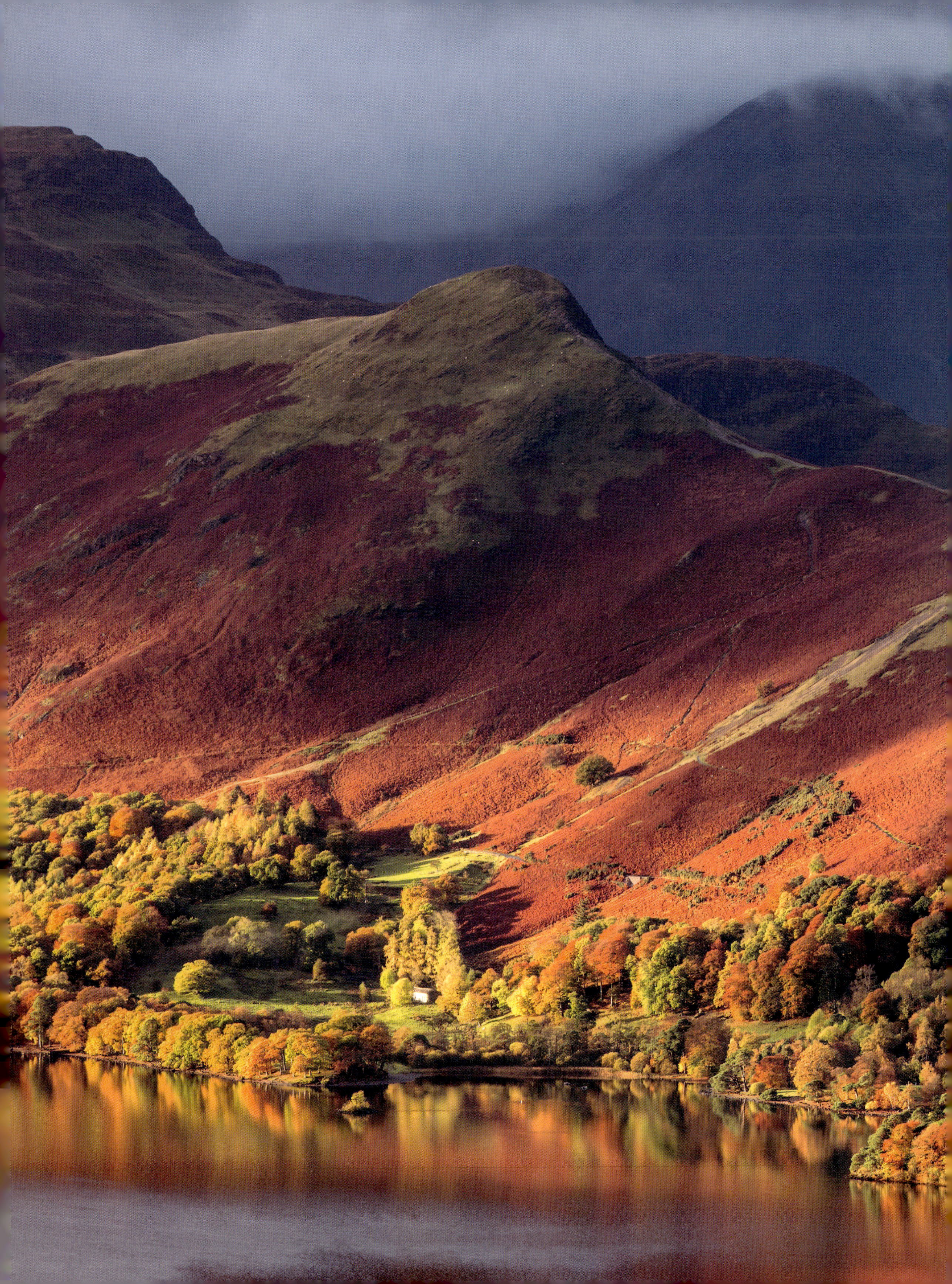

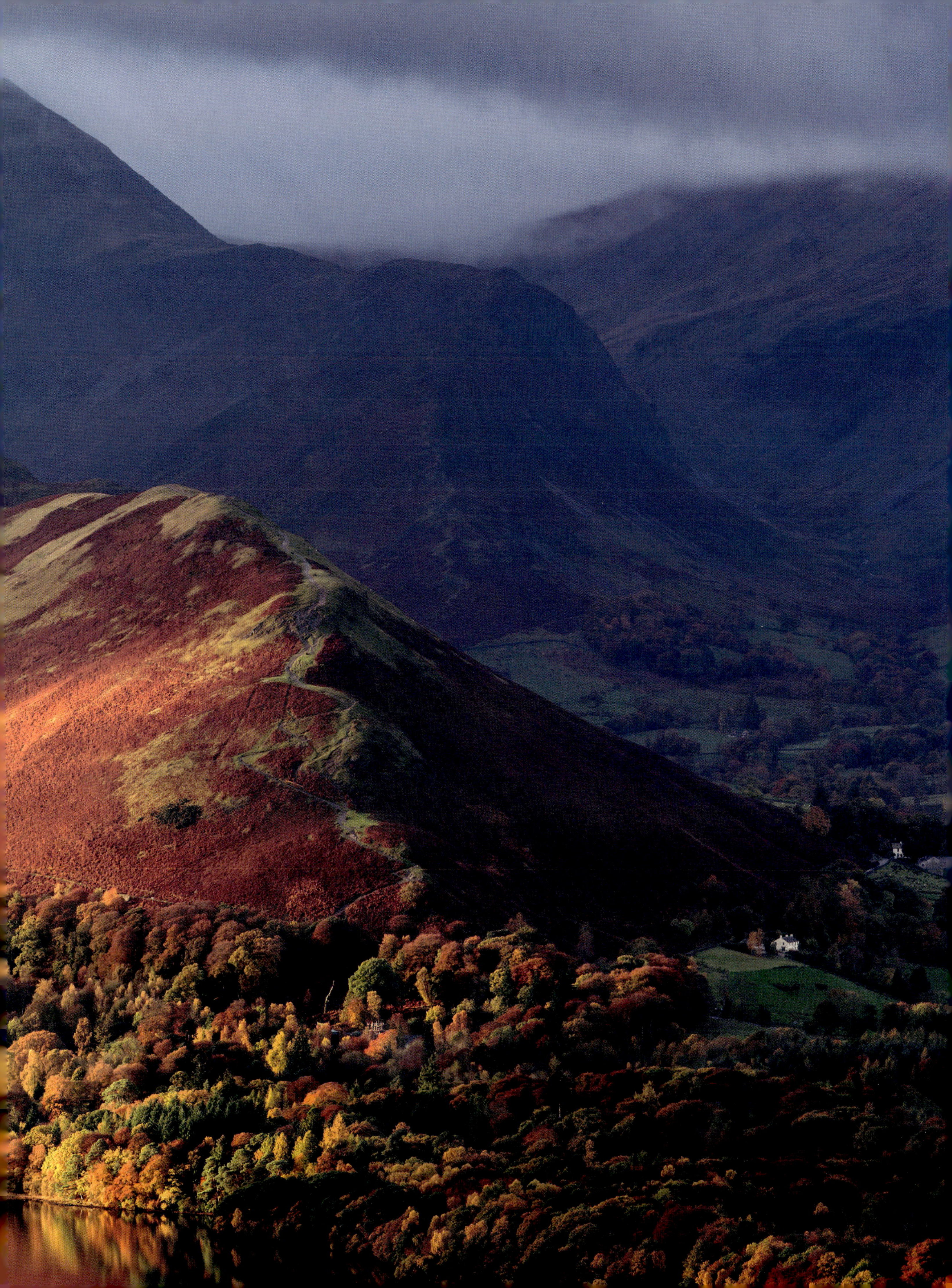

A motionless grey heron waits patiently for prey next to a Lakeland waterfall.

Ospreys disappeared from England in the 1830s, but a pair returned in 2001 to successfully breed in the Lake District thanks to conservation efforts. They have bred there every year since and spread to other locations.

Opposite:
Water thunders down Dungeon Ghyll in Great Langdale.

Overleaf:
Pastures and hill farms give way to the open fells in the Newlands Valley. Despite the tranquil and tourist-friendly image of the Lake District today, it still contains remnants of a more hard-bitten industrial past. The Newlands Valley is pockmarked with old metal mines, the most famous being Goldscope, which was originally excavated by German miners hired during the reign of Elizabeth I.

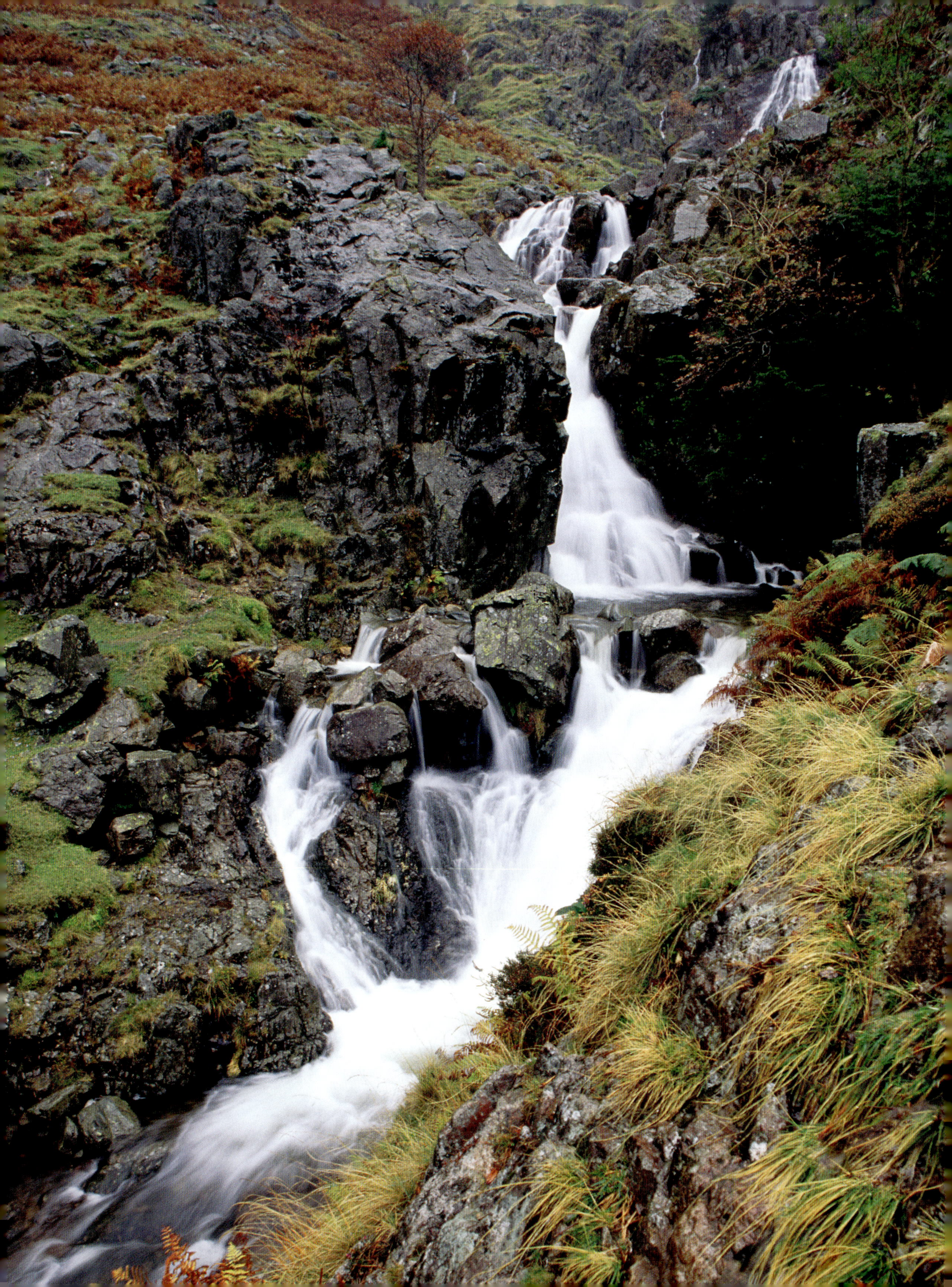

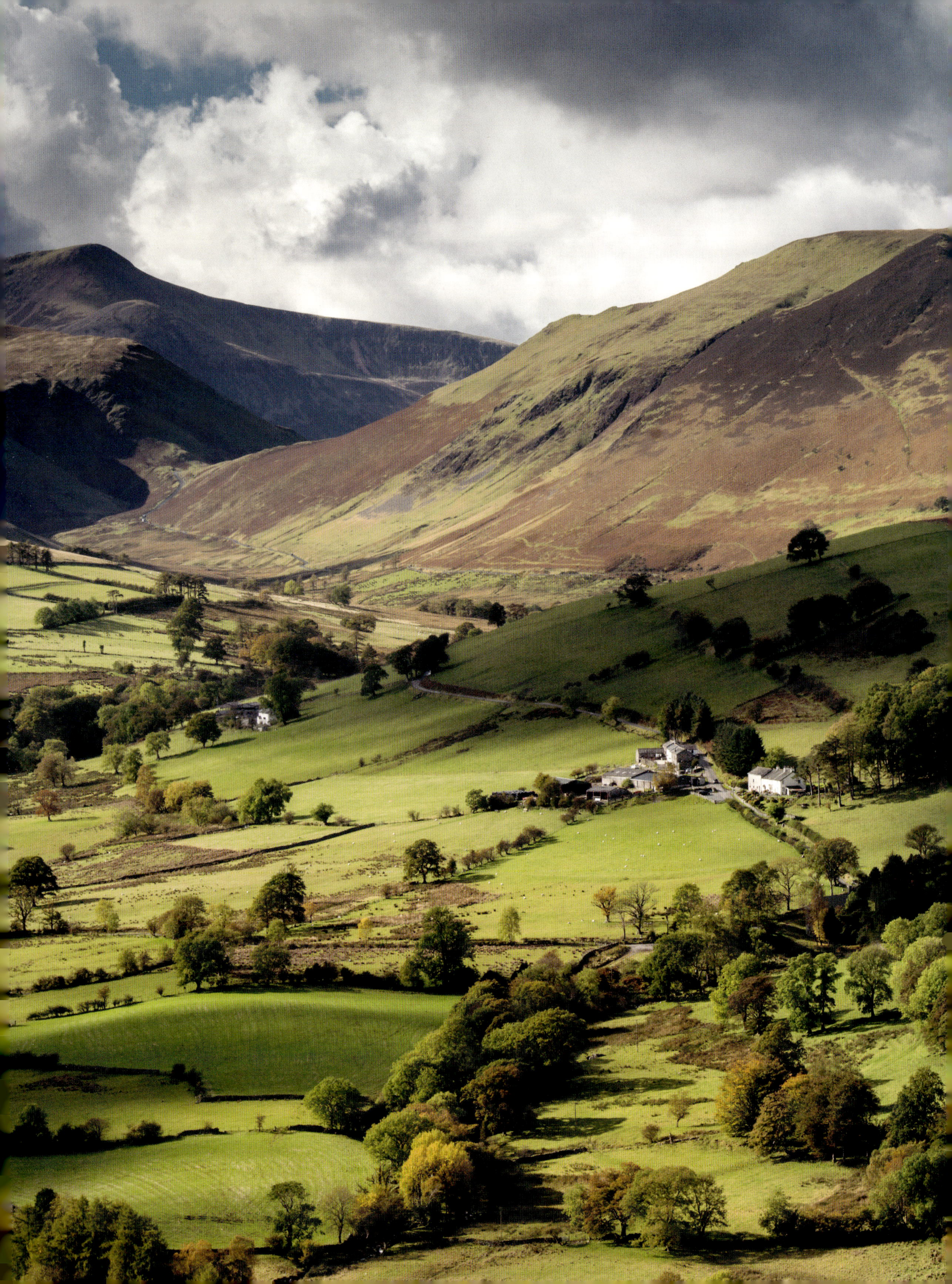

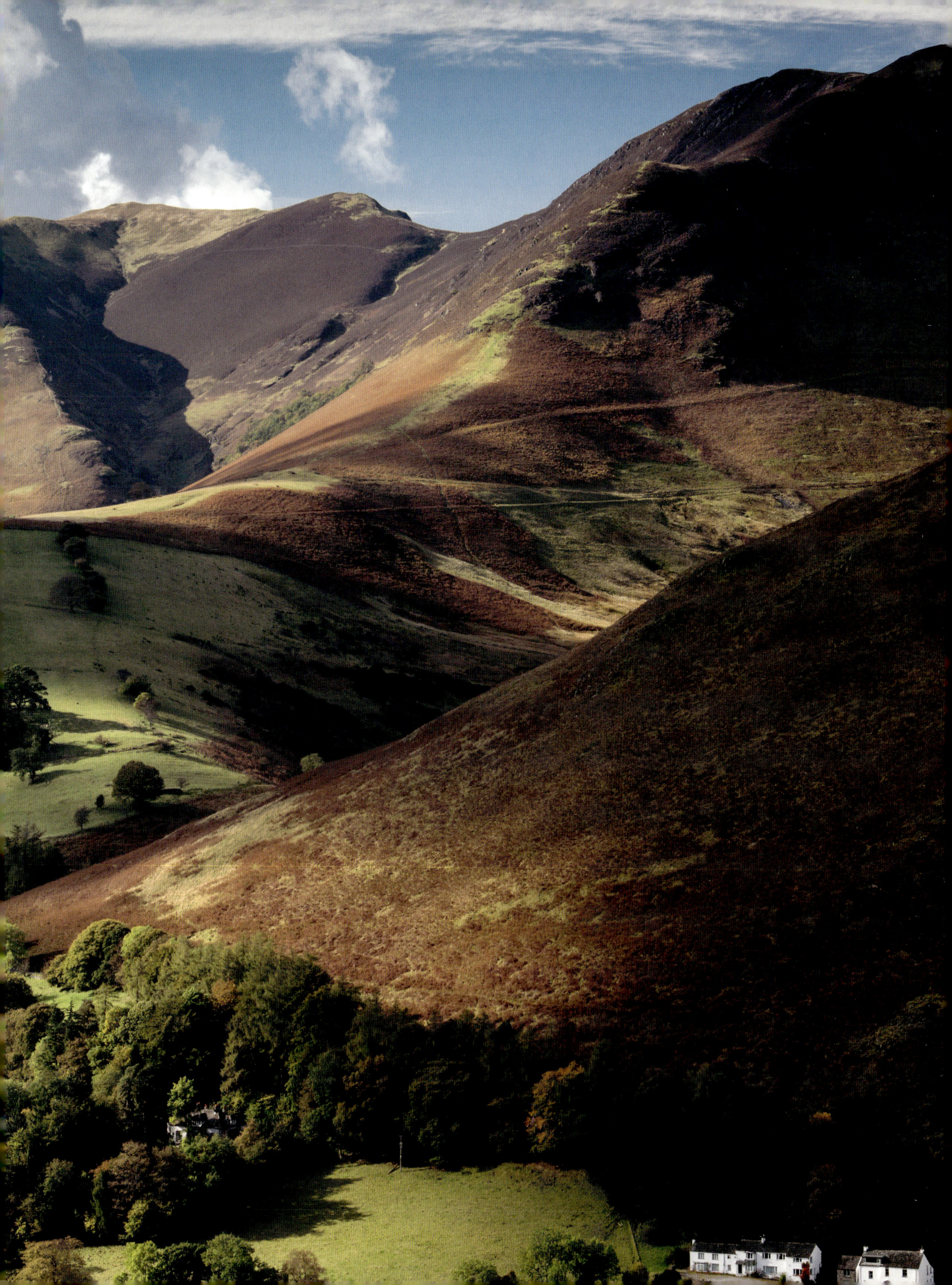

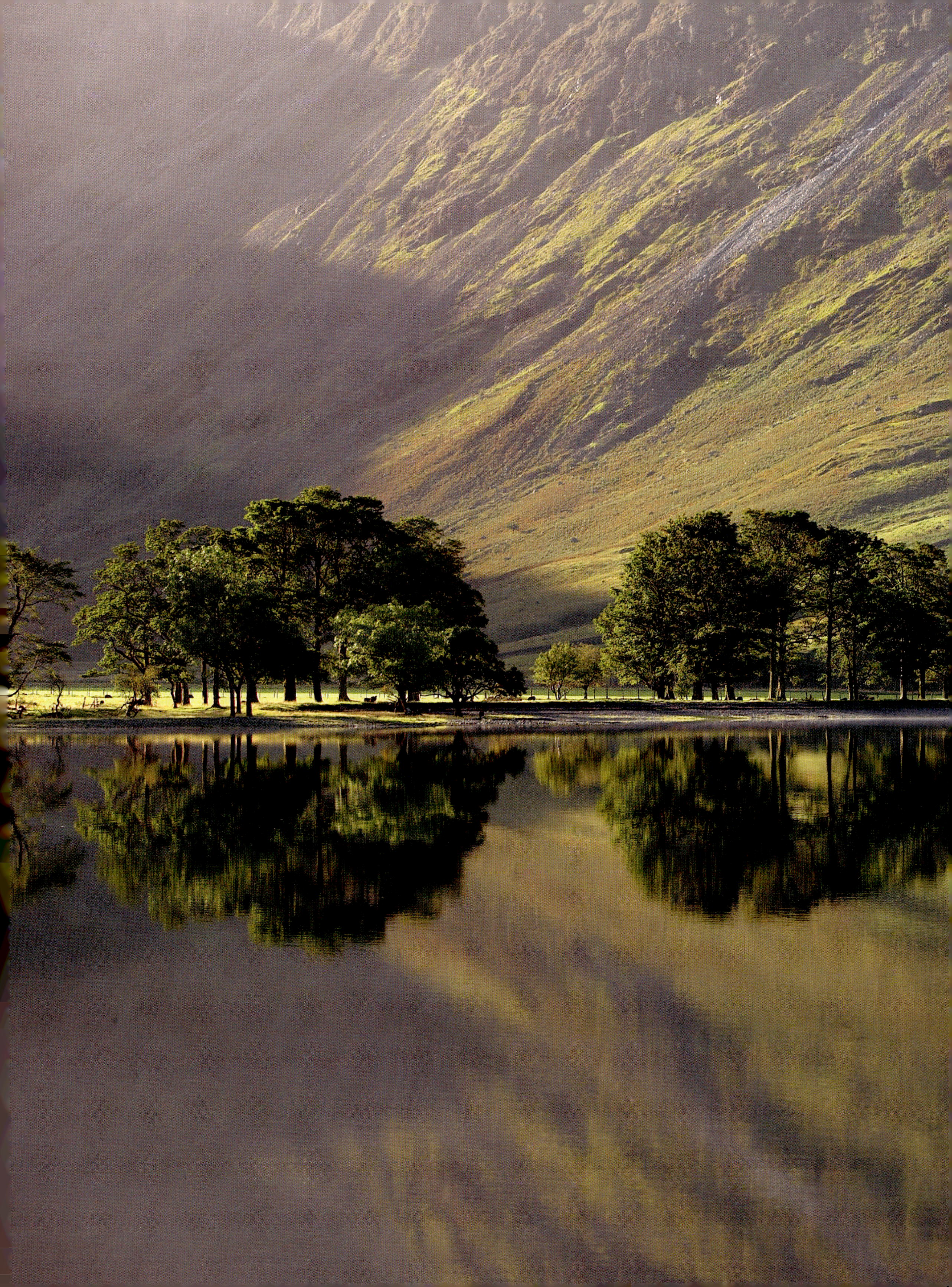

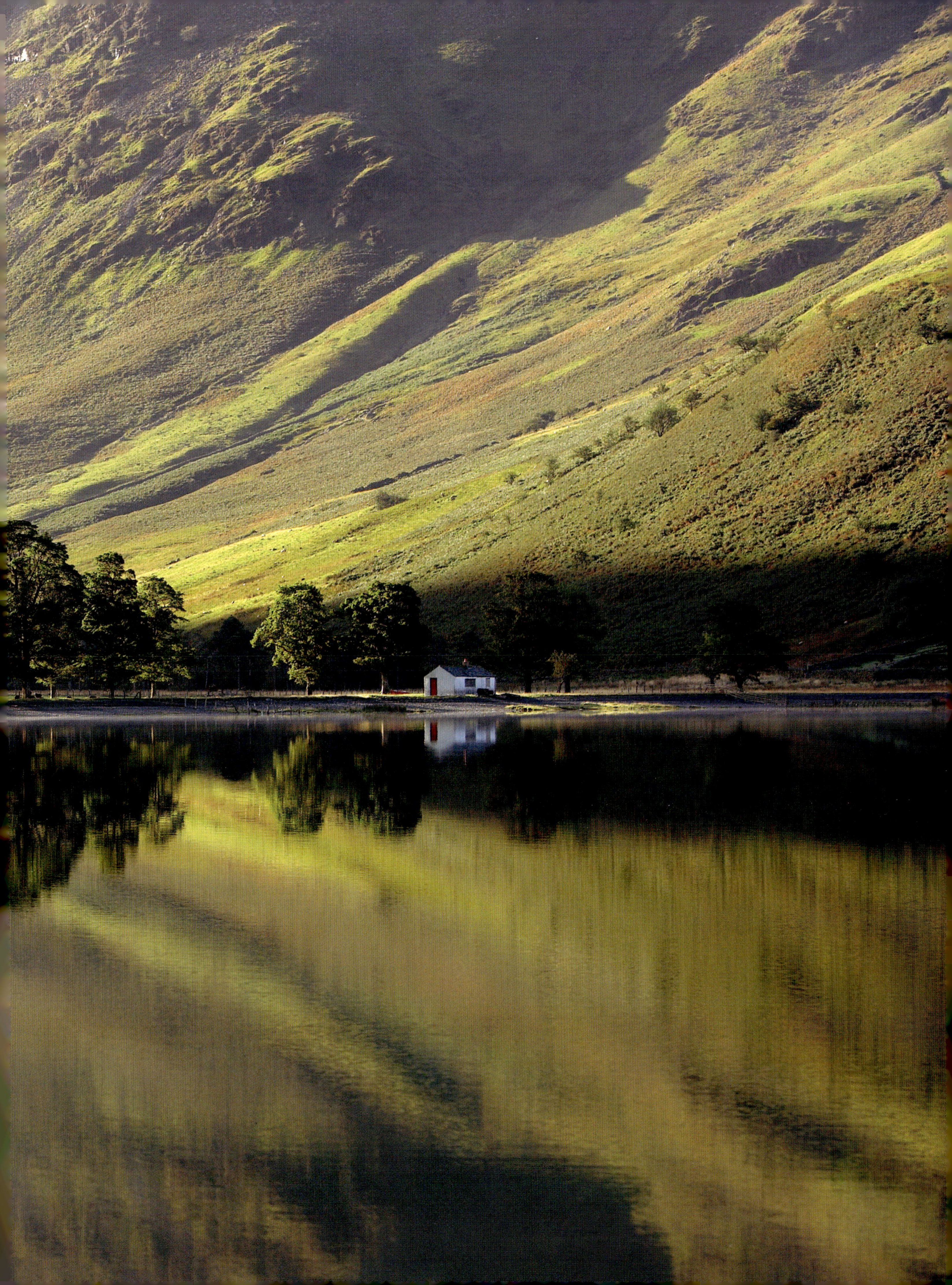

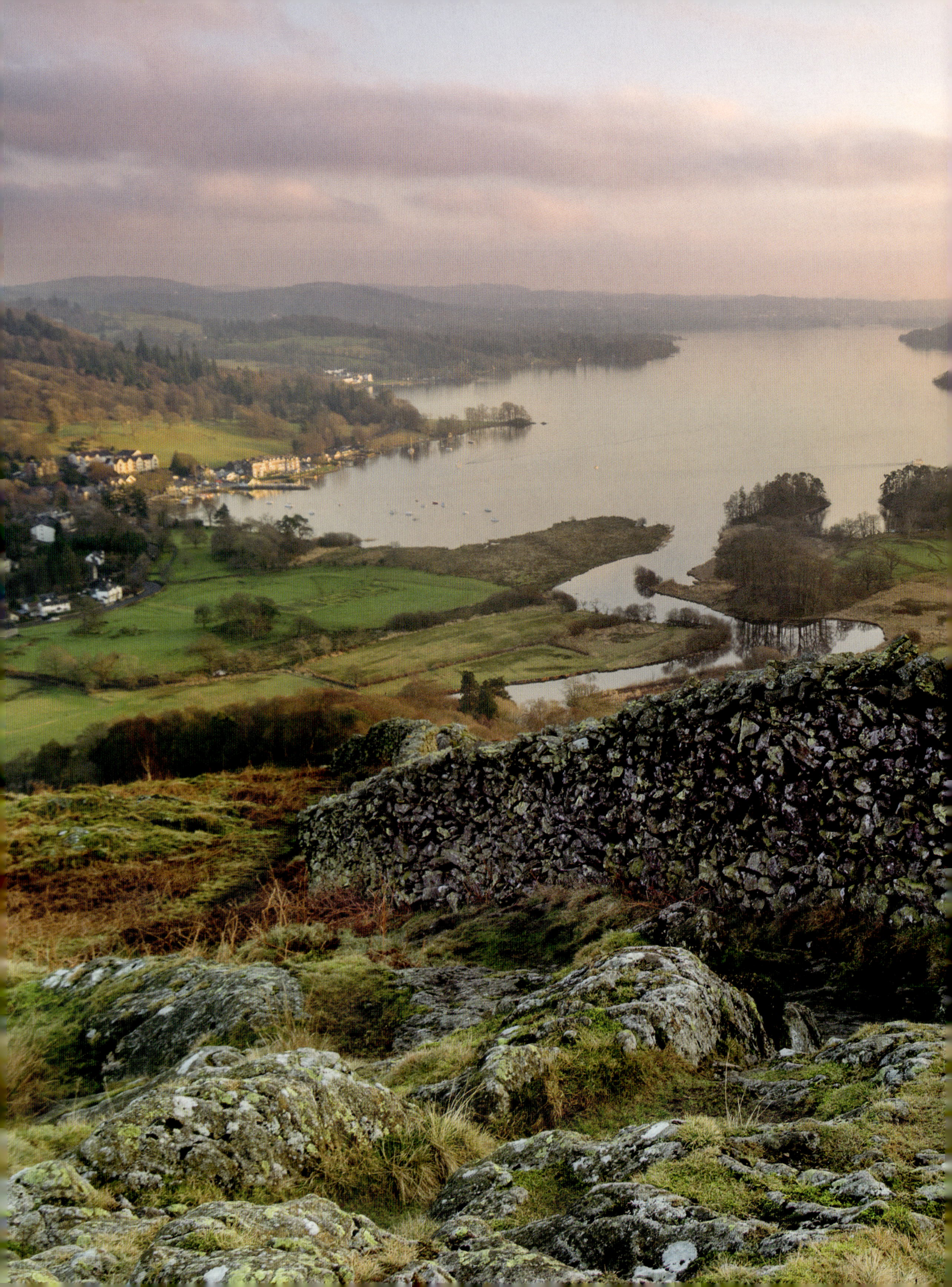

Previous page:
A cluster of trees stand at the southern end of Buttermere. Above, the imposing rocky slopes of High Crag, Haystacks and Fleetwith Pike surround the head of the valley.

A stile (now missing) spanning a drystone wall on the slopes of Loughrigg, looking down the length of Windermere, England's largest lake, from its northern shore.

Overleaf:
Mist drifts through the winter-gripped landscape of Langdale, with snow coating the tops of Pike of Blisco and Crinkle Crags in the distance. Valley fog like this in mountain regions can often be the result of temperature inversions, where cold air becomes trapped below a layer of warmer air. Often sought by photographers, 'cloud inversions' are most common on calm autumn and winter days, but can occur in high pressure conditions all year round.

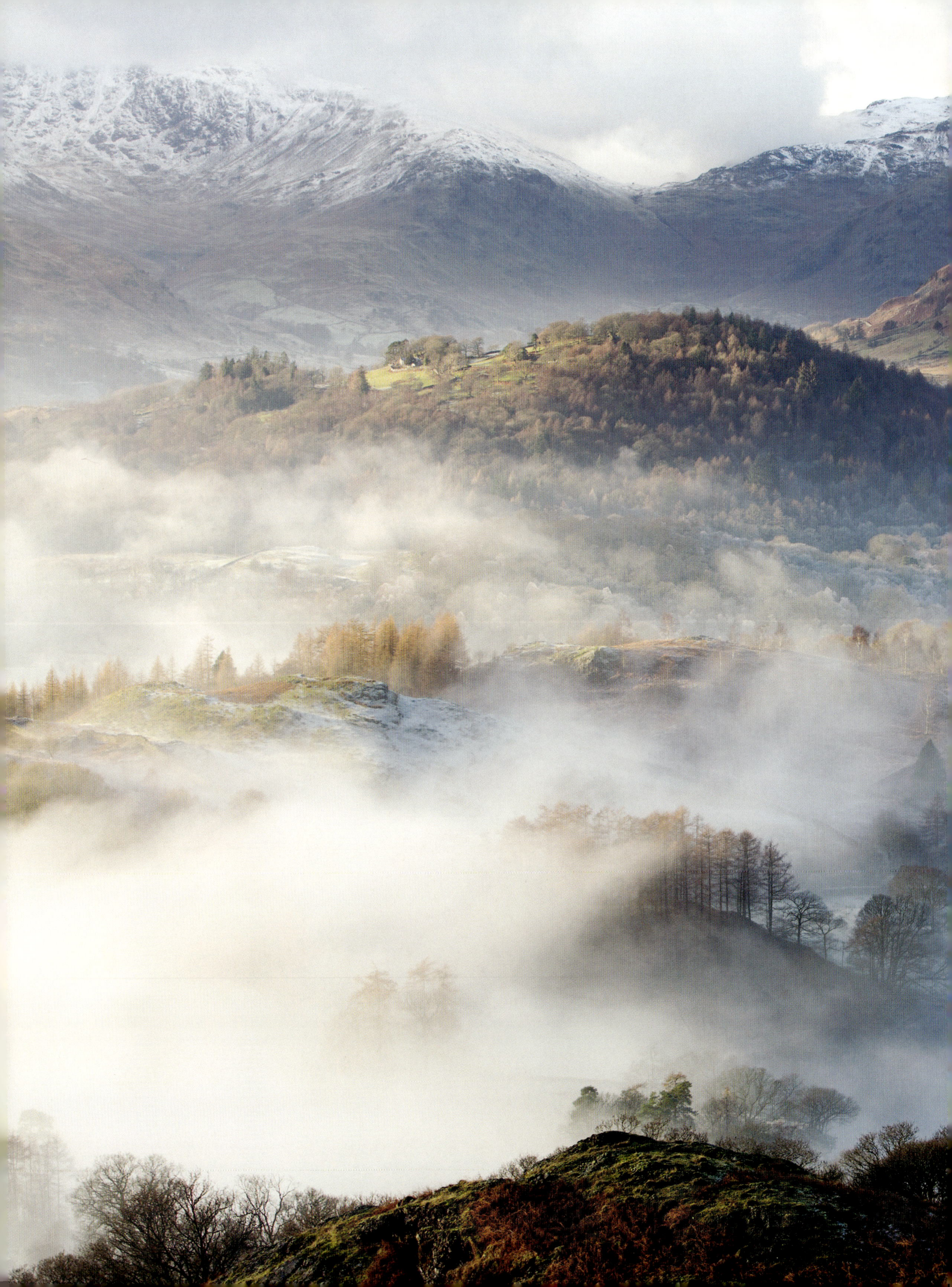

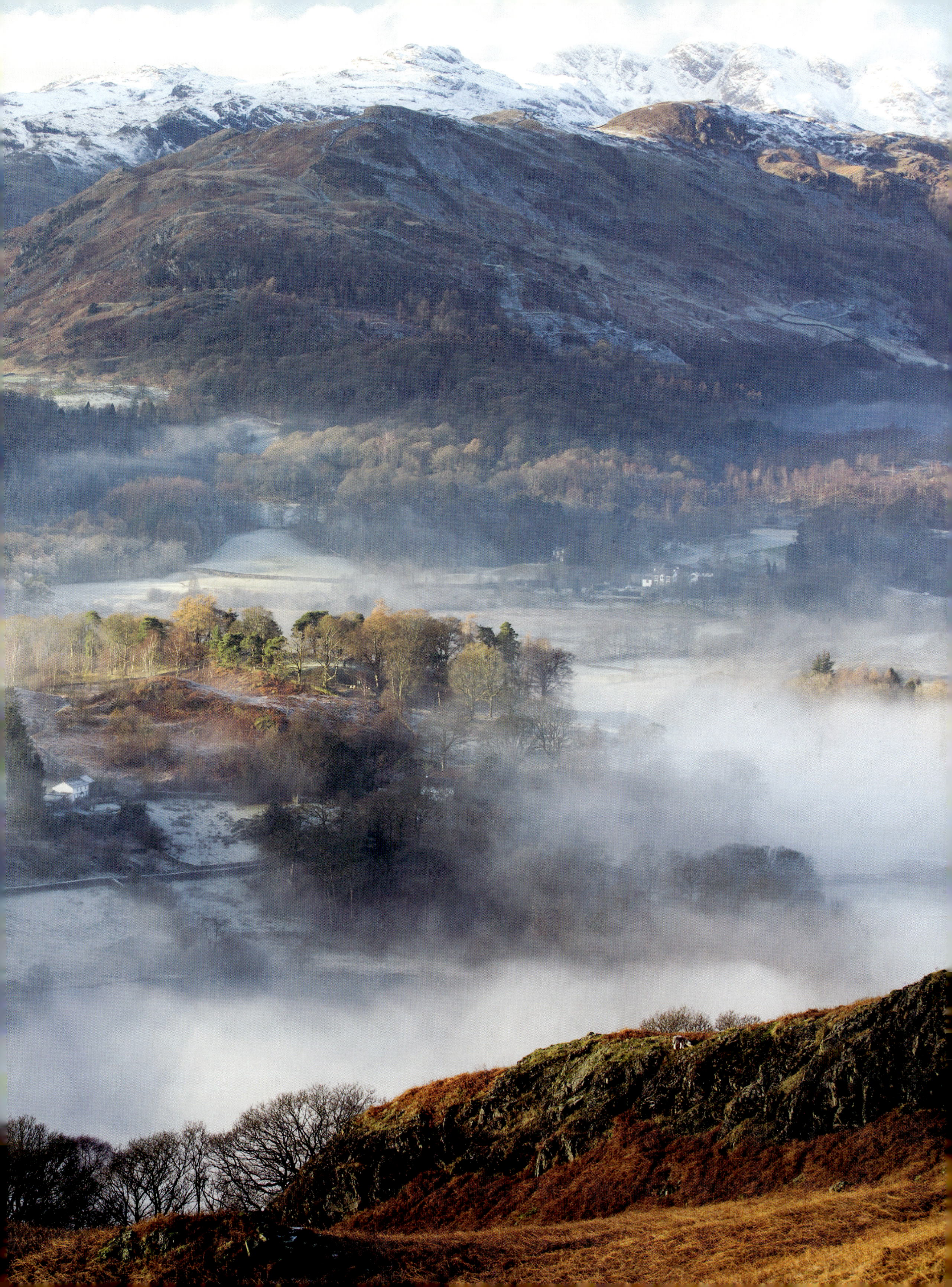

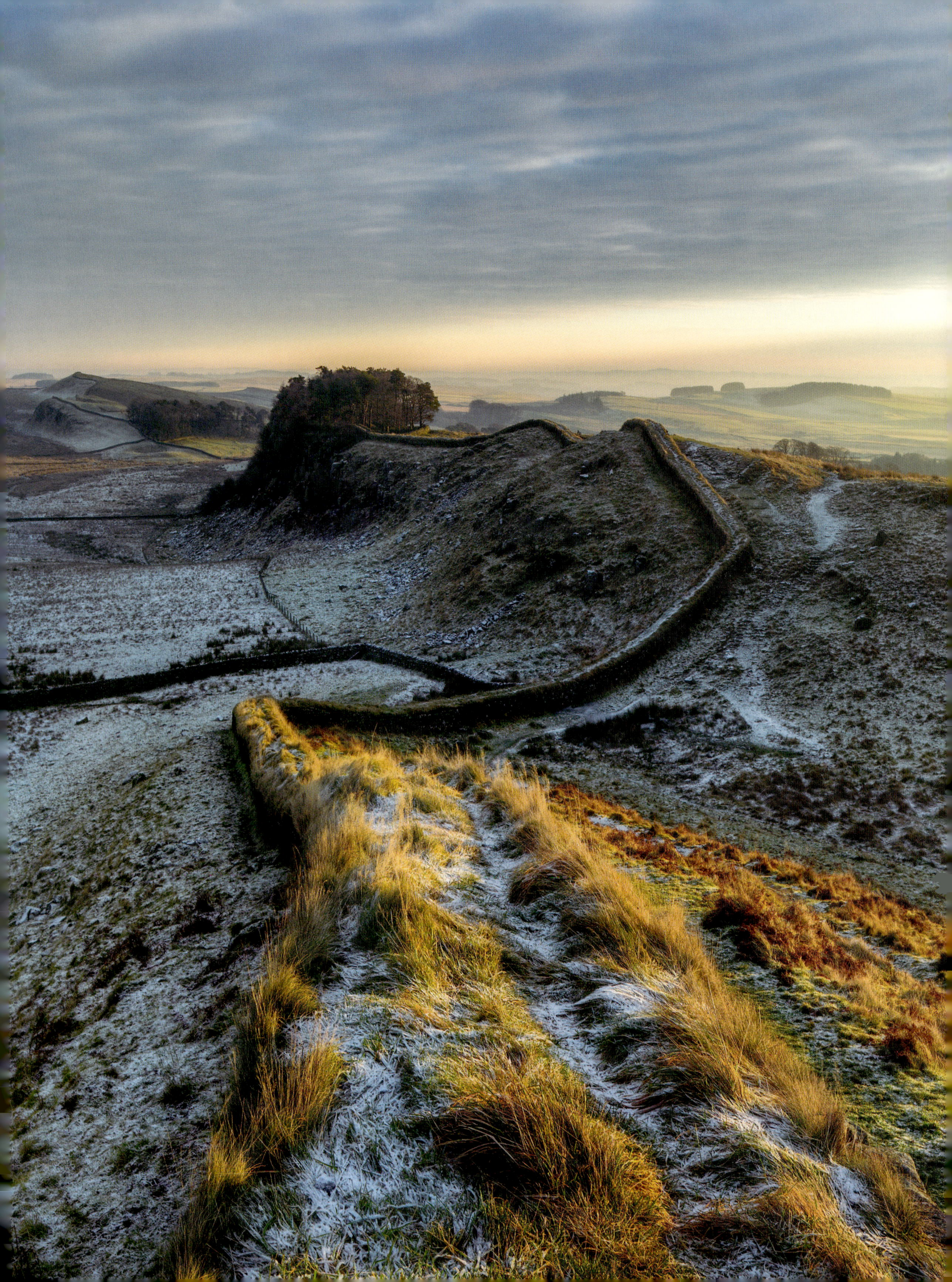

Northumberland

On dark, moonless April nights in the Northumberland hills, away from streetlights, you can see our corner of the universe in all its glory. Jupiter and Venus stand out like bright pearls; the Milky Way shines above the jagged black shapes of the moors, a bridge of light so dense it can be hard to recognise constellations. It might be difficult to imagine that there are still places in England where the night sky is largely unaffected by light pollution from surrounding cities and conurbations, but the Northumberland National Park, a rugged upland landscape of granite hills, volcanic sills, clean rivers and remote valleys in the far north-east of England, bordering Scotland, is one of them.

Together with the neighbouring Kielder Water and Forest Park, it forms the largest 'International Dark Sky Park' in Europe, a designation awarded to places with exceptionally good views of the night sky. The skies in this heart of darkness are rated in the 'Gold' tier, meaning that even the faintest stars and astronomical phenomena are visible. On moonless winter nights when the solar winds are blowing strong, the colours of the aurora borealis can even be seen shimmering on the northern horizon. On summer nights, when the below-the-horizon sun illuminates ice high in the atmosphere, eerie noctilucent clouds shine in the dark sky. At twilight you can sometimes see shafts of zodiacal light – a ghostly glow produced by the dust left in the wake of comets.

This is top-quality darkness. In fact, it is the same clear and unblemished night sky a Roman soldier on night duty might have seen almost 2,000 years ago. And the lack of pollution extends beyond light: four out of the five cleanest rivers in the whole of Britain rise from within this landscape, and they support thriving populations of Atlantic salmon and otter. This is undoubtedly connected to the lack of habitation; just 2,000 people live within the Northumberland National Park, or 0.02 people per hectare, which makes the population one tenth of any other English national park. If you are looking for seclusion and tranquillity, there are few better places to find it.

But the peace of the landscape today belies its often volatile history – for many centuries this was a frontier world, a rugged, even ungovernable, borderland straddling the space between cultures, powers and nations.

The most famous feature of this national park, and the key to its history and identity, is Hadrian's Wall. This World Heritage Site runs for 117 kilometres (73 miles) from coast to coast across northern England, spanning the isthmus

The World Heritage Site of Hadrian's Wall runs from coast to coast across northern England, spanning the isthmus between the Solway Firth and the mouth of the River Tyne. Completed in AD 128, it became the most enduring northern frontier of the Roman Empire, garrisoned by up to 10,000 soldiers from as far away as modern-day Syria.

In a collision of history and geology, Hadrian's Wall undulates over the top of the craggy escarpments created by the Great Whin Sill, an outcrop of volcanic dolerite rock with origins dating back 300 million years. More resistant to erosion than the surrounding sedimentary rocks, the Whin Sill often forms dramatic and conspicuous landforms as it runs across the north of England. Elsewhere, outcrops of the Whin Sill can be seen in the glacially formed cliffs of High Cup Nick in Cumbria; the waterfall of High Force in County Durham; and the lofty protrusions supporting Northumberland coastal castles like Bamburgh and Lindisfarne.

between the Solway Firth and the mouth of the River Tyne. It was the most enduring outer limit of the Roman Empire in northern Europe, and the Northumberland National Park, most of which lies between Hadrian's Wall and the Anglo-Scottish border, encloses the most well-preserved and often jaw-dropping central section of this ancient imperial frontier.

Hadrian's Wall was built over a period of six years from AD 122, under the reign of the eponymous emperor, to provide a secure defensive fortification on the northern edge of the Roman province of Britannia. Beyond it was the realm of Caledonia, inhabited by Pictish tribes, who fiercely resisted imperial rule and ultimately rebuffed every Roman attempt to conquer them. Most of the masonry of Hadrian's Wall and its accompanying fortifications has disappeared – often having been removed and reused for other constructions – but substantial parts of it have endured through the centuries.

In a spectacular collision of geology and history, the wall runs over the top of the natural defensive line of the Great Whin Sill, a long chain of dark cliffs created by an upwelling of volcanic rock 300 million years ago. Following the natural contours of the wavelike escarpment, the wall rises over high crags and periodically dips down into saddles and gaps where the remains of 'milecastles' – fortifications placed at regular intervals along the wall – are nestled. This rollercoaster middle section of the structure is flanked by paths and trails, allowing you to walk with the wall, soaking up views of the high pastures and moors that now surround it. One of England's most celebrated national trails, the 135-kilometre (84-mile) Hadrian's Wall Path, closely follows the route of the fortification across its whole intercoastal length.

Despite being built 2,400 kilometres (1490 miles) away from Rome itself, Hadrian's Wall and the relict landscape around it have yielded internationally significant insights into the nature of Roman society. To its builders, Hadrian's Wall represented the frontier of the known world, and the Romans brutally enforced this barrier against what they saw as the 'barbarians' beyond. Visiting it today, with only the watery calls of curlews or the trills of skylarks interrupting the upland silence, it can be easy to imagine this would have felt like a remote place for the Romans garrisoned here, and for many of them – drawn from as far away as modern-day Syria and North Africa – it would have felt a long, long way from home. But with up to 10,000 soldiers stationed along the wall's length, it gave rise to a society of its own, attracting families, traders and merchants, and supporting significant settlements. Some Roman soldiers are known to have intermarried and started families with the local population, settling in Britain permanently, and becoming incorporated into the cultural mix of these islands.

Hadrian's Wall was abandoned not long after the Roman legions withdrew from Britain in AD 410, but the landscape around it continued to be a contested borderland. The kingdoms of England and Scotland emerged in the 9th century, giving rise to several centuries of conflict and border skirmishing in which landmarks like Humbleton Hill would see bloody battles. Within this war-scarred landscape, central authority was often weak, and communities relied on their own guile and strength for survival. For around 400 years, the border region was dominated by a culture of clan conflict, the era of the famed and feared Border Reivers – cattle raiders who lived by plundering the surrounding region, and each other.

The border country straddled England and Scotland, but neither government exercised full authority within their portion. Instead, the region became governed by a specific cross-border body of law and custom – the 'March law' – which brought some semblance of order to the raiding culture. A physical legacy of this era are the peel towers, small fortified keeps and castles, and bastle houses – farmhouses with inbuilt protections against raiders – found within the national park.

The thick-walled fortified farmhouse of Woodhouses Bastle. During the volatile time of the 'Border Reivers', buildings were often designed with measures to provide protection from raids and conflict.

Opposite:
Lichens covering the branches of an oak tree in Northumberland. Epiphytic lichens, which grow on tree trunks and branches, are sensitive to pollution, and their presence is often a sign of good air quality.

Overleaf:
Northumberland National Park is sparsely populated; just 2,000 people live within its boundaries, the fewest of any national park. Settlements often take the form of quiet hamlets, farmsteads and rural houses. The Edwardian-built Hethpool House – now run as a bed and breakfast – sits within a typical Northumberland landscape of sheep pastures, mixed woods and open moorland.

This tumultuous era is long gone, but a military dimension still persists in this landscape. The Otterburn Training Area takes up around a fifth of the park, a large swathe of moorland between the A68 and Coquetdale dotted with fragments of woodland. It is owned by the Ministry of Defence and is used for army training. Access on roads and public rights of way is permitted outside of times when live firing is underway.

The roof of the Northumberland National Park is the Cheviot, a hulking granite giant of a hill with broad, rotund slopes covered in heather moorland and peat bogs. This mountain is the heavily eroded remnant of an ancient stratovolcano, which may once have been as big as Mount Etna. Time has weathered it down to a lowly 815 metres (2,674 feet) and smoothed out its contours, but it remains the highest thing for many miles around, and on a clear day it provides expansive views into Scotland's southern uplands and England's wild far north.

The Anglo-Scottish border cuts across the high and wild watershed of the Cheviot Hills, but only the English side is enclosed by the Northumberland National Park. In the middle and southern parts of the park, the volcanic geology gives way to sedimentary sandstones and limestones from the Carboniferous era, which form lower hills, and contain some of the most unsung corners of landscape in England. Winding valleys such as Coquetdale, with pockets of ancient woodland, blooming spring meadows, stone villages and lonely farmsteads, are for connoisseurs of quiet country. If you like to walk all day to the sounds of moorland birds and barely see another soul, this is the place for you. Fans of birdlife stand a better chance of spotting some species here than in other parts of upland England: a partnership project involving the Northumberland National Park Authority, the RSPB, Forestry England and others is supporting the resurgence of the local population of hen harrier, providing a haven for the UK's most intensely persecuted bird of prey.

There are no large settlements within the Northumberland National Park, and habitation comes in the form of small hamlets and scattered farmsteads, most of which are historically connected to sheep and cattle farming. Around three-quarters of the park is farmed, and traditional practices like hefting – where flocks of sheep 'know' their territory on the open hillside and pass this knowledge on to subsequent generations – continue to survive here. Around 98 per cent of farmed land within the park is under some form of stewardship scheme to benefit nature and heritage, including initiatives to preserve hay meadows, protect water quality and repair traditional farm buildings.

The Northumberland National Park is a place to experience space in all its forms: the space of the granite moors; the space between past and the present; the space between nations; the space between the stars and galaxies. Yet the paradox of this landscape is how packed it is in other ways: with human history, with distinctive culture and with natural interest. There may be ample space, but it is far from empty.

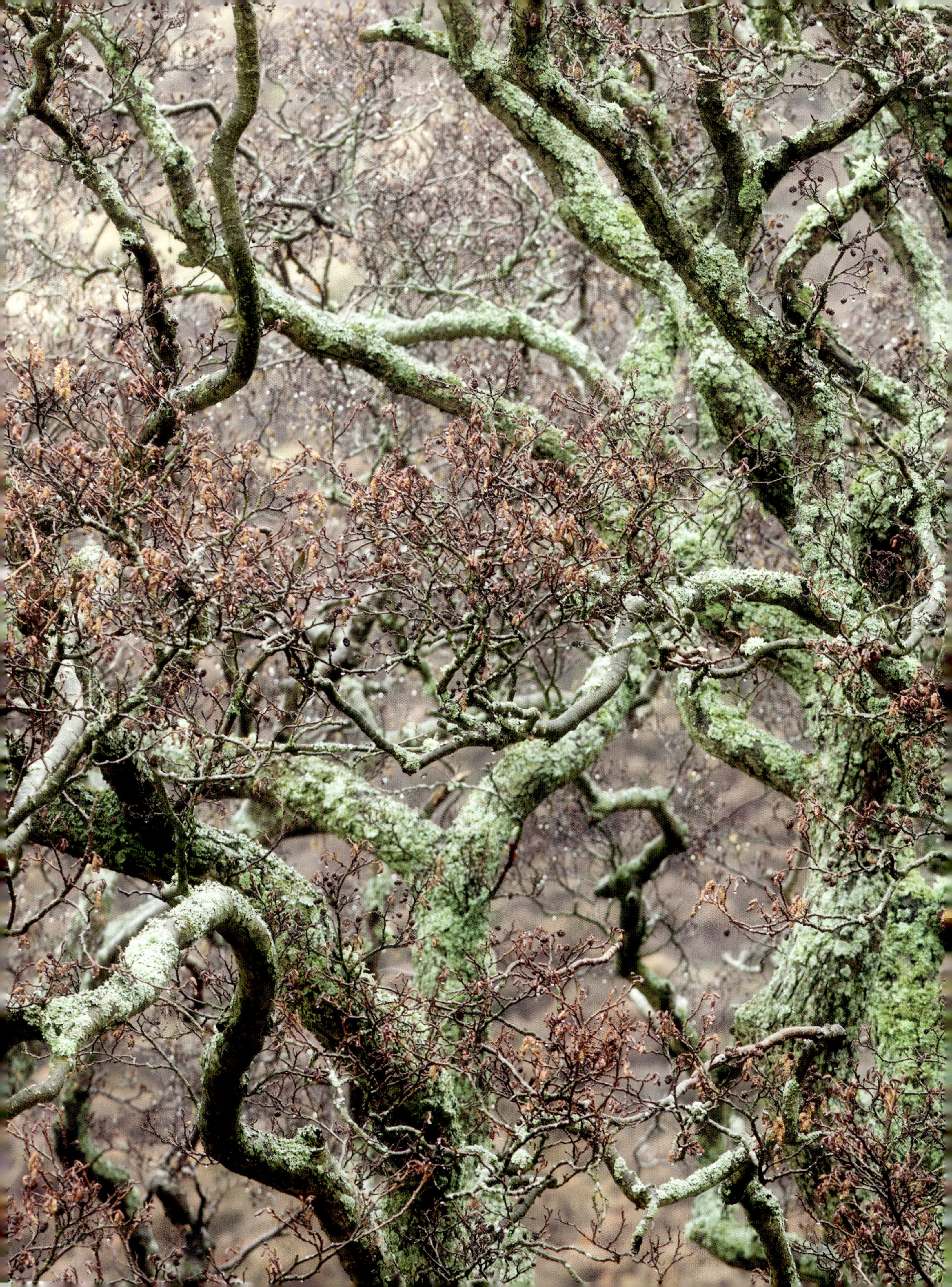

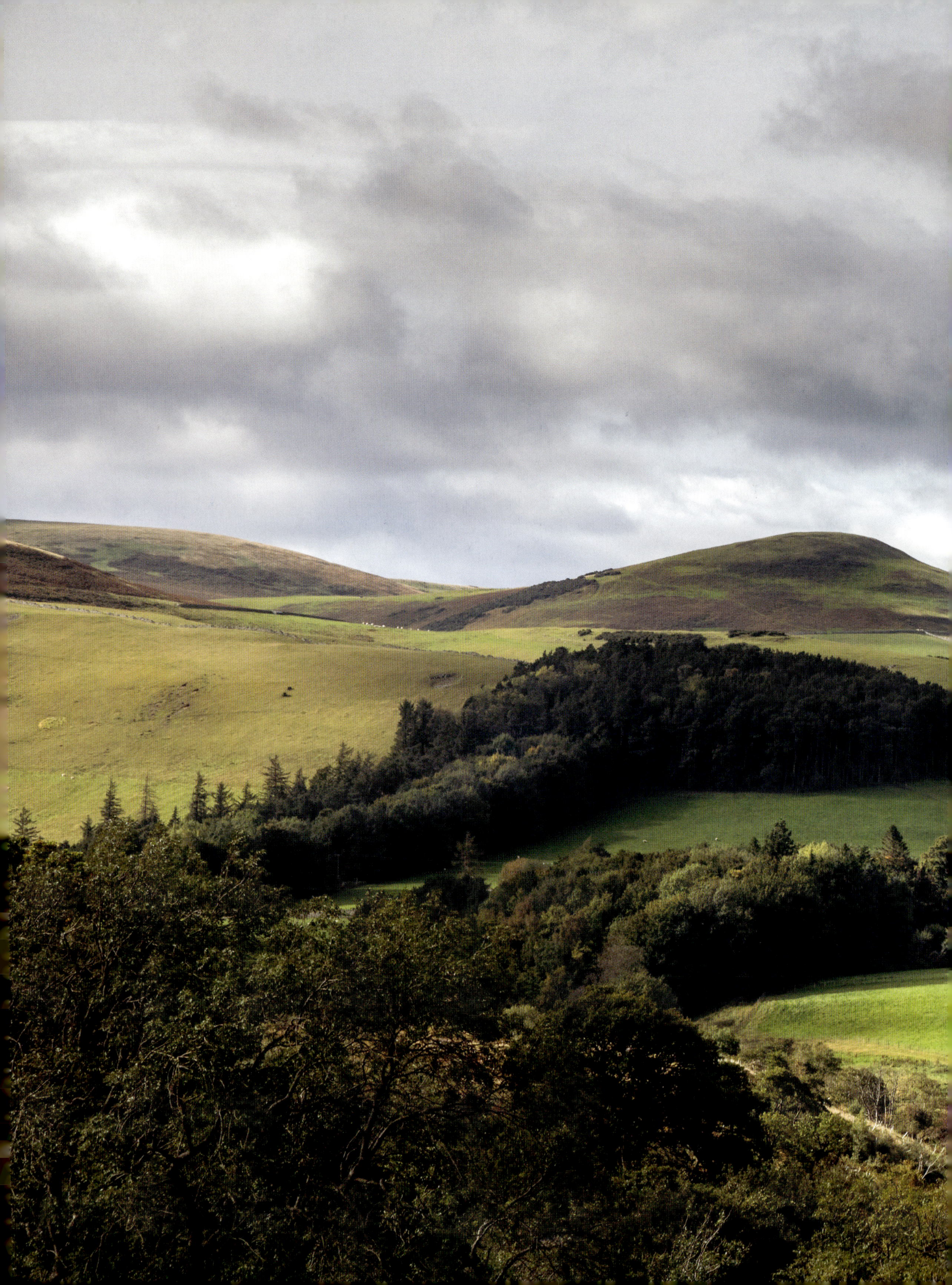

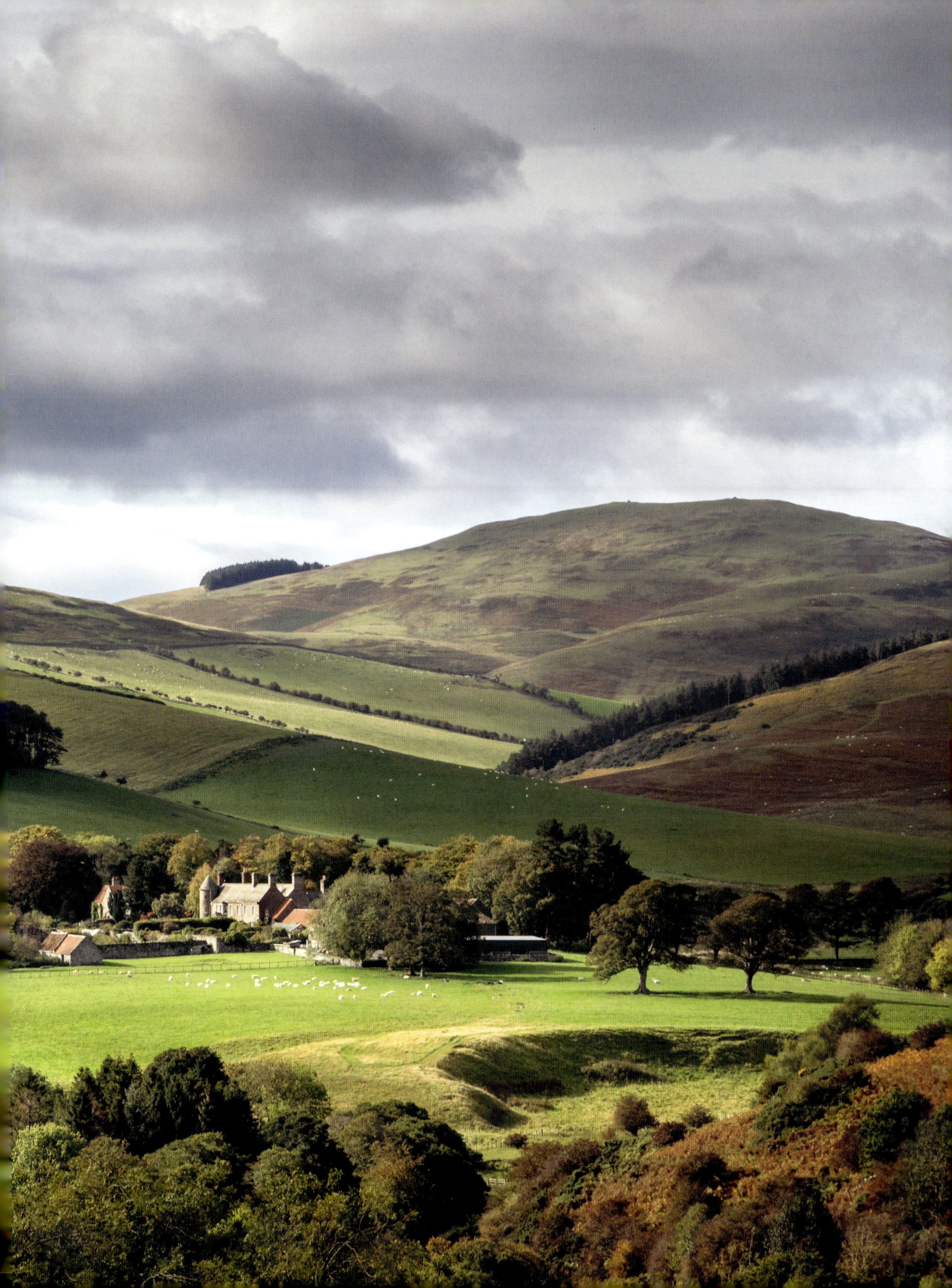

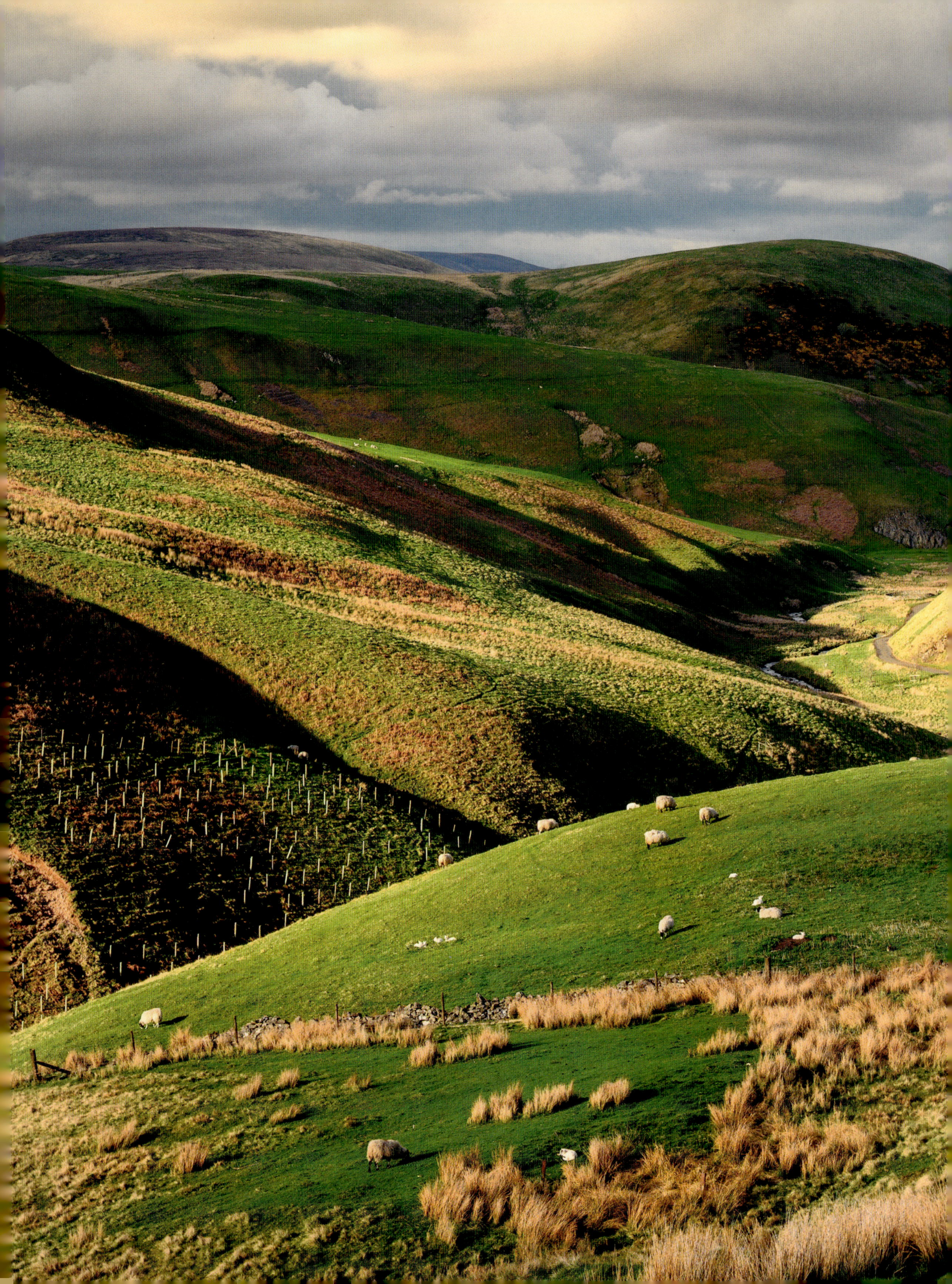

The quiet, tightly winding river valley of Coquetdale carves through the sandstone and limestone hills to the south of the Cheviots.

Overleaf:
Most visible in arctic latitudes, the electrifying sight of the aurora borealis – or Northern Lights – in the skies above Northumberland is a rare one, but the region's exceptionally low levels of light pollution make for unimpeded views when it does appear. This image shows the aurora above Sycamore Gap, a photogenic dip in the Whin Sill. The location was famously featured in the 1991 movie Robin Hood: Prince of Thieves, *with Kevin Costner and Morgan Freeman's characters conversing under the tree as they wander across Hadrian's Wall. Heavily photographed, the sycamore became an icon of North East England, but today the heart of the image shown here is missing. In September 2023, in what authorities described as an act of vandalism, the tree was felled near its base, causing a widespread outpouring of anger and sadness.*

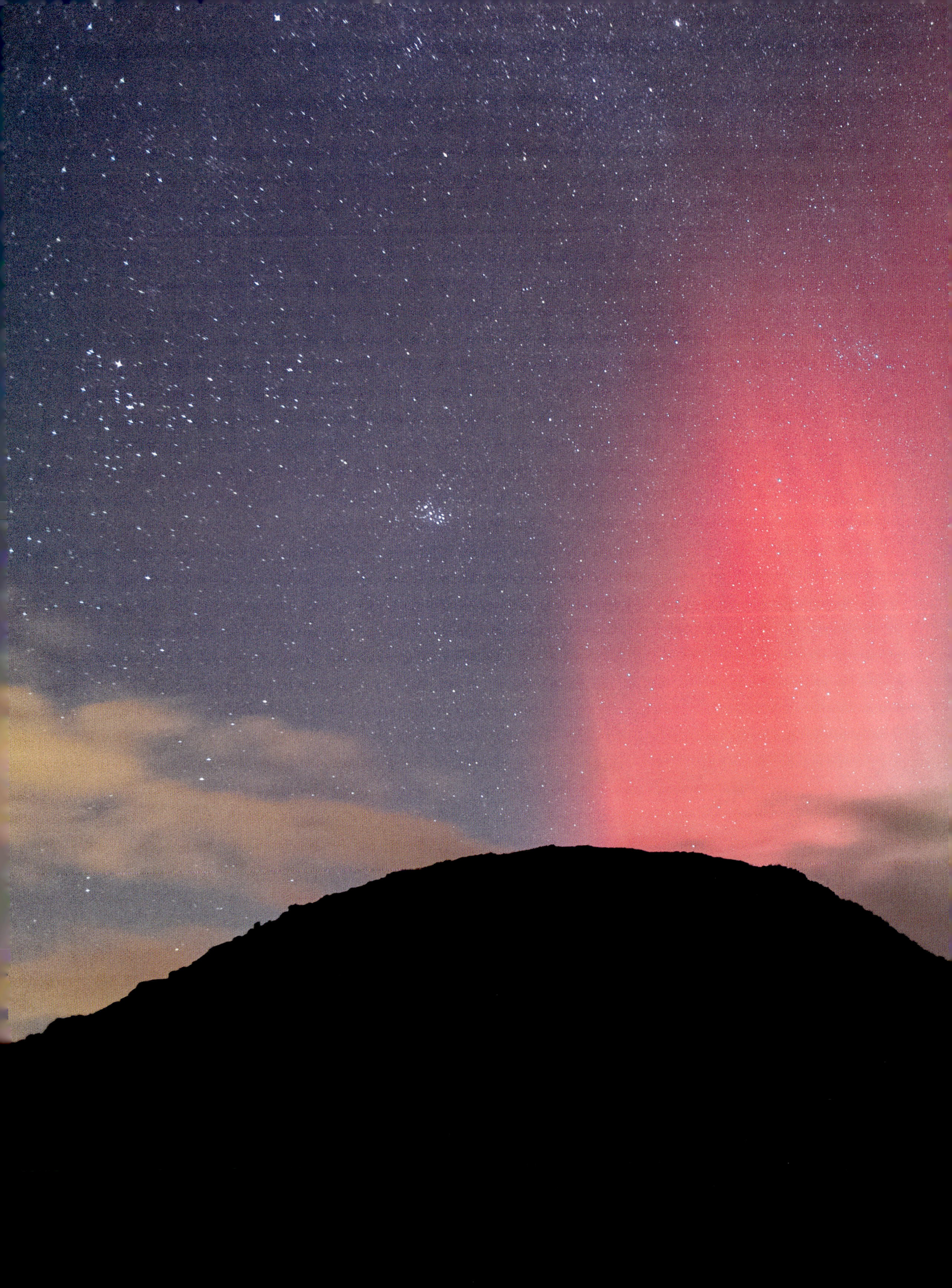

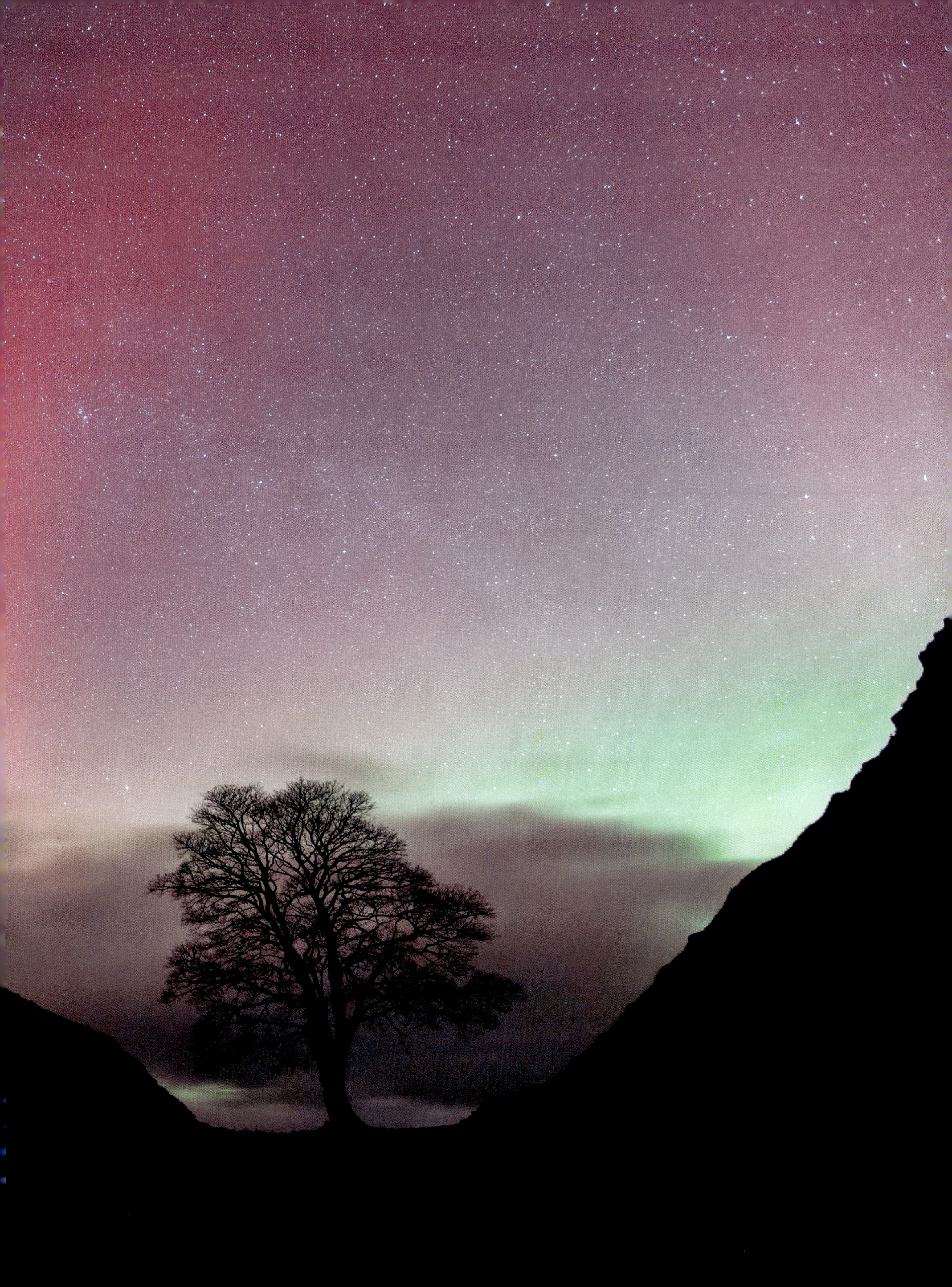

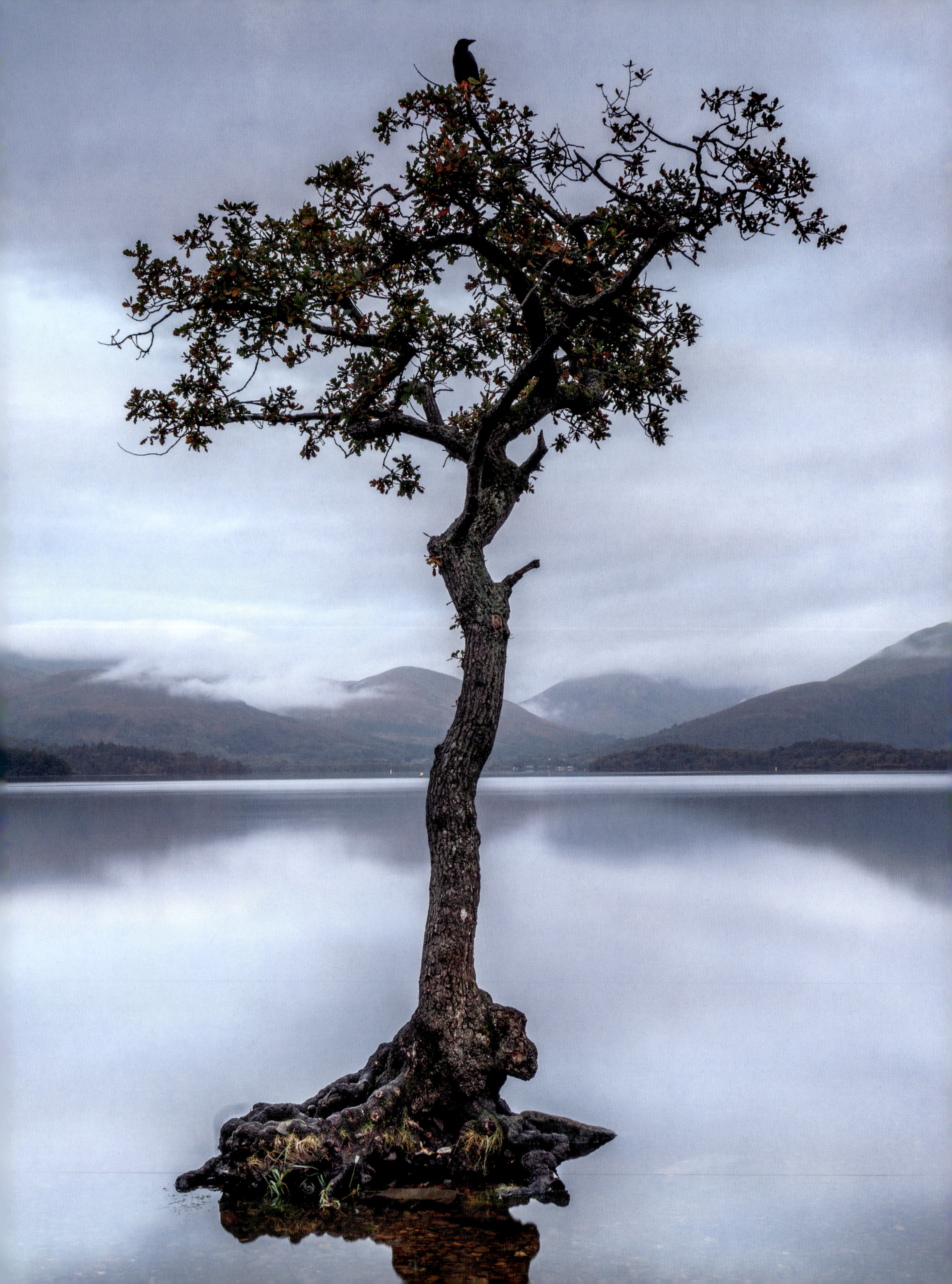

Loch Lomond & The Trossachs

Journeying north from Glasgow, the transition is sudden and spectacular. At some point, the suburbs, fields or rolling hills abruptly give way to something else altogether: a grand world of craggy-summited mountains, lush forests, glacier-carved glens and beautiful lochs jewelled with emerald islands. You have reached the edge of the Scottish Highlands. From here, a chain of hundreds of ancient mountains stretches north for 400 kilometres (249 miles), until the far tip of the British landmass.

This gateway to the Highlands is Loch Lomond & The Trossachs National Park. The change in the landscape stems from crossing the Highland Boundary Fault, the tectonic divide between Scotland's Lowlands and Highlands – not only a geological boundary, but a historic and cultural one too. This national park has the Highlands on the doorstep, an otherworld of lochs and mountains, islands and forests, waterfalls and woods; a place encapsulating all the natural wonder of Scotland's wild places, on the outskirts of a great city.

Loch Lomond, enjoys international cultural fame, in large part through the eponymous song. The loch and its 'bonnie banks' serve as a poignant symbol of Scotland for a Jacobite soldier languishing in an English prison, doomed to take the 'low road' of death back to the Highlands:

O ye'll tak' the high road, and I'll tak' the low road,
And I'll be in Scotland afore ye,
But me and my true love will never meet again,
On the bonnie, bonnie banks o' Loch Lomond.

The mountain-framed Loch Lomond is one of the great natural wonders of Scotland and Britain as a whole, and it serves as a spectacular welcome to the Highlands. Great Britain's largest lake by surface area, stretching for 71 square kilometres (27 square miles) from Balloch to Ardlui, Loch Lomond starts out broad, shallow and island-filled in the south, then narrows into a deep trench of 190 metres (623 feet) in its northern end as it is squeezed between mountain massifs. Venerable oak woods cloak the flanks of many of the mountains surrounding the loch, and its shores are dotted with sandy beaches and fine little hamlets with piers and promenades.

Loch Lomond also contains an archipelago of almost fifty islands and islets, a water world which can be explored by cruise, kayak, boat, or other marine means. It includes Britain's largest inland island, Inchmurrin; the conservation

A lone oak tree perches on a rock in Milarrochy Bay, Loch Lomond. Stretching for 40 kilometres (25 miles) from Balloch to Ardlui, Loch Lomond is the largest lake by surface area in Britain. The loch has a maximum depth of 190 metres (623 feet) – deep enough to submerge the Great Pyramid.

A panorama of Loch Lomond from its south-east corner, showing its fleet of islands, with the Luss Hills rising above the loch to the left and Ben Lomond to the right.

refuge of Inchcailloch, where spectacular carpets of bluebells blanket the floors of dense woods in spring; and Inchlonaig, where the island's population of yew trees is a legacy of Robert the Bruce, who planted them 900 years ago to supply wood for bows used in the First War of Scottish Independence. The Highland Boundary Fault is spectacularly visible as a fleet of wooded islands stretching across the south of the loch like a convoy of green ships, culminating in the miniature mountain of Conic Hill (361 meters / 1,184 feet) on the eastern shore of the loch. In this national park, land and water blend together in some of the most enchanting ways to be found anywhere in Britain.

Some of the smaller islets are thought to be 'crannogs', the remains of ancient artificial islands built to provide a platform for dwellings. The construction of substantial paved roads through the intractable terrain of the Highlands is relatively new, and historically, lochs, waterways and seaways were important thoroughfares through the landscape. Islands like those in Loch Lomond would have been places of convergence. The island of Clairinsh, for example, was the medieval seat of Clan Buchanan, which held the land to the east of Loch Lomond. The adjacent crannog, 'the Kitchen', is thought to have been where they held meetings of council.

Much of the Scottish Highlands has seen historic deforestation, but this national park contains some of the largest remaining tracts of native Atlantic oakwood on the western side of the Highlands. The combination of mountainous topography and proximity to the Gulf Stream makes this one of the wettest landscapes in Britain, producing temperate rainforests where epiphytic plants – plants that grow from other plants – thrive. These oak woods are not 'untouched', but they provide a glimpse into what large areas of western Scotland would once have looked like. The islands of Loch Lomond and its sylvan shores contain some of the most beguiling examples of these waterwoods. Boughs of sessile oaks overhang sandy beaches; moisture-loving trees, mosses, ferns, fungi, flowers, liverworts and lichens tangle indistinguishably together in a lush chaos of growth; eldritch-looking goblin forests of alder and willow thrive in boggy mires.

Much of Loch Lomond is surrounded by hills and mountains, but one summit above all is identified with this beautiful lake. Rising to the east side of the loch, its lower flanks skirted by forest, is the quartz-topped form of Ben Lomond (974 metres / 3,196 feet), the most southerly of Scotland's Munros – the 282 mountains in Scotland above 914 metres (3,000 feet); a list first compiled by Sir Hugh Munro in 1891. Ben Lomond gives its name to the huge body of water below it and dominates the scene from many of its shores, while the sight of the island-scattered loch spread out below you from the mountain's summit is one of the most magnificent views offered by the high places of Scotland. Ben Lomond and Loch Lomond have a kind of intertwined identity: it is hard to think of one without the other. As with the loch, it is a popular landmark within relatively easy reach of the central belt; sometimes dubbed 'Glasgow's Mountain', it holds a special place in the heart of the city.

The Glasgow-born climber, author and broadcaster Tom Weir is closely associated with Loch Lomond, and is credited with introducing countless people to the beauty of the Scottish landscape through his writings and long-running TV series *Weir's Way*. Scotland's 'best-loved walker' lived on the shores of Loch Lomond and beautifully evoked its surroundings: 'wage slaves no longer, but with hearts light as the blue sky… we set off on the high contouring path in a scent of bluebells and rowan blossom'. Weir campaigned for the designation of this national park, a goal fulfilled in 2002, four years before his death. He is memorialised with a bronze statue on the shores of the loch in Balmaha.

With wingspans of more than two metres, golden eagles are a breathtaking sight across the Scottish Highlands. Despite their vast size, these eagles can be surprisingly hard to spot, but are unforgettable when they are.

The other landscape in the double-billing of this national park's title is the Trossachs. Concentrated around a single glen, but generally held to refer to a wider area, the Trossachs is intricate and deeply photogenic. Mini-mountains

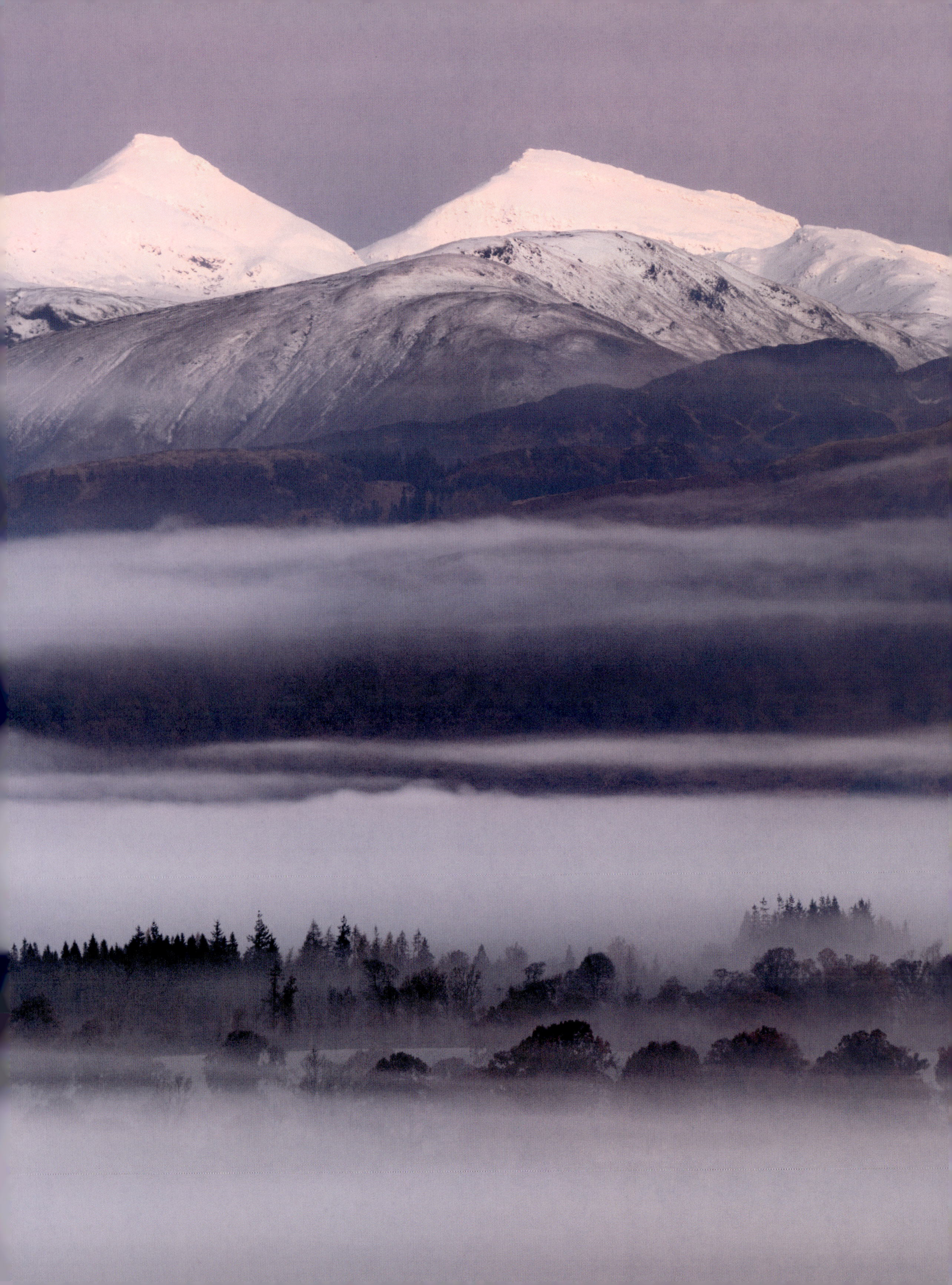

poke up from swathes of forest; braes are blanketed in purple heather; rocky rivers and waterfalls course through woods; and exquisite lochs steam with mist in the morning sun.

Filtered through the imaginations of artists, this small pocket of landscape – often described as 'the Highlands in miniature' – has had an important cultural impact, influencing modern perceptions of the Highlands, and serving as a blueprint for an idealised vision of Scotland. Its beauty and relative accessibility made it a favourite haunt of Romantic poets and painters, most famously Walter Scott, who set his 1810 long poem 'Lady of the Lake' here, where the landscape is described as 'so wondrous wild, the whole might seem / the scenery of a fairy dream'. Scott's work – which follows three intertwined narratives involving a love rivalry, a plot against King James V and the conflict between Lowland Scots and Highlanders – helped to trigger the Highland Revival, a surge of interest in the customs, culture and dress of the Scottish clans, albeit in romanticised form. In the midst of the turbulence of industrialisation, the alluring myth of the Highlands as a place of wild landscapes and noble traditions served as an antidote to the pressures of the age. As the 19th century progressed, the Trossachs became one of Scotland's first tourist destinations. Scott's 1817 novel *Rob Roy* also did much to popularise and shape the image of the Jacobite-era cattle raider and outlaw as a loveable Highland rogue.

Today, the real-world Trossachs remains a beautiful place to visit, as well as a natural bastion. There are extensive tracts of commercial forestry here, but as with the shores of Loch Lomond, the Trossachs glen and its surroundings also contain significant swathes of ancient and semi-natural broadleaved woodland, particularly at the head of Loch Katrine, where waves of oak and beech push high up the sides of Ben A'an and Ben Venue, the fiery foliage creating one of the most spectacular scenes in the Highlands when autumn arrives.

Red deer are a natural icon of Scotland, long celebrated in the arts. In autumn, their rutting calls echo around the glens. With no natural predators, deer are culled in large numbers both for sport and conservation, as overly high numbers of deer suppress the growth of vegetation. Along with other deer species, red deer numbers are thought to be at an all-time high, leading to heated debate around how best to address their environmental impact.

Opposite:
The first creeping rays of winter sunlight touch the tops of Ben More (right) and Stob Binnein. The former is the highest peak in the national park, and climbing it via the usual route from the north is a steep and sustained effort, but one rewarded by extensive views across the Southern Highlands and beyond.

The Scottish Highlands are a stronghold of the pine marten, which has been spreading further across Scotland and Britain since it became legally protected in the 1980s. A relative of weasels and stoats, they are nocturnal and notoriously difficult to spot. Pine martens prey on both native red squirrels and invasive grey ones, but they find the latter easier to catch - meaning that red squirrels tend to do better in areas with pine martens than without.

Opposite:
A burn tumbles through temperate rainforest near Inversnaid, on the east bank of Loch Lomond. Poet Gerard Manley Hopkins evoked the atmosphere of these lush Atlantic oakwoods in his poem named after the area:
'What would the world be, once bereft / Of wet and of wildness? Let them be left, / O let them be left, wildness and wet; / Long live the weeds and the wilderness yet.'

Several of the iconic species associated with Scotland's mountain areas can be found in the Trossachs, including the slinky, chestnut-brown pine marten, and the iconic red deer, whose monstrous-sounding rutting calls reverberate through the woods in autumn. Along with the national park as a whole, the Trossachs have a healthy population of red squirrels: their non-native grey squirrel competitors, who have done so much damage to the red squirrel population elsewhere in Britain, are rarely found north of the Highland Boundary Fault.

This national park has also played is part in the resurgence of wild beavers in Scotland, which has seen the numbers of this celebrated aquatic animal rise to more than 1,000 across the country after having been extinct for 400 years. Evidence of them has been found in Loch Earn, along the River Dochart, and in Trossachs lochs including Loch Achray. A planned translocation of a beaver family to Loch Lomond also took place in 2023.

As well as Loch Lomond and the Trossachs, the west side of this national park also encompasses a large section of the Cowal peninsula, where rugged hills overlook Loch Eck and the two sea lochs of Goil and Long, where pilot whales, porpoises and dolphins can occasionally be glimpsed. The national park also stretches north of Ben Lomond, incorporating the Southern Highlands, with 21 Munros in total. Significant mountain clusters include the rugged Arrochar Alps, the Crianlarich Hills (at 1,174 metres / 3,852 feet, Ben More is the highest summit in the national park), and the magnificently throne-shaped Ben Lui massif. This southern swath of the Highlands, its summits often visible from the tops of Glasgow's tenements, has played an important role in the formation of Scotland's outdoor culture.

One such landmark is the formidable-looking peak of the Cobbler (or Ben Arthur) in the Arrochar Alps. Crowned by a triple-summited craggy fortress of quartzite rock, it is said to resemble a shoemaker at work, but it could also be

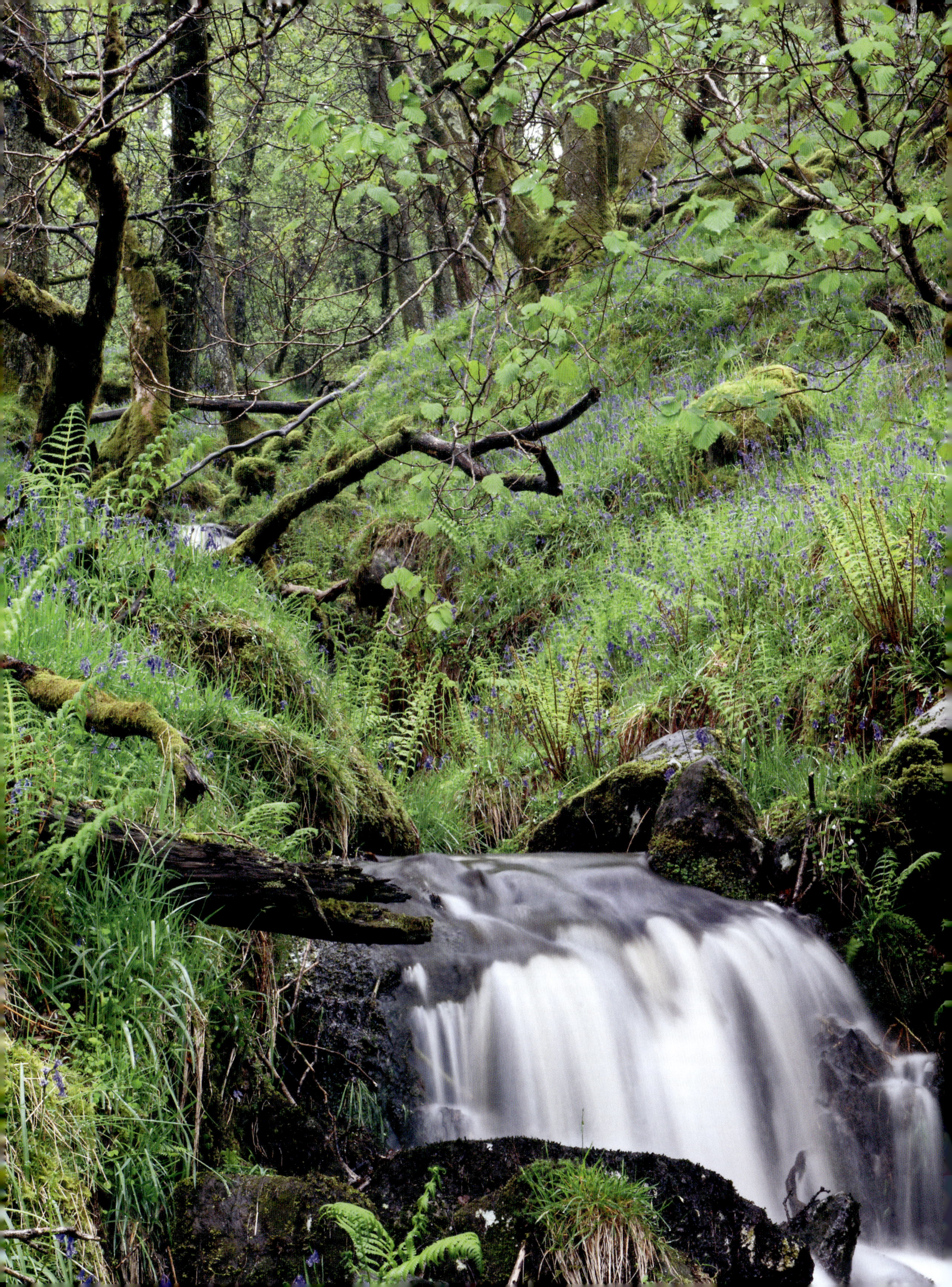

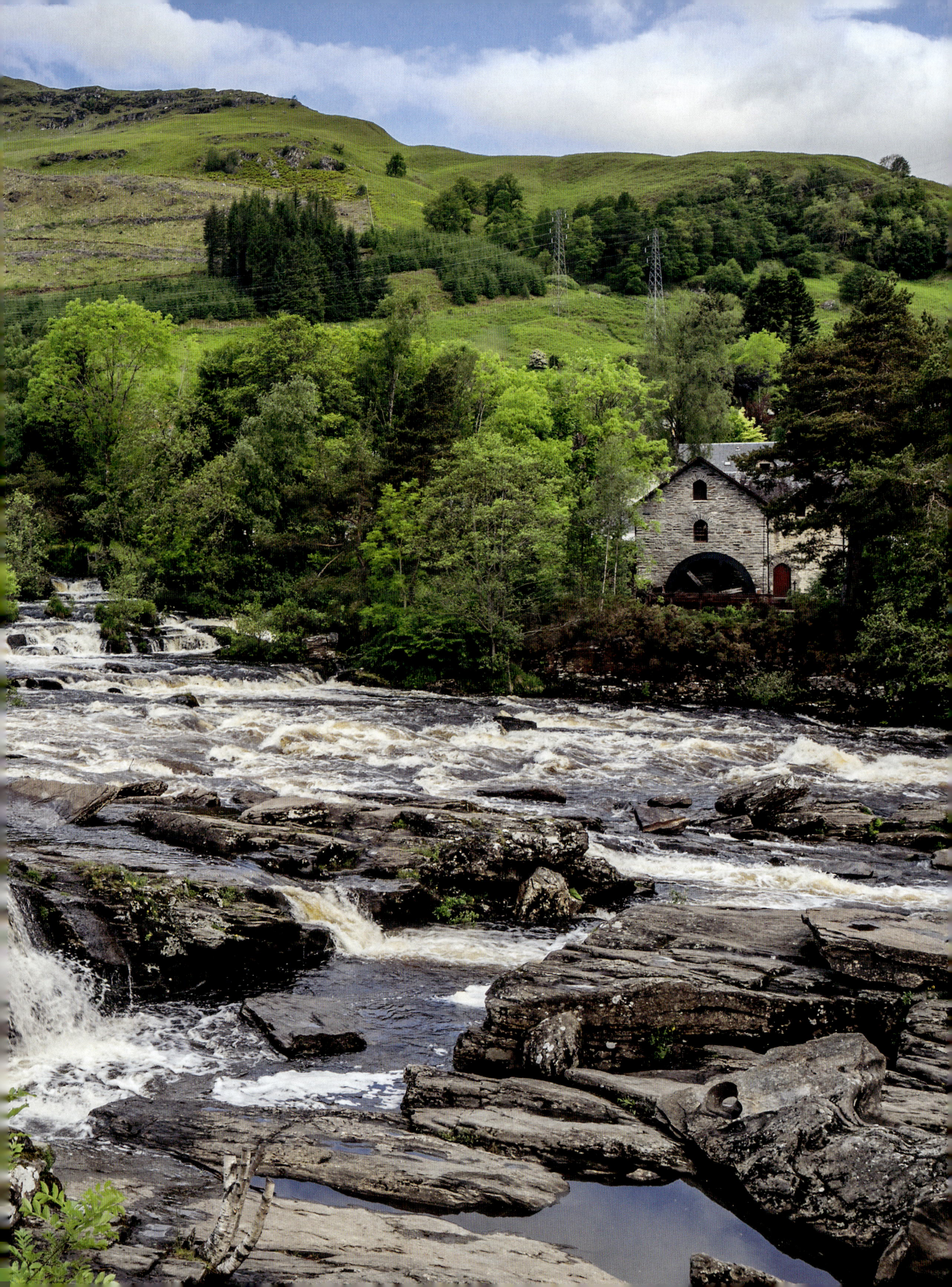

The unmistakeable schist summits of The Cobbler. Steeped in climbing history, the mountain is also one of the most popular hillwalks in the Southern Highlands - though reaching its 'true' summit requires a careful scramble up an exposed rocky spire.

The West Highland Way approaches Conic Hill near Loch Lomond. Running from the outskirts of Glasgow to Fort William, the famous 154km-long route is walked by around 35,000 people a year.

Opposite:
At the village of Killin, the river Dochart flows through the tumultuous Falls of Dochart. The force of the river was harnessed by a local textile industry; the mill visible here was built in 1840 and last saw industrial use as a tweed mill. Now used as a museum and crafts centre, it is also where the stones of St Fillan are kept: eight river-eroded stones shaped like an organ of the body, which are reputed to have healing powers.

the outstretched wings of an eagle swooping on prey. Scotland's first climbing club, founded in 1866, was named after this mountain, but the depression era of the 1930s saw it become the focus of attention for underemployed workers from Glasgow's shipbuilding communities. With time on their hands, they channelled their energies into climbing and mountaineering, pioneering hard new routes on the Cobbler's summit crags and bedding down amid the boulders of neighbouring Beinn Narnain. A politicised working-class outdoor movement was burgeoning across Britain at the time, personified in Scotland through influential figures like Sir Robert Grieve, a pioneering town planner and mountaineer, and Jock Nimlin, a cutting-edge climber who made many important first ascents in the Arrochar Alps. A legacy of this era is the campaigning energy that eventually led to the long-standing 'right to roam' on land and water being enshrined in Scottish law in 2003.

The popularity of this national park for recreation naturally creates pressures on the landscape, but it has also directly contributed to its protection. Established in 1980 as Scotland's first official long-distance trail, the West Highland Way is 154 kilometres (96 miles) long, and its route between the Glasgow suburbs and Fort William passes alongside Loch Lomond. The route's founder, Glaswegian Tom Hunter, believed that having an official trail in place would protect the woodland on the eastern shore of Loch Lomond from development. 'There's enough walking country for our lifetime,' he said, 'but if we don't do something now there will be none for future generations.' The West Highland Way is now an internationally celebrated attraction, bringing in millions of pounds of revenue to the region every year, and acting as an effective shield for the natural and scenic value of the landscape along the way.

It is a fitting example of the loyalty and affection the landscape of this national park has fostered in so many people. As Tom Weir wrote, 'At the end of the day the wondrous beauty of Loch Lomond is a public responsibility in which all of us must play a part.'

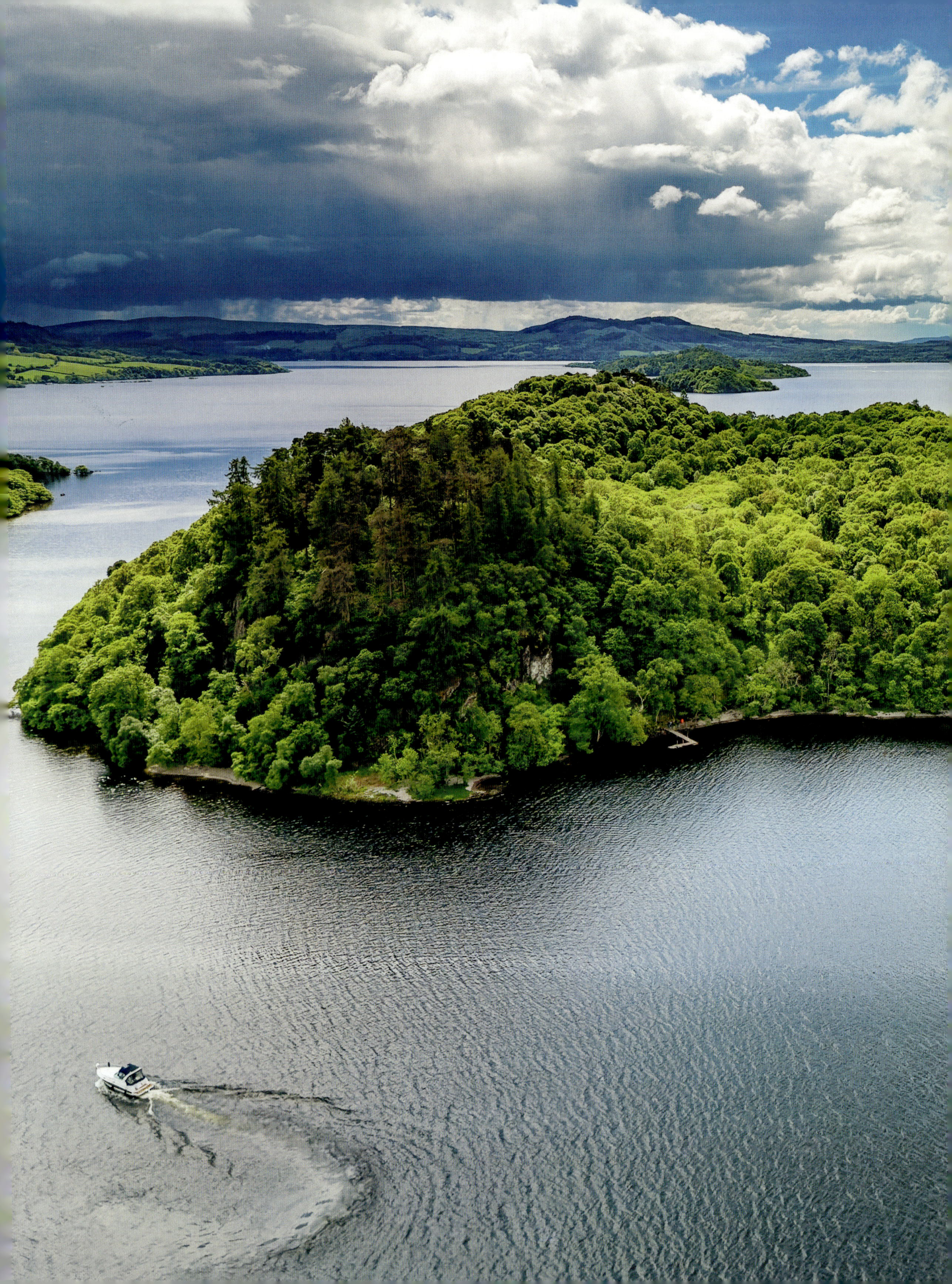

Loch Lomond is dotted with 22 main islands and a host of smaller islets. Inchcailloch ('Isle of the old woman') is one of the largest and most often-visited, thanks to its accessibility across a short channel from the nearby village and tourist hub of Balmaha. Like most of the loch's islands, it is densely wooded, and is spectacularly carpeted in bluebells in spring. Inchcaillioch is one of a line of islands that form part of the Highland Boundary Fault, along with the lochside summit of Conic Hill.

Overleaf:
At 454 metres (1,491 feet) high, Ben A'an is a small hill by the standards of the Scottish Highlands, but the view offered by its rocky summit across Loch Katrine and the forests of the Trossachs is one of the most beautiful outlooks anywhere in these islands.

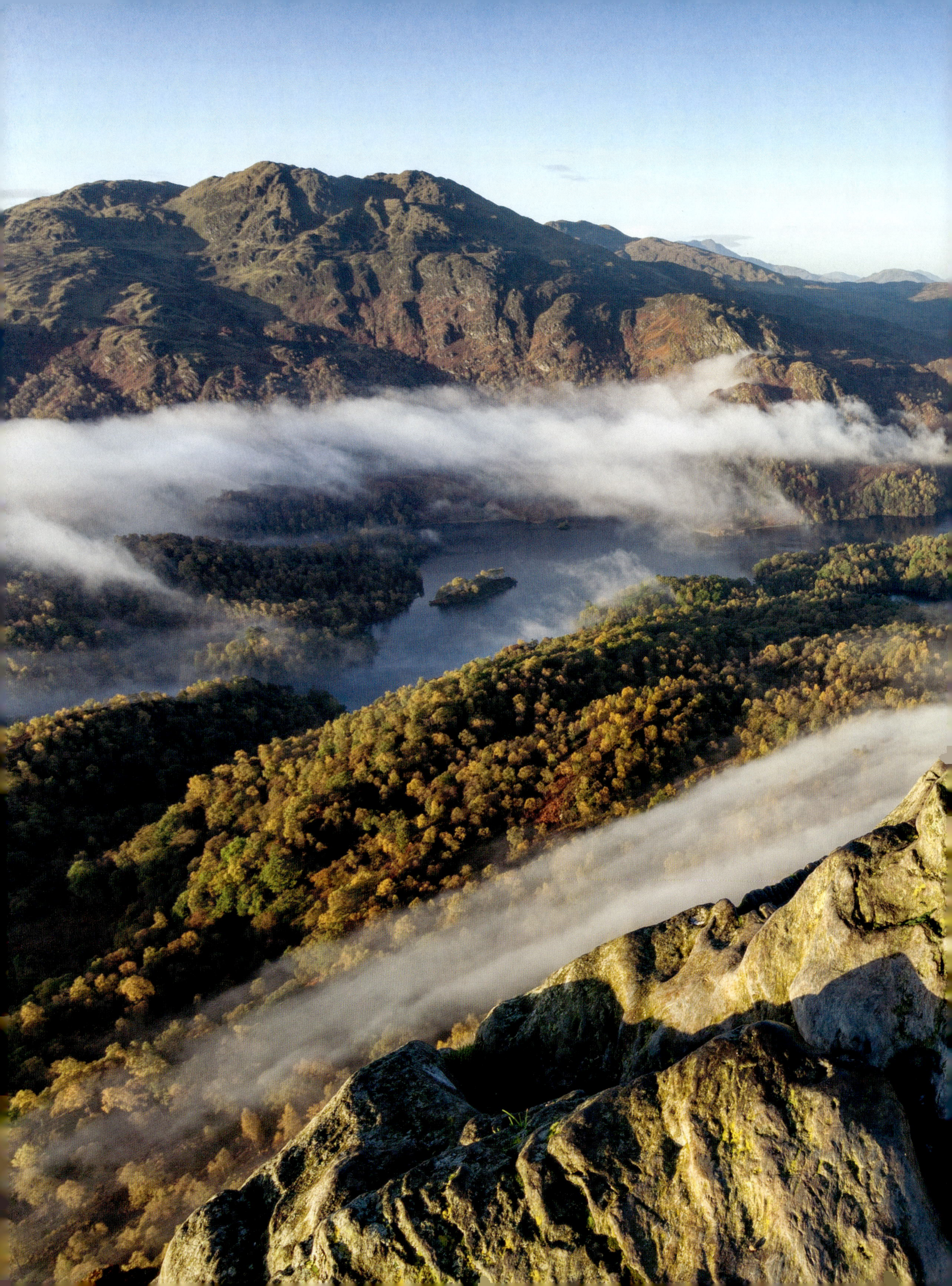

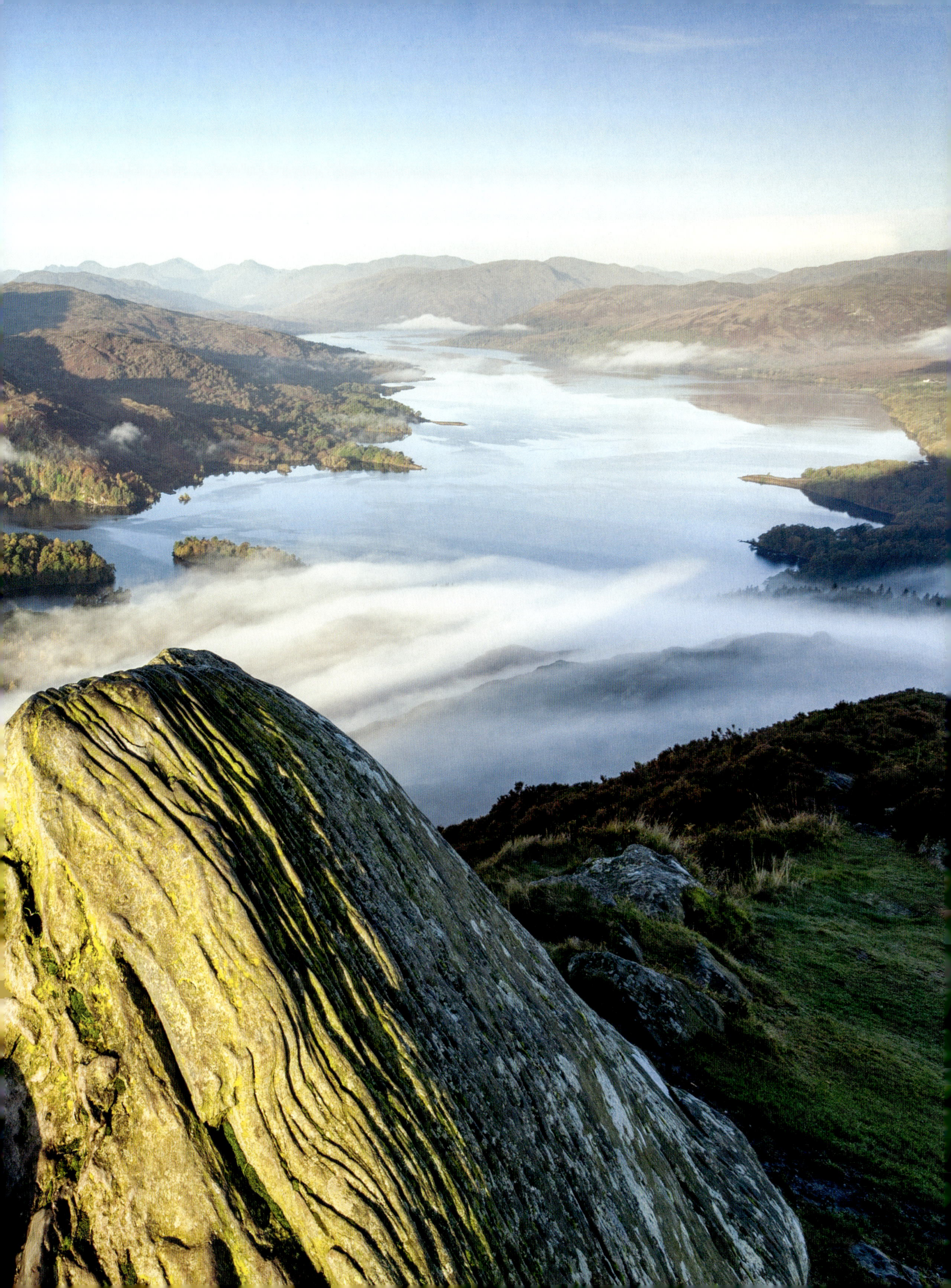

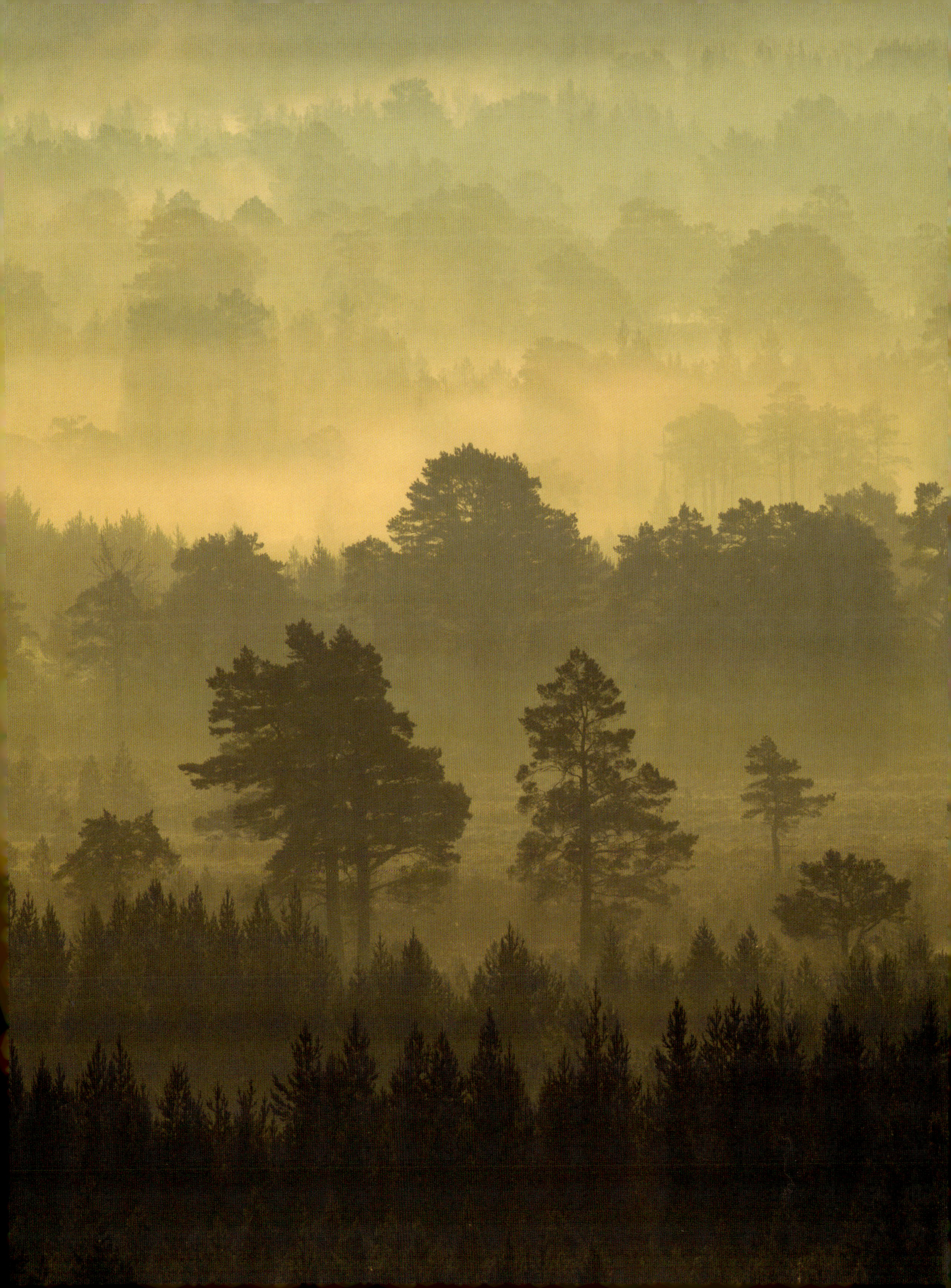

Cairngorms

Around 6,000 years ago, Scotland, along with much of Britain, would have resembled the wildest parts of Scandinavia today. It was widely covered in 'boreal' woodland dominated by Scots pine, interspersed with bogs, marshes, heaths and grasslands. Salmon leapt from rich rivers into the waiting jaws of bears; wolves prowled the landscape and aurochs – now-extinct wild cattle – grazed through the grasslands and marshes. Many of these beasts have vanished today, but still wander through our language and mythology. Human-driven destruction and natural climate change both diminished these coniferous forests and pushed them northwards, but around half of Scotland is thought to still have been wooded when the Romans unsuccessfully attempted their conquest of Caledonia, with soldiers reporting of their campaigns being frustrated by impregnable tracts of forest.

By the 20th century, this 'Caledonian forest' had been reduced to a handful of isolated enclaves – as little as 1 per cent of its historic extent across the Scottish Highlands. Yet in the Cairngorms, Britain's highest, wildest, biggest and coldest national park, the Caledonian forest has clung on, and is even experiencing a resurgence. In a corridor running from the upper reaches of Glen Feshie to Grantown-on-Spey – via the forests of Rothiemurchus, Glenmore and Abernethy – large swathes of pine woodland cover thousands of hectares, filling the floor of the wide mountain basins and pushing high into glens and mountain passes. These forests give a tantalising glimpse of a lost world. Reefs of heather, bilberry and cowberry cover the ground; click-clacking calls of lekking capercaillie echo through the understory; pine martens slink along the gnarled branches of veteran trees. The Caledonian forest is also a vital refuge for Scotland's threatened population of wildcats, Britain's only remaining native wild feline (its near relative, the Eurasian lynx, was hunted to extinction in Britain centuries ago). Dozens of wildcats are currently being released into secret forest locations across the Cairngorms as part of a programme to revive the drastic decline of the species, which has suffered from habitat loss, persecution and hybridisation with domestic cats.

In ecological terms, most of the Scottish Highlands forms part of the taiga, the great unbroken belt of forest that encircles the high latitudes of the earth. In the Cairngorms, standing on the shores of an exquisite forest-fringed water like Loch Morlich or Loch an Eilein, with the broad backs of sub-arctic mountains beyond, you can feel the landscape's natural affinity with the great boreal expanses of Siberia, Scandinavia and North America. An Lochan Uaine – 'the green loch' – is a jewel of a tarn nestling under Meall a' Bhuachaille on the

Hazy early morning light washes over the pines of Rothiemurchus, one of Scotland's largest remnants of native Caledonian forest.

Regenerating forest in the upper reaches of Glen Feshie pushes high up the mountain slopes. The Cairngorms contain some of the last remaining 'natural' treelines in Scotland and wider Britain, where trees and montane shrubland reach 800 metres (2,625 feet) or higher. Forest restoration efforts are helping to spread these high-altitude treelines.

A rock ptarmigan in its white winter plumage. With this natural camouflage, the birds blend seamlessly and almost invisibly into a backdrop of snow.

Ryvoan Pass, flanked by hillsides swathed in Scots pines – its emerald hue is said to be the result of bathing fairies, but it also seems to distil the colours of the trees around it, as if the water were infused with the forest itself.

As wondrous as these time-capsule forests are, they only comprise a relatively small part of this national park, which is twice the size of Lake District, the next-largest UK national park. The eponymous Cairngorms, or Am Monadh Ruadh in Gaelic – roughly meaning red mountains, referring to the pinkish tinge of the range's rock – are a range of hulking granite giants whose sprawling heights suddenly give way to plunging crags and deep glacial troughs. Crowned by Ben Macdui (1,309 metres / 4,295 feet) the UK's second-highest mountain, the tops of the Cairngorms form a kilometre-high sub-arctic tundra, which is Britain's largest continuous area of high ground, a sea of granite with a climate and ecology more akin to Iceland than many other parts of the UK. As well as the Cairngorms themselves, this national park also encompasses a host of other mountain areas including the mighty Lochnagar; Beinn a'Ghlo and the hills of the Forest of Atholl; the Glenshee hills; and parts of the remote moorlands of the Monadhliath. This national park includes 55 of Scotland's 282 Munros, including four of the five highest, all of which are in the main Cairngorms range.

This massive mountain landscape can be an unforgiving place. Winter temperatures approaching -30°C are not uncommon, wind speeds of up to 173mph have been recorded on the summits, and blizzarding snows regularly swathe the upper reaches of the mountains in disorientating white-outs – 'white rooms', where all reference points in the landscape terrifyingly vanish. Yet life still finds a way here: these mountains are home to astonishingly hardy wildlife like the snow bunting, the rock ptarmigan and the mountain hare, all animals that change their colour from summer to winter to better blend in with their rocky or snowy surroundings.

Vegetation can also be found in the upper reaches of the mountains: low-growing arctic–alpine plants like creeping azalea, starry saxifrage and alpine lady's mantle nestle cushion-like between rocks or run in mats across the ground, having adapted to a climate that sees them buried in snow for six months of the year. Even on the highest summits, trees manage to survive, although they are easy to miss: the dwarf willow has been whittled down by the snows and the incessant winds to miniature proportions, growing to no more than a few centimetres high, making it possibly the world's smallest tree.

According to legend, colour-changing animals and tiny trees are not the only extraordinary inhabitants of the high Cairngorms. The Big Grey Man (Am Fear Liath Mòr), a sinister supernatural creature said to dwell on the remote summit of Ben Macdui, has been the subject of a host of sightings and encounters over the last 100 years. Hillwalkers and mountaineers have reported fleeing the mountain after hearing loud footstep sounds around them; feeling a malevolent presence nearby; or waking in a tent at night to see the creature silhouetted against the moon, a wiry ten-foot-tall giant with long dark hair. It is not difficult to imagine the Cairngorms plateau as a place of mists and monsters, but more materially grounded explanations for the Old Grey Man include exhaustion, discomfiting ultra-low frequency sounds caused by wind, or Brocken spectres – the illusion of a tall figure caused by a person's shadow projected onto cloud.

One person who did not flinch from the mysteries these mountains beg was Nan Shepherd. Her book *The Living Mountain* contemplates the Cairngorms as observed in the 1940s and is often described as one of the finest works of British landscape and nature writing. 'However often I walk on them, these hills hold astonishment for me,' she wrote. 'There is no getting accustomed to them.' Shepherd's descriptions of the Cairngorms range from the minutest details of cup lichens and saxifrages to powerful evocations of its high places: 'Summer on the high plateau can be delectable as honey; it can also be a

Purple saxifrage is an arctic–alpine plant of the Cairngorms that can form large colourful 'cushions', typically across rocky ground. A species of cold extremes, it is the highest known flowering plant in Europe, found at 4,500 metres (15,000 feet) in the Swiss Alps, and it also grows on Greenland's Kaffeklubben Island, the northernmost permanent point of land on earth.

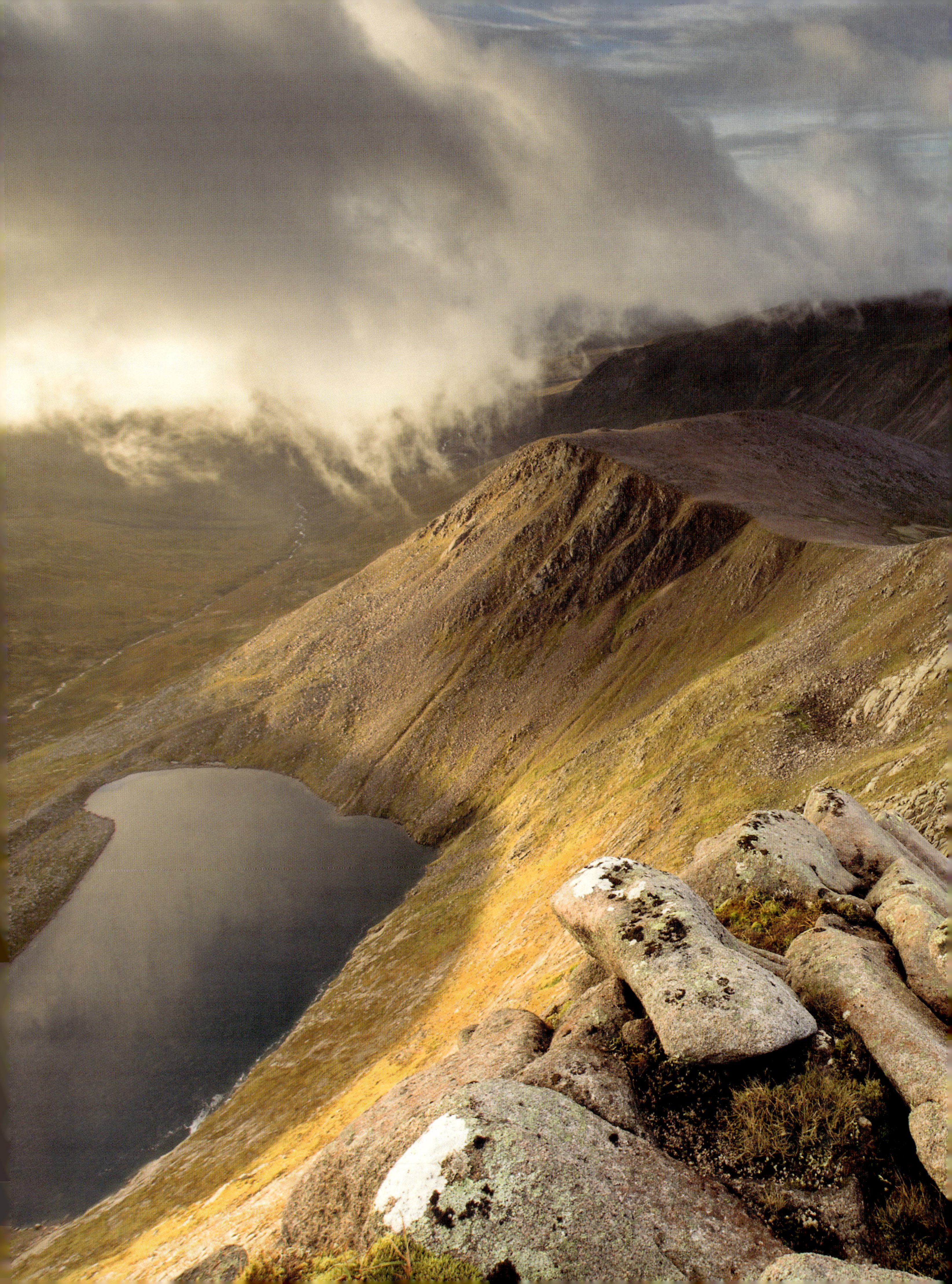

roaring scourge.' For her, the immensity of the Cairngorms was something to be embraced, a way of fusing with the infinite.

Formed from 400-million-year-old granite, and thought to have been exposed to the surface for most of that the time, these weathered, rounded mountains are in contrast to the more jagged and pronounced summits of Scotland's west coast. Yet glaciers have also taken huge bites out of the granite plateau, forming the plunging crags and corries that give the land much of its dramatic power. The Cairngorms are often wide and horizontal and then suddenly vertical. The relatively accessible rock walls of the Northern Corries, often ice-clagged in winter, are a mecca for climbers and mountaineers; the Lairig Ghru pass is overlooked by the vertiginous flanks of Ben Macdui, Braeriach and Cairn Toul, some of the most spectacular and remote mountain architecture in Scotland. The icy flows have also carved out awesome glacial troughs like the ones cradling Loch Avon and Loch Eanaich, both of which are hemmed in by sheer mountainsides 600 metres (2,000 feet) high.

The sheer scope and size of this landscape has meant it has always been one of Scotland's great hillwalking and mountaineering heartlands. The Cuillin of Skye are more jaggedly alpine; the Fisherfield or Torridon hills are Atlantic-facing giants; Ben Nevis is a taller stand-alone mountain. But few places match the Cairngorms and its neighbours for sustained grandeur and remoteness. As Scottish climber W. H. Murray wrote in his 1947 classic *Mountaineering in Scotland*, 'On a wind-swept plateau we may drink the living waters of freedom and learn of our heritage.'

The main Cairngorms range alone stretches roughly from the River Feshie and Mullach Clach a' Bhlair to the River Avon and Ben Avon in the east, between which is a sea of mountains studded with high lochans, plunging corries and high passes, a labyrinthine mountain realm that can sustain whole lifetimes

Reaching 835 metres (2,740 feet) at its rocky high point, the Lairig Ghru is a mountain pass that cuts through the wild heart of the Cairngorms, squeezing between the hulking masses of Braeriach and Cairn Toul on one side, and Ben Macdui on the other. A 30-kilometre (19-mile) walk over Lairig Ghru connects Speyside with Deeside, a classic hiking route often broken up with an overnight stay in Corrour Bothy.

Opposite:
Morning light drifting over Lochan Uaine and the southern flanks of Ben Macdui, Scotland's second highest Munro. This is a high and remote place; reaching the nearest road or settlement from this location would entail a three to four hour hike across challenging terrain in any direction.

of exploration. The longest straight-line distance between paved roads in Britain, almost 130 kilometres, crosses this remote vastness. The lack of roads means that many summits and crags often demand long walk-ins or overnight wild camps, giving a backcountry-expedition feel to adventure here, which is rare in Britain. But the park is also dotted with volunteer-maintained bothies – buildings used by walkers and climbers for shelter in remote areas. These camaraderie-filled shelters offer emergency refuge, easier access to the bigger mountains or crags, or stopover points on popular hiking routes – like the Lairig Ghru crossing, a north–south traverse through the wild heartland of the Cairngorms via a pass that is a breathtaking 800 metres (2,600 feet) high.

Bothies also have the great benefit of putting four sturdy walls and a roof between you and Scotland's population of midges. Although small, these notorious biting insects form frenzied clouds of irritation: in their summer prime, they are capable of overwhelming even the hardiest mountaineer in minutes. Another way to avoid the midges is simply to visit in winter – as Britain's snowiest place, the Cairngorms is one of Scotland's winter sports heartlands. The national park contains three ski resorts, and is also one of the few places in Britain that can lend itself well to ski-touring, either across the high plateau or through the forests.

The Cairngorms National Park may be Britain's wildest landscape, but it is far from a wilderness. Around 18,000 people live within its borders, largely in the Strathspey and Deeside corridors. For all its vastness, it remains a landscape in human hands. Yet those hands have, in recent decades, done some exemplary work to make this a wilder place. The Caledonian forest is experiencing a resurgence, thanks to restoration work aimed at expanding it and connecting its disparate fragments. There have already been visible and sometimes astonishing successes. On Meall a' Bhuachaille, the treeline pushes more than 700 metres up the mountain's flanks, giving way to a rich montane zone of dwarf birches, shrubs and wildflowers that almost touches the 810-metre (2,657-foot) summit, dispelling the myth that the mountains of Scotland cannot support trees at high elevations. In Glen Feshie, where deer numbers have been reduced to lessen grazing pressure, 300-year-old 'granny pines' that survived the centuries of deforestation have been joined by a layer of vibrant new growth: countless young pines sprout from reefs of bright purple heather; open areas are vibrant with the colours of devil's-bit scabious, harebell and yarrow; golden eagles are glimpsed through the airy pine canopy, drifting over the glen and quartering the lush hillsides for prey.

The Cairngorms National Park is unquestionably one of Britain's greatest mountain landscapes. But if arduous mountain adventure is not your thing, don't be put off: lower-level walking within this national park can also be wonderful, thanks to the many accessible trails, forest hikes and lochside walks that thread through the great belt of Caledonian forest. Or you could opt for the more contemplative and exploratory approach favoured by Nan Shepherd; after all, as she wrote, 'to aim for the highest point is not the only way to climb a mountain'.

Scots pine saplings growing as part of a regenerating area of Caledonian forest in the Cairngorms.

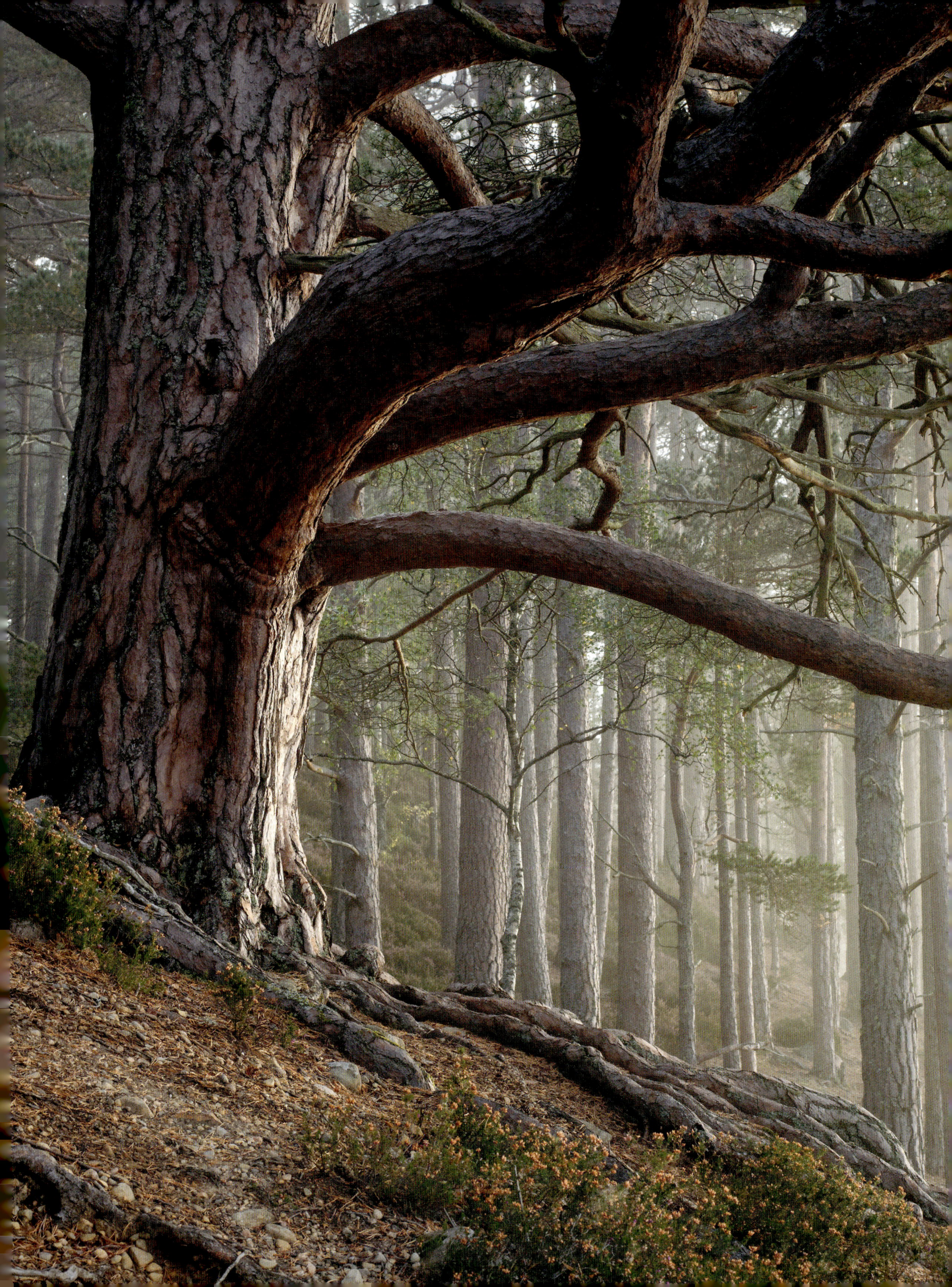

A mature Scots pine tree surrounded by younger trees on the shores of Loch an Eilein. Britain's only native pine, this evergreen tree is the dominant tree species of the Caledonian forest, and as such it is the linchpin of a habitat that supports red squirrel, pine marten and capercaillie. Scots pines can reach 35 metres (115 feet) in height and live for up to 700 years, growing knotted and gnarled; the oldest individuals are affectionately called 'granny pines'. Although it is one of the iconic natural symbols of Scotland, Pinus sylvestris *grows extensively across Eurasia, from Spain to the Pacific coast of Russia.*

Overleaf:
Fringed by forests, with views of sub-arctic mountains beyond, Loch an Eilein – whose name means 'loch of the island' – is one of the most beautiful bodies of water in Scotland. The eponymous island contains the ruins of a 13th-century castle.

249

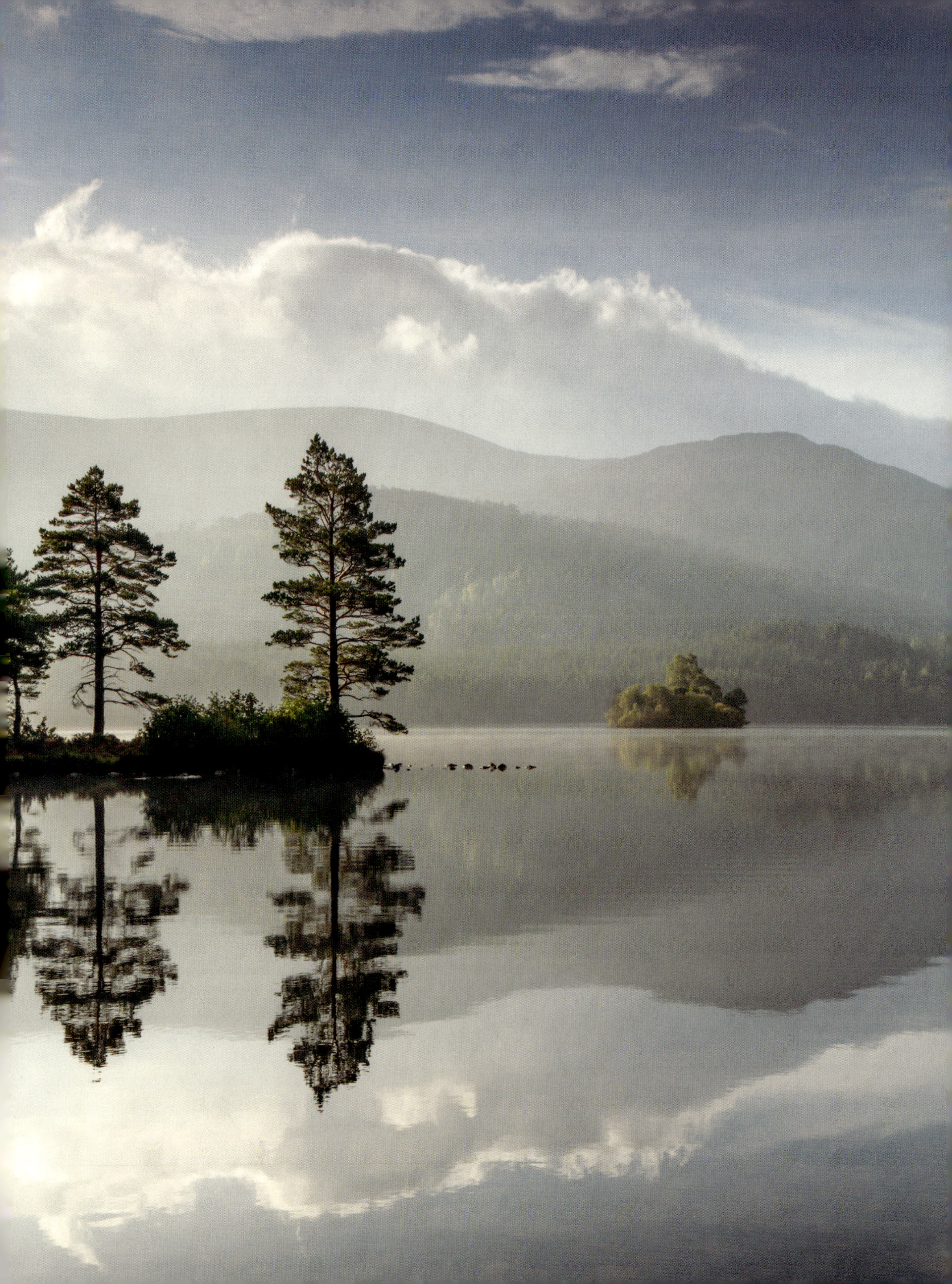

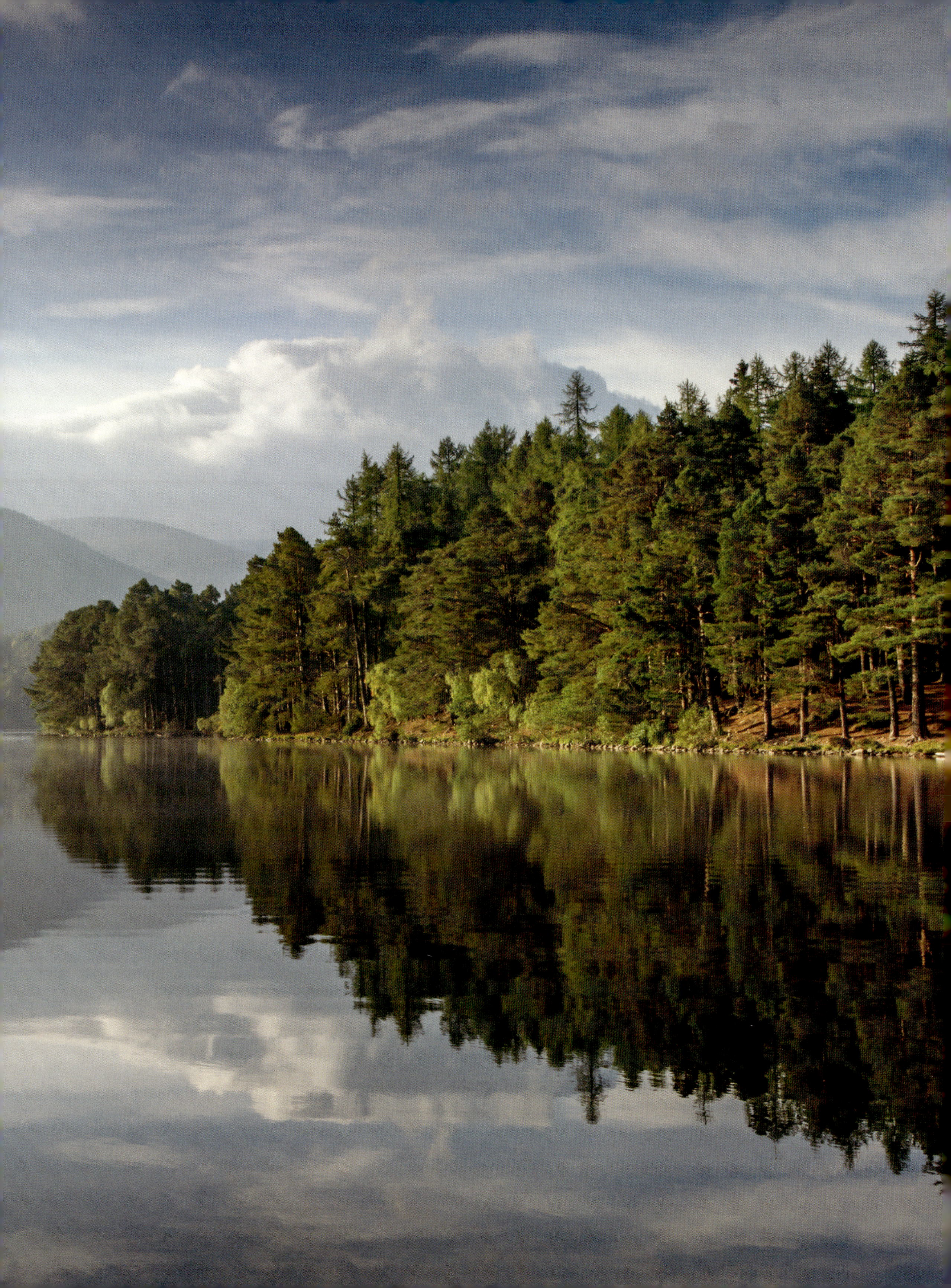

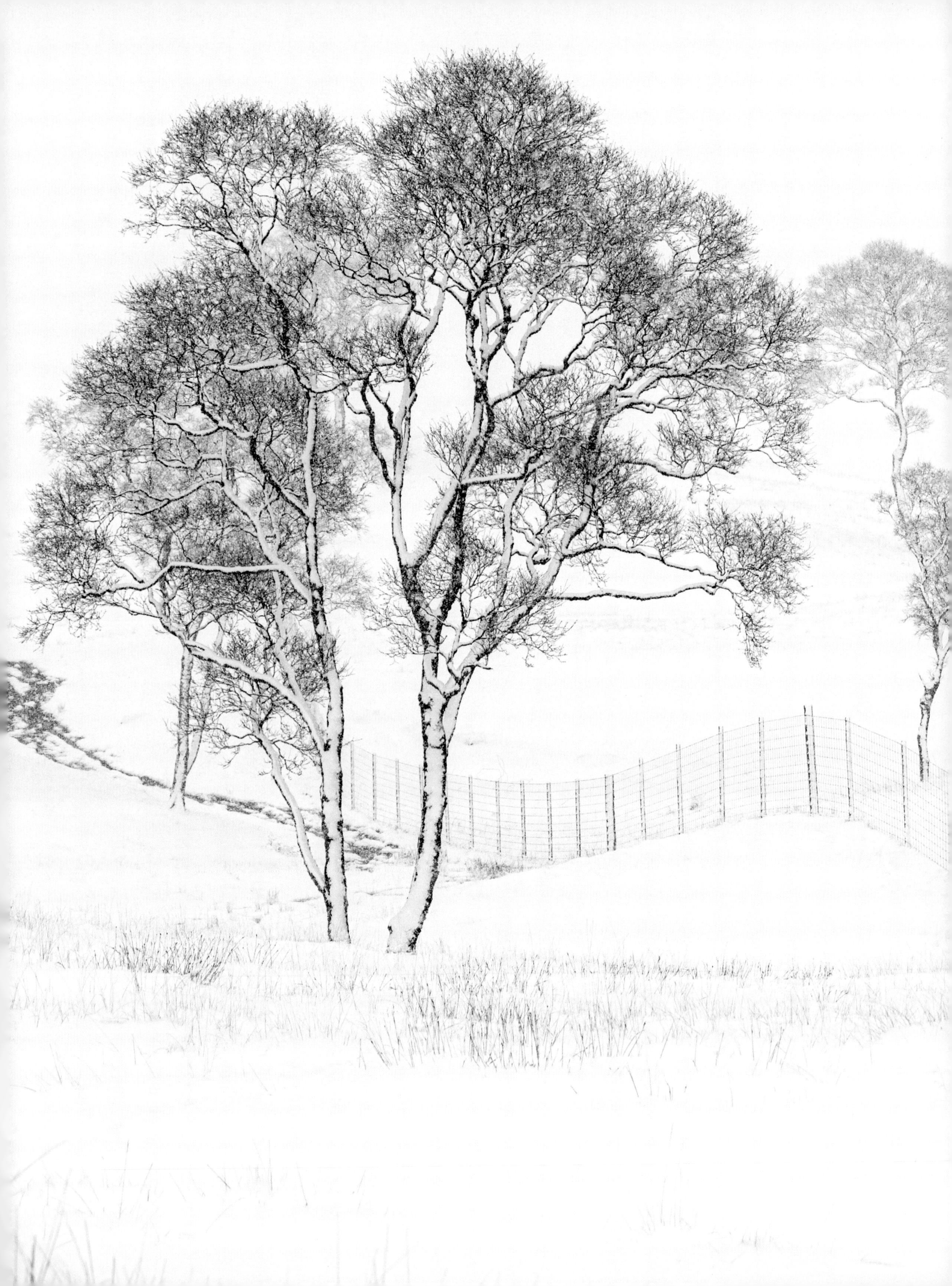

Corrour bothy provides sanctuary for walkers and climbers and is maintained by the Mountain Bothies Association. It is overlooked by the pyramid-shaped summit of Bod an Deamhain, which means 'Penis of the Demon' in Gaelic, but is said to have been known as the milder 'Devil's Point' in English following a visit to the area by Queen Victoria. The queen reputedly asked what its name was and was given a euphemistic answer to avoid embarrassment.

A mountain hare in its winter colours. They were granted protected status in 2020 following a public outcry over the numbers being killed by gamekeepers, whose aim was to protect red grouse in the Scottish Highlands.

Opposite:
A blizzard envelops the landscape. The Cairngorms are the UK's coldest national park. Braemar in Deeside has recorded Britain's lowest ever temperature three times: -27.2°C.

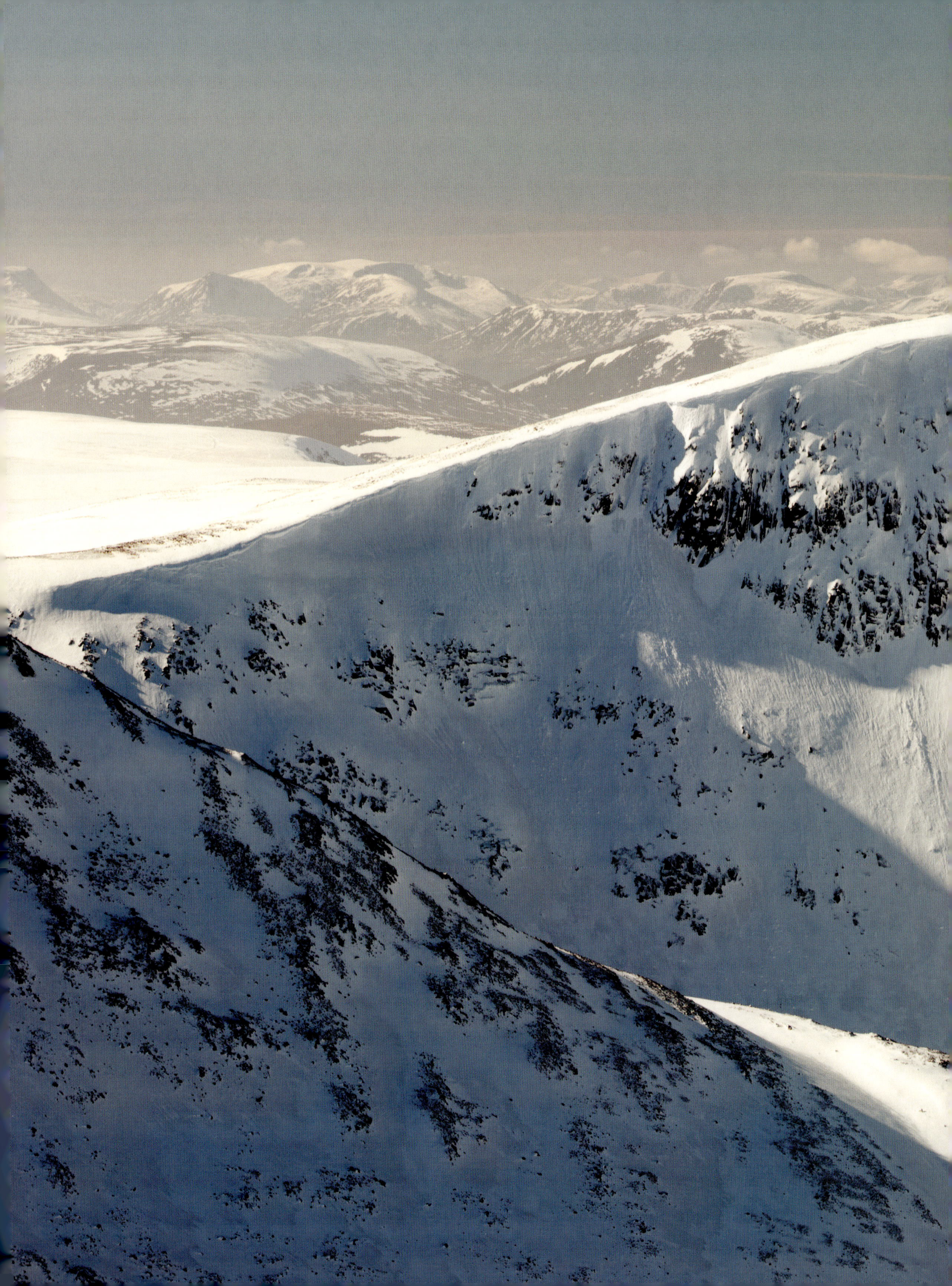

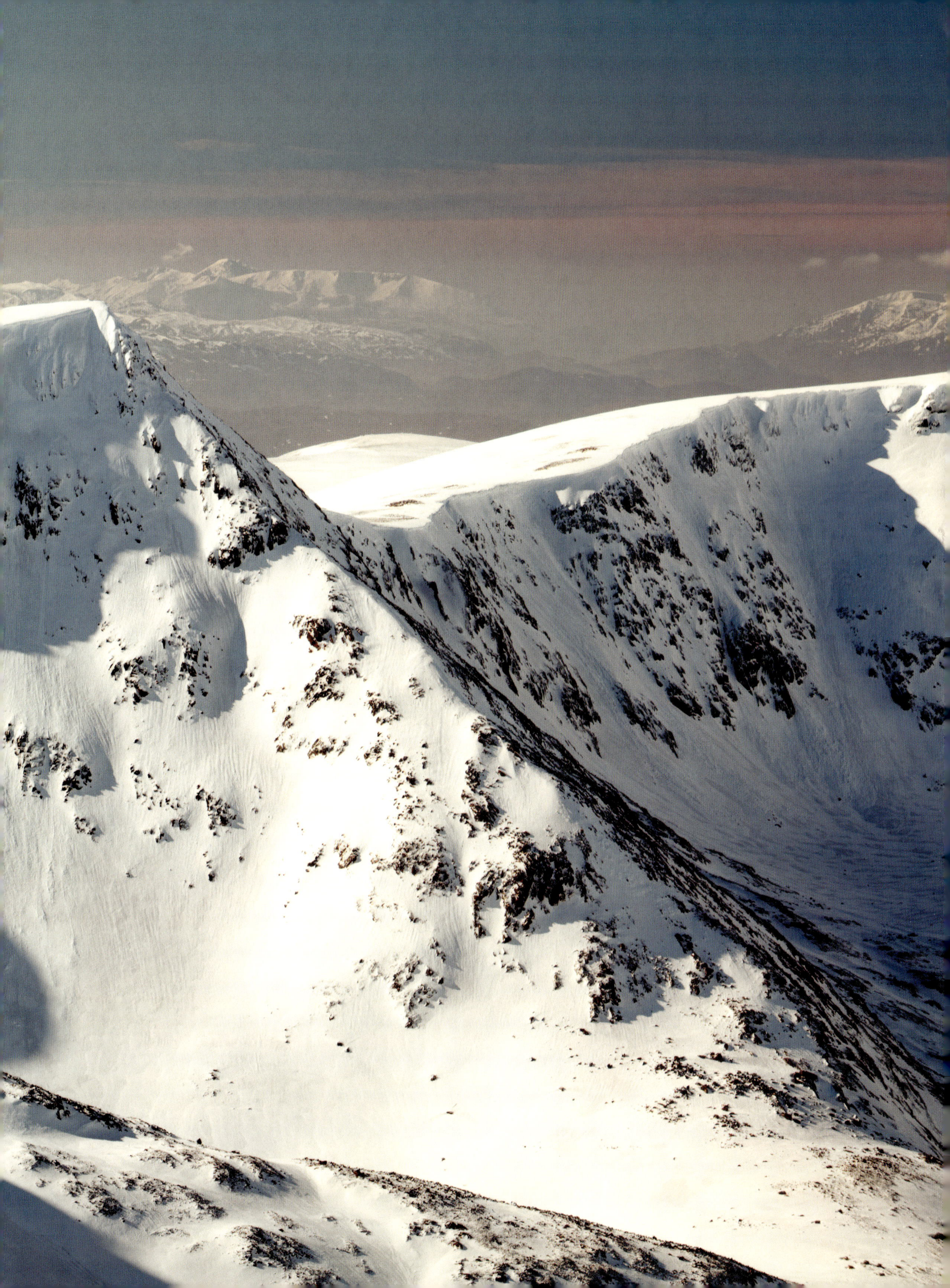

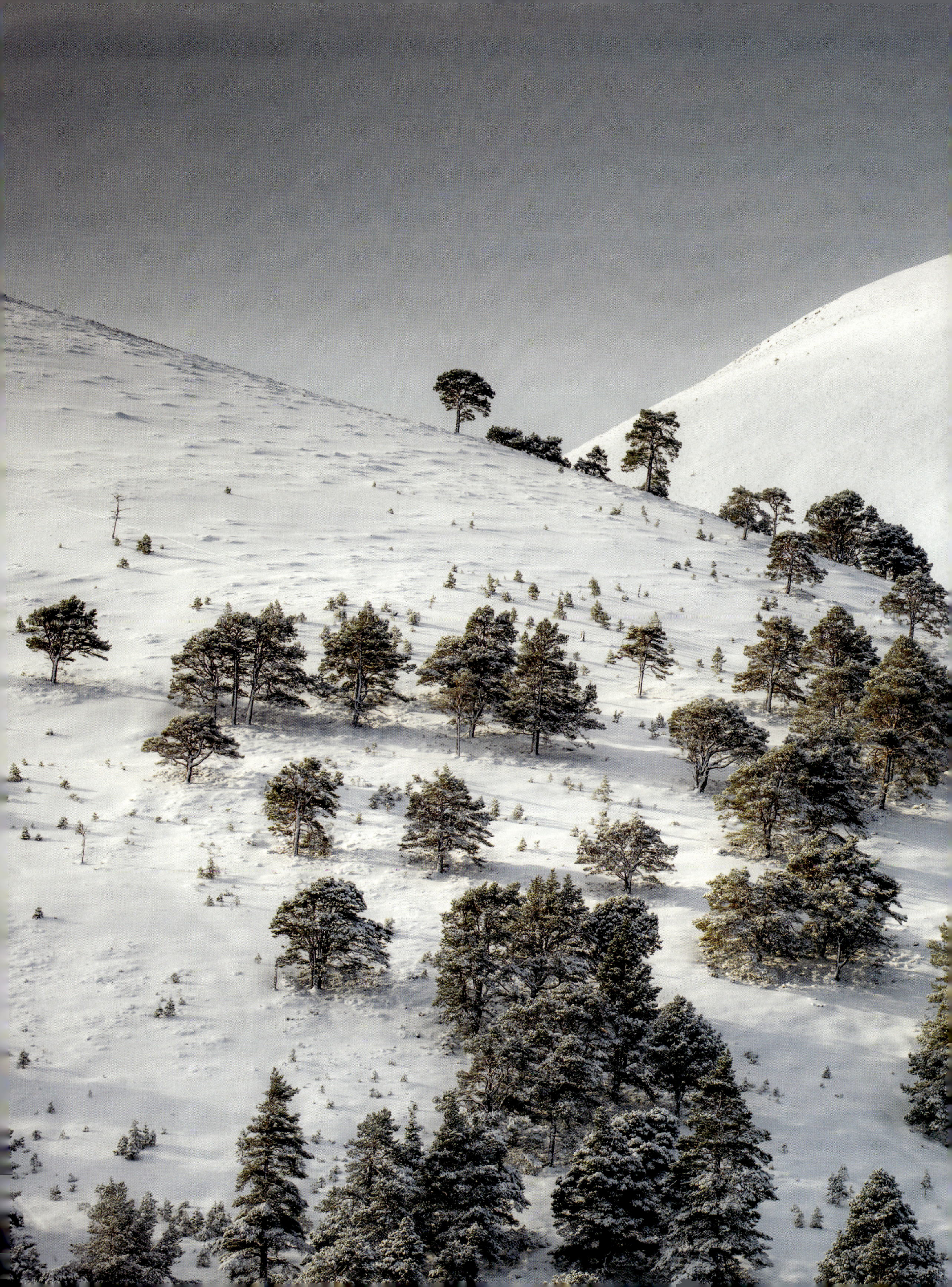

Previous page:
Looking across to Cairn Toul from Ben Macdui. The tops of the Cairngorms form a kilometre-high sub-arctic plateau, often extensively snow-covered for six months of the year or more, while patches of snow linger all year round.

A natural and regenerating high-altitude treeline above Glen Feshie. Younger Scots pine can be seen growing amid the older trees.

Overleaf:
Climbing Meall a' Bhuachaille ('Hill of the Herdsman') in winter. Abernethy, one of the Cairngorms' big surviving remnants of Caledonian forest, can be seen carpeting the snowy contours of the terrain below, a natural contrast to the blocky conifer plantations in the far distance.

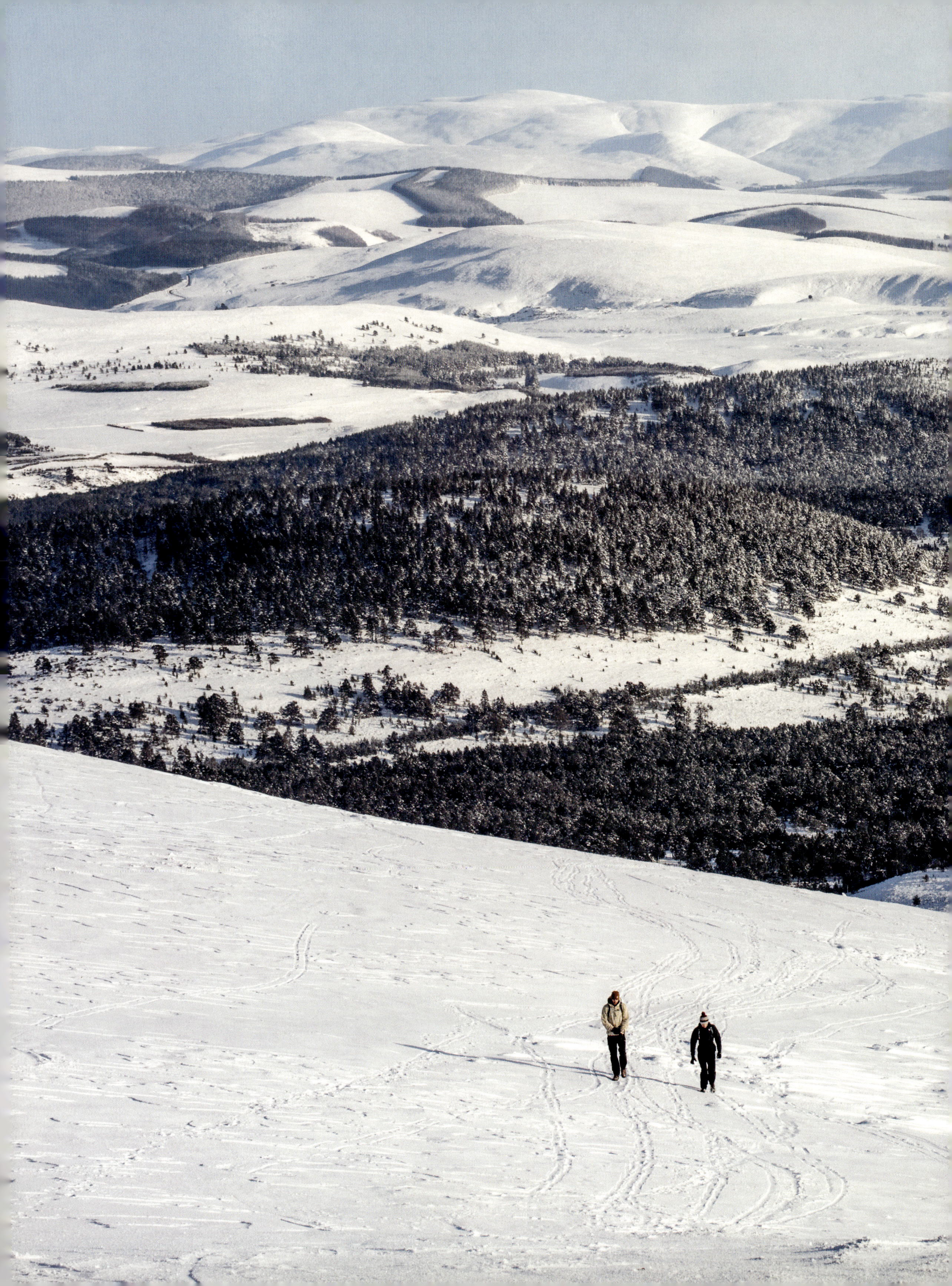

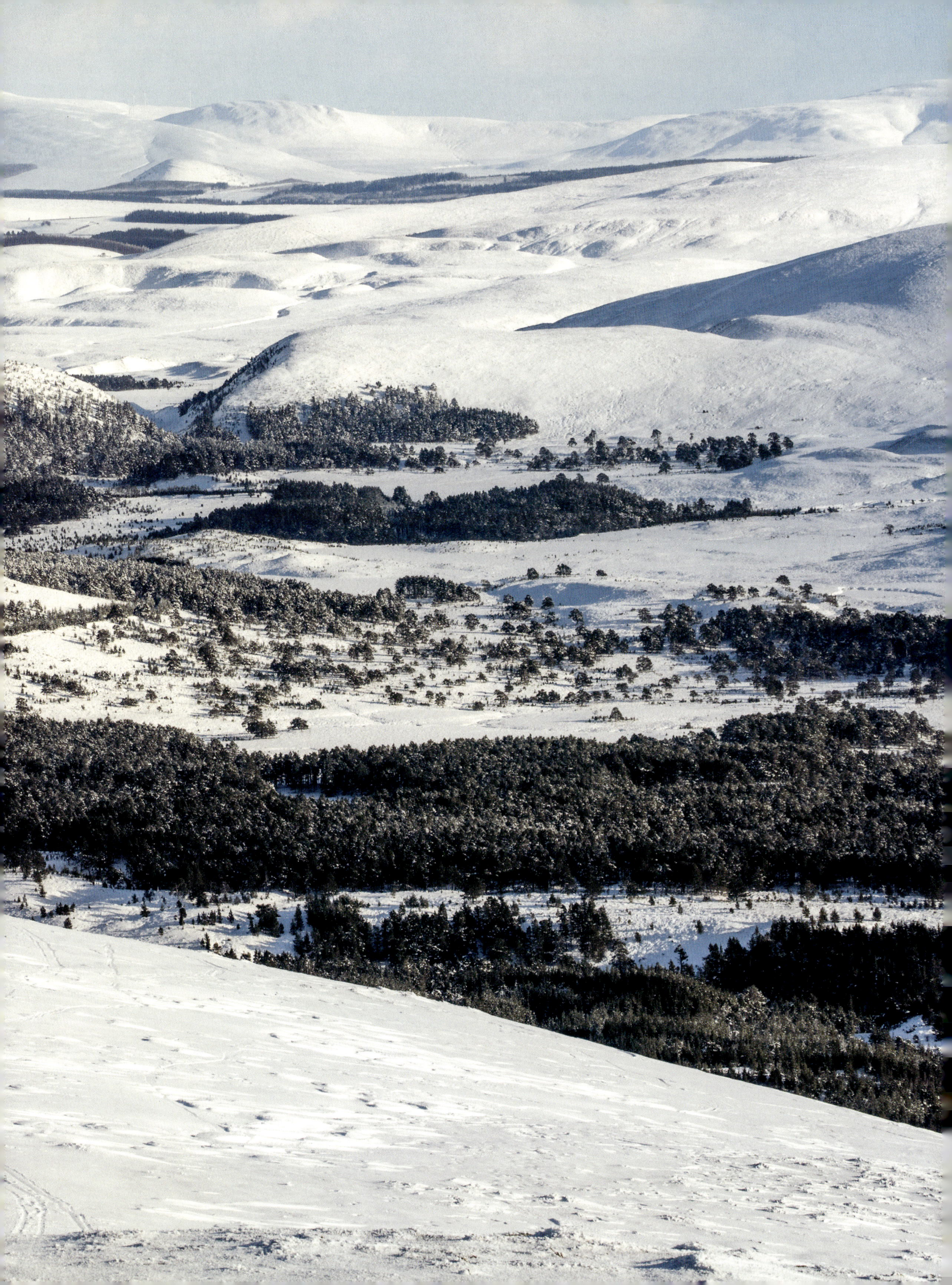

National Parks
in brief

National parks in the UK have over 200 routes specified as suitable for those with limited mobility such as wheelchair users, families with pushchairs, and less agile walkers.

See what each national park offers here:
www.nationalparks.uk/accessibility

Definitions:
Sights: *Scenic locations that can be readily accessed from a road, town or village. Some walking or hiking may be involved.*
Attractions: *Paid-for activities or attractions.*
Towns or villages: *Settlements in or close to the national park which can be used as a holiday base.*

Dartmoor

Location: *South Devon, South-West England*
Established: *1951*
Area: *95,400 hectares*
Special features: *open moorland, granite tors, prehistoric and medieval archaeology*
Main habitats: *Largely high moorland dominated by grasses and heather, with a significant proportion on deep peat. Small remnants of high-altitude oakwood and temperate rainforest. Farmland at lower levels with ancient broadleaved woodland in some valleys.*
Interesting animals: *ring ouzel, blue ground beetle, adder, high brown fritillary butterfly, moorland birds like snipe and curlew, ash-black slug, cuckoo, otter*
Interesting plants: *horsehair lichen, wild daffodil, greater butterfly orchid, old-growth pedunculate oak, epiphyte (plants that grow on other plants) ferns, mosses and lichens*
Activities: *hiking, mountain biking, cycling, rock climbing*
Sights: *Haytor Rocks, Merrivale stone row, St Michael's Church (Brentor), Burrator Reservoir, Lydford Gorge*
Attractions: *Buckfast Abbey, River Dart Country Park, Dartmoor Prison Museum, Pennywell Farm*
Towns or villages: *Princetown, Okehampton, Ashburton, Widecombe-in-the-moor, Tavistock, Bovey Tracey*
Visitor centres: *main national park visitor centres at Postbridge, Princetown and Haytor*
Getting there: *Driving times: approx. 30 mins from Exeter, 4 hours from London, 5 hours from Manchester. Train line from Exeter to Okehampton. Local service buses.*

www.dartmoor.gov.uk

New Forest

Location: *In the south of England, mostly in South-West Hampshire, with some in South-East Wiltshire*
Established: *2005*
Area: *56,720 hectares*
Special features: *Extensive area of largely unenclosed forest, heath and pasture, with a stretch of wildlife-rich coastline.*
Main habitats: *ancient broadleaved woodland, coniferous forest, lowland heath, coastal salt marsh and wetland*
Interesting animals: *free-roaming ponies and other livestock, European honey buzzard, northern goshawk, smooth snake, sand lizard, Dartford warbler, heathland dragonfly species, wide range of bat species, overwintering wading birds and wildfowl*
Interesting plants: *old-growth oak trees, ancient yew trees, imported ornamental trees like giant sequoia and redwood, wide range of fungi including rarities like nail fungus and devil's fingers, bog pimpernel, coral necklace, Hampshire purslane, small fleabane, pillwort, marsh clubmoss, bluebells and other woodland ground flora*
Activities: *hiking, cycling, horse-riding, watersports, birdwatching, bushcraft, foraging, archery*
Sights: *Views over open heathland like Piper's Wait, Bratley View and Ibsley Common. Woodland walks with famous old trees like the Knightwood Oak. Coastal views at Keyhaven and Lepe.*
Attractions: *New Forest Heritage Centre, Beaulieu National Motor Museum, New Forest Wildlife Park, Furzey Gardens, Hurst Castle*
Towns or villages: *Brockenhurst, Lyndhurst, Ashurst, Burley, Beaulieu, Sway*
Visitor centres: *A host of local information points – see national park website*
Getting there: *Driving times: approx. 15–30 mins from Southampton, 1 hour 45 mins from London, 4–5 hours from Manchester. Train line with stops at Ashurst, Brockenhurst and Sway. Good bus connections from Southampton, including open-top bus tours in summer.*

www.newforestnpa.gov.uk

South Downs

Location: *Spread across Hampshire, West Sussex and East Sussex in the south of England*
Established: *2010*
Area: *162,651 hectares*
Special features: *rolling chalk grassland hills, patchwork of farmland and woods, large coastal cliffs, historic sites including Iron Age hillforts and Bronze Age burial sites*
Main habitats: *species-rich chalk grasslands, ancient woodlands, lowland heath, chalk streams and rivers, farmland and coastland*
Interesting animals: *wide range of bat species including Bechstein's and Barbastelle; Adonis blue, Duke of Burgundy and a wide range of other butterflies; all native reptiles and amphibians, including the sand lizard and natterjack toad; otter, skylark, red kite and buzzards*
Interesting plants: *chalk grassland species like orchids, wild thyme, birds-foot trefoil, dropwort, salad burnet, vetches and rampions; ancient oak and yew trees; heathland species such as the sundew, heather and cranberry*
Activities: *hiking, cycling, horse-riding*
Sights: *Seven Sisters cliffs, Devil's Dyke, Long Man of Wilmington, Kingley Vale yew trees, Blackdown Hill, Old Winchester Hill, Chanctonbury and Cissbury Iron Age Hill Fort sites*
Attractions: *Arundel Castle, Weald and Downland Living Museum, Jane Austen's House, Queen Elizabeth Country Park, various vineyards like Rathfinney, Ridgeview, Stopham, Hambledon*
Towns or villages: *Lewes, Petersfield, Alfriston, Arundel, Midhurst, Seven Sisters Country Park Visitor Centre*
Visitor centres: *South Downs Centre in Midhurst*
Getting there: *Nearest national park to London. Approx. 1–1.5 hours by train. Close to Winchester, Portsmouth, Eastbourne, Brighton, Worthing and Chichester. Well served by trains from London, Portsmouth and Brighton.*

www.southdowns.gov.uk

Exmoor

Location: *North Devon, West Somerset, South-West England*
Established: *1954*
Area: *69,300 hectares*
Special features: *Large areas of moorland with winding river valleys and a high-cliffed coastline.*
Main habitats: *moorland (including blanket mire), heathland, broadleaved oak woodland and temperate rainforest, rivers, woodland-covered coastal cliffs, coastal heaths, farmland*
Interesting animals: *Exmoor ponies, large red deer, Atlantic salmon, heath fritillary, cuckoo, moorland birds, heathland birds like whinchat and stonechat, cliff-nesting coastal birds like fulmar, kittiwake, razorbill and guillemot*
Interesting plants: *rare whitebeams; blanket bog species like sundew, sphagnum mosses and bog asphodel; epiphytes in woodland*
Activities: *hiking, road cycling, fishing, kayaking, mountain biking*
Sights: *Valley of the Rocks, Dunkery Beacon, Tarr Steps, Heddon's Mouth*
Attractions: *Dunster Castle, Watersmeet House, Lynton and Lynmouth Cliff Railway, Lynton and Barnstaple Railway, Exmoor Pony Centre*
Towns or villages: *Lynton, Lynmouth, Dunster, Combe Martin, Porlock, Dulverton*
Visitor centres: *national park visitor centres in Dulverton, Dunster, Lynmouth*
Getting there: *Driving times: approx. 1 hour from Exeter, 1.5 hours from Bristol, 4.5 hours from Manchester. Nearest rail is Taunton or Tiverton Parkway. Bus connections to Minehead, then onwards to Lynmouth.*

www.exmoor-nationalpark.gov.uk

Pembrokeshire Coast

Location: *South-West Wales*
Established: *1952*
Area: *62,936 hectares*
Special features: *Rocky coastline interspersed with beaches, with some areas reaching inland to encompass estuaries and uplands. Prehistoric megalithic monuments.*
Main habitats: *coastal cliffs and beaches, intertidal habitats, seabird colonies, moorland, estuaries and mudflats, sand dune systems, farmland*
Interesting animals: *Vast colonies of Manx shearwater, Atlantic puffins and northern gannet, plus wide range of other seabirds. Passage seabirds like arctic and great skua, Sabine's gull and Leach's petrel. Porpoises, dolphins, whales and sharks in the coastal waters. Atlantic grey seal on the coast. Wading birds and wildfowl in estuaries.*
Interesting plants: *halophytes (salt-tolerant plants) like sea thrift and sea campion*
Activities: *hiking, climbing, kayaking, coasteering, surfing, swimming, birdwatching, sea safaris*
Sights: *St David's Head, Green Bridge of Wales, Barafundle Bay, St Govan's Chapel, megalithic monuments like Pentre Ifan and Carreg Samson*
Attractions: *St Davids Cathedral, Strumble Head Lighthouse, boat trips to Ramsey and Skomer islands, Carew Castle, Tidal Mill, Castell Henllys Iron Age Village*
Towns or villages: *Tenby, St Davids, Newport, Solva*
Visitor centres: *Oriel y Parc gallery and visitor centre, St Davids*
Getting there: *Driving times: approx. 1–1.5 hours from Swansea, 2–2.5 hours from Cardiff, 5–6 hours from Manchester or London. Rail stations at Tenby, Haverfordwest and Fishguard. Range of coastal bus services.*

www.pembrokeshirecoast.wales

Bannau Brycheiniog

Location: *South Wales, spread across various counties, with a large part in Powys.*
Established: *1957*
Area: *134,420 hectares*
Special features: *extensive moorland with steep escarpments, secluded pastoral valleys and waterfalls, medieval castles and prehistoric archaeology*
Main habitats: *moorland, reservoirs, farmland, coniferous woodland, ancient woodland fragments*
Interesting animals: *red kite, buzzard, peregrine, nightjar, feral ponies, wide range of moorland birds*
Interesting plants: *rare whitebeams, melick, mossy saxifrage, pink meadowcap and olive earthtongue fungi, moorland plants like sundews and butterworts*
Activities: *hiking, mountain biking, caving, canyoning, fishing, rock climbing*
Sights: *Talybont Reservoir, Gospel Pass, waterfalls around Pontneddfechan and Ystradfellte*
Attractions: *Tretower Castle, Carreg Cennen, Llanthony Priory, Penderyn distillery, red kite feeding station at Llandeusant*
Towns or villages: *Brecon, Crickhowell, Abergavenny, Llandovery, Hay-on-Wye*
Visitor centres: *national park visitor centre in Libanus*
Getting there: *Driving times: approx. 1 hour from Cardiff, 4 hours from London or Manchester. Trains to Abergavenny, Merthyr Tydfil and Llandovery. Various local buses.*

https://bannau.wales

Broads

Location: *East Anglia, mostly in Norfolk with parts in Suffolk*
Established: *1989*
Area: *30,300 hectares*
Special features: *largest area of protected wetland in the UK, 200 kilometres of navigable waterways, stretch of sandy coastline*
Main habitats: *lakes, rivers, wetlands, reedbeds, wet woodland, grazing marsh, farmland*
Interesting animals: *Common crane, swallowtail butterfly, marsh harrier, bittern, starling murmurations, great white egret, cormorant, kingfisher. Wide range of dragonflies and damselflies, including Norfolk hawker and banded demoiselle. Whooper swan, pink-footed goose, brent goose, varied duck species and large numbers of other overwintering wildfowl. Grey seals at the coast.*
Interesting plants: *Plants of marshes and dykes like marsh fern, cowbane, round-leaved wintergreen, southern marsh orchid, early marsh orchid, frogbit, arrowhead, water soldier. Sprawling reedbeds dominated by common reed and other plants like meadowsweet and herb agrimony. The willows, alders, sedges and ferns of wet 'carr' woodland, including royal fern and crested buckler fern.*
Activities: *boating, kayaking, sailing, birdwatching, hiking, cycling*
Sights: *Thurne Mill, St Benet's Level Mill, Hickling Broad, view from top of St Helen's Church*
Attractions: *St Benet's Abbey, BeWILDerwood, Fairhaven Woodland and Water Garden, boat hire in marinas and villages*
Towns or villages: *Wroxham and Hoveton, Acle, Ludham, Reedham, Brundall, Great Yarmouth*
Visitor centres: *national park visitor centres at Hoverton, Ranworth and How Hill*
Getting there: *Norwich is next to (and even contains a part of) the national park. Driving times: approx. 2.5–3 hours from London, 4–5 hours from Leeds or Manchester. Train to all the villages and towns listed above (and others) except Ludham. Some local bus services.*

www.visitthebroads.co.uk

Eryri

Location: *North Wales, mostly in Gwynedd but with parts in Conwy.*
Established: *1951*
Area: *213,156 hectares*
Special features: *dramatic mountains, picturesque lakes, rivers and waterfalls, industrial heritage, coastline with dunes and estuaries*
Main habitats: *moorland and mountainous terrain; mountain crags with arctic-alpine plant communities; coastal mudflats, marshes, shingle spits and sand dunes; steep-sided gullies and gorges; ancient woodland and fragments of temperate rainforest; farmland*
Interesting animals: *Welsh mountain goat, chough, rainbow leaf beetle, raven, peregrine, wild ponies*
Interesting plants: *lili'r Wyddfa (Snowdon lily), saxifrage (purple, mossy, starry), roseroot, butterwort, dwarf willow, northern rockress, alpine chickweed, lungwort lichens (e.g.* Lobaria pulmonaria*), stinky sticta (e.g.* Sticta sylvatica*)*
Activities: *hiking, rock climbing, scrambling, winter climbing, mountain biking, kayaking, paddleboarding, fishing*
Sights: *Cwm Idwal, Aber Falls, Dolgoch Falls, Rhaeadr Ewynnol (Swallow Falls), Ffos Anoddun (Fairy Glen), Aberglaslyn gorge*
Attractions: *Snowdonia Mountain Railway, Harlech Castle, Yr Ysgwrn (Hedd Wyn house). Attractions relating to slate industry just outside park boundary, e.g. National Slate Museum, Zip World (Penrhyn quarry)*
Towns or villages: *Beddgelert, Betws-y-Coed, Llanberis, Dolgellau, Barmouth, Conwy*
Visitor centres: *national park visitor centres at Betws-y-coed, Beddgelert and Aberdyfi*
Getting there: *Driving times: approx. 15–30 mins from Bangor, 1.5–2 hours from Liverpool, 3 hours from Cardiff, 5–6 hours from London. Rail to Bangor, then Conwy Valley Line as far as Blaenau Ffestiniog. Local bus services, including the Sherpa'r Wyddfa (Snowdon Sherpa), which connects locations around the mountain.*

www.snowdonia.gov.wales

Peak District

Location: *Middle of England, mostly in Derbyshire, but with parts in five other counties.*
Established: *1951*
Area: *143,744 hectares*
Special features: *large areas of mountainous or semi-mountainous open moorland with extensive blanket peat bog, rocky escarpments, limestone gorges and caves, large reservoirs*
Main habitats: *moorland, blanket peat bog, broadleaved and conifer woodland, limestone grassland, meadows, farmland, rivers, rocky outcrops*
Interesting animals: *ring ouzel, short-eared owl, mountain hare, bilberry bumblebee, dingy skipper butterfly, water vole, merlin, dipper, curlew, pied flycatcher, green hairstreak butterfly*
Interesting plants: *Jacob's ladder, rare hawkweeds (Dales, Derby and leek-coloured), sphagnum mosses, sundew, bog asphodel, cotton grass, cloudberry, cranberry, three heather species*
Activities: *hiking, mountain biking, cycling, caving, rock climbing, bouldering, accessible trails*
Sights: *Kinder Downfall, The Woolpacks (Kinder Scout), Mam Tor, Stanage Edge, Win Hill, Derwent Edge, Lud's Church, The Roaches, Ramshaw Rocks, Dovedale, Thor's Cave, Ladybower Reservoir*
Attractions: *Chatsworth House, various show caves (Peak, Treak, Speedwell, Poole's, Blue John), Lyme Park, Monsal Trail, Eyam 'Plague Village' Museum, Haddon Hall*
Towns or villages: *Bakewell, Edale, Flash, Tideswell, Tissington, Hartington, Hathersage, Hayfield, Castleton, Buxton, Chapel-en-le-Frith*
Visitor centres: *national park visitor centres at Bakewell, Castleton, Edale, Upper Derwent*
Getting there: *Driving times: 15–30 mins from Sheffield, 1.5–2 hours from Birmingham, 3–4 hours from London.*

www.peakdistrict.gov.uk

Yorkshire Dales

Location: *North of England, mostly in North Yorkshire but with north-west part in Cumbria and a small part in Lancashire*
Established: *1954*
Area: *217,818 hectares*
Special features: *secluded glacier-carved dales; mountainous or semi-mountainous terrain; limestone crags, caves, pavements and other karstic landforms; wildflower meadows; characterful villages; distinctive farming heritage*
Main habitats: *moorland and peat bog, limestone grassland, ash woods, extensive areas of limestone pavement, rivers, farmland*
Interesting animals: *black grouse, curlew, peregrine, golden plover, redshank, lapwing, red squirrel, northern brown angus butterfly, red kite, Atlantic salmon, Swaledale sheep*
Interesting plants: *lady's slipper orchid, Nowell's limestone moss, long-leaved flapwort, frog orchid, lesser butterfly orchid, small white orchid, birds-eye primrose, rigid buckler fern, globeflower, baneberry*
Activities: *hiking, caving, rock climbing, mountain biking*
Sights: *Malham Cove, Gordale Scar, Janet's Foss, Aysgarth Falls, Ribblehead Viaduct*
Attractions: *show caves (White Scar, Ingleborough, Stump Cross Caverns) Ingleton Waterfalls Trail, Hardraw Force, Bolton Abbey, Gaping Gill, Wensleydale Creamery*
Towns or villages: *Ingleton, Settle, Hawes, Malham, Grassington, Kettlewell, Reeth, Aysgarth*
Visitor centres: *national park visitors centres at Aysgarth Falls, Grassington, Hawes, Malham and Reeth*
Getting there: *Driving times: approx. 30 mins–1 hour from Bradford or Leeds, 5–6 hours from London, 3–4 hours from Glasgow or Edinburgh. Rail to Settle and onwards on the Settle–Carlisle line. Bus services connecting to nearby towns and cities via the DalesBus network.*

www.yorkshiredales.org.uk

North York Moors

Location: *North of England, North-East Yorkshire and a small part in Redcar & Cleveland*
Established: *1952*
Area: *143,485 hectares*
Special features: *extensive areas of heather-dominated moorland, widely wooded valleys, a high-cliffed Jurassic coastline, International Dark Sky Reserve, ancient trees, abbey ruins, Roman fortifications, medieval castles, secluded waterfalls, rural settlements, distinctive stone buildings, ancient moorland crosses*
Main habitats: *heather moorland, broadleaved ancient woodland, rivers, rocky coastal cliffs and coves, limestone grassland, farmland*
Interesting animals: *snipe, beaver, merlin, ring ouzel, white-clawed crayfish, Atlantic salmon, curlew, golden plover, meadow pipit, skylark, minke whale, water vole, otter, turtle dove, keeled skimmer dragonfly, emperor moth, six-spotted longhorn beetle, nightjars, adder, freshwater pearl mussels, large heath butterfly, Duke of Burgundy butterfly, Alcathoe bat*
Interesting plants: *wild daffodil, sphagnum mosses, bog myrtle, bog asphodel, butterwort, three heather species*
Activities: *hiking, mountain biking, road cycling, birdwatching, surfing, paddleboarding, stargazing, Tramper (all-terrain mobility scooter) experiences*
Sights: *Sutton Bank, Mallyan Spout, Kilburn White Horse, Boulby cliffs*
Attractions: *North Yorkshire Moors Railway, Goathland Station, Dalby Forest, Ryedale Folk Museum, Rievaulx Abbey, Byland Abbey, Helmsley Walled Garden, Helmsley Castle, Mount Grace Priory, House and Gardens*
Towns or villages: *Helmsley, Robin Hood's Bay, Staithes, Grosmont, Goathland, Runswick Bay, Whitby*
Visitor centres: *national park centres at Danby Lodge and Sutton Bank*
Getting there: *Driving times: 30 mins from Middlesbrough, 40 mins from York, 2–2.5 hours from Manchester, 4–5 hours from London. Rail from Middlesbrough via the Esk Valley and North Yorkshire Moors railways. Daily bus services from Middlesbrough, Scarborough and York.*

www.northyorkmoors.org.uk

Lake District

Location: *North-West England, in Cumbria*
Established: *1951*
Area: *229,205 hectares*
Special features: *dramatic mountains, large scenic lakes, cosy pastoral valleys, characterful towns and villages, literary heritage, distinctive farming traditions and heritage*
Main habitats: *mountainous moorland and grassland, blanket bogs, mountain crags and gullies, rocky screes, broadleaved and coniferous woodland, Atlantic oakwood / temperate rainforest, large lakes, upland tarns, rivers, limestone grassland, beaches and dune systems*
Interesting animals: *osprey, red squirrel, peregrine, red deer, otter, ring ouzel, raven, natterjack toad, goldeneye, great-crested grebe, buzzard, red kite, kingfisher, butterflies (marsh fritillary, meadow downs, orange-tip), Herdwick sheep*
Interesting plants: *floating water-plantain, moss campion, roseroot, alpine cinquefoil, alpine meadow grass, black alpine sedge, alpine saxifrage, oblong woodsia fern, alpine catchfly, pyramidal bugle, interrupted clubmoss, killarney fern, touch-me-not balsam, alpine enchanter's nightshade, epiphytic mosses and liverworts*
Activities: *hiking, mountain biking, cycling, rock climbing, scrambling, gorge scrambling, winter climbing, kayaking, paddleboarding, boating, sailing, birdwatching*
Sights: *Windermere, Derwentwater, Buttermere, Blea Tarn, Tarn Hows, Wastwater, Orrest Head*
Attractions: *Dove Cottage, Rydal Mount, The World of Beatrix Potter, Aira Force, Honister Slate Mine, Lakeland Motor Museum, Ruskin Museum, boat trips and tours on various lakes including Windermere, Ullswater and Derwentwater*
Towns or villages: *Windermere / Bowness-on-Windermere, Ambleside, Grasmere, Hawkshead, Keswick, Buttermere, Glenridding*
Visitor centres: *national park visitor and information centres at Brockhole, Bowness, Keswick, Ullswater and Hawkshead*
Getting there: *Driving times: approx. 30 mins–1 hour from Carlisle or Lancaster, 1.5–2 hours from Manchester, 2–2.5 hours from Glasgow, 4–5 hours from London. Rail to Windermere and Penrith, with bus connections onwards.*

www.lakedistrict.gov.uk

Northumberland

Location: *North-East England*
Established: *1956*
Area: *106,190 hectares*
Special features: *high rolling moors, quiet valleys, ancient archaeology*
Main habitats: *moorland, rivers, rough pastures, broadleaved and coniferous woodland, farmland*
Interesting animals: *Cheviot wild goats, oystercatcher, lapwing, curlew, redshank, adder, barn owl, black grouse, red squirrel, hen harrier, dipper, redwing, fieldfare, ring ouzel, Atlantic salmon, trout, moss-carder bee*
Interesting plants: *aspen, Jacob's ladder, wood cranesbill, wood anemone, sphagnum mosses, frog orchid, southern marsh orchid, epiphytic lichens*
Activities: *hiking, mountain biking, cycling, stargazing*
Sights: *Hadrian's Wall World Heritage Site, Hareshaw Linn waterfall, Linhope Spout waterfall, Harthope Valley, Coquetdale*
Attractions: *museums and exhibits connected with Hadrian's Wall (e.g. Vindolanda, Housesteads Roman Fort), The Sill: National Landscape Discovery Centre*
Towns or villages: *most bases just outside the national park boundaries, e.g. Wooler, Bellingham, Rothbury, Haltwhistle, Hexham*
Visitor centres: *visitor centres at The Sill and Walltown*
Getting there: *Driving times: approx 30 mins–1 hour from Newcastle, 1.5 hours from Edinburgh, 5–6 hours from London.*

www.northumberlandnationalpark.org.uk

Loch Lomond & Trossachs

Location: *West Central Scotland, located on the highland boundary fault that links the Highlands and Lowlands.*
Established: *2002*
Area: *186,479 hectares*
Special features: *dramatic mountain terrain, large lochs, ancient woodlands and wetlands*
Main habitats: *mountain moorland and grassland, mountain crags and gullies, Atlantic Oakwood / temperate rainforest, large freshwater lochs, sea lochs, upland lochans, wetland, wet woodland, rivers*
Interesting animals: *golden eagle, osprey, hen harrier, black grouse, red squirrel, beaver, pine marten, Greenland white-fronted geese, raven, cuckoo, pied flycatcher, Atlantic salmon, powan, lamprey, Arctic charr, otter, water vole, mountain hare, ptarmigan, mountain ringlet butterflies*
Interesting plants: *purple saxifrage, yellow mountain saxifrage, elongated sedge, six-stamened waterwort, cowbane, Loch Lomond dock, mudwort, mountain avens, butterwort, bluebell, epiphytic mosses and lichens*
Activities: *hiking, mountain biking, walking, cycling, kayaking, paddleboarding and swimming*
Sights: *Loch Lomond, Loch Katrine, Ben A'an, Falls of Falloch, Falls of Dochart*
Attractions: *Benmore Gardens (Cowal), RSPB Loch Lomond (Gartocharn), Loch Lomond Bird of Prey Centre (Balloch), Sea Life Loch Lomond Aquarium (Balloch), various boat trips and tours on Loch Lomond and Loch Katrine*
Towns or villages: *Balmaha, Balloch, Killin, Crianlarich, Tyndrum, Callander, Aberfoyle*
Visitor centres: *National Park Visitor Centre in Balmaha, The Lodge Forest Visitor Centre in Aberfoyle, VisitScotland Centres in Balloch and Aberfoyle and Woodland Trust Visitor Centre at Glen Finglas*
Getting there: *Driving times: 45 mins–1 hour from central Glasgow, 3 hours from Aberdeen, 4–5 hours from Manchester.*

www.lochlomond-trossachs.org

Cairngorms

Location: *Eastern Highlands of Scotland, covering five council areas*
Established: *2003*
Area: *452,729 hectares*
Special features: *dramatic mountainous terrain of broad-backed granite mountains and plunging corries, surrounding glens with extensive remnants of Caledonian pine forest*
Main habitats: *sub-arctic plateau, heather moorland, montane heath and scrub, mountain crags and gullies, Caledonian forest, other coniferous forest, lochs, wetlands, wildflower grasslands*
Interesting animals: *Scottish wildcat, golden eagle, white-tailed eagle, osprey, capercaillie, black grouse, beaver, pine marten, raven, red kite, snow bunting, ptarmigan, otter, water vole, mountain hare, whooper swan, Atlantic salmon, various butterflies (Kentish glory, dark bordered beauty), scabious mining bee, pine hoverfly, northern damselfly, freshwater pearl mussel*
Interesting plants: *twinflower, one-flowered wintergreen, waxcaps, marsh saxifrage, alpine blue sow thistle, alpine lady's mantle, small cow wheat, woolly willow, witch's hair lichen, downy willow, dwarf willow, woolly willow, moss campion, wide range of moorland species (butterwort, heathers, cowberry, cloudberry, bog asphodel, etc.)*
Activities: *hiking, rock climbing, mountain biking, cycling, skiing (downhill and cross-country), kayaking, backpacking*
Sights: *Loch Morlich, Loch an Eilein, Loch Muick, Uath Lochans, Northern Corries, Meall a' Bhuachaille, An Lochan Uaine, SnowRoads scenic route*
Attractions: *Highland Folk Museum, Highland Wildlife Park, Cairngorm Mountain, RSPB Loch Garten, Ruthven Barracks, Cairngorm Reindeer Herd, Balmoral Castle, Mar Lodge Estate, Blair Castle*
Towns or villages: *Aviemore, Kingussie, Newtonmore, Grantown-on-Spey, Braemar, Ballater, Pitlochry*
Visitor centres: *VisitScotland visitor information centres at Pitlochry (on the southern boundary) Ballater and Aviemore*
Getting there: *Driving times: approx. 30–45 mins from Inverness, 2–3 hours from Glasgow, 5–7 hours from Manchester. Rail to Dalwhinnie, Newtonmore, Kingussie, Aviemore and Carrbridge. Trains from London stop at Kingussie or Aviemore; Caledonian Sleeper stops at Aviemore.*

www.cairngorms.co.uk

Picture Credits

Cover photos:
Wasdale Head and Wast Water, Lake District NP.
Guy Edwardes/naturepl.com
Wensleydale, Yorkshire Dales NP.
Guy Edwardes/naturepl.com

7	*Linwood, New Forest NP.* Guy Edwardes/naturepl.com
8–9	*Mutton's Mill, Norfolk Broads NP.* Tom Barrett
10–11	*Gwynant Valley, Eryri NP.* Alan Williams/naturepl.com
12–13	*Marloes Sands, Pembrokeshire Coast NP.* Mark Hamblin/naturepl.com
14–15	*Wensleydale, Yorkshire Dales NP.* Guy Edwardes/naturepl.com
16–17	*Wardlow Hay Cop, Peak District NP.* Alex Hyde/naturepl.com
24–27	Ross Hoddinott/naturepl.com
28	Artur Niedzwiedz/Shutterstock.com
29	Ross Hoddinott/naturepl.com
30	Steve Nicholls/naturepl.com
31	Jitchanamont/Shutterstock.com
32–37	Ross Hoddinott/2020VISION/naturepl.com
38–40	Mike Read/naturepl.com
41	Guy Edwardes/naturepl.com
42:1	Guy Edwardes/naturepl.com
42:2	Mike Read/naturepl.com
44	Mike Read/naturepl.com
45	Colin Varndell/naturepl.com
46–47	Ross Hoddinott/naturepl.com
48–49	Guy Edwardes/2020VISION/naturepl.com
50–51	Matt Roseveare/naturepl.com
52	Guy Edwardes/naturepl.com
54:1	Matthew J. Thomas
54:2	Colin Varndell/naturepl.com
55	Daniel Greenwood
56	Andy Rouse/naturepl.com
57	Guy Edwardes/2020VISION/naturepl.com
58–59	Glenn Driver/Moment via Getty Images
60–61	Guy Edwardes/naturepl.com
62–63	Guy Edwardes/2020VISION/naturepl.com
64–65	Guy Edwardes/naturepl.com
66–69	David Noton/naturepl.com
70–71	Nick Garbutt/naturepl.com
72	Ross Hoddinott/naturepl.com
73	Nathan Danks/Shutterstock.com
74–75	John Waters/naturepl.com
76–77	Ross Hoddinott/naturepl.com
78–79	tanya_tatyana/Shutterstock.com
80	Elgol/E+ Via Getty Images
82	Ross Hoddinott/naturepl.com
83	Danny Green/naturepl.com
84:1	Hawlfraint y Goron/Crown Copyright
84:2	Alex Mustard/naturepl.com
85	Alex Mustard/naturepl.com
86	Graham Eaton/naturepl.com
87	Henley Spiers/naturepl.com
88	Ashley Cooper/The Image Bank via Getty Images
89	Michael Roberts/Moment via Getty Images
90–91	Birdsonline via Getty Images
92–93	Hawlfraint y Goron/Crown copyright
94–95	inigocia/Shutterstock.com
96–97	Photos by R A Kearton/Moment Open via Getty Images
98	Emma Hurren/Shutterstock.com
100	Will Watson/naturepl.com
101	Guy Edwardes/naturepl.com
102	Phil Savoie/naturepl.com
103–107	Guy Edwardes/naturepl.com
108–109	Merryn Thomas/naturepl.com
110–113	Guy Edwardes/naturepl.com
114	Ernie Janes/naturepl.com
116	Mike Page
117	Robin Chittenden/naturepl.com
118:1	Tom Barrett
118:2	Nick Upton/naturepl.com
120	Steve Knell/naturepl.com
121	Ernie Janes/naturepl.com
122–123	Helen Hotson/Shutterstock.com
124–125	Yackers1/Shutterstock.com
126–127	Oscar Dewhurst/naturepl.com
128	Alan Williams/naturepl.com
130	Matthew E Simmons/Shutterstock.com
131	Chris Goddard/Shutterstock.com
132	Graham Eaton/naturepl.com
133	Mike Potts/naturepl.com
134	Guy Edwardes/naturepl.com
135	Ross Hoddinott/naturepl.com
136:1	David Noton/naturepl.com
136:2	Photos by R A Kearton/Getty Images
138	Alan Williams/naturepl.com
139:1	LGagePhotography/Shutterstock.com
139:2	Mark Palombella Hart/500px Plus via Getty Images
140–143	Dilwyn Williams
144–147	Alan Williams/naturepl.com
148–149	Ross Hoddinott/naturepl.com
150	Alex Hyde/naturepl.com
152:1	John Finney Photography/Moment via Getty Images
152:2	Alex Hyde/naturepl.com
153–154	Alex Hyde/naturepl.com
156	Graham Eaton/naturepl.com

157	Paul Hobson/naturepl.com		230	SCOTLAND: The Big Picture/naturepl.com
158	Alex Hyde/naturepl.com		231	Petr Jelinek/Shutterstock.com
159	Gary K. Smith/naturepl.com		232	SCOTLAND: The Big Picture/naturepl.com
160–161	Dave Massey/500px Plus via Getty Images		233	David Tipling/naturepl.com
162–163	Alex Hyde/naturepl.com		234	Philippe Clement/naturepl.com
164–165	Ben Hall/2020VISION/naturepl.com		235:1	Anderl/Shutterstock.com
166	Guy Edwardes/naturepl.com		235:2	Michael Warren/Moment via Getty Images
168:1	Andy Kay		236–237	Richard Whitcombe/Shutterstock.com
168:2	David Pike/naturepl.com		238–239	Guy Edwardes/naturepl.com
169	SCOTLAND:The Big Picture/naturepl.com		240	Mark Hamblin/2020VISION/naturepl.com
170	Guy Edwardes/naturepl.com		242:1	SCOTLAND: The Big Picture/naturepl.com
171:1	Photos by R A Kearton/Moment via Getty Images		242:2	Peter Cairns/naturepl.com
			243	Niall Benvie/naturepl.com
171:2	Alex Hyde/naturepl.com		244	SCOTLAND: The Big Picture/naturepl.com
172:1	Andy Sands/naturepl.com		245	Peter Mulligan/Moment via Getty Images
172:2	Guy Edwardes/naturepl.com		246–251	SCOTLAND: The Big Picture/naturepl.com
173	Gary K. Smith/naturepl.com		252	Brais Seara/Moment via Getty Images
174–177	Guy Edwardes/naturepl.com		253:1	SCOTLAND: The Big Picture/naturepl.com
178–179	Daniel Kay		253:2	Brais Seara/Moment via Getty Images
180	Danielle Robinson		254–255	Ashley Cooper/naturepl.com
182:1	Mark Taylor/naturepl.com		256–259	SCOTLAND: The Big Picture/naturepl.com
182:2	Milosz Maslanka/Shutterstock.com		261–265	Mapelio // https://mapelio.com
183	Gary K. Smith New/naturepl.com			
184	Paul Hobson/naturepl.com		268–269	*Slufters Inclosure, New Forest NP.* Mike Read/naturepl.com
185	Gary K. Smith/naturepl.com			
186	Frank Fell/robertharding/Collection Mix Subjects via Getty Images		270–271	*Green Loch, Cairngorms NP.* SCOTLAND: The Big Picture/naturepl.com
187–189	Gary K. Smith New/naturepl.com			
190–191	Helen Hotson/Shutterstock.com			
192	Guy Edwardes/naturepl.com			
194	Peter Atkinson/500px via Getty Images			
195	Linda Pitkin/2020VISION/naturepl.com			
196	Julian Carnell/Shutterstock.com			
197	Merryn Thomas/naturepl.com			
198–199	Ashley Cooper/naturepl.com			
200–201	Guy Edwardes/naturepl.com			
202–203	Ross Hoddinott/naturepl.com			
204:1	Ben Hall/2020VISION/naturepl.com			
204:2	Andy Rouse/naturepl.com			
205	Michael Hutchinson/naturepl.com			
206–207	Ross Hoddinott/naturepl.com			
208–209	David Noton/naturepl.com			
210–211	Daniel_Kay/Shutterstock.com			
212–213	Ashley Cooper/naturepl.com			
214	Guy Edwardes/naturepl.com			
216–217	Ann & Steve Toon/naturepl.com			
218	Daniel_Kay/Shutterstock.com			
219	Guy Edwardes/2020VISION/naturepl.com			
220–221	Ann & Steve Toon/naturepl.com			
222–223	Dave Head/Shutterstock.com			
224–225	Guy Edwardes/naturepl.com			
226	Paul C Stokes/Moment via Getty Images			
228	David McElroy/Shutterstock.com			
229	Melvin Grey/naturepl.com			

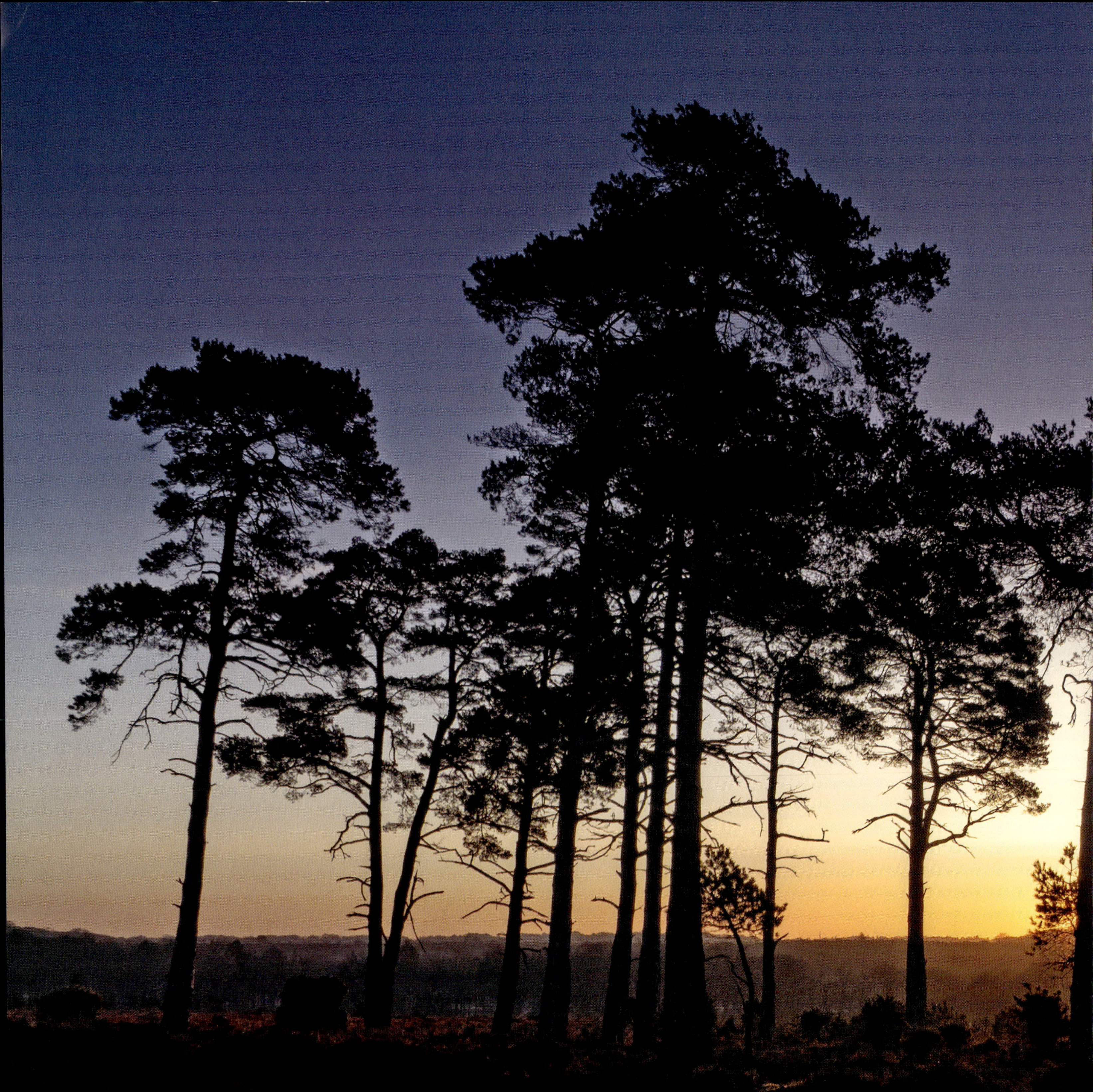